Rebuilding the State Institutions

Juan Antonio Le Clercq ·
Jose Pablo Abreu Sacramento
Editors

Rebuilding the State Institutions

Challenges for Democratic Rule of Law in Mexico

Editors
Juan Antonio Le Clercq
Departamento de Relaciones
Internacionales y Ciencia Política
Centro de Estudio sobre Impunidad y
Justicia, Universidad de las Américas
Puebla (UDLAP)
Cholula, Puebla, Mexico

Jose Pablo Abreu Sacramento
Departamento de Derecho, Escuela
de Ciencias Sociales y Gobierno
Tecnológico de Monterrey
Campus Santa Fe
Mexico City, Mexico

More on this book is at: http://afes-press-books.de/html/SA_05.htm.

ISBN 978-3-030-31316-6   ISBN 978-3-030-31314-2   (eBook)
https://doi.org/10.1007/978-3-030-31314-2

© Springer Nature Switzerland AG 2020
This work is subject to copyright. All rights are reserved by the Publisher, whether the whole or part of the material is concerned, specifically the rights of translation, reprinting, reuse of illustrations, recitation, broadcasting, reproduction on microfilms or in any other physical way, and transmission or information storage and retrieval, electronic adaptation, computer software, or by similar or dissimilar methodology now known or hereafter developed.
The use of general descriptive names, registered names, trademarks, service marks, etc. in this publication does not imply, even in the absence of a specific statement, that such names are exempt from the relevant protective laws and regulations and therefore free for general use.
The publisher, the authors and the editors are safe to assume that the advice and information in this book are believed to be true and accurate at the date of publication. Neither the publisher nor the authors or the editors give a warranty, expressed or implied, with respect to the material contained herein or for any errors or omissions that may have been made. The publisher remains neutral with regard to jurisdictional claims in published maps and institutional affiliations.

The cover photo of this book was photographed by the first coeditor Juan Antonio Le Clercq who granted permission to use his photo in his own book. The photographer retains the copyright.

Copy Editor: PD Dr. Hans Günter Brauch, AFES-PRESS e.V., Mosbach, Germany
Language Editor: Dr. Vanessa Greatorex, England

This Springer imprint is published by the registered company Springer Nature Switzerland AG
The registered company address is: Gewerbestrasse 11, 6330 Cham, Switzerland

Foreword

Literally every single day people talk more about the necessity of establishing the rule of law. Some think it should be a kind of primary setting. Others believe that it is more a process that implies a broad transformation to enforce something that is incomplete or dysfunctional. Yet there are diverse possibilities between these two extremes. The narratives of these moments have an element in common: the identification of absences. Practically nobody believes that Mexico has managed to build, operate, establish, work with, or, indeed, perform any similar expression related to what has historically been defined as the rule of law.

It would be relatively easy to compile a list of authors who have discussed the numerous deficiencies and the damaged or disastrous status that rule of law has or does not have in our society. If we take as the starting point, let's say, twenty years ago, the list would be enormous. Many topics would appear, one or multiple times, in an isolated or cyclical way: security or insecurity of contracts, police action, lack of resources, violation of due process, the disruption of federalism or separation of powers, the expansion of crime, legalization of drugs, accountability, a career civil service, the use of the Army for public security tasks, informal economy, regulatory proliferation, but also the absence of regulation, corruption, migration, human rights violations, absence of referendums among indigenous minorities, irregular extractions, corporatization of political parties, spread of political and electoral clienteles, depredation of natural resources, cybernetic insecurity, unmarked graves, kidnaps, disappeared people, murdered journalists, human trafficking, black markets, extrajudicial executions, and a literally profound etcetera.

The items in the aforementioned list, along with other topics and variables that could easily be included, have been advanced as deficiencies in the rule of law. Beyond relevant viewpoints and thematic differences, what it is shown is the perception, and sometimes a full demonstration, of a series of national problems linked to the law. Each person sees only what is personally or professionally relevant to him or her, and that obliviousness is so great that it should be regarded as the antithesis of the situation that should ideally prevail.

The challenge of facing those problems in that way generates additional complications. The first and most evident one consists of the turmoil caused by trying to turn any deficiency into a legal, normative, or practical damage to the rule of law. If we imagine this legal-political-social possibility as one piece composed of many parts, it could be said that the whole ends up being adversely affected by the inadequacy of one of its elements.

This metaphoric approximation highlights that many authors maintain that the rule of law to which we aspire as a totality is normatively and practically non-existent, or else does exist but deficiently because it lacks that central element.

Several things that have been discussed in recent years are situated in this foggy condition. The underlying issue is not so much the difficulty of identifying such topics, but the reasons for considering these particular topics, and not others, as deficient and, what is more, why those issues affect the "rule of law" as a whole.

Perhaps, it could be said that this analysis is, in fact, a meta-discussion. According to this logic, we would not be discussing the problems with the rule of law, but what individuals believe to be more disruptive, in an analytical way. This perspective leads us to a second discussion about how it affects the whole, and not about what it is important to adjust or correct in the legal-cultural mode.

Possibly, it could be said the two discussions are different and independent. And I would agree. But I disagree about the confusion of some authors when they draw a line between the necessity of correction and of description. I should insist on the fact that if everything that is done fits within the "rule of law" zone and there is limited awareness of how the part affects the whole, we would not know which specific part should be corrected or how it should be corrected in order to achieve that whole.

I am elaborating on the above considerations, maybe quite extensively, to contextualize the book which I am about to introduce. It is a compilation of essays where, in my opinion, three elements converge. First, it seeks to define what could nowadays be conceptually understood as the rule of law in this geographic area. This is not a trivial feat. There is a large number of works on the possible list to which I previously referred which, before embarking on the analysis of successes and failures, do not explain what is going to be understood by the rule of law. This gives the impression that those who act in that way assume the existence of a natural state of affairs, as if everybody is thinking, both conceptually and practically, the same thing when they talk about the rule of law. But, in fact, this is not true.

If we look closely at what I will call the underlying discourse, wide and profound differences could be identified in the components of the rule of law or its objectives and functions. For some people, it is an instrument of contractual execution; for others, it is a control and coaction mechanism; for still others, it is the normative realization of the democratic State.

The book's main strength is that it makes explicit the whole theoretical scaffold of what is going to be understood by the rule of law. The essays in the first part focus on this concept and what conforms to it and what does not. This does not mean that we have to accept the authors' ideas. It simply enables us to know, explicitly, the authors' ideas and arguments and to avoid erroneous suppositions.

The second advantage of the book is that it provides concrete examples of some specific issues to demonstrate what is defined as the rule of law. At this stage, we move on from the theory to see how these failures take place. Does the number of constitutional reforms generate an affectation, in a kind of understanding as Marx did, where the quantitative become qualitative? Is the absence of security or the lack of civic culture destructive of what is construed and done as rule of law?

The third aspect of this work has a more specific dimension by asking what should be done socially, and in some cases legally, to establish or reestablish equilibrium in the country, either by geography or subject. There are valuable arguments that also, of course, have a practical dimension.

What has just been mentioned could give the impression that the book possesses a sort of unity: a whole perfectly formed from the general and abstract to the concrete, through the particular. But the fact that diverse authors present their ideas about related topics does not automatically lead to complete cohesion. In other words, what is said by one author in the first part may not necessarily be accepted by another author in a different part of the book.

Anyone who decides to read this book cannot simply assume its total unity. On the contrary, the reader has to extract from each chapter the elements of particular use and relevance to them. What certainly has been done is to structure the parts in a differentiated manner and, for me, this is the chief merit of the collection. This is not a common feature; however strange this may sound. It is delightful and valuable that authors and editors have made an effort to mark the differences. It is a relevant analytic step forward. This could foster further reflections to comprehend and generate consensuses to modify the situation of a fundamental theme of our time: simply, from my perspective, the rational and ordered social coexistence among all or quite a few of us.

Mexico City, Mexico
January 2019

Dr. José Ramón Cossío Díaz
Ministro de la Suprema Corte
de Justicia de la Nación
Miembro de El Colegio Nacional

Acknowledgements

We are grateful to colleagues from Mexico and different countries who participated in the review of all the chapters: Alejandra Díaz de León, Alejandro Ramírez, Belem Guerrero, Benito Sotelo, Claudio López-Guerra, César Borja, Dieter Enríquez, Edgar Valle, Edith Mercado, Elisa Gómez, Elizabeth Espinoza, Emilio Zacarías, Fernando Ojesto, Francisco Esquinca, Gerardo Rodríguez, Gerardo Toache, Guillermo Casillas, Isabel Fulda, Jorge Andere, José Ojeda, Kira Ciofalo, Ludwig Von Bedoya, Laura Romero, Mayra Cabrera, Miguel Casillas, Mohamed Badine, Nancy Nieira, Nicolás Corona, Rebecca Sophie, Ronald Guy Emerson, Sofía Ballesteros, Tania Ramírez, Wendy Jarquín, and Ximena López. We appreciate the support of Celeste Cedillo, Dahyane Galindo, Daniela Hernández, Santiago Martinez, Alexis Murrillo, Eduardo Poltolarek, Elena Munive, Emilia Quijano, Santiago Torres, and Amado Tress, who helped throughout the editing process. Without them, this book could not end in your hands.

We are also thankful to UDLAP authorities for all their support for this project, especially Dr. Luis Ernesto Derbez Bautista, President; Cecilia Anaya Berríos, Academic VicePresident; and Raphael Steger Cataño, Dean of the Social Sciences School.

Finally, we want to thank Springer Nature in Heidelberg for their faith in this project, especially to Dr. Johanna Schwarz, Dr. Christian Witschel, and Ms. Aurelia Heumader and the book editor, PD Dr. Hans Günter Brauch as well as the book producer in Heidelberg, Ms. Doerthe Mennecke-Buehler, and the author would like to thank Ms. Jayanthi Krishnamoorthi and Ms. Manopriya Saravanan and the production team in Chennai, Tamil Nadu, India.

They were patient and supportive during the whole process. Also, we recognize the effort and engagement of all the authors.

Cholula, Puebla, Mexico	Dr. Juan Antonio Le Clercq
Mexico City, Mexico	Dr. Jose Pablo Abreu Sacramento
August 2019	

Contents

1 **Introduction: Understanding the Lack of Rule of Law in Mexico** 1
Juan Antonio Le Clercq, Jose Pablo Abreu Sacramento and Fernando Miguel Herrera Rosado

Part I The Concept of Rule of Law and Its Measurement

2 **Conceptualizing the Rule of Law** 19
Rodolfo Sarsfield

3 **Rule of Law and "Estado Constitucional" Indicators. Does Law Rule Effectively in Mexico?** 39
Rafael Estrada Michel

4 **Measuring the Rule of Law in Mexico** 57
Camilo Gutiérrez, Joel Martinez, Alejandro Ponce and Leslie Solís

Part II Explaining the Fragility of the Rule of Law in Mexico

5 **How Many Constitutional Reforms Produce Rule of Law?** 81
Juan Antonio Le Clercq

6 **Security** 107
Vidal Romero

7 **Human Rights and Unreliable Institutions in a Globalized World: The Case of Irregular Migrants in Mexico** 123
Mauricio Olivares-Méndez and Radu-Mihai Triculescu

8 **Amparo and Administrative Trials as Accountability Mechanisms in Mexico** 141
Ana E. Fierro

9   Citizenry, Civic Education and Rule of Law 155
Jose Pablo Abreu Sacramento

10   The Challenge of Developing a New Human Rights Culture
in Future Mexican Lawyers 175
Eduardo Román González

Part III   Structural Reforms and Their Implementation Challenges

11   How Does Criminal Justice Work in Mexico? 193
María Novoa and Karen Silva Mora

12   The Monster Within: Mexico's Anti-corruption National
System... 207
Cristopher Ballinas Valdés

13   Institutional Path Dependence in the Failure of the
"War on Drugs" in Mexico................................ 223
Jorge Javier Romero

14   Reversal of Fortunes: Changes in the Public Policy
Environment and Mexico's Energy Reform 241
Tony Payan

15   The Rule of Law in Economic Competition 265
María Solange Maqueo Ramírez

Universidad de las Américas Puebla (UDLAP)..................... 281

About the Editor... 283

About the Co-Editor... 285

About the Contributors 287

Index 293

Contributors

Jose Pablo Abreu Sacramento Department of Law, Tecnológico de Monterrey, Mexico City, Mexico

Ana E. Fierro Management and Public Policy and Research, CIDE, Mexico City, Mexico

Eduardo Román González Government and Public Policy, Universidad Autónoma de Madrid, Madrid, Spain

Camilo Gutiérrez World Justice Project, Washington, D.C., USA

Juan Antonio Le Clercq Department of International Relations and Political Science, UDLAP. Ex hacienda de Sta. Catarina Mártir, Puebla, Mexico

Joel Martinez World Justice Project, Washington, D.C., USA

Rafael Estrada Michel Escuela Libre de Derecho, Mexico City, Mexico

Karen Silva Mora UNAM, Mexico City, Mexico

María Novoa Universidad Simón Bolívar, Caracas, Venezuela

Mauricio Olivares-Méndez Universidad Autónoma de Querétaro, Querétaro, Mexico

Tony Payan Baker Institute, Rice University, Houston, USA; Universidad Autónoma de Ciudad Juárez, Ciudad Juárez, Mexico

Alejandro Ponce World Justice Project, Washington, D.C., USA

María Solange Maqueo Ramírez Economic Research and Teaching Center (CIDE), Mexico City, Mexico;
National Institute for Transparency, Access to Information and Personal Data Protection (INAI), Mexico City, Mexico

Jorge Javier Romero Department of Politics and Culture, Universidad Autónoma Metropolitana Xochimilco, Mexico City, Mexico;
Faculty of Political and Social Sciences, UNAM, Mexico City, Mexico

Vidal Romero Political Science Department, ITAM, Mexico City, Mexico

Fernando Miguel Herrera Rosado School of Social Sciences and Government of Tecnológico de Monterrey, Monterrey, Mexico

Rodolfo Sarsfield Autonomous University of Querétaro, Querétaro, Mexico

Leslie Solís World Justice Project, Washington, D.C., USA

Radu-Mihai Triculescu University of Twente, Enschede, The Netherlands

Cristopher Ballinas Valdés Philosophy in Politics, University of Oxford, Oxford, UK

Abbreviations

ACHR	American Convention of Human Rights
ARP	Administrative Responsibility Penalties
ASF	Superior Federal Audit (Auditoría Superios de la Federación)
CAPI	Computer-assisted personal interviewing
CCINM	Citizen Council of the National Institute of Migration (Consejo Ciudadano del Instituto Nacional de Migración)
CEAV	Executive Commission for Victims Assistance (Comisión Ejecutiva de Atención a Víctimas)
CEEAD	Center for Studies on Teaching and Law Learning (Centro de Estudios Sobre Enseñanza y Aprendizaje del Derecho)
CENACE	National Center for Energy Control (Centro Nacional de Control de Energía)
CENAGAS	National Center for Natural Gas Control (Centro Nacional de Control de Gas Natural)
CIDAC	Research Center for Development (Centro de Investigación para el Desarrollo, A.C.)
CIDE	Center for Research and Teaching in Economics (Centro de Investigación y Docencia Económicas, A.C.)
CIDH	Inter-American Court of Human Rights
CJF	Mexican Council on Administration of the Federal Judicial Branch (Consejo de la Judicatura Federal)
CNDH	National Commission for Human Rights (Comisión Nacional de los Derechos Humanos)
CNH	National Hydrocarbons Commission (Comisión Nacional de los Hidrocarburos)
CNPJE	National Census of Local Prosecution Offices (Censa Nacional de Procuración de Justica Estatal)
COFETEL	Federal Telecommunication Commission (Comisión Federal de Telelecomunicaciones)

COFECE	Federal Competition Commission (Comisión Federal de Competencia Económica)
COLMEX	College of México (Colegio de México)
CONAPRED	National Council Against Discrimination (Consejo Nacional contra la Discriminación)
CONEVAL	National Council for the Evaluation of Social Development Policy (Consejo Nacional de Evaluación de la Política de Desarrollo Social)
CRE	Energy Regulatory Commission (Comisión Reguladora de Energía)
CSG	Carlos Salinas de Gortari
ELD	Free School on Law (Escuela Libre de Derecho)
ENVIPE	National Victimization Survey (Encuesta Nacional de Victimización y Percepción sobre Seguridad Pública)
EPN	Enrique Peña Nieto
EZP	Ernesto Zedillo Ponce de León
FCH	Felipe Calderón Hinojosa
FLACSO	Latin American Faculty of Social Sciences (Facultad Latinoamericana de Ciencias Sociales)
FMP	Mexican Petroleum Fund (Fondo Mexicano del Petróleo)
GCM	Global Compact for Safe, Orderly and Regular Migration
GII	Global Impunity Index (Índice Global de impunidad)
GPP	General Population Poll
HPR	Homologated Police Report
IAHRC	Inter-American Human Rights Commission
IEDF	District Federal Electoral Institute
IFECOM	Federal Institute of Experts in Mercantile Contests (Instituto Federal de Especialistas en Concursos Mercantiles)
IFETEL	Federal Institute for Telecomunications (Instituto Federal de Telecomunicaciones)
INACIPE	National Institute of Criminal Sciences (Instituto nacional de Ciencias Penales)
INAI	Instituto Nacional de Acceso a la Información (Instituto Nacional de Acceso a la Información)
INE	National Electoral Institute (Instituto Nacional Electoral)
INEE	National Institute for Educational Evaluation (Instituto Nacional para la evaluación Educativa)
INEGI	National Institute for Statistics and Geography (Instituto Nacional de Estadística y Geografía)
INM	National Institute of Migration (Instituto Nacional de Migración)
IPSA	International Political Science Association
ITAM	Autonomous Technological Institute of México (Instituto Nacional Autónomo de México)
ITESM	Monterrey Institute of Technology and Higher Education (Instituto Tecnológico Y de Estudios Superiores de Monterrey)

LACC	Latin America and Caribbean Centre
LFCE	Federal Law of Economic Competition (Ley Federal de Competencia Económica)
LSE	London School of Economics and Political Science
MORENA	National Regeneration Movement (Movimiento de Regeneración Nacional)
MP	Federal Prosecutor (Ministerio Público)
NAFTA	North American Free Trade Agreement (Tratado de Libre Comercio)
OECD	Organization for Economic Cooperation and Development
PAN	National Action Party (Partido Acción Nacional)
PEMEX	Mexican Petroleum (Petróleos Mexicanos)
PF	Principle of Fairness
PPD	Drug Policy Program (Programa de Política de Drogas)
PRI	Institutional Revolutionary Party (Partido Revolucionario Institucional)
QRQ	Qualified Respondent's Questionnaires
REDODEM	Documentation Network of Migrant Advocacy Organizations (Red de Documentación de las Organizaciones Defensoras de Migrantes)
RLI	Rule of Law Index
SCJN	Court of Justice of the Nation (Suprema Corte de Justicia de la Nación)
SEGOB	Ministry of National Affairs (Secretaría de Gobernación)
SESNSP	Executive Secretariat of the National Public Security System (Secretariado Ejecutivo del Sistema Nacional de Seguridad Pública)
SETEC	Technical Secretariat for the Implementation of Criminal Justice Reform (Secretaría Técnica del Consejo de Coordinación para la implementación del Sistema de Justicia Penal)
SFP	Ministry of Public Function (Secretaría de la Función Pública)
SNA	National Anti-corruption System (Sistema Nacional Anticorrupción)
SNI	National System of Researchers (Sistema nacional de investigadores)
SPT	Subcommittee on Prevention of Torture and other Cruel Inhuman or Degrading Treatment or Punishment
TFJA	Federal Court of Administrative Justice (Tribunal Federal de Justicia Administrativa)
UAM	Metropolitan Autonomous University (Universidad Autónoma Metropolitana)
UANL	Nuevo León Autonomous University (Universidad Autónoma de Nuevo León)
UDLAP	University of the Americas Puebla (Universidad de las Américas Puebla)

UIA	Iberoamerican University (Universidad Iberoamericana)
ULSA	La Salle University (Universidad de La Salle)
UMECAS	Supervisory Units for Precautionary Measures (Unidades Estatales de Supervisión a Medidas Cautelares y Suspensión Condicional del Proceso)
UN	United Nations
UNAM	National Autonomous University of Mexico (Universidad Nacional Autónoma de México)
UNDP	United Nations Development Programme
UNHRC	United Nations Human Rights Council
UNLA	Latin University of America (Universidad Latina de América)
UNODC	United Nations Office on Drugs and Crime
UP	Panamerican University (Universidad Panamericana)
UPM	Pontifical University of Mexico (Universidad Pontifica de México)
USAL	University of Salamanca (Universidad de Salamanca)
VFQ	Vicente Fox Quezada
WGI	Worldwide Governance Indicators
WJP	World Justice Project
WVS	World Value Survey

Chapter 1
Introduction: Understanding the Lack of Rule of Law in Mexico

Juan Antonio Le Clercq, Jose Pablo Abreu Sacramento and Fernando Miguel Herrera Rosado

1.1 The Complex Development of the Rule of Law

The rule of law has been established as a central feature of modern states and democracies; it represents an ideal linked to political development. The rule of law rests on the idea that a society adopts through legislation a set of formal rules and norms and decides to adhere to those rules in order to regulate the behavior and interaction of individuals, public institutions and private organizations, including conflict resolution mechanisms. This represents the basic social contract crystallizing a common aspiration of modern democracies.

In some of its canonical definitions, the rule of law refers to at least five fundamental processes: lawmaking in coherence with principles such as clarity, publicity, stability, consistency, transparency or prospectivity; equal protection of citizens' rights and interests; impartial and universal access to justice; public officials' behavior and decisions in adherence to law; and institutional rules of the game to regulate social, political and economic interactions – something North (1990) called a timeless certainty horizon.

Prof. Dr. Juan Antonio Le Clercq, Ph.D. in Political and Social Sciences, Department of International Relations and Political Science, UDLAP. Ex hacienda de Sta. Catarina Mártir, 72810, San Andrés Cholula, Puebla, México. E-mail: juan.leclercq@udlap.mx.

Prof. Dr. Jose Pablo Abreu Sacramento, Ph.D. in Law. Department of Law, Tecnológico de Monterrey, Campus Santa Fe, Mexico City. E-mail: jpabreu@tec.mx.

Fernando Herrera holds a B.A. in Marketing and International Business from the Universidad Autónoma de Yucatan (UADY), and a Master in Latin American Studies from Université Paris III Sorbonne Nouvelle. He has collaborated at Higher Education Institutions such as UADY and CIDE. He has also worked as a consultant for non-profit organizations participating in projects related to transparency and accountability, education and social policy. He currently works at the School of Social Sciences and Government of Tecnológico de Monterrey. E-mail: fernandoherrera@tec.mx.

© Springer Nature Switzerland AG 2020
J. A. Le Clercq and J. P. Abreu Sacramento (eds.), *Rebuilding the State Institutions*, https://doi.org/10.1007/978-3-030-31314-2_1

But thick and critical descriptions[1] of the liberal negative concept of legal order, centered on restraints, rights, checks and balances, view the rule of law in a more extended way, a perspective that involves more complex elements, such as the development of institutional capabilities, the provision of public goods, a culture of legality, market regulation, containing corruption and patrimonialism, promotion and protection of human rights, principles of social justice and equality and the legal and political consequences of economic inequality and social exclusion (Tamahana 2004; Bingham 2010; Waldron 2016).

Beyond the differences and advantages of thick and thin approaches to the rule of law, a central problem in contemporary academic and political discussions is the difficulty of extending and consolidating the rule of law where tradition, political informality or autocracy have been the basis of the social contract. This is why it is very relevant to focus our attention on the key institutional conditions and social circumstances that allow the development of an effective rule of law, especially in developing countries and post-authoritarian regimes.

Is it possible to establish the rule of law successfully in developing countries or young democratic regimes? Does the rule of law depend on high degrees of economic development, related to particular political histories or conditioned by specific legal traditions? Is it possible to design public institutions according to legal principles where problems of corruption, patrimonialism, informality or lack of a culture of legality persist? What is the relationship between an effective rule of law and deep economic inequalities?

Answering these questions requires the study of successful and failed experiences as well as deeper comparison between different national cases. One of the main issues in the debate on the rule of law, as the reader will notice throughout the articles in this book, has to do with its measurement. What is the optimal framework of variables and attributes that would enable us to capture reality? Why is it important to measure the rule of law? The authors of the book will attempt to address these questions.

It is particularly relevant to reopen this discussion when disappointment with democracy is clearly rising in different regions of the world.

Beyond a Political Sciences and Law perspective, the intensification of global dynamics has significant effects on the rule of law. Migration is one of the key issues of our time. But also, we cannot ignore the fact that de facto or agreed supranational norms are defining national ones. HiTech companies play globally but constrain to local norms. International treaties and regional institutions force interactions between people to change and this requirement starts to be distrusted.

---

[1]Thick descriptions (a term first coined by British philosopher Gilbert Ryle in an essay entitled "The Thinking of Thoughts: What is 'Le Penseur' Doing?" [1968] and expanded on by American anthropologist Clifford Gertz in *The Interpretation of Cultures* [1973]) are based on contextualized scientific observation of human behavior, whereas thin descriptions offer only surface level observations.

In addition, we cannot ignore the prominence gained around the world over the past few years by strong quasi authoritarian leaderships like Turkey, Russia, and China, or the rise of populist/nationalist political actors and parties like Trump (USA), Bolsonaro (Brazil), Kurz (Austria), Le Pen (France), the League (Italy) and VOX (Spain).

In Latin America, this discussion acquires more relevance when we focus our attention on the complicated regional context. The consolidation of democracy in different countries seems to pass through a delicate moment. The high levels of inequality, the growing security crisis, the generalized environment of corruption, and the political conflicts in specific countries like Nicaragua and Venezuela are just some examples of the issues we are facing.

Although there is no unique model and the rule of law is considered not a final stop but a continuing construction, there is a never-ending risk of regression, and fundamental elements are threatened.

In Mexico, the rule of law is still an aspiration. In spite of several structural reforms adopted during the last three Presidencies, public institutions still have significant deficiencies. The inauguration of a left-wing government in December 2018 – which could be considered a second pivotal moment in the transition to democracy – is starting to provoke questions about its economic model, its security strategy and its political attitude of distrust/intolerance to other ideologies.

Mexico represents a case of the persistence of weak rule of law in a context of problematic democratic consolidation and unequal economic development. Several rankings, indexes, and reports have continually shown the endurance of widespread corruption, ineffective institutions, impunity and globally feeble rule of law. These studies are additional evidence of the relevance of discussing the rule of law in Mexico, which is the aim of the book.

For example, the Corruption Perception Index that studies this phenomenon in 180 countries around the world classifies Mexico in the 138th position, behind Latin American countries like El Salvador, Honduras, and Bolivia (Transparency International 2018). The World Bank's World Governance Indicators includes a rule of law indicator in which Mexico has worsened its score from 38 points out of 100 in 2007 to 32 in 2017. In the Economist Intelligence Unit Democracy Index (2018), Mexico scores 6.19 and ranks within Latin American and Caribbean countries in the 16th position out of 24. This is the worst score among "flawed democracies" – not far from El Salvador with 5.96, which is considered a "hybrid regime". In the Freedom in the World Index (Freedom House 2018) Mexico scores 62 points out of 100 and is classified as "partly free", along with other nations in the region, such as Bolivia, Paraguay, Colombia, Ecuador and Central American countries. In the Fragile States Index Mexico scores 71.5 out of a maximum of 120, ranking in the 94th position of 178 countries, and is classified in the 'warning' category like the majority of countries in Latin America.

In addition to these reports, there are two valuable initiatives understand Mexico's performance on the rule of law: The *World Justice Project* (WJP) Rule of Law Index and the Global Impunity Index. Analyzing the data of both within their various editions, it is possible to observe not only the evolution of scores but how the methodology has changed. This illustrates the complex task of measuring the rule of law. Interestingly, both indexes launched subnational indexes throughout the years to measure the performance of the Mexican states and obtain more in-depth insights.

The first edition of the WJP Index was launched in 2009 (Agrast et al. 2009). In the first edition WJP did not provide a general score for each country. Instead, factor scores were presented.

Table 1.1 presents the four highest and four lowest subfactor scores for Mexico in the 2009 edition, comprising four factors and 16 subfactors. As these data show, the highest subfactor involved the design of laws. The lowest scores, in contrast, involved the effectiveness and accountability of public agencies and actors.

The WJP index evolved and began to rank countries and provide a general score. In the 2017–2018 edition, Mexico occupied position 92 out of 113 countries. Its highest factor was open government and its lowest criminal justice and absence of corruption. The subfactor scores reveal that accountability and corruption control are still relevant challenges that have changed little in a decade (Tables 1.2 and 1.3).

On the other hand, the Global Impunity Index[2] shows that Mexico ranks very poorly against other countries on impunity. Since the 2015 edition Mexico has had the worst position in the Americas (Table 1.4).

Beyond the deficiencies of Mexican government institutions, the behavior of Mexican citizens does not appear to contribute towards closing the gap to reach an effective rule of law. For example, Mexicans' perception of what could be called democratic values is very revealing. In 2001 the Secretaria de Gobernación – National Affairs – launched the Encuesta Nacional sobre Cultura Política y Prácticas Ciudadanas. The answers to some of the questions are very interesting: 44% of the participants considered that neither authorities nor citizens respect the law. 68% considered that both politicians and citizens were involved in corruption. The questions varied in subsequent editions, but the results show a similar pattern. In the 2008 edition, 64% considered that people did not respect or barely respected the laws. 68.2% considered that the laws were enforced to the benefit of a minority (SEGOB 2008). In the 2012 edition, 80.3% of the participants answered that they had no or very little trust in Mexican laws.

As the readers shall see in Section 1.3, for the first time WJP launched a subnational index for Mexico. One of the questions in the survey asked people which three words they thought of when they hear "rule of law". The most frequent words

---

[2]The Global Impunity Index was launched in 2015 by the Centro de Estudio sobre Impunidad y Justicia belonging to the Universidad de las Américas Puebla. The index evaluates security and justice systems in Mexico.

Table 1.1 World Justice Project (WJP) Rule of Law Index (2009)

Subfactor	Factor score
Government powers limited by constitution	0.87
Compliance with international law	0.63
Laws are clear, publicized and stable	0.62
Governmental and non-governmental checks	0.56
Accountable government officials and agents	0.38
Accountable military, police, and prison officials	0.36
Fair and efficient alternative dispute resolution	0.34
Fair and efficient administration	0.31

Source WJP (2009)

Table 1.2 WJP Rule of Law Index 2017–2018

Factor	Factor score
Open government	0.61
Order and security	0.59
Fundamental rights	0.52
Constraints on government powers	0.46
Regulatory enforcement	0.44
Civil justice	0.40
Absence of corruption	0.31
Criminal justice	0.30
Position in ranking	92/113

Source WJP (2018)

Table 1.3 WJP Rule of Law Index 2017–2018

Factor	Factor score
Absence of civil conflict	1.00
Freedom of religion	0.74
Publicized laws and government data	0.68
Right to information	0.63
Absence of violent redress	0.29
Sanctions for official misconduct	0.25
Absence of corruption (in the legislature)	0.19
Effective correctional system	0.19

Source WJP (2018)

Table 1.4 Global Impunity Index 2015

	Position/Number of countries	Score
2015	58/59	75.7
2017	65/69	69.21

Source Le Clercq/Rodriguez (Coords.) (2018)

were: respect, rights, and justice. However, 52% of the participants did not have an answer to the question.

The relevance of evaluations and measurements, as some of the authors will advocate, lies in the fact that diagnosis allows direction to be given and priorities to be set for public policies. Measuring also allows Mexico to be contextualized and put into perspective against other nations.

1.2 Understanding the Proposal of Rebuilding the State Institutions – An Overview

Having established the relevance of discussing the rule of law nowadays, globally and locally, we should say that this book is an attempt to contribute to the public debate on the fragility of the rule of law. Its purpose is to identify the key factors which explain the endurance of its fragile condition in Mexico, opening possible routes to possible solutions and further research. Three axes are proposed: first the concept and measurement of the rule of law, second some factors that explain its fragility in Mexico, and third specific cases of policy implementation in the country.

The opening section of this book is dedicated to examining the concept of the rule of law and the difficulties of measuring it. It is generally accepted that there is no consensus on the definition of the concept of rule of law. Its multidimensional nature allows the inclusion or exclusion of several competing attributes and the adoption of distinctive analytical perspectives. Consequently, there is no consensus on how to measure the health of the rule of law in a given country or society. Conversely there is no argument about the importance and the necessity of measurement tools. As we shall see in Chap. 4, the more information we have, the more accurate the diagnosis that can be made.

In the first chapter in the section, Sarsfield opens the discussion by presenting the main attributes and perspectives that leading authors advance when they deal with the concept of the rule of law. He highlights that, along with other major concepts in political science, there is no agreed or accepted definition. Following Sartori, he takes as a starting point the delimitation of what is not considered rule of law. Societal arrangements with the presence of the "rule by men" or "special interest-based laws" are incompatible with the idea of the rule of law. This implies that one's actions must be regulated by external norms. Norms should not be captured by subjective or arbitrary considerations. The enactment of a law and its application should respect equality before the law – a condition that is broken when laws are aimed at specific groups or individuals.

One of the most debated questions is how many and which attributes should be included within the rule of law notion. Some conceptions favor thinner definitions, whereas others prefer thicker ones. It is a very relevant question because the answer will affect the applicability and the measurement of the concept, as we shall see later in the book. An essential attribute addressed by Sarsfield is institutional equilibrium: "laws must be able to domesticate, transform or constrain the behavior of powerful actors". This is particularly relevant in contexts where the executive branch tends to concentrate power, as we can see in Latin American countries.

Finally, following Raz (1979), the author suggests that paramount attributes, such as democracy, fundamental rights or justice, that can be included as part of the rule of law should not be confused or regarded as synonyms. To do so would be to risk losing the particularity of the rule of law concept.

Chapter 3 introduces a key issue of this book: does law effectively rule in Mexico? In his article, Estrada Michel argues that Mexico lacks indicators to measure compliance with the rule of law. The author also underlines the necessity of addressing the rule of law within the constitutional theory, surpassing the borders of other disciplinary approaches (political science or economics). Following these ideas, he proposes a set of indicators covering a variety of relevant areas: human rights, impunity, corruption control and the performance of specific government bodies, such as the agency in charge of performing financial audits of government offices.

In his view, the rule of law must not ignore Mexico's transition process to democracy. A positive achievement of the past decade is the human rights 2011 reform that created a network of agencies in the country to promote and guarantee human rights at state level. Another positive step forward is the autonomy of Prosecutor Offices. To conclude, the author maintains that the key to straightening the rule of law in Mexico is combating impunity.

The final chapter in Part 1 reminds us that, beyond the conceptual debates, the rule of law notion is related to essential aspects of everyday life, such as walking without danger in our neighborhoods, practicing religion and enforcing contracts. Granted the lack of consensus, the *World Justice Project* (WJP) attempts to fill the aforementioned conceptual and measurement gap by introducing a comprehensive framework of indicators to capture its multidimensional nature and monitor the performance of countries. The purpose is to facilitate evidence-based policy-making.

The authors present an overview of the WJP's efforts to measure the rule of law in Mexico. Since 2009, the country's performance has been measured every one or two years, along with more than 100 nations worldwide as part of its Rule of Law Index. For the first time, the WJP adapted its methodology to produce a subnational index to obtain specific country insights, resulting in the Mexico States Rule of Law Index. The new index covers the same standard eight factors as the global study: constraints on government powers, the absence of corruption, open government, fundamental rights, order and security, regulatory enforcement, civil justice, criminal justice. These factors were adapted to the Mexican context in order to produce relevant data that would identify which states and what specific factors show the greatest opportunities and weaknesses.

The WJP index stands out because country reports are based on the collection of primary data: the perception of the general public along with country experts' opinions. One of its limitations is the fact that the study covers only the three largest cities in each country. The Mexico States Rule of Law Index is a decisive effort to overcome this issue.

Overall, the rule of law in Mexico shows a prevailing precarious performance with significant negative effects on the everyday life of Mexicans. Results for each state can be found in detail in this article. In the future, the WJP envisions producing thematic data reports. The WJP's experience is a clear demonstration that, regardless of conceptual and methodological challenges, the measurement of the rule of law is invariably essential to facilitate more effective policy design. The Mexico States Rule of Law Index should be a relevant reference for state governments that would seriously embrace the objective of straightening the rule of law.

The second section of the book covers the most substantive contributions to the debate on the structural fragilities of the rule of law in Mexico. The section opens with a crucial issue: How many constitutional reforms produce rule of law?

The Mexican constitution is one of the most long-living fundamental laws in the world that are still in effect. Since it was adopted in 1917 after the Mexican Revolution, it has shown great vitality and is to be transformed by incorporating new rights and institutional change which echo political and social changes. Yet constitutional change does not necessarily produce positive effects. The Mexican constitution has undergone 233 amendments which reform 698 articles, damaging its order and coherence. The author suggests that reforming the constitution has become a fetish: "political actors assume that everything that is integrated (in the constitution) updates, strengthens, improves or even guarantees coherence, generating a process that reinforces itself through time", the main assumption being that changing the text will change the reality. The WJP Rule of Law Index along with other measurements like The Global Impunity Index (Le Clercq/Rodriguez 2018) have clearly demonstrated that Mexico suffers significant and pervasive deficiencies in enforcing laws and actually applying changes that were introduced in the fundamental law. The third section of the book will provide some relevant examples.

The first chapter in the section presents an extensive quantitative analysis of institutional reforms of Mexican fundamental law, including constitutional reforms by presidential period, by decade, and by topic, and the most reformed articles. One of the main conclusions of the chapter is that amendments show that the Mexican constitution represents more a battlefield of competition driven by political aspirations and projects rather than a milestone in the rule of law. This conclusion is complemented by indicators presented in the previous section: several surveys have shown the feeble trust of Mexicans towards theirs own laws and the lack of respect for them.

In this context, the main challenge for Mexico regarding this matter is understanding the gap that prevents the translation of constitutional change into significant improvements to the rule of law. Relying on several scholars, the author notes some of the challenges which need to be overcome: design issues, difficulties in implementation related to secondary legislation, poorly coordinated and underfunded agencies, social conflicts, and high levels of corruption and impunity.

The next contribution in this section is an overview of Mexico's current insecurity crisis. Vidal Romero presents a broader perspective of violence during the twentieth century. He reminds us that one of the primary tasks of a state is to impose order within its territory, a *sine qua non* to the flourishing of society. According to this logic, citizens would rationally prefer democratic order to alternative forms or organization as a means for securing respect for basic rights and enjoying favorable conditions for economic prosperity. As the WJP Rule of Law Index shows, even in democratic settings, adherence to law and order results in a variety of performances across nations. Failures of the rule of law open the gates for illicit behavior, a trend that could get out of control when impunity and economic incentives work in a negative way, as the case of Mexico shows.

For some authors, Mexico's security crisis can be explained by political pluralism. The transformation of the Mexican political system brought major changes to the structure of the Mexican state. Others focus more on the failures of the Mexican government's strategy to deal with criminal organizations. Vidal Romero maintains that, in addition to these possible explanations, there are other factors that contribute to the rising violence in Mexico. Relevant changes in the strategy and the operational function of cartels, and the disconnection between the taxing authorities and the specific public bodies that actually spend government budgets also lead to corruption and undermine local authorities' capabilities to fight crime. The combination of a fragile rule of law and uncontained violence creates a vicious cycle, deteriorating law and order even further. On the whole, Mexico's biggest challenge is to create institutions and the right incentives so that individuals, organizations, and public officials adhere to the norms. Fixing fiscal arrangements and regulating drugs could also be game changers.

In the next chapter, Olivares-Mendez and Triculescu plunge into one of the most sensitive topics of our times on a global stage: irregular immigration and human rights. Irregular migrants end up involved in a "grey area" at the crossroad between globalization, sovereignty, and the rule of law. Although Mexican constitution acknowledges protection for all, not just for its citizens, the constitution's content is disconnected from reality, as many Central Americans passing through the country experience day by day.

The authors signal a key issue that came after the adoption of the Human Rights Reform in 2011. The *pro personae* principle was undermined in 2013 when the Mexican Supreme Court constrained the application of international treaties to those rules that do not contradict exceptions contained in the Constitution. According to the authors, this represents a setback to the application of the *pro personae* principle in the country.

The Migration Act, adopted in 2011, was indeed a step forward in the right direction. Unfortunately, weak institutional capacities, unqualified staff, and a limited budget, among other obstacles, have seriously damaged the effective implementation of the law. Audits by the National Institute of Migration had reported significant deficiencies. Mexican immigration officers repeatedly detain people for longer periods than the rules allow and do not provide proper assistance to migrants. This is relevant if we bind it with the report of the United Nations Subcommittee on Prevention of Torture and other Cruel, Inhuman or Degrading Treatment or Punishment, acknowledging that torture in Mexico is generalized.

Migration is by nature a transnational issue, as migratory flows between the United States, Mexico, and Central America or African and European Nations clearly show. Mexico's condition as a country that is simultaneously origin, passage, and destination for migrants places it in a unique position to push forward the global agenda, securing the protection of the rule of law for both regular and irregular migrants.

The next chapter presents an infrequent and sometimes ignored discussion about the rule of law: the role of citizens. This contribution invites us to reflect on the role that the members of a society as individuals have in public affairs. The author maintains that the effectiveness of government bodies is not the only condition to achieve a forceful rule of law; another necessary one is the participation of the people motivated by an individual moral obligation.

However, Mexicans do not seem to be cooperative or show sufficient involvement, beyond showing up to vote on elections. Existing mechanisms that empower citizens, such as the possibility of proposing legislation or demanding referendums on relevant topics, are scarcely used.

The chapter provides a thought-provoking discussion with other scholars on the principle of fairness, a principle that is proposed as the foundation of the moral obligation to participate and cooperate in a community. Citizenry tends to ignore the fact that public goods are the result of an "unbroken chain of coordinated actions" that demand the participation of its members. "When an individual enjoys a benefit available for everybody and this benefit exists just because of the sacrifice of others, then that person will have an obligation to do her fair share to maintain that benefit". Minimal actions such as voting, reporting crimes, paying taxes or collaborating with neighbors and organizations are the proposed fair share. The promotion of a broad civic education policy in Mexico could be a joint effort by schools and universities, along with civil society organizations and relevant public agencies, to set a starting point for building the social construct of the rule of law.

According to Fierro (Chap. 8), democratization and the end of the hegemonic political party system in Mexico lead to further demands, such as transparency and accountability mechanisms, the necessity of a civil service and the promotion of human rights. Accountability mechanisms should be an essential component of the rule of law as a means to increase society's control over government bodies and to get better results. The Mexican legal system adopts the French tradition oriented towards control of powers and the protection of human rights.

Fierro refers to administrative law as a domain where conflict resolution was dominated mostly by informal means until the end of the twentieth century. Underfunded courts, the lack of qualified staff, restraints on independence and the limitations in dealing with administrative activities are some of the main challenges that limit the potential benefits of administrative law in Mexico. In this context, the administrative courts' purpose is to determine whether government acts guarantee human rights protection and comply with norms fixed by the constitution. To this end, 'nullity', "state liability" and 'amparo' trials are mechanisms available to Mexican citizens to control public bodies protecting them from the negative consequences of their actions. Financial compensation, for example, is established by the Mexican constitution to repair damages.

The *amparo* trial is the mechanism by which citizens are entitled to challenge actions they considered contrary to the constitution. It is considered the most powerful accountability mechanism in the Mexican legal system because it is applicable to all branches and orders of government. The 2011 human rights amendment made *amparo* mechanisms more flexible. Nowadays, class actions and legally pursuing private entities as providers of public services are possible. However, more flexibility is needed since sixty per cent of *amparo* cases are dismissed due to case overloads and the excessive formalities of the legal system.

All in all, Mexican citizens' ignorance of the available accountability mechanisms, coupled with technicalities, are major barriers for its broader use.

To close the second section of the book, Roman Gonzalez brings to our attention the importance of the education of future lawyers. He maintains that having a significant number of law schools and lawyers in Mexico has not led to greater strengthening of the rule of law in the country. According to the author, this situation suggests that something is wrong. Training lawyers is more a matter of quality than quantity. Therefore, enhancing the quality of the education of law students would have positive effects across the Mexican legal system. As an example, the next generation of lawyers could be trained to be more sensitive and get more technical skills to promote human rights.

Excessive focus on content-memorizing, lack of context, weak analytical and argumentative skills and poor knowledge of international norms are some of the educational deficiencies that law school students show – deficiencies that, in time, result in interpretation and application mistakes once in the labor market.

The aforementioned 2011 Humans Rights amendment makes addressing this well-known situation especially timely. To Roman Gonzalez, without pertinent efforts to redress law students' education in Mexico, the possibilities of the reform succeeding are very limited. Law schools can play a decisive role to improve the likelihood of success, given the social relevance of the profession as intermediaries between the legal apparatus and the people seeking for justice.

The third and last section of the book covers relevant analysis of so-called "structural reforms" introduced in Mexico over the past decade: criminal justice system, anti-drugs strategy, corruption control, energy sector, and economic competition. All of them are relevant domains that illustrate the challenges of translating the rule of law into concrete public policies.

The section's opening chapter (Novoa and Silva) discusses the Mexican criminal justice system. More than ten years have passed since Mexico introduced major changes in 2008. The aim was to improve the quality and to guarantee respect of the rights of both victims and suspects of crime. Several statistics and reports show the disturbing condition of the criminal justice system in Mexico. Only ten per cent of crimes are reported by victims, mainly because people consider it a waste of time and do not trust the authorities. As an illustration, according to the Impunity Global Index (2018), the State of Mexico has the highest impunity levels. This state has the largest amount of cases (202,205) in the country. Of those, only 0.59% (1,209) resulted in a sentence.

The judicial system reform was adopted to promote the transition from an inquisitorial system to an adversarial and accusatorial one. Mexican Congress fixed 2016 as the deadline for full implementation. Today, the implementation is still in its early stages.

According to the authors, one of the main obstacles to the success of the reform was the feeble political will of state governors towards the reform. This could suggest that they expected the reform would be abandoned. Coordination issues, low budgets, and poor investigative capacities are additional deficiencies that limit the potential of the reform.

Another major obstacle is the current legislation of *amparo* trial, which does not operate coherently with the criminal reform system. On the whole, the authors maintain that the greatest limitations of the system are not to be found in the regulation but in the day-to-day operational and institutional failures.

Christopher Ballinas presents a review of the National Anti-corruption System (SNA). "Mexico has no tradition of checks and balances or independent watchdogs, and corruption was endemic". Ballinas provides a description of Mexican political institutions where, for many decades under PRI, the president held privileged legal and extralegal powers. In this context, institutional change was more a mechanism to maintain power than a path to transformation and prosperity. The behavior of political actors and public officials was indeed motivated by particular interests and a desire to maintain the status quo.

Former Mexican President Enrique Peña Nieto (2012–2018) launched an ambitious reform agenda which managed to obtain the cooperation of the main opposition political parties (The Pacto for Mexico). However, the Casa Blanca and other political scandals resulted in corruption control becoming a mainstream topic in the country, forcing the president's agenda to take more decisive steps to foster corruption control: The introduction of the SNA was the consequence. The SNA was conceived as an entity to coordinate the anti-corruption capabilities of existing government bodies with the participation of civil society both nationally and at the level of the individual states. Yet the SNA has not tackled major political scandals – not just the Casa Blanca case but also others such as the Odebrecht. According to Ballinas, the SNA is symptomatic: "the government creates a panel to address a major issue, only to starve it of resources, inhibit its progress or ignore it, or make rules so convoluted as to make the system unworkable".

The next contribution, by Jorge Romero, takes a critical perspective of the so-called "war on drugs" initiated by the Mexican Federal Government during Felipe Calderon's (2006–2012) administration. This strategy has been criticized from different angles: as a human rights crisis and for its social and economic implications. Romero presents a new perspective: institutional analysis, bringing attention to the distribution of power at the local level and its relationship with the drug policy.

The author introduces the figure of the 'cacique', a form of political intermediary. In its origins, the 'cacique' referred to a person who had legitimate leadership over a certain territory. This figure illustrates the relationship between formal institutions and de facto power allocation mechanisms that have been in place in Mexico for centuries. Taking a path-dependence approach, the author shows how the cacique figure evolved from a formal institution to an informal one. "The *cacicazgo* emerges as a mechanism of clientele administration that exercises control over local populations as a bargaining chip in perpetual negotiation with federal political leaders".

Jorge Romero provides an overview of the evolution of the drug policy in Mexico. He subscribes to the argument of other scholars, highlighted by Vidal Romero in his article about Security, who relate the significant increase in the power of drug cartels to the democratization process and the end of the political monopoly of PRI. Several authors had underlined that political changes disrupted local agreements. Romero remarks on the necessity of more research to analyze Mexican State cases, such as Michoacan, where the "drug on wars" began in 2006. Since then, Mexican armed forces have been deployed throughout the territory without clear legislation. For Romero, Mexico is in the midst of a transition process to establish an open access social order.

The final chapters present a review of economic reforms. First, Tony Payan presents an analysis of the relationship between politics and public policy. Taking as a case study the reform of the Mexican energy sector, he shows that policies produce incentives, and resources and influence actors (opposition, interest groups, citizens), provoking consequences in politics. In parallel, political changes affect the design and implementation of policies. "Public policy and politics produce feedback loop dynamics that end up changing the policy environment and threatening the implementation and consolidation of a policy path".

The reduction in Mexico's oil production coupled with international factors led the Government to reform the energy sector. The author identifies poverty and pervasive inequality, along with corruption, organized crime, and impunity, as domestic factors that undermined the implementation of the energy sector reform. External factors such as changes in USA politics also had consequences in Mexico. The sluggish economic results damaged the support of Mexican people for neoliberal economic reforms introduced over the previous decades, which contributed to the election of a left-wing candidate to the presidency in 2018. The energy sector was, in a way, the ultimate stage of an aggressive economic agenda launched by PRI and PAN.

The aforementioned factors have a strong relation to the rule of law. For Payan, the understanding of the evolution of political, social and economic indicators cannot be separated from keeping track of the shifts in the public policy environment.

In the closing chapter of the book, Solange Maqueo presents a comprehensive overview of the evolution of economic competition legislation in Mexico. Over the past three decades, Mexico's political system has undergone major changes that some of the authors of the book have described. These transformations in politics were accompanied by no less significant changes in the Mexican economy. Successive reforms gave place to the Federal Law in Economic Competition in 1992 and the creation of special public agencies in charge of its implementation. Significant amendments followed in 2006, 2011 and 2013. This twenty-year period shows how the agencies in charge of enforcing economic law (the Federal Competition Commission, the Federal Telecommunication Commission, and their successive names) were adjusted and acquired more autonomy and legal powers, placing Mexico on a par with best international practices. In this gradual process, the author highlights the importance of the creation of specialized economic competition courts. Economic competition law represents a domain where the rule of law has evolved in the right direction.

This book represents a common effort of scholars who, in recent years, have been working on different topics relevant to greater understanding of the complex Mexican context. We strongly believe that the arguments, data, and analyses that are presented in this book could lead to serious reflection by stakeholders and, maybe, facilitate public policy design.

Although the authors have different perspectives and conclusions, we share a common ideal: the desire to foster coordinated actions to change the state of affairs that govern us and keep us far from an authentic rule of law.

References

Agrast, Mark; Botero, Juan; Ponce, Alejandro (2009). *The Rule of Law Index: Measuring Adherence to the Rule of Law Around the World* (Washington, D.C.: The World Justice Project).
Bingham, Tom (2010). *The Rule of Law* (London: Penguin).
Freedom House (2018). *Freedom in the World Index*; at: https://freedomhouse.org/report/freedom-world/freedom-world-2018 (15 January 2019).
Freedom House (2019). *Freedom in the World Index 2018*; at: https://freedomhouse.org/report/freedom-world/freedom-world-2018 (15 January 2019).
Gertz, Clifford (1973). *The Interpretation of Cultures* (New York: Basic Books).
International Transparency (2018). *The Corruption Perception Index*; at: https://www.transparency.org/cpi2018 (15 January 2019).
Le Clercq, Juan Antonio; Rodríguez, Gerardo (Coords.) (2018). *La impunidad subnacional en México y sus dimensiones IGI-MEX 2018* (Puebla, México: Fundación Universidad de las Américas).
North, Douglass C. (1990). *Institutions, Institutional Change and Economic Performance* (New York: Cambridge University Press).
Ryle, Gilbert (1968). "The Thinking of Thoughts: What is *Le Penseur* Doing?", in: *Collected Essays, 1929–1968*, Vol. 2 (Abingdon: Routledge): 494–510.
Secretaría de Gobernación (2012). *Encuesta Nacional Sobre Cultura Política y Prácticas Ciudadanas*; at: www.encup.gob.mx/es/Encup/Documentacion (15 January 2019).
Tamanaha, Brian Z. (2004). *On the Rule of Law* (New York: Cambridge).

The Economist Intelligence Unit (2018). *Democracy Index*; at: http://www.eiu.com/topic.aspx?topic=democracy-index&zid=democracyindex2018&utm_medium=social&utm_source=twitter&utm_name=democracyindex2018&linkId=100000004653972 (15 January 2019).
The Fund for Peace (2018). *Fragile States Index*; at: http://fundforpeace.org/fsi/ (15 January 2019).
Waldron, Jeremy (2016). *Political Political Theory* (Cambridge: Harvard University Press).
World Bank (2018). *World Governance Indicators*; at: http://info.worldbank.org/governance/wgi/#reports (15 January 2019).
World Justice Project (2018). *The WJP Rule of Law Index 2017–2018* (Washington, D.C.); at: https://worldjusticeproject.org/sites/default/files/documents/WJP-ROLI-2018-June-Online-Edition_0.pdf (15 January 2019).

Part I
The Concept of Rule of Law and Its Measurement

Chapter 2
Conceptualizing the Rule of Law

Rodolfo Sarsfield

Abstract With the rise of research on the rule of law during recent years, the meaning of that concept has become a subject of much debate. The lack of consensus becomes quickly noticeable when some of the existing concepts of the rule of law are examined. This chapter seeks to explore the different concepts of the rule of law – and its definitional prerequisites – present in the literature. This review is organized according to two competing accounts of conceptual analysis used in political science, hierarchical structures (e.g., Møller/Skaaning 2014), and radial categories (e.g., Collier/Mahon 1993). Hierarchical structures organize different definitions of a concept along a continuum from the thinner (or minimalist) definitions to the thicker (or maximalist) definitions, while the conceptual analysis of radial categories proposes the existence of a "primary category" (Collier/Mahon 1993) with different "diminished subtypes" of the concept (Collier/Levitsky 1997). Thick and thin conceptualizations "involve trade-offs between generality and specificity, quantity and quality, and absolutes and matters of degree" (Coppedge 2002: 1).

Rodolfo Sarsfield is an Associate Professor at the Autonomous University of Querétaro. His research focuses on the study of social norms, preference formation, and political attitudes, with an emphasis on the attitudes toward democracy, corruption, informal rules, and the rule of law in Latin America. Also, he studies concepts and methods in political science. He is the editor of the special issue for Justice System Journal on "The Rule of Law" (with Ryan E. Carlin). He also is the author of *Research Design* (with G. Dave Garson, Statistical Associate Publishing, Asheboro, NC). He has published more than two dozen journal articles and contributions to edited volumes. He received his Ph.D. in Political Science from the Facultad Latinoamericana de Ciencias Sociales [Latinamerican Faculty of Social Sciences] (FLACSO) in 2004. He has been Associate Researcher of the Latin American Public Opinion Project at Vanderbilt University, and Affiliated Researcher of the Department of Legal Studies at the Centro de Investigación y Docencia Económicas [Center for Research and Teaching in Economics] (CIDE). He is currently a Board Member of the Committee on Concepts and Methods at the International Political Science Association (IPSA), and he collaborates with the Mass Survey team for Team Populism. Email: rodolfo.sarsfield@uaq.mx.

Keywords Rule of law · Rule by law · Democracy · Individual rights · Equality · Law

2.1 Introduction

Along with other major concepts in political science, such as democracy (Collier/Levitsky 1997; Munck/Verkuilen 2002), ideology (Gerring 1997), and populism (Mudde/Rovira 2017; Weyland 2001), the rule of law seems to be an essentially contested concept (Collier et al. 2007; Fallon 1997; Gallie 1956; Møller/Skaaning 2012, 2014; Waldron 2002). Several contesting conceptions of the rule of law have been provided by Fuller, Finnis, Raz, and Dworkin, with as few as eight dimensions (Fuller 1981), and as many as fourteen (Lauth 2001). Consensus on this essentially contested concept may not be rapidly forthcoming.

With the rise of research on the rule of law during recent years, the meaning of that concept has become a subject of much debate. The lack of consensus becomes quickly noticeable when some of the existing concepts of the rule of law are examined. Thus, many legal scholars think of formal legality – understood as the attribute according to which laws must be general, public, prospective, certain, and consistently applied – when they refer to the rule of law. Meanwhile, contemporary economists (e.g. Fukuyama 2010) emphasize, as an attribute of the rule of law, what they term established property rights. Others, instead (e.g. Belton 2005; Bingham 2010), regard a list of liberal rights – or, more generally, human rights – as a definitional prerequisite for the concept of rule of law. Also, some political theorists (e.g. Habermas 1996) claim that rule of law must be based on the sovereignty of the people, affirming that the authority of laws ultimately rests on democratic consent. Finally, other scholars, especially within the field of political science, propose that the presence of public order – or legal behavior – must be considered a basic attribute of the rule of law – i.e., a state of the world in which people typically obey the law (e.g. Maravall/Przeworski 2003) and where individuals are appropriately safeguarded from crime and violence (e.g. Belton 2005; cf. Møller/Skaaning 2014: 4).

Although some scholars increasingly list the rule of law as a critical element of a liberal democracy, others claim that it is possible for the rule of law – or at least some of the attributes of this concept – to exist in non-democratic regimes, such as China or Chile under Pinochet's regime (Barros 2003; Chavez 2008; Peerenboom 2002, 2004). In this vein, there is a tradition that defines the rule of law merely as the system of order imposed by states on their populations whatever character that order happens to have. Thus, the rule of law would simply mean the 'existence of public order'. According to this stance, all modern societies would live under the rule of law, regardless of whether their regimes are fascist, socialist or liberal states (Friedmann 1952: 281; Kelsen 2009 [1967]; cf. Lovett 2016: 4).

This chapter seeks to explore the different conceptions of the rule of law – and its definitional prerequisites – present in the literature. Thus, in the first part of this work, and following Sartori's dictum, according to which an important first step for having a concept is "distinguishing A from whatever is not-A" (Sartori 1984: 74), this chapter aims to identify what is *not* the rule of law. Subsequently, in the second section, this work provides a review of different attributes of the rule of law proposed for different definitions of this concept. This review is organized according to two competing accounts of conceptual analysis used in political science, hierarchical structures (e.g. Møller/Skaaning 2014), and radial categories (e.g. Collier/Mahon 1993). Hierarchical structures organize different definitions of a concept along a continuum from the thinner (or minimalist) definitions to the thicker (or maximalist) definitions. The conceptual analysis of radial categories proposes the existence of a "primary category" (Collier/Mahon 1993) with different "diminished subtypes" of the concept (Collier/Levitsky 1997). Finally, some conclusions on the different conceptualizations of the rule of law are presented.

2.2 What is *Not* the Rule of Law?

Little or no consensus exists with regard to the definition of the rule of law. What occurs with the rule of law concept is, of course, not uncommon in this respect. Most concepts in the social sciences are characterized by significant conceptual debates (Gallie 1956). Therefore, the most valuable advice is to "treat the conceptual disagreement in what Sartori (1970) refers to as a (methodologically) self-conscious way" (Møller/Skaaning 2014: 7). In this vein, the classic work of Giovanni Sartori suggests that in order to understand the singularity of any phenomenon it is important to distinguish its opposites. When it comes to the rule of law, the clearest two are the *rule of men* and *special-interest laws*.

2.2.1 Rule of Law, Not of Men

A frequent interpretation of the rule of law is set out it by contrast to the rule of men. This contrast is presented as different antitheses: 'the rule of law, not men'; 'a government of laws, not men'; 'law is reason, man is passion'; 'law is not-discretionary, man is arbitrary will'; 'law is objective, man is subjective' (Tamanaha 2004: 122). The inspiration underlying this idea is that to live under the rule of law is to not be subject to the vagaries of other individuals.[1]

---

[1] It is worth noting that this conception of the rule of law seems be grounded on a negative view of the human being. As it occurs with different ideological visions, often concepts in positive political theory are based on different underlying assumptions about human nature. These different assumptions "lead not only to different conclusions on particular issues, but also to wholly different meanings to such fundamental words as 'justice' [or] 'equality'" (Sowell 2007: xi).

"The rule of law, not men" is, in some way, "the antithesis of the arbitrary use of the power" (Hamara 2013: 16). The rule of law is conceived as objective and in conformity with reason, and as such is the opposite notion to the rule of men, which is assumed to be subjective and arbitrary. To live under the rule of law – instead to live under the rule of men – means to be protected from human nature, which tends to be characterized by "bias, passion, prejudice, error, ignorance, cupidity, or whim" (Tamanaha 2004: 122). A ruler who typifies the rule of law behaves according to "factors external to himself – existing rules, principles, and reason". By contrast, a ruler who rules in concordance with the rule of men does not behave according to "factors external to himself, but only to internal factors such as his own needs, desires, or predilections" (Hamara 2013: 16–17).

However, the idea of "the rule of law, not men," powerful as it is, has been forever dogged by the fact that laws are not self-interpreting or applying. Since laws cannot be applied without human interpretation and participation (Hampton 1994), the boundaries between the rule of law and the rule of men become complex and blurred. The operation of law cannot be sequestered from human participation. The inevitably of such participation provides the opportunity for the reintroduction of the very weaknesses sought to be avoided by resorting to law in the first place.

Additionally, the ideal of the rule of law – as the opposite concept of the rule of men – is eroded by the often dual nature of the laws. On the one hand, in concrete disputes, the demands of laws are often obscure, complex, and controversial. This inescapable characteristic of the laws produces contentious legal decisions in terms of their normative appropriateness (internal criticism). On the other hand, a legal decision can be contested according to exogenous factors of the legal decision itself (external criticism), such as "ideology or ethnicity of judge, the sex or social status of the losing party, and the wealth or power of the victorious party" (Schedler 2004: 246). Legal decisions can be controversial from both an internal perspective and an external perspective.

Therefore, establishing a clear boundary between the rule of law and the rule of men is often very difficult, if not impossible. Despite the fact that human interpretation and application of the law is unavoidable, it should not be concluded that the rule of law is inevitably reduced to the rule of men (Waluchow 2007). Hence, the principle of "the rule of law, not men", although complex, should be considered as a fundamental *regulative* model of the application of the laws.

2.2.2 Equality Before the Law, Not Special Interest Law

Equality before the law has a huge normative force in modern societies. In legal theory, this principle has largely been proposed as a definitional prerequisite of the rule of law (e.g. Fuller 1982; Lauth 2001).[2] It is important to distinguish between

---

[2]Joseph Raz is an important exception to this general rule.

two different dimensions of equality before the law: enactment of law and application of law. A well-known characterization of equality before the law in terms of legislation is *negative*: equality before the law and special-interest laws are mutually exclusive. Hence, it would be unjustified to say that a particular country is characterized by the rule of law if particular interests are enshrined within the laws. For instance, when "white legislators attach harsh penalties to the consumption of drugs consumed by blacks and lenient penalties to the consumption of drugs consumed by whites, they are promoting special-interests legislation" (Holmes 2003: 48). At the level of the application of laws, equality before the law is the opposite of legislation that it will never be applied to specific groups or individuals. If legislators attach penalties to the consumption of drugs consumed by any citizen – without special distinction regarding race, gender, socio-economic status or whatever other characteristic – but in its application by government officials only the poor, women or immigrants are penalized, then we do not have equality before the law.[3]

It seems to be inevitable that the generality of rules often results in both over-inclusiveness and under-inclusiveness. The first problem emerges when a rule stated in general terms applies to some situations that do not fit the purpose behind the law. The second dilemma occurs when the same general rule fails to cover a situation that it should. These two problems that characterize what Nonet/Selznick (1978) call "Autonomous Law" are less likely to occur in the exercise of what those authors identify as "Responsive Law", that is, a thoughtful consideration of substantive justice.[4]

---

[3] Achieving equality before the law is a very difficult task. A first puzzle appears when it is argued that laws are inherently special-interests-based because organized interests, with varying degrees of power, inevitably emerge in every society (Holmes 2003). A few powerful groups naturally sprout forth and cannot be prevented from manipulating law to their private advantage. Special-interests legislation, however unjust, "is not the exception but the rule". It has been said that "since human beings cannot escape from Original Sin", man-made laws will always reflect special interests, and that "[t]o be ruled impartially – that is, by laws not men – would be possible only for a population of gods" (Holmes 2003: 47–48).

[4] To avoid both over-inclusiveness and under-inclusiveness it can be useful to introduce the distinction between norms, standards, and rules. A rule "is like a numerical speed limit, whereas a standard is like a norm that requires people to drive at a 'reasonable' speed" (Waldron 2016: 8). Legal systems use both types of norm (Sunstein 1994): use standards for cases where the appropriate decision may vary with ambient circumstances and it seems better to trust the judgement of those who face a particular situation, rather than laying it down in advance.

2.3 What *Is* the Rule of Law? Contesting Definitions of the Concept

Several contesting definitions of the rule of law characterize the literature in political science, legal studies, and other social sciences.[5] Different meanings of that notion have been provided by Fuller, Finnis, Raz, and Dworkin, among other scholars. The lack of conceptual clarity of the rule of law has not, however, stopped empirical analysis of its causes and consequences. In spite of the limited systematic accounts of what is the rule of law, the term is abundantly present in political and legal research as a dependent variable (Barros 2000; Joireman 2001, 2004; Hansson/Olsson 2006; Hayo/Voigt 2005; Hoff/Stiglitz 2004; Lovett 2016; Møller/Skaaning 2014; Sandholtz/Taagepera 2005), as well as an independent variable (Carothers 1998, 2006; Barros 1997; Haggard et al. 2008).

Examination of the recent literature on the rule of law shows an increasing interest in the discussion about the measurement of that concept (Carothers 1998, 2006; Lovett 2016; Møller/Skaaning 2010; Skaaning 2009; Waldron 2002). However, much less work has been done on conceptualization of the rule of law.[6] One reason for the absence of research on the concept of rule of law could be the aforementioned fact that several authors have considered the rule of law as an essentially contested concept (e.g. Fallon 1997; Waldron 2002). As a synthesis of the state of affairs in this matter until relatively recently, it has been said that the debate on the conceptualization of the rule of law is a task that "should be abandoned and replaced with the individual concepts from which it is constituted" (Ríos-Figueroa/Staton 2008: 1), since that notion is broad and multidimensional.

Attention to disputes over the meaning of concepts is a fundamental aspect of political science. A growing body of work considers the systematic analysis of concepts to be an important component of political methodology (Adcock 2005; Collier/Levitsky 1997; Collier/Mahon 1993; Gerring 1997; Goertz 2006; Sartori 1970, 1984; Sartori et al. 1975; Schaffer 1998). The clarification and refinement of concepts is a "fundamental task in political research, and carefully developed concepts are, in turn, a major prerequisite for meaningful discussion about

---

[5]With regard of the contested meaning of the concept, it is worth noting that no government in the world today rejects the notion of the rule of law. Those in power repeatedly espoused the virtue of being bound by the law. However, a good percentage of those governments are far from showing respect for some basic principles of the rule of law. The widespread use of the notion seems to reflect the considerable legitimacy that the rule of law has around the world at present. Also, the extensive utilization of that concept could be reflecting ignorance or disagreement about the characteristics of the rule of law. As government officials do not explicate the ideas that they associate with the rule of law, its substantive meaning remains unclear, especially when political use is made of it alongside other socially desirable concepts, such as democracy (Schedler/Sarsfield 2007). However, even when it is more rhetoric that realistic, the use of the term is of fundamental significance.

[6]Significant exceptions to this general rule are Møller/Skaaning (2012, 2014) and Tamanaha (2004, 2007).

measurement validity" (Adcock/Collier 2001: 529–532). As Giovanni Sartori established in a seminal paper, "concept formation stands prior to quantification" (Sartori 1970: 1038).

However, researchers often tend to propose attributes for a concept without careful consideration of the theoretical adequacy of such definitional prerequisites or the logical relationships between those attributes. To avoid this shortcoming, discussion of the existing alternative conceptions of the rule of law should include both an examination of the mostly mentioned attributes in the literature as well as a review on the conceptual analysis behind the relationships between those attributes.

Regarding the conceptual analysis of the rule of law, examination of the literature shows that some scholars have proposed the existence of a hierarchical structure behind that concept (e.g. Møller/Skaaning 2014), whereas other authors have explored definitions based on the conceptual logic of what have been termed "radial categories" – or family resemblances – (Collier/Mahon 1993) that suggest the existence of trade-offs between those attributes (e.g. Lauth/Sehring 2009).

Hierarchical structures derive from the classical Aristotelian logic of the conceptual analysis employed by Sartori (1970), which organizes the different definitions proposed in the literature along a continuum from the thinner (or minimalist) definitions to the thicker (or maximalist) definitions. Such conceptual analysis entails thinner definitions being included in thicker definitions. In other words, such logic is conceptually premised on the existence of a hierarchy between the attributes of a concept.

The conceptual analysis of radial categories involves the existence of tensions between the attributes of a certain concept. Thus, such trade-offs between the attributes of rule of law imply a "radial concept" or a "primary category" (Collier/Mahon 1993) with different "diminished subtypes" (Collier/Levitsky 1997), each of which is defined by a missing attribute. In the realm of radial categories what matters is "to tease out diminished subtypes from a comprehensive primary category, with each diminished subtype representing functionally different combinations that deserve individual attention" (Møller/Skaaning 2014: 30).

The next section surveys existing definitions of the rule of law. In this part of the chapter, different attributes that have been proposed as forming part of that concept are examined, and the conceptual analysis behind those definitions is revised. Following an accepted analytical distinction for some concepts in political science (e.g. democracy, populism, political regime) that include the very notion of rule of law (e.g. Tamanaha 2004; Møller/Skaaning 2012, 2014), this section begins with the thinner definitions before presenting the thicker definitions.

2.3.1 Rule of Law, Rule by Law, and Formal Legality

A well-known version of the rule of law is the notion that law is the mean by which the state conducts its affairs (e.g. Kelsen 1960). In this sense, the meaning of the rule of law is equivalent to a state in which all-state agencies' actions are done through laws (Reynolds 1989). As a consequence, the rule of law means that all of the government's actions must be authorized by the law (Raz 1979). This meaning of the rule of law has received two kinds of criticism. On the one hand, Joseph Raz has asserted that the rule of law, understood in those terms, has no real meaning since it collapses into the notion of rule of government: "If government is, by definition, government authorized by the law, the rule of law seems to amount to an empty tautology" (Raz 1979: 212–213). On the other hand, Brian Tamanaha claims that this conception of the rule of law "carries scant connotation of legal *limitations* on government, which is the *sine qua non* of the rule of law tradition". A more apt label for that version of the concept of the rule of law therefore seems to be "rule *by* law". Hence, rule by law is just "a partial meaning of the German *Rechtsstaat* (law state), but no Western legal theorist identifies the rule of law entirely in terms of rule *by* law" (Tamanaha 2004: 92).[7]

In order to expand our understanding of the difference between rule of law and rule by law, it is important to introduce the distinction between rule by law and formal legality (e.g. Tamanaha 2004, 2007; Møller/Skaaning 2012, 2014). Rule by law means that the exercise of power is carried out through laws, whereas formal legality means that those laws satisfy the principles of generality, prospectivity, clarity, certainty, and equality in its application. It is worth noting that such definitions of rule by law and formal legality imply that the former is thinner and included in the latter, since "formal legality also entails that rulers exercise power via positive law [i.e. rule by law] but then adds certain requirements concerning the characteristic of these rules" (Møller/Skaaning 2014: 17). In terms of conceptual analysis, there are two consequences of those definitions. Firstly, rule of law is not confined to the presence of rule by law but also requires the presence of formal legality. Secondly, rule by law is included in formal legality, which entails a hierarchical structure for the concept of rule of law.[8] In other words, "rules of law and rule by law occupy a single continuum and do not present mutually exclusive options" (Holmes 2003: 49). Therefore, "rule by the law is arguably the minimalist definition *par excellence* within the literature" (Møller/Skaaning 2012: 139).

Rule by law and formal legality – the latter including the former – seem to encompass the concept of rule of law. Rejecting thinner definitions of the rule of law, other scholars nevertheless deny that the scope of the rule of law is limited to only those two attributes. According to Dworkin, the "rule book" conception of the rule of law is incorrect. Law consists of more than just rules. It also consists of immanent moral and political principles embodied within or standing behind the rules and the cases. Law represents the customs and morals of the community (Dworkin 1977, 1985, 1986). Law constitutes not just a coherent and integrated scheme of rules but also moral principles that reflect the life and vision of the community.

---

[7]Italics in the original.
[8]For a systematic discussion of this topic, see Møller/Skaaning (2012).

However, there has also been much criticism of thicker theories of the rule of law. One well-known criticism claims that in a "deeply pluralistic society Dworkin's conception has questionable value, since in such societies there are competing sets of moral principles" (Tamanaha 2004: 80–81). Beyond this controversy, there would be some agreement that it is not possible to conceptualize the rule of law without rule by law and formal legality. Accordingly, it would be possible to affirm that, on the one hand, both rule by law and formal legality are individually *necessary conditions* for the rule of law. On the other hand, no consensus exists on whether rule by law and formal legality are jointly *sufficient conditions* for the rule of law. When thicker conceptions add additional attributes (for instance, individual rights), such definitions wouldn't accept that rule by law and formal legality are jointly sufficient conditions for the rule of law.[9]

2.3.2 Rule of Law, Legal Behavior, and Institutional Equilibrium

Another attribute of the concept of the rule of law that has been proposed in the literature – at least among political science scholars – is the existence of an *institutional equilibrium*. This attribute is understood as a *state of the world* in which both actors within the state and societal actors typically behave according the law. In other words, there is an institutional equilibrium in a country when the behavior of both governmental agents and societal agents typically converges with its political institutions, understood as the existing formal and written rules (e.g. Maravall/Przeworski 2003; Maravall 2003; Sánchez-Cuenca 2003).[10] Equilibrium is institutional *only if* all the powerful interests customarily channel their conflict through law.

Hence, institutional equilibrium permits the set of *possible* actions of actors to be defined. In particular, laws must be able to domesticate, transform or constrain the behavior of powerful actors. Thus, institutional equilibrium requires that organized groups act obeying the laws. Unless "political, including legal, institutions are at least somewhat independent from military or economic power, the effect of

---

[9]Ironically, rule by law is perhaps best appreciated by comparing it with situations in which it is lacking. In the absence of some other source of predictability (like widely shared social norms or customs), not knowing how government officials will act in response to one's conduct or the behavior of others is to be perpetually insecure. A society without rule by law will be condemned to a disagreeable state of uncertainty. For a revision of this question, see Tamanaha (2004).

[10]However, some scholars have claimed that the state of the world in which state actors and societal actors "recognize and act following the law" is an attribute of another concept rather than the rule the law, that is, social order or public order (e.g. Møller/Skaaning 2014). The extent to which laws can keep violence or crime at bay in the relationships between individuals and groups is a possible result or outcome of the functioning of the rule of law (basically understood as formal legality). Therefore, that result should be conceptualized as a *consequence* of the rule of law but not as the rule of law *itself*.

institutions cannot be distinguished from the effects of powerful actors" (Maravall/ Przeworski 2003: 8). In other words, a society comes closer to the rule of law when power is not monopolized and the law is not used by the few against the many (Holmes 2003).[11] In contrast, when governmental actors and/or societal actors defend their interests by extralegal means (i.e. informal institutions, corruption, violence), a country will be far distant from the rule of law. When actors act according to an uneven distribution of power and the source of their behavior is external to institutions – for instance, the Mafia in the Italian case (Guarnieri 2003) – a country becomes distant from institutional equilibrium.

As a definitional prerequisite of the rule of law, institutions must be independent of "brute power" (Sánchez-Cuenca 2003). In other words, powerful non-state actors must obey the law. As is well-known, different countries face different dangers depending where economic and political power is concentrated. In many new democracies, some members of the private sector with a monopoly on the means of production are a major threat. In the case of El Salvador, for example, "the judiciary has been more focused on preserving the privileges of the economic elite than on protecting the rights of all citizens" (Chavez 2008: 66). A different scenario is represented by Colombia, a country in which "drug lords along with guerrilla and paramilitary groups present a danger to established political institutions" (Chavez 2008: 66).

Actors in the state must also, of course, obey the law. In Russia and other post-Communist nations in Central and Eastern Europe, including Albania, Belarus, and Romania, the major challenge is the presidency, which may be elected democratically but is thereafter subject to few constraints (Herron/Randazzo 2003; Schwartz 1998). Executive dominance is also a threat to the rule of law in Tanzania and Zambia (Gloppen 2003). In Bulgaria, the parliament interferes with judicial autonomy (Melone 1996). In the case of Hungary, state administrative apparatus violates the rule of law (Orkeny/Scheppele 1999). In Venezuela, the armed forces remain a potential hazard alongside the executive, even though for most Latin American countries the major challenge to the rule of law is no longer a military coup. Across Latin America as a region, however, the concentration of power in the presidency is a principal challenge to the rule of law. As a result of executive supremacy, other state actors lack effective means to check the president. In the

---

[11] Although conceptualization of the rule of law is relatively the same, Maravall and Przeworski's *explanation* differs from Holmes's *explanation*. According to Holmes, "power politics incubate the rule of law" (cf. Maravall/Przeworski 2003: 8). From his optimistic perspective, as organized interests multiply, these interests will become organized, power will be dispersed, and the law will be an instrument used by everyone. From the Maravall and Przeworski points of view, institutional equilibrium will emerge only when "those groups that have the capacity to defend their interest by extralegal means are also those best protected by the law". In other words, "once law become an effective instrument of some interest", institutional equilibrium – rule of law – will emerge (Maravall/Przeworski 2003: 8).

context of Latin American ultrapresidentialism, judges should have the capacity to act as controls on the executive (Kapiszewski/Taylor 2006).[12]

The achievement of an institutional equilibrium seems to be logically subsequent to rule by law and formal legality. Obedience to the laws (legal behavior) among governmental and societal actors presupposes the existence of rule by law and formal legality. Consequently, the two latter attributes are thinner and subsumed by the former, as an institutional equilibrium requires governmental actors to exercise power through laws (i.e. rule by law) and these laws to satisfy certain requirements concerning the characteristics thereof (i.e. formal legality). Therefore, it seems there is a hierarchical structure between these attributes.

It is worth mentioning that this hierarchical definition of the rule of law that includes institutional equilibrium as an attribute nevertheless might also be analysed from the competing conceptual analysis of radial categories. Thus, it is possible to propose two "diminished subtypes" (Collier/Levitsky 1997) of the rule of law. When the threats to the rule of law come from governmental agencies – for instance, as in the Venezuelan case, with the Maduro's government – what might be termed an *internally weak rule of law* emerges. In a different manner, when threats come from non-state actors – for instance, from drug trafficking organizations in the case of Mexico – what might be termed an *externally weak* rule of law arises. Accordingly, this conceptual logic leads to those two diminished subtypes being teased out from the comprehensive primary category of the rule of law.[13]

2.3.3 Rule of Law, Judicial Independence, and the System of Checks and Balances

Some scholars have highlighted the presence of an autonomous judiciary as a prerequisite for rule of law. In the same vein, other authors have suggested that independent courts are the essential attribute of the rule of law (e.g. Chavez 2008; Ríos-Figueroa/Staton 2008). Hence, the rule of law requires judicial independence, and judicial independence entails impartiality and political insularity (Fiss 1993). The courts must be independent of all actors that tend to monopolize the power in both state and society, "including the other branches of government, the military, or powerful agents of private sector" (Chavez 2008: 65). It is interesting to note,

---

[12]Although this chapter does not analyze the necessary inputs to making the rule of law possible, it is worth noting that generality of rules is threatened by economic inequality. In countries characterized by widespread economic hardship and social distress, the wealthy tend to have advantages in the legal system while courts often fail to protect vulnerable groups (Méndez et al. 1999; Ungar 2002). In their study of democratizing regimes, "scholars would do well to expand their conception of rule of law to include greater emphasis on access to justice" (Chavez 2008: 76).

[13]It is worth noting that these two diminished subtypes of rule of law are not mutually exclusive conceptually (or empirically). Those countries in which threats come from both state actors and non-state actors could be defined as nations with a *very weak rule of law*.

however, that this definition of the rule of law does not take into account the possibility that the judiciary itself might tend to monopolize the power.

Regarding the attribute of judicial independence as a definitional prerequisite of the rule of law, an important issue emerges when considering the conceptual relationship with the system of checks and balances, a fundamental condition that has also been proposed as an attribute of that concept (e.g. Møller/Skaaning 2012, 2014; Nino 1996). In this sense, it is worth considering that the very notion of judicial independence seems to be in conflict with the system of checks and balances.[14] If public authority as a whole is to be limited, there must be no "unchecked checked". In other words, there must be no agencies within the state that can check others without being themselves subject to checks. Are we asked to believe that judges have no interests other than to implement "the law", that their power to make decisions is nondiscretionary or that independence guarantees impartial decisions? Because the legitimacy of non-elected authorities rests on their impartiality, the courts have an institutional self-interest in appearing to be impartial, or at least non-partisan. However, "there are no grounds to think that independent judges always act in a nondiscretionary, impartial manner" (Maravall/Przeworski 2003: 12).[15] If the interpretation of the laws becomes the exclusive domain of unchecked bureaucrats, the risk to the rule of law is evident; it is also evident with regard to horizontal accountability and, consequently, the democracy (Guarnieri 2003).

The theory of the separation of powers asserts that only a sovereign whose authority is divided will be a limited, moderated one. This theory defends clear and stable boundaries between different branches of power. Power must be divided, limited, and stable. Power must avoid the unconstrained will of rulers. Only a divided state can be a limited one. In "opposition to Hobbes's argument, those conditions are the foundations of the rule of law" (Maravall/Przeworski 2003: 10; Hampton 1994; Kavka 1986).[16]

Whereas the theory of the separation of powers is in favor of functional and well-designed limits between the different branches of power in order to prevent interference from one public authority on the functions assigned to another, the theory of checks and balance asserts that each branch of government should

---

[14]Checks and balances are also proposed as part of a constitutional system of the separation of powers and democracy (Cameron 2002).

[15]It is worth noting that the emerging literature on the rule of law in political science highlights the fact that judicial independence depends on more than constitutional guarantees. In order to determinate the degree of judicial autonomy in a given country, a consideration of informal rules must accompany the analysis of rules outlined in national constitutions. Informal practices that allow elected officials to control the courts often overshadow formal guarantees of judicial independence. Informal practices can shape the incentive structure facing judges in such a way that they are unlikely to oppose government policies. An understanding of informal practices that shape behavior and incentives is essential where actual behavior is inconsistent with constitutional provision. Actual practices "may reveal that formal institutions are mere façades that hide the subordination of courts" (Chavez 2008: 67; Chavez 2004).

[16]In such a case, a sovereign whose powers are circumscribed would be an individually *necessary attribute* for the existence of the rule of law.

exercise some influence on the others (Vile 1967). Hence, a mere separation of powers is not enough because separation of powers endows each branch with unlimited latitude. For this reason, only if each public authority is allowed to "exercise a part of the function primarily assigned to another, could [it] inflict a partial loss of power on another" (Manin 1997: 54). Without a system of checks and balances, it is possible for any particular authority to undertake actions unilaterally, even though this authority does not have the consent or cooperation of some other authorities.

Paradoxically, the rule of law might be weakened by the presence of *unlimited* judicial independence. Instead, an attribute of the rule of law should be a system of checks and balances that can ensure that each branch of government exercises some influence on the others, *including* the judiciary. As a central issue, the very notion of judicial independence might be problematic. There is no guarantee that the judicial branch will be impartial if no accountability mechanisms for judiciary exist. In this instance, the concern would be where the boundary between *judicial accountability* and *judicial independence* should lie.

Finally, there are reasons to suggest that a conceptual trade-off between judicial independence and the system of checks and balances exists.[17] Hence, it seems plausible to consider the concept of rule of law as a radial category with two diminished subtypes, that is, a rule of law *with an unchecked judiciary* – or an *unchecked rule of law* – (where the system of checks and balances for the judicial power is missing but *rule by law* is present) on the one hand, and a rule of law *with a controlled judiciary* – or a *checked rule of law* – (where the judicial independence is missing but *rule by law* is present), on the other hand.[18]

2.3.4 Rule of Law, Democracy, and Individual Rights

Other accounts of the rule of law include two additional attributes for that concept: democracy and individual rights. Of these two attributes, democracy (Tamanaha 2004) – or consent (Møller/Skaaning 2012, 2014) – has been the more controversial. The very inclusion of democracy as a definitional requisite of the rule of law is conceptually dubious. Instead, there are reasons to suggest that democracy and the rule of law are two different concepts. In this vein, it has been affirmed that "[r]ule of law and democracy are both desirable attributes of a political system" (Ferejohn/Pasquino 2003: 242).

Democracy has been defined as "the inclusive election of law-givers and governors" (Møller/Skaaning 2014: 23). Thus, "democratic rule minimally requires

---

[17]It is worth mentioning that since none of those attributes lends itself to a hierarchical structure in which the thicker attribute subsumes the thinner one, the conceptual logic of the rule of law seems to be different from a classical hierarchy.

[18]The inclusion of rule by law in the definition of both diminished sub-types means, of course, that we are considering the former attribute to be the minimalist definition of the rule of law.

government by the people or their representative, elected on a broad franchise". However, "in some conceptions, it too may require more than that" (Ferejohn/ Pasquino 2003: 242). For instance, on some counts, a genuine democratic political system requires that the citizenry be regularly consulted on fundamental legal changes. So, the judicial branch should be prepared to enforce such new laws by striking down the old laws. Therefore, more comprehensive conceptualizations of democracy and rule of law can bring them into conflict with one another. Additionally, since the supremacy of law (i.e. rule of law, not men) requires the lawgiver to be bound by higher laws, such as those of the constitutions, and since an effective system of checks and balances entails rulers being checked, laws cannot be a product of democratic consent. As some scholars have suggested (e.g. Barros 2003; Ferejohn/Pasquino 2003), there would be tension between the *rule of the majority* and the rule of law.

Also, some scholars have highlighted the notion of individual rights as an attribute of the rule of law. This attribute has different labels: "individual rights", "rights of dignity and/or justice", and/or "social welfare" (Tamanaha 2004), "human rights" (Belton 2005; Bingham 2010), and "substance of the rules", "negative rights", and "positive rights" (Møller/Skaaning 2012, 2014).[19] The inclusion of this attribute seems to come from the classic concern of political theorists over the limitations on liberty that could be imposed by very formal legality if the laws are repressive (cf. Caldwell 2004). Consequently, some scholars have proposed augmenting the attribute of formal legality by adding the notion of individual rights to the definition of the rule of law. It is worth noting that individual rights are typically conceived among these scholars as *pre-political* and/or *constitutionally sanctioned rights*, which means that such individual rights cannot be modified through the democratic channel (Bingham 2010). Accordingly, it seems there is a trade-off between individual rights and democracy. Considering that democratic consent is defined – at least, in some accounts of this concept (e.g., Habermas 1996) – as the ideal according to which the *sources* of the laws rest on the *sovereignty of the people*,[20] and that "the people is only sovereign insofar as it can alter (or even overrule) rights" (Møller/Skaaning 2014: 23–24), a (paradoxical) conflict emerges between the notion of democracy and the notion of individual rights.

---

[19] All these labels have their conceptual advantages and disadvantages. One of the most compelling ways to present this definitional prerequisite is proposed by Møller and Skaaning. Following Isaiah Berlin's classic distinction, these scholars divide the dimension of what they term as the *substance of the rules* between two attributes, negative liberal rights on the one hand and positive social rights on the other (Berlin 1969). Hence, according to these authors, this distinction "is expressly hierarchical in that negative rights" are conceptually "prior to positive rights" (Møller/Skaaning 2014: 20). In other words, positive social rights incorporate negative political rights.

[20] According to Møller/Skaaning (2012, 2014), this idea seems to have its historical origins and background in the feudalist notion of the right of resistance.

2.4 Conclusions

This chapter has sought to explore different attributes that have been proposed as forming part of the concept of the rule of law. Analysis of the meanings of the rule of law in the literature made it possible to identify some of the areas of consensus on and disagreement over the definitional prerequisites of that concept. Regarding the presence of consensus, this work found that there is extensive agreement on what should *not* be regarded as rule of law. Thus, it is widely claimed that *rule by men* and *special interest-based laws* are incompatible with the rule of law. Both the presence of the rule by men and the presence of special-interest laws imply the absence of the rule of law for a good part of the scholars.

Also, several of the central controversies about the conceptualization of the rule of law were identified. One of these controversies is analytical and it has to do with *which* attributes should be considered as part of the rule of law. An important step to define a concept is identifying a set of individually necessary and jointly sufficient attributes (Adcock 2005; Sartori 1975, 1984). A list of potential attributes of the rule of law was presented throughout this work. Another of these controversies is methodological and it has to do with *how many* attributes should be considered as part of the rule of law. This chapter found the existence of some conceptions that emphasize thinner (or minimalist) definitions of the rule of law and other conceptions that highlight thicker (or maximalist) meanings of the rule of law.

Conceptual analysis matters. Thick and thin conceptualizations "involve trade-offs between generality and specificity, quantity and quality, and absolutes and matters of degree" (Coppedge 2002: 1). One of the trade-offs between thick and thin conceptualizations was spelled out long ago by Sartori (1970). The more multifaceted a concept is, the smaller the number of objects to which it applies. For instance, Weyland (2001) offers a good example of the concept of populism: if the term is equated only with a style of discourse exalting "the people", most Latin American politicians and many beyond the region would qualify as populists. But "the more one adds on additional characteristics – spell-binding oratory from balconies, working-class support, neglect of party-building, redistributionist policies, military background, authoritarian proclivities – the fewer qualifying populists there are" (Coppedge 2002: 5). Consequently, on the one hand, thick conceptualizations add meaning to a concept, but at the expense of wide applicability. Thin conceptualizations, on the other hand, have more general applicability, but tell us less about the objects they describe (Weyland 2001; Coppedge 2002).

Many conceptualizations of the rule of law are thick. For instance, in a classic study, Fuller (1981: 158; cf. Skaaning 2009: 5) proposes eight attributes that laws must satisfy in a country characterized by the rule of law: generality, publicity, prospectivity, clarity, non-contradictoriness, capability of compliance, stability, and congruence between declared rules and the acts of administrators. More contemporarily, Lauth (2001: 33; cf. Skaaning 2009: 18) recognizes those eight attributes and expands the list to fourteen attributes: general laws and not *ad personam*; publicly promulgated laws; prohibition against retrospective laws; clear and comprehensive laws; no contradictory or inconsistent laws; no law should be impossible to respect; relative stability in the lawmaking; proportionality in the law; equality before the law; precedence of law; no one is above the law; independent and effective juridical control; due process; liability to pay compensation for any damage caused; and absence of arbitrary state action and promotion of legality.

Additionally, Belton (2005) distinguishes five attributes of a country characterized by the rule of law: the state must be subordinated to law, the existence of the equality before the law, formal legality, law and order, and human rights. At the same time, Tamanaha (2004) identifies six different attributes of the rule of law. First, rule by law; second, formal legality; third, democracy; fourth, individual rights; fifth, rights of dignity and/or justice; and sixth, social welfare. Also, Møller/Skaaning (2012, 2014) propose five attributes: formal legality, checks and balances, sovereignty of the people, negative rights, and positive rights.

Finally, and considering the advantage and disadvantage of thin and thick conceptualizations, it is important to note that thick conceptualizations "tend to be multifaceted, multidimensional, and imbued with theory", whereas thin conceptualizations "tend to be simple, one-dimensional, and more theoretically adaptable" (Coppedge 2002: 1). With regard to the addition of more attributes to thinner definitions of the rule of law, Raz has made a decisive objection concerning any kind of thicker definitions of that concept: the rule of law "is not to be confused with democracy, justice, equality (before the law or otherwise), human rights of any kind or respect for the person or for the dignity of the man" (Raz 1979: 211). Raz's assertion seems to anticipate Sartori's ideas on the inherent danger of choosing too thick a definition of a concept, as it could rob the conception of rule of law of its distinct meaning, to the point that it becomes a term which means everything and thus means nothing (Sartori 1970; cf. Møller/Skaaning 2014: 26). This argument would involve excluding thicker definitions and their attributes (i.e. consent, negative rights, positive rights) from the semantic field of the rule of law and reducing this concept to thinner definitions and their attributes (i.e. rule by law, formal legality).

References

Adcock, R.; Collier, D. (2001). "Measurement Validity: A Shared Standard for Qualitative and Quantitative Research", in: *American Political Science Review,* 95, 3: 529–546.
Adcock, R. (2005). "What is a Concept?", in: *Committee on Concepts and Methods Working Paper Series,* IPSA-CIDE, 1 (April).
Barros, R. (1997). *Determinants of Economic Growth: A Cross-Country Empirical Study* (Cambridge: MIT Press).
Barros, R. (2000). "Rule of Law, Democracy, and Economic Performance", in: G.P. O'Driscoll Jr., K.R. Holmes, and Melanie Kirkpatrick, *2000 Index of Economic Freedom* (Washington and New York: Heritage Foundation and Wall Street Journal).
Barros, R. (2003). "Dictatorship and the Rule of Law. Rules and Military Power in Pinochet's Chile", in: A. Przeworski and J.M. Maravall (Eds.), *Democracy and the Rule of Law* (New York: Cambridge University Press): 188–219.

Belton, R.K. (2005). "Competing Definitions of the Rule of law: Implications for Practitioners", in: *Carnegie Papers*, 55 (January).
Bingham, T. (2010). *The Rule of Law* (London: Allan Lane).
Caldwell, B. (2004). *Hayek's Challenge: An Intellectual Biography* (Chicago and London: The University of Chicago Press).
Cameron, M. (2002). "Strengthening Checks and Balances: Democracy Defense and Promotion in the Americas", Paper for a conference on The Inter-American Democratic Charter: Challenges and Opportunities, at the Liu Institute for the Study of Global Issues, University of British Columbia, Vancouver, BC, Canada, November: 12–13.
Carothers, T. (1998). "The Rule of Law Revival", in: *Foreign Affairs*, 77: 95–106.
Carothers, T. (2006). *Promoting the Rule of Law Abroad: In Search of Knowledge* (Washington: Carnegie Endowment for International Peace).
Collier, D.; Mahon, J.E. Jr. (1993). "Conceptual Stretching 'Revisited': Adapting Categories in Comparative Analysis", in: *American Political Science Review*, 87 (December): 845–855.
Collier, D.; Hidalgo, F.D.; Maciuceanu, A.O. (2007). "Essentially Contested Concept. Debate and Application", *Committee on Concepts and Methods Working Paper Series*, IPSA-CIDE, 12 (January).
Collier, D.; Levitsky, S. (1997). "Democracy with adjectives. Conceptual Innovation in Comparative Research", in: *World Politics*, 49, 3: 430–451.
Coppedge, M. (1999). "Thickening Thin Concepts and Theories: Combining Large N and Small in Comparative Politics", in: *Comparative Politics*, 31, 4: 465–476.
Coppedge, M. (2002). "Thickening Thin Concepts: Issues in Large-N Data Generation", at: https://www3.nd.edu/~mcoppedg/crd/CollMunckIII1.pdf.
Chaihark, H. (2004). "Rule of Law in South Korea: Rhetoric and implementation", in: R. Peerenboom (Ed.), *Asian Discourses of Rule of Law* (London: Routledge): 385–416.
Chavez, R.B. (2004). *The Rule of Law in Nascent Democracies: Judicial Politics in Argentina* (Stanford: Stanford University Press).
Chavez, R.B. (2008). "The Rule of Law and Courts in Democratizing Regimes", in: K.E. Whittington; R.D. Kelemen; G.A. Caldeira (Eds.), *The Oxford Handbook of Law and* Politics (New York: Oxford University Press): 63–80.
Dworkin, R. (1977). *Taking Rights Seriously* (London: Gerald Duckworth & Co).
Dworkin, R. (1985). *A Matter of Principle* (Cambridge: Harvard University Press).
Dworkin, R. (1986). *Law's Empire* (Cambridge: Harvard University Press).
Fallon, R. (1997). "'The Rule of Law' as a Concept in Constitutional Discourse", in: *Columbia Law Review*, 97, 1: 1.
Ferejohn, J.; Pasquino, P. (2003). "Rule of Democracy and Rule of Law", in: J. Maravall; A. Przeworski (Eds.), *Democracy and the Rule of Law* (Cambridge: Cambridge University Press): 242–260.
Fiss, O. (1993). "The Right Degree of Independence", in: I.P. Stotzky (Ed.), *Transition to Democracy in Latin America: The Role of the Judiciary* (Boulder, CO: Westview): 56–60.
Friedmann, W. (1951). *Law and Social Change in Contemporary Britain* (London: Stevens & Sons, Ltd.).
Fukuyama, F. (2010). "Transitions to the Rule of Law", in: *Journal of Democracy*, 21, 1: 31–44.
Fuller, L.L. (1964). *The Morality of Law* (New Haven, CT: Yale University Press).
Fuller, L.; Winston, K. (1981). *The Principles of Social Order: selected essays of Lon L. Fuller* (Durham, NC: Duke University Press).
Gallie, W. (1956). "Essentially Contested Concepts", in: *Proceedings of the Aristotelian Society*, 56: 167–198. Retrieved from http://www.jstor.org/stable/4544562.
Gerring, J. (1997). "Ideology: A Definitional Analysis", in: *Political Research Quarterly*, 50, 4: 957–994.
Gloppen, S. (2003). "The Accountability Function of The Courts in Tanzania and Zambia", in: *Democratization*, 10: 112–136.
Goertz, G. (2006). *Social Science Concepts: A User's Guide* (Princeton, NJ: Princeton University Press).

Guarnieri, C. (2003). "Courts as an Instrument of Horizontal Accountability. The Case of Latin Europe", in: A. Przeworski; J.M. Maravall (Eds.), *Democracy and the Rule of Law* (New York: Cambridge University Press): 223–241.
Habermas, J. (1996). *Between Facts and Norms: Contributions to a Discourse Theory on Law and Democracy* (Cambridge, MA: MIT Press).
Haggard, S.; MacIntyre, A.; Tiede, L. (2008). "The Rule of Law and Economic Development", in: *Annual Review of Political Science*, 11: 205–234.
Hahm Chaihark (2004). "Rule of Law in South Korea: Rhetoric and Implementation", in: Randall Peerenboom (Ed.), *Asian Discourses of Rule of Law. Rhetoric and Implementation of the Rule of Law in Twelve Asian Countries, France, and the US* (London and New York: Routledge): 385–416.
Hamara, Courtney T. (2013). "The Concept of the Rule of Law", in: Flores, Imer B.; Himma, Kenneth E. (Eds.), *Law, Liberty, and the Rule of Law* (Dordrecht: Springer): 11–26.
Hampton, J. (1994). "Democracy and The Rule of Law", in: Shapiro, I. (Ed.), *The Rule of Law* (New York: New York University): 36: 13–44.
Hansson, G.; Olsson, O. (2006). *Working Paper 200* (Göteborg: School of Economics, Göteborg University).
Hayo, B.; Voigt, S. (2005). "Explaining de facto judicial independence", *Working Paper No. 200507* (Marburg: Philipps-Universität Marburg).
Herron, E.S.; Randazzo, K.A. (2003). "The Relationship between Independence and Judicial Review in Post-Communist Countries", in: *Journal of Politics*, 65: 422–438.
Hoff, K.; Stiglitz, J. (2004). "After the Big Bang? Obstacles to the Emergence of Rule of Law in Post-Communist Societies", in: *American Economic Review*, 94: 753–763.
Holmes, S. (2003). "Lineages of the Rule of Law", in: Przeworski, A.; Maravall, J.M. (Eds.), *Democracy and the Rule of Law* (New York: Cambridge University Press): 19–61.
Joireman, S.F. (2001). "Inherited Legal Systems and Effective Rule of Law: Africa and the Colonial Legacy", in: *Journal of Modern African Studies*, 39: 571–596.
Joireman, S.F. (2004). "Colonization and the Rule of Law: Comparing the Effectiveness of Common Law and Civil Law Countries", in: *Constitutional Political Economy*, 15: 315–338.
Kapiszewski, D.; Taylor, M.M. (2006). "Doing Courts Justice? Studying Judicial Politics in Latin America". Paper presented at the Annual Meeting of Political Science Association, Philadelphia (August 31-September 3).
Kavka, G. (1986). *Hobbesian Moral and Political Theory* (Princeton: Princeton University Press).
Kelsen, H. (2009) [1967]. *Pure Theory of Law* (Clark, NJ: The Lawbook Exchange Ltd).
Lauth, H-J. (2001). "Rechtsstaat, Rechtssysteme und Demokratie", in Becker, M.; Lauth, H-J.; Pickel, G. (Eds.), *Rechtsstaat und Demokratie: Theoretische und empirische Studien zum Recht in der Demokratie* (Wiesbaden: Westdeutscher): 21–24.
Lauth, H-J.; Sehring, J. (2009). "Putting Deficient Rechtsstaat on the Agenda: Reflections on Diminished Subtypes", in: *Comparative Sociology*, 8, 2: 165–201.
Lovett, F. (2016). *A Republic of Law* (Cambridge: Cambridge University Press).
Manin, B. (1997). *The Principles of Representative Government* (Cambridge: Cambridge University Press).
Maravall, J.M.; Przeworski, A. (2003). "Introduction", in: Przeworski, A.; Maraval, J.M. (Eds.), *Democracy and the Rule of Law* (New York: Cambridge University Press): 1–16.
Melone, A.P. (1996). "The Struggle for Judicial Independence and the Transition toward Democracy In Bulgaria", in: *Communist and Post-Communist Studies*, 29: 231–243.
Méndez, J.E.; O'Donnell, G.; Pinheiro, S. (Eds.) (1999). *The (Un)Rule of Law and the Underprivileged in Latin America* (Notre Dame, IN: University of Notre Dame Press).
Merryman, J.H. (1985). *The Civil Law Tradition: An Introduction to the Legal Systems of Western Europe and Latin America* (Stanford: Stanford University Press).
Møller, J.; Skaaning, S. (2010). *On the Limited Interchangeability of Rules of Law Measures* (Unpublished Manuscript).
Møller, J.; Skaaning, S. (2012). "Systematizing Thin and Thick Conceptions of the Rule of Law", in: *The Justice System Journal*, 33, 2: 136–153.

Møller, J.; Skaaning, S. (2014). *The Rule of Law: Definitions, Measures, Patterns and Causes* (London: Palgrave Macmillan).
Mudde C.; Rovira, C. (2017). *Populism: A Very Short Introduction* (New York: Oxford University Press).
Munck, G.L.; Verkuilen, J. (2002). "Conceptualizing and Measuring Democracy. Evaluating Alternative Indices", in: *Comparative Political Studies*, 35, 1: 5–34.
Nonet, P.; Selznick, P. (1978). *Law and Society in Transition: Toward Responsive Law* (New York: Harper Torch Books).
Nino, C. (1996). *The Constitution of Deliberative Democracy* (New Haven: Yale University Press).
O'Donnell, Guillermo (1998). "Horizontal Accountability in New Democracies", in:. *Journal of Democracy*, 9, 3: 112–126.
Orkeny, A.; Scheppele, K.L. (1999). "Rules of Law: the Complexity of Legality in Hungary", in: Krygier, M; Czarnota, A. (Eds.), *The Rule of Law after Communism: Problems and Prospects in East-Central Europe* (Brookfield: Ashgate).
Peerenboom, R.P. (2002). *China's Long March toward Rule of Law* (New York: Cambridge University Press).
Peeremboom, Randall (2004). "Varieties of Rule of Law: An Introduction and Provisional Conclusion", *School of Law Research Paper Series* (Los Angeles: University of California).
Raz, J. (1979). *The Authority of Law* (Oxford: Clarendon Press).
Reynolds, N.B. (1989). "Grounding the Rule of Law", in: *Ratio Juris*, 2, 1: 1–16.
Ríos-Figueroa, J.; Staton, J. (2008). "Unpacking the Rule of Law. A Review of Judicial Independence Measures", *Committee on Concepts and Methods Working Paper Series*, IPSA-CIDE, 21 (September).
Rose-Ackerman, S. (2004). "Establishing the Rule of Law", in: Rotberg, R. (Ed.), *When States Fail: Causes and Consequences* (Princeton: Princeton University Press): 183–221.
Sánchez-Cuenca, I. (2003). "Power, Rules, and Compliance", in: Przeworski, A.; Maravall, J.M. (Eds.), *Democracy and the Rule of Law* (New York: Cambridge University Press): 62–93.
Sandholtz, W.; Taagepera, E. (2005). "Corruption, Culture, and Communism", in: *International Review of Sociology/Revue Internationale de Sociologie*, 15, 1: 109–131.
Sarsfield, Rodolfo (2010). "The *Mordida* Game: How Institutions Incentivise Corruption". Paper for the symposium on The Rule of Law: Concepts, Measures, and Theory, Georgia University State, Atlanta (June).
Sartori, G. (1970). "Concept Misformation in Comparative Research", in: *American Political Science Review*, 64 (December): 1033–1053.
Sartori, G.; Riggs, F.; Teune, H. (1975). *Tower of Babel: On the Definition and Analysis of Concepts in the Social Sciences* (Pittsburgh: University of Pittsburgh/International Studies Association.
Sartori, G. (Ed.) (1984). *Social Sciences Concepts: A Systematic Analysis* (Beverly Hills: Sage).
Schaffer, F.C. (1998). *Democracy in Translation: Understanding Politics in an Unfamiliar Culture* (Ithaca, NY: Cornell University Press).
Schedler, A. (2004). "Arguing and Observing: Internal and External Critiques of Judicial Impartiality", in: *The Journal of Political Philosophy*, 12, 3: 245–265.
Schedler, A.; Sarsfield, R. (2007). "Democrats with Adjectives: Linking Direct and Indirect Measures of Democratic Support", in: *European Journal of Political Research*, 46: 637–659.
Schwartz, H. (1998). "Eastern Europe Constitutional Courts", in: *Journal of Democracy*, 9, 4: 100–114.
Shapiro, M. (2008). "Law and Politics: The Problem of Boundaries", in: Whittington, K.E.; Kelemen, R.D.; Caldeira, G.A. (Eds.), *The Oxford Handbook of Law and Politics* (New York: Oxford University Press): 767–774.
Skaaning, S-E. (2009). "Measuring the Rule of Law", in: *Committee on Concepts and Methods Working Paper Series*, IPSA-CIDE, 29 (April).
Skaaning, S-E. (2010). "Measuring the Rule of Law", in: *Political Research Quarterly*, 63, 2: 449–460.

Sowell, T. (2007). *A Conflict of Visions: Ideological Origins of Political Struggles* (New York: Basic Books).

Sunstein, C.R. (1994). "Rules and Rulelessness", in: *Coase-Sandor Institute for Law and Economics Working Paper No. 27* (Chicago: University of Chicago Law School).

Tamanaha, B.Z. (2004). *On the Rule of Law: History, Politics, and Theory* (Cambridge: Cambridge University Press).

Tamanaha, B.Z. (2007). "A Concise Guide to the Rule of Law", in: *St. John's University School of Law Legal Studies Research Paper Series*, No. 07-0082.

Ungar, M. (2002). *Elusive Reform: Democracy and the Rule of Law in Latin America* (Boulder: Lynne Rienner).

Vile, M.J.C. (1967). *Constitutionalism and the Separation of Powers* (Oxford: Clarendon Press).

Waldron, J. (2002). "Is the Rule of Law an Essentially Contested Concept (in Florida)?", in: *Law & Philosophy*, 21: 137–164.

Waldron, J. (2016). "The Rule of Law", in Zalta, Edward N. (Ed.), *Stanford Encyclopedia of Philosophy*, at: https://plato.stanford.edu/archives/fall2016/entries/rule-of-law/.

Waluchow, W.J. (2007). *A Common Law Theory of Judicial Review: The Living Tree* (Cambridge: Cambridge University Press).

Weyland, K. (2001). "Clarifying a Contested Concept – Populism in the Study of Latin American Politics", in: *Comparative Politics*, 34, 1: 1–22.

Chapter 3
Rule of Law and "Estado Constitucional" Indicators. Does Law Rule Effectively in Mexico?

Rafael Estrada Michel

Abstract The fulfillment of the law has always been the aspiration of every State but this does not necessarily imply the emergence of a constitutional and democratic State, since the fulfillment of the letter of the law, in the Roman-Germanic-Canonical tradition, does not automatically mean the existence of a legal status that guarantees the enjoyment of fundamental rights. In this sense, what has the Mexican State done to guarantee the enjoyment of these basic individual rights? How can we measure the success or failure of the government in this matter? There is no other answer but the establishment of the rule of law. Rule of law is a complex topic that cannot be treated in isolation since it encompasses civil law, criminal law, human rights, administrative law, corruption combat, and interior, public and national security issues. Therefore all indicators and formulas to achieve rule of law should take these factors into account. In Mexico we lack indicators capable of measuring compliance with the rule of law. If we add up the problems that the legal substance faces when encountering the typical forms of Mexican legalism, the problem of indicators intensifies, since we require much more substantive measurements than those that only calibrate quantitative advances and regulate

---

Rafael Estrada Michel is a lawyer from the Escuela Libre de Derecho (ELD), Mexico, and received his doctorate in the History of Law and Legal, Moral and Political Philosophy program at the University of Salamanca (USAL) in Spain. He studied a Diploma in Legal Anthropology at the National School of Anthropology and History (ENAH) and since 1997 has been teaching public law and legal history at his alma mater and at Universidad Iberoamericana [Iberoamerican University] (UIA), Universidad Panamericana [Panamerican University] (UP), Universidad Nacional Autónoma de México [National Autonomous University of Mexico] (UNAM), Universidad Autónoma Metropolitana [Metropolitan Autonomous University] (UAM), Instituto Tecnológico Autónomo de México [Autonomous Technological Institute of Mexico] (ITAM), Universidad La Salle (ULSA) [La Salle University], Instituto Tecnológico y de Estudios Superiores de Monterrey [Monterrey Institute of Technology and Higher Education] (ITESM), Universidad Latina de América [Latin University of America] (UNLA), Universidad Autónoma de Nuevo León [Nuevo León Autonomous University] (UANL), and Universidad Pontificia de México [Pontifical University of Mexico] (UPM). Between 2009 and 2016 he was a Counselor of the National Commission of Human Rights, appointed by the Senate, and between 2012 and 2016 he served as Director General (dean) of the National Institute of Criminal Sciences (INACIPE), appointed by the President of Mexico. In 2018 he was designated Visiting Research Professor at the University of Pisa, Italy. A member of the National Researchers System, level 2. Email: restradam@up.edu.mx

formalities. We do not have enough indicators, and those that we do have do not allow us to adequately measure the serious and substantive problems in Mexico. In this hypothesis, if we develop and use more relevant indicators, we shall see, in a few decades, a substantial increase in the rule of law. It is a matter of governability.

Keywords Constitutionalism · Governability · Human rights · Indicators · Legalism · Rule of law

3.1 Introduction: From Traditional Legalism to the Rule of Law in Mexico

Complying with the law has always been the aspiration of the two-hundred-year-old Mexican State. As we will try to prove in this work, even of this had been possible (which it was not) it would not have implied the emergence of a constitutional and democratic State, since the fulfillment of the letter of the law, in Roman-Germanic-Canonical tradition, does not automatically mean the existence of a legal status that guarantees the enjoyment of fundamental rights.

We will start from the base that we lack, in Mexico, indicators capable of measuring compliance with the rule of law. If we add up the problems that the legal substance faces when encountering the typical forms of Mexican legalism, the problem of indicators intensifies, since we require measurements which are much more substantive than those that only focus on calibrating quantitative advances and regulating formalities.

We do not have enough indicators and those that we have do not allow us to adequately measure the serious and substantive problem we have. According to this hypothesis, if we develop and use more relevant indicators we shall see, in a few decades, a substantial increase in the rule of law. It is a matter of governability.

In his book *Governability, Constitutional Aspects* (2018), as in *The Norm and Normality* (2018) and *Cabinet Government and Coalition Governments* (2018), Diego Valadés speaks of our "constitutional vicissitudes". This is not strange: let us look at what has happened in the very important issue of the autonomy of the Public Ministry and in the lack of regulation, at regulatory level, of the coalition governments. Everything is contained in our Constitution, but it has been half-finished, in the inkwell.

The book *Governability* begins by distinguishing between governability (which is proper to constitutional states) and governance (typical of private companies), and even governability from mere stability, which can exist in non-constitutional states.

That is why institutional designs (for instance, ministerial autonomy in criminal procedures) are fundamental to ensure that violence does not impede the enjoyment of public goods, in Rotberg's sense: that violence does not lead to the failure of the states.

Thucydides spoke of the crisis of *stasis*, of paralysis, of lack of constitutional dynamism – a crisis derived from the commercialization of the *polis* in Athens. He, like Aristotle, Plato, Xenophon and Polybius, knew that it was necessary to moderate the principles of government through a mixed constitution that, without being of anyone, was at the same time of all (Fioravanti 2001).

On the other side was (and is) *anomie*, which is contrary to the norm (and, therefore, to society, because *nomói* is society): the interruption of the spontaneous observance of the norm. All of this is about the loss of solidarity articulated around the rationality of the norm.

Merton proved that if the channels of vertical mobility are closed, if the institutional system is the barrier for the excluded, the adaptive and logical reaction – the Pareto optimum – is rebellion.

But all this is Sociology. Valadés affirms that the constitutional nature is based on finding the appropriate institutional arrangement for each country. It is a topic of tools in the hands of constitutionalists of the stature of Brewer-Carías in Venezuela and García Belaúnde in Perú, as shown by the Ibero-American cases he analyzes in one of the important essays in the book.

Dahrendorf argues that governability is the effective capacity of governments to give direction to economy and society. Of course it is essential to safeguard this faculty from the forces that Ferrajoli (2011) calls 'wild'. The "Fourth Transformation" heralded by President López Obrador intends to achieve that. And this aim is noble, as long as no one forgets "Transformation 3.5": the institutional and agreed democratic transition that, from 1977 to date, opened the doors of democratic sense in the wake of the Mexican Revolution.

The philosophy and goal today must be: better to consolidate than dismantle. Better to create plural paths to equality than to eliminate fundamental freedoms. But to achieve this we need indicators.

3.2 Human Rights Compliance Indicators

In terms of the "rule of law" or – more accurately with Civil Law tradition – "Estado constitucional de Derecho",[1] an issue that crystallized in the great Mexican constitutional reform of 2011 is that of "the unrestricted recognition of human dignity as the only Reason of State in Mexico".

---

[1]We need to be careful, since "rule of law" does not stand exactly for "Estado de Derecho", but for Latin *Ordo iuris*: "And if we have talked about it (the difficulty) for the term *lex*, a no less difficult speech is what could be done for the term law, which still today has meant misunderstanding, indicating both an entire system of legal norms (in ancient times: the law, *ius*/law), and the specific legislative act of the legislator (formerly: a law), and in fact a concept so central to Western legal culture as the rule of law is translated – we use the French expression to better understand – as *le règne du droit*, but also as *le règne de la loi*" (Cavina et al. 2016). In fact, 'Law' equals "Rule of

The active promotion of the aforementioned constitutional reform, as well as the System for Attention to Victims of Crime, the Mechanism to Prevent and Punish Trafficking in Persons, and the System for Attention to Unaccompanied Migrant Children and Adolescents, has continued, with lots of attention given to the various developments, in very broad areas, of the 2011 reform. In fact, the fight against feminicide and the violence exercised over women are the axis of governmental programs, and Mexico can presume an experience of decades.

We can be optimistic about reform because its beneficent development literally jumps out: in all Mexican States we now have *Ombudsman* public institutions (called "Comisiones de Derechos Humanos") that have managed to form a functional network for the defense of human rights in the republic, transcending the inflexible molds that for many years tried to paralyze the work by appealing to a misunderstood federalism.

The reform of 2011 is based on a philosophical platform for which many of us fought for many years: that fundamental rights take precedence over the State and, therefore, the public apparatus must not only recognize them unambiguously, but proceed with granting guarantees of their effective validity (Estrada Michel 2014: 214–252).

But we cannot be satisfied, since the distance between norms and reality is still enormous. In 2018, in the case of independent candidates running for Presidency and Congress, for example, the electoral authority blocked in practice what it claimed to recognize in terms of normative victories. In order to compete successfully in a Mexican election, it is still necessary to belong to a political party or, at least, to build a structure organized as an institutional public movement or coalition.

So that this does not happen in even more delicate areas, such as eliminating torture or upholding social rights (the right to health and an end to the worrying reality of gynecological-obstetric violence are good examples), the reform of 2011 gave us invaluable instruments. We have, for instance, the above-mentioned correctly functioning network of public organizations for the defense and protection of human rights, but also the constitutional autonomy that both the National Commission and the local Commissions have reached, and the opening of legal sources towards that modern *Ius Commune* that is the International Law of Human Rights.

The autonomy of the Commissions includes safeguarding the sufficiency of their material and budgetary conditions (which is still a distant goal in some Union entities), and also, thanks to the decided support of administrative bodies, freely conducting research to facilitate the implementation of recommendations that for some authorities (the President, the Attorney General or the Governors) may be uncomfortable.

Rights", but its Latin equivalent, 'Ley' or "principio de legalidad", is not always synonymous with 'derecho' or 'derechos'. Zagrebelsky (2009: 24–27).

When a public authority refuses to accept the recommendations issued by the *Ombudsman's* office, the right seat to discuss the correctness of the recommendations is, at federal level, the Senate. A fine indicator may be constantly following up the determinations that the *Ombudsman* organisms issue and complaining at the Senate if a recommendation is contravened, in addition, of course, to the instances of mediation between citizens and authorities that have been functioning discreetly and effectively since 1992.

This is not only autonomy, but recognition of the effective and functional value of constitutional autonomy. I see a huge area of opportunity in the autonomy – already approved but not yet delivered – of the Public Ministry.[2]

Why? What can one thing have to do with the other? Much, in terms of due process, and the proper work of law enforcement, but also with regard to the effective compliance of the recommendations issued by the National Commission for Human Rights (CNDH), the national *Ombudsman*.

Indeed, for some years now, the human rights organizations have had the positive initiative of including in their recommendations the presentation of the corresponding denunciations to determine the criminal responsibilities of the case. However, it is no secret that as long as Attorney General's and Prosecutor's Offices are subordinate to the Executives, these determinations become practically impossible. With the autonomy of the Public Ministry, the opportunities for positive synergy between Commissions and Prosecutor's Offices will begin to fulfill a very positive role in the scope of Government's control. No official who has been denounced as a human rights violator by the *Ombudsman* may remain in the Administration, after the violation committed by him has been proved beyond any reasonable doubt. Here is a good formula for obtaining the fair and effective rule of law:

$$ERLHR = CD + DFD$$
$$ERLHR = CC$$

where:

ERLHR = Effective Rule of Law in terms of respect for Human Rights
CD = Criminal denunciations filed by the CNDH after a recommendation
DFD = Due foreseeing of the Denunciation before the Public Ministry
CC = Criminal Condemnation regarding violations of Human Rights.

The 2011 reform also brought us openness to fundamental rights from a supranational source through the operation of the *pro persona* criterion. The administration, and not only the judge or the legislator, is now required in each case

---

[2]Above all, it is necessary to analyze the infamous Iguala case, related to the still unclear enforced disappearance of 43 students from the Rural Normal School of Ayotzinapa on September 26, 2014 (see, for example, Garibian et al. 2017).

to look for the solution that more broadly protects the basic rights of the people, according to our constitutional text, notwithstanding that the mentioned solution is contained in an international source, such as a Treaty or Convention signed by the Republic, or in a subnational one, for instance, indigenous consuetudinary Law.

The perspective that we will have to assume will be, unequivocally, a perspective of basic rights and, at the same time, it will contribute to the universal validity of the principles of progressivity, interdependence and integrality of fundamental rights, to which the first article of our Constitution also refers.

"Universal validity" implies an authentic crusade for the definitive extension of social rights to all layers of the population. It is time for us to take seriously the eradication of hunger, universal access to health services and quality education, and the effective promotion of the right to decent work, as had been claimed through the example of domestic work that unfortunately remains in the scope of a profound extension beyond mere formality. Due to the reform of 2011, doors of Human Rights Commissions were opened to the labor claims.

Particularly in the field of social rights, in which our country was a century-old constitutional pioneer, the fight against corruption has become necessary. We are not going to achieve the social development goals that we set for ourselves at the dawn of the new millennium, until we decisively operate budget control and severely punish deviations in terms of budget allocations. Human Rights Commissions should turn their attention to the expense budgets and to their concrete applications, and should issue the recommendations that they consider appropriate. A general recommendation for the 2019 fiscal year in the area of fundamental social rights would be a valuable guide for governments and legislatures. It should contain indicators on best budget practices in order to ensure universal cover for health and education public services.

Non-discrimination for any reason that relates to human dignity (fifth paragraph of Article 1) has been considered the clause for opening and closing any constitutional reasoning and, therefore, for the human rights system. No one can be discriminated against for any of the reasons mentioned in the Constitution or in the terms specified by the Commissions or the Supreme Court of Justice. No persons at all: not because of their ethnic origin, nor because of their age, nor because of their religious creed, nor because of their sexual orientation, nor because of their disabilities, nor because of their gender. Neither can people be discriminated against because of their procedural or penitentiary situation, so the rights of victims, defendants and inmates in Social Reintegration Centers must be object of special attention.

In such regard, the axis of public security can and must be approached from the perspective of fundamental rights. The system must be inflexible with regard to the prohibition of torture and degrading treatment, and also with regard to the right of victims to the truth, to memory and to the reparation of the damage that has been caused to them. Special attention should be paid to satisfactory implementation of the initiative that the CNDH recommended to the Executive Commission for Victims Assistance (CEAV): the access of victims to the Reparation Fund legally established since 2013. But this alone is not enough: we must guarantee them and all the inhabitants of the country, including those who transit through it, full protection of their right to security. And this can only be achieved through a determined fight against impunity:

RL = EFI

Here, RL is "Rule of Law" and EFI stands for "Effective Fight against Impunity".

Standing emphatically for a due process of law, in an accusatory and effective way as the 2008 procedural reform ordered, also raises concern over incorrect implementation. Mexican citizens have a fundamental right to the correct administration and delivery of justice, that drastically and immediately reduces the levels of impunity and that imposes sanctions on both the corrupt officials and those who violate, kill, traffic people, torture, disappear people, execute, misuse personal data, and a long and painful et cetera.

This list includes, of course, not just drug trafficking, but organized crime in all its forms, including that affecting the most vulnerable populations: elderly persons, minors, migrants, people living on the streets, and inmates of Reintegration Centers. The pernicious tendency to dismantle a police force that, at a federal level, took many years to build, has obligated administrations to use the armed forces, many of whose members have no perspective of human rights in main issues, as we have seen in Tlatlaya and Tanhuato.

Regulation of Internal Security, as seen in polemics towards the recent expedition of the "Ley de Seguridad Interior", must undergo a more cautious analysis, especially with regard to the suspension of guarantees through procedures other than strictly constitutional ones. Above all, rights that Article 29 has declared non-suspendable under any circumstances may be *de facto* violated through opaque and informal procedures. This, and other important questions, remain *sub iudice* at the Supreme Court, as per constant constitutional complaints, one of which was delivered by the CNDH.

The principle of progressivity on human rights, included in the constitutional text after the seminal reform of 2011, has suffered a worrying challenge. This controversial Internal Security Law adds to the confusion between "national security" (one of whose ramifications is, by constitutional mandate, "internal security") and "public security", amplifying (and pretending to justify) the areas of intervention by the armed forces in tasks that are alien to them and establishing a regime in which the guarantee of human rights is suspended, contrary to regulations and delimited by the Constitution itself.

3.3 Administrative Justice Indicators

Let us move from Constitutional issues to the area of Administrative Law by asking a few questions. First of all, are human rights being respected in the administration of administrative justice?

It is necessary to distinguish two areas in the question. If we are talking about respect for the fundamental elements of due process within administrative procedures, it can be said that most administrative courts comply with them. This is the case of the Federal Court of Administrative Justice (TFJA), a body that was reformed to adapt to the requirements of the 2011 reform on human rights and the anti-corruption reform of 2016. It must be said, moreover, that the judgments of the administrative Courts are frequently reviewed by way of the *amparo* procedures resolved by a Federal Court, and the same occurs with the resolutions of autonomous bodies such as the Instituto Nacional de Acceso a la Información (INAI), the Instituto Federal de Telecomunicaciones (IFETEL) and the Federal Institute of Competition (IFECOM). However, at local level the situation is very varied. Some States lacked a local contentious-administrative court as recently as 2017. In others, the contentious-administrative court that resolves complaints is completely subordinate to the local administration. In those cases, the rights of the governed against the administration cannot be asserted except through civil reparation, often a very inefficient method.

The second area of the question centres on whether administrative justice is an appropriate channel for the guarantee and protection of basic rights. In that regard, it must be said that the 2011 reform was one of the great milestones of the democratic transition. Although it has been questioned and even used for electoral purposes, the truth is that it forces all the authorities in the country to promote, respect and guarantee fundamental rights. The TFJA and other contentious-administrative courts have been given the task of diffusely controlling the constitutionality of administrative laws and discarding those that they consider contrary to the constitutional and conventional order of human rights. The Federal Circuit Courts have done the same with administrative matters and, of course, so has the Supreme Court.

The challenge is to refrain from denaturalizing the concept of "human rights" by distinguishing fundamental rights from those that are a matter of mere legality. To assist with this, the Constitution offers keys in the very first article: basic rights are universal, unavailable, unconditioned and fundamental for human coexistence in terms of dignity and non-discrimination. They admit the application of the principles of interdependence, indivisibility, universality and comprehensiveness. Unless we want to sweeten the constitutional and democratic rule of law, we cannot affirm that the right not to undergo torture or arbitrary detentions is just the same as the possibility of consuming marijuana.

Second question: in administrative matters, are judgments handed down with a gender perspective? This has been a constant concern of the Gender Equality Commission created in the TFJA, which also has an Ethics Commission. Both support the transversal and generalized application of the perspective to the resolutions of the various chambers of the Court. Not only in administrative matters, but also in other matters, such as the criminal or the properly constitutional, the Supreme Court has ruled by the need to judge from a gender perspective.

A breakthrough occurred when a stipulation that concepts such as the "suspicious category" (which prompts the judging body to go beyond the evidence presented by the parties and to question whether the context is too risky for gender equality) should not result in violations to the presumption of innocence was finally recognized at constitutional level after the reform of Article 20 on the criminal prosecution system (2008). The principles and values of the new criminal justice system, which is more democratic and transparent, are applicable to the rest of the procedures in whatever is analog by their various forms of operation.

The gender perspective issue must, moreover, be approached in the context of the prohibition of all types of negative discrimination (the above mentioned fifth paragraph of the first constitutional article) and the operation of the *pro dignitate* principle as the sole and definitive *raison d'etre* of the Mexican State.

Is there full access to administrative justice? Access to justice continues to be a problem – and not only in the administrative area, but also in the civil and criminal fields – because it shows the limitations that we face as a country due to marginality and social exclusion. The Bar Associations have a lot to say about this. Perhaps it would not hurt a reform to promote compulsory licensing accompanied by instruments such as the shift of office, which requires the lawyer to take *pro bono* cases. Italian, Brazilian and Spanish cases yield interesting lessons in that regard.

The TFJA has courts in practically all the states of the Republic, and has pioneered the so-called "online trial", in which individuals can participate from practically any computer terminal. It is still important that procedures and argumentation become less complex, despite the technical difficulties that this entails. It is, however, very difficult even for a lawyer to make a Mexican municipality respond effectively to complaints about the damage suffered by vehicles due to the poor condition of the streets. In addition to that, there are hundreds of other examples, not to mention the factors required to promote administrative protection or to litigate before specialized committees in financial, telecommunications or economic competition matters.

From the moment of hiring an expensive lawyer who is well-known in judicial and administrative circles, costs accumulate exponentially, and few people are wealthy enough to afford their fees. Understandably, the offices of the public defender prioritize family and criminal cases, so in this matter there is still much to be done.

Are there exemplary sanctions in administrative matters for those who violate human rights? Again, we must particularize. If the question refers to deterrent exemplariness as a method of general prevention, we must remember that, at this point, we are not talking about criminal matters. There have been, however, cases of very high fines for companies and private organizations that violate fundamental rights in terms of the protection of personal data. The Federal Court of Administrative Justice, with the endorsement of the Supreme Court, has managed to get the Mexican State to apologize for the poor performance of the Public Prosecutor's Office[3] (that the public event was intended to be used for political purposes, and that Mr Peña Nieto's administration shot itself in the foot by insulting the Mexican people is another story). There have been some cases of corrupt public servants being dismissed, but in general we can say that impunity is far from being eradicated, and therefore the incentives for the proper exercise of public service are far from adequate. The sanctioning Administrative Law is still in the process of formation.

How has the constitutional reform on human rights in administrative justice been interpreted? As is clear from the TFJA precedents to which I have referred, it can almost be said that the 2011 reform has been interpreted in the sense that the administrative tribunals are obliged to control the conventionality and constitutionality of the laws, but also their interpretation according to the *pro persona* principle, seeking the solution that more fully guarantees the fundamental rights of the defendant. This is another of the great advances that we owe to the reforms that were introduced in the Constitution during the past years.

Finally, can it really be asserted that, in administrative matters, respect for human rights and the rule of law is guaranteed? There is still some distance to go, but I think that in general it can, especially compared to other procedural areas in which the situation is much more worrying (I'm thinking, of course, of criminal matters, but also local ones). Now that the issue of the fight against corruption assigns a role of high relevance to administrative justice, we will see if the administrative judges are up to the challenge of generating, for Mexicans, an authentic fundamental right to enjoy a correct and efficient public administration.

3.4 Formulas for Indicators in Criminal Matters Against Corruption

The challenges are huge – almost infinite – not just for the TFJA, but also for the Auditoría Superior de la Federación (ASF, a Congress Agency in charge of undertaking inspections and financial examinations of all government offices), the Ministry of Public Function (SFP) and the Special Prosecutor against Corruption ("Fiscal Anticorrupción", an office partially autonomous from the Attorney General's, whose leader has not been appointed since the legal reform was issued between 2014 and 2016). All of these offices, as well as a Citizen Committee ("Comité de Participación Ciudadana"), the Consejo de la Judicatura Federal ('CJF', Mexican Council on Administration of the Federal Judicial Branch), the

---

[3]This is a reference to the case of *Jacinta, Alberta and Teresa*, and to the "Hasta que la dignidad se haga costumbre" speech by Estela Hernández at the Attorney General's office in February, 2017. See, for instance, https://actualidad.rt.com/actualidad/231827-hoy-chingamos-al-estado-demoledor-discurso-indigena-mexico.

TFJA and the INAI are part of the "Sistema Nacional Anticorrupción", a comprehensive system presided over by the Citizenship Committee with a remit to combat corruption. As this mission involves both administrative and criminal prosecution channels, the following indicators are proposed:

Indicator: Strength of the foundation by the Superior Federal Audit (ASF) of the files that sustain criminal accusations

- SCDASF = DA + FIE + CSO + CC + IP
- CJF = SCDASF + CGRI

Where:

- SCDASF stands for Conviction Sentences derived from Complaints made by the ASF (Superior Federal Audit)
- DA are the Adequate Complaints regarding their motivation and typical criminal grounds (due description of crimes)
- FIE means Formulation of Successful Imputation
- CSO equals Sufficient and Timely help granted to the Attorney General Office
- CC means respect for the Chain of Custody in terms of proving material
- IP is equal to Procedural Impulse
- CJF means the Final and Definitive Sentence Favorable to the interests of the Government on Corruption combat
- CGRI means Correct Management of Appeals and Procedural Instances.

Indicator: Effectiveness of the challenges of the ASF against the resolutions of the Public Prosecutor's Office on not prosecuting probable corruption crimes

- AGDR = NRI − RNC
- AGDR = RP − (RI − M)

Where:

- AGDR = Appropriate Management of the Appeals Law
- NRI = Number of Resources and Challenges to Public Ministry resolutions
- RNC = Resolutions not exercising the criminal action Never Communicated to the ASF
- RP = Number of successful Resources
- RI = Number of Wrongful Resources
- M = Motivation of the resolution of no exercise of the Criminal action.

Indicator: Formula of Responsibilities of the different actors in the procedures

- IR = ID + FMA
- RASF = FA − EMP

Where:

- IR = Responsible Instance
- ID = Denying Instance

- FMA = Lack of Motivation in its Arguments
- RASF = Responsibility of the Superior Audit of the Federation
- FA = Lack of Accreditation of a fact that the law indicates as a crime and probability of commission
- EMP = Errors in the chain of custody and in the formulation of the imputation from the Public Ministry.

Indicator: Impact of the Superior Inspection in judgments

- RASF = CJEC − ECCNI − EVMP
- DA = DHT + Dprob + PP

Where:

- RASF = Responsibility of the ASF
- CJEC = Sentence Judged Against ASF's petition
- ECCNI = Errors in Chain of Custody Not Imputable to the ASF
- EVMP = Errors or Violations of the Federal Prosecutor (MP) from a complaint properly formulated and followed
- DA = Adequate complaint duly followed by the ASF as a coadjuvant of the MP
- DHT = Contains the Data that establish that a Typified Event has been committed as a crime
- Dprob = Contains the Data that there is likelihood that the suspect committed or participated in it
- PP = Test Principle (according to the standard of the new criminal justice system), with evidence properly expressed and safeguarded.

Indicator: Contribution to the identification of corruption networks

- RASF = ACSD − EVPMP

Where:

- RASF is the responsibility of the ASF for judicial denial of the existence of networks of corruption in the court
- ACSD = Argumentation, Custody of evidence and Monitoring of the Complaint
- EVPMP = Errors or Procedural Violations attributable to the MP.

3.5 Prospective

Rule of law is a complex topic that cannot isolate civil law from criminal law, human rights from administrative law or corruption combat from interior, public and national security issues. The name of the game should be "effective combat on impunity" (Romero Gudiño 2007), and all indicators and formulas should take into account the intricacies of such a complicated goal.

Let's address the most important and difficult question: the war on organized crime and its ramifications for pardon, amnesty and effective drug control (Begné Guerra 2007).

At what point does defending citizens with the Army become an apology for violence and, above all, a celebration of illegitimate violence?

There are two basic reasons why it is said that the armed forces must continue to support the efforts of the people of Mexico to combat crime: one, of a pragmatic nature, is the enormous predicament in which the recent administration (2012–2018) has left us: there are not enough police elements with which to face the seriousness of the problem. This is the harsh reality, which is obstinate in prevailing over our illusions and desires.

But the transcendent motive derives from a deep and ancient conviction shared by millions of Mexicans of goodwill: all, absolutely all public organisms are at the inescapable service of human dignity. As we have stated, this is the principle that must underpin all aspects of our legal reasoning and all of our public policies: the Army has been made for man, and not man for the Army.

Beyond statistics, critical essays and measurement models, the truth is that at the end of Felipe Calderón's administration (2006–2012), the panorama of our country began to change. The Chapultepec dialogues (2011) created an arena for the effective and systematic validation of the rights of victims. A lot of desirable details were missing, but the route was drawn.

However, this path was abandoned and, five years later, we see the results: a terror so constant that, hampered by the indolence of the civil authority, it affects every facet of security: citizen, national, interior, public… Human, in short. The threat that we failed to manage and to eliminate unfortunately appears today to be overflowing and merciless.

Given this, which extremes have the capacity to encapsulate a peace proposal which is both effective and respectful of the principle that Law, and only Law, rules? Armed forces, yes, but only if they operate within ethical boundaries and are inexorably respectful of human dignity. Mexico needs armed forces that do not replace the areas of law enforcement, administration and execution, but that contribute to the search for what belongs to each person due to the shared human condition.

In parallel, we need a strategy that establishes an efficient civil force which is compact, supportive, sufficient, strategic, and capable of having a positive impact on justice and peace. The State has to take prime responsibility not just for this, but also for the effective prevention of crime, guaranteeing the right to the truth, and commemorating victims with justice and dignity. We cannot continue to turn away our gaze while conveniently forgetting about the compensation funds and the legal, psychological and integral medical assistance that were promised between 2006 and 2012, only to be replaced by the quarrels of senior bureaucrats and the inefficient use of resources during the government of president Peña. During his administration, the strategy was not the same as the one instrumented by presidents Zedillo, Fox and Calderón. In 2012 all the statistics suggested that the Chapultepec route was beginning to function. We had before us a great opportunity to achieve peace via justice and dignity, as crime victims' organizations used to say years ago.

Today, with the recent change of government, this precious opportunity is renewed. We cannot allow it to be thrown overboard again.

There is a lot of talk about the enormous social concern over violence, insecurity and injustice in our country, but few efforts seek to be systematic when analyzing the various proposals of those who have reached a position of influence through popular election. In fact, in terms of judicial review of constitutionality and conventionality, we should ask ourselves whether or not it is desirable for a Constitutional Court to replace or supplement the Supreme Court. President López Obrador seems willing to do so and has referred in unkind terms to the current justices of the highest federal court. Attacks on the Supreme Court and the Judicial Branch are the order of the day, and numerous scandals related to the development of the jurisdictional career follow one another. A radical change with regard to our Constitutional Justice and the jurisdictional protection of fundamental rights does not, however, seem foreseeable in the short term. If structural reform is envisaged, the CJF – the body in charge of administering the federal Judicial Branch, placed under severe scrutiny in recent months on account of denunciations of nepotism and networks of undue influence (Borrego Estrada 2018) – will undoubtedly constitute one of the topics for discussion during the next campaigns.

The autonomy and effectiveness of the Public Prosecutor's Office are now unplayable to such a degree that the national anti-corruption system outlined a couple of years ago after the scandals perpetrated by the group in power, and seen as a panacea by many leaders of opinion outside the field of criminal and administrative proceedings, could be reduced to the serious and technically viable proposal of an accusatory ministry that is truly public and autonomous. The autonomies of numerous prosecutors at local level and, of course, the autonomic design of the federal Public Ministry have been pending. Proposals for this by various advocates were coming and going even before the Organic Law of the new Attorney General of the Republic, stuck in Congress, was issued. The social collective "Fiscalía que sirva" has launched a call to 'deepen' the autonomic reform. Mr López Obrador, on the other hand, has made known triple proposals for the appointment of the Attorney General, the Electoral Prosecutor and the Anti-Corruption Prosecutor in advance exercise of a faculty which, at present, the Executive of the Union lacks. Meanwhile, the 'forced' landing of the 2008 criminal reform in an adversarial and accusatory sense is still pending and increasingly provokes a greater degree of dissatisfaction among the population.

A genuinely structural reform, that of the professionalization of public justice services, must be built on the understanding that there should no longer be access to government positions except on accredited merit, either through direct appointments that fall on irreproachable people who are not related to improper interests, or through opposition examinations in which the interest, expertise and ability to share values held by those who aspire to make the public function their career path are evaluated.

In this last respect, the scope of the functions related to justice enjoys undeniable areas of opportunity and characteristics in its favor, since it deals with very specific aspects of the life of human communities with a margin of surprise lower than that which corresponds to legislative or executive activities. In other words, the judiciary is a structure that has performed more consistently and more continuously similar activities (and, in most cases, predictable and systematizable) throughout its historical development. It is no coincidence that the Mexican Jurisprudence, to cite a very plastic example, is ordered by 'epochs' generally much more extensive than those that correspond to the exercise of a Legislature and, of course, to a sexennial administration. Needless to say, in arenas of high constitutional development, the jurisdictional authorities are strangers to political ideological struggles, at least those that have a marked electoral bias.

In this regard, it is highly desirable that all those who hold a position in the Judiciary, starting with the administrative officers, know the mystique of the work, endeavor to share the values of justice and equity that should permeate judiciary tasks, and, in addition to displaying competence in generic administrative duties, express enthusiastic dedication to the tasks that specifically relate to the administration of justice.

Thus, people who enter the judiciary as administrative officers should be chosen with complete impartiality from a list of 'authorized' candidates, that is, people declared fit to enter the Judicial School, who have received appropriate training and can present proof of competency that enables them to ascend (and, in time, be declared permanent) to the administrative management tasks of a complex body such as the CJF. This would weaken many of the perverse incentives that currently exist for the configuration of nepotism networks or for updating potential conflicts of interest. We are talking about the creation of foundations that construct a clear framework for the development of a civil service administrative career within the Judicial Power. This would strengthen the mechanisms of transparency and accountability, for example in matters of appointments and ascriptions.

I mean, if district judges and circuit magistrates are constrained to select only 'authorized' officers who have passed stringent exams after a period of strict and academically irreproachable training, the risk of appointing unsuitable personnel is minimized. The current scheme of free selection, on the other hand, has provoked the infamous triangular movements, the exchanges of favors, the simulations and the more than symptomatic confluences of kinship between the members, administrative or not, of the Judicial branch.

With a school of knowledge for the first-level judicial management, taking advantage of the advances made by the Federal Judicial Institute since the seminal reform of the jurisdictional apparatus of 1995, as well as the experiences of the main educational institutions of our cultural environment (France, Spain, Canada, Colombia, Italy, Brazil), the Federal Judicial branch would be able to serve as an example of best practice not only to the other two branches of the Union, but also to the local judicial powers and to constitutionally autonomous organisms like the Prosecutor's Offices. This paradigm demonstrates the vital role that the creation of an authentic professional service plays in the consolidation of a democratic transition and in a system of constitutionally guaranteed freedoms. It also underlines the extraordinary importance of irreproachable administrative activity in modern and renewed jurisdictional services.

A strict regime of formation, appointment, ascription and permanence for the administrative officials of the Judicial Power is something that our country deserves and that the citizenship demands. It will translate, no doubt, into a very appreciable increase in the quality of the administration services of justice in the Republic. It is not possible to have excellent justice without institutions that comply with high standards of ethical, technical and administrative quality.

- EJ = TBD + FDPL − PCIRNC

Where:

- EJ = Excellent Justice.
- TBD = Well-equipped technicians.
- FDPL = Fairness in Due Process of Law.
- PCIRNC = Potential conflict of interest derived from nepotism or clientele networks.

3.6 Conclusion

Although in the normative and organizational order the rule of law in Mexico seems well grounded, above all in terms of the areas analyzed (Human Rights, Administrative Justice, Fight against Corruption and the structure of the Judiciary), much remains to be done in order to translate public policies into effective progress in what, for example, Diego Valadés has discussed under the heading 'Governability' or in what corresponds to the rule of law in the analytical sense of the World Justice Project, which continues to place Mexico among the last places in all the categories and scales that it uses. A first step to reverse the current situation would be the serious, effective and impartial application of indicators such as those proposed in this study, in which the Republic is almost completely lacking.

References

Begné Guerra, Cristina (2007). *Neoliberalismo y política criminal en México* (Mexico: Miguel Ángel Porrúa).
Borrego Estrada, Felipe (2018). *Informe sobre Nepotismo y Redes clientelares en el Consejo de la Judicatura Federal* (Mexico: UNAM, in press).
Cavina, Mario; Ferrante, Riccardo; Tavilla, Elio (2016). "Dalla crítica umanista all paradigma della Modernità", in: *Tempi del Diritto* (Torino: Giapichelli Editore).

Estrada Michel, Rafael (2014). "La historia del Derecho en México. Un estado de la cuestión en la formación de los operadores jurídicos", in: *Storia e Diritto. Esperienze a confronto. Atti dellíncontro internazionale di studi in occasione dei 40 anni dei Quaderni Fiorentini a cura di Sordi, Bernardo* (Milano: Giuffré editore).

Ferrajoli, Luigi (2011). *Los poderes salvajes: La crisis del Estado constitucional* (Madrid: Trotta).

Fioravanti, Maurizio (2001). *Constitución: de la antigüedad a nuestros días* (Madrid: Trotta).

Garibian, Sévane; Anstett, Élisabeth; Dreyfus, Jean Marc (Eds.) (2017). *Restos humanos e identificación: Violencia de masa, genocidio y el "giro forense"* (Buenos Aires: Miño y Dávila editores).

Romero Gudiño, Alejandro (2007). *Innovación judicial: Profesionalización, rendición de cuentas y ética* (México: Porrúa/Universidad Panamericana).

Valadés, Diego (2018). *Gobernabilidad. Aspectos constitucionales* (México: UNAM/Porrúa).

Valadés, Diego (2018). *El gobierno de gabinete y los gobiernos de coalición* (México: IIJ-UNAM).

Valadés, Diego (2018). *La norma y la normalidad* (México: Porrúa).

Zagrebelsky, Gustavo (2009). *El derecho dúctil: Ley, derechos, justicia* (Madrid: Trotta).

Chapter 4
Measuring the Rule of Law in Mexico

Camilo Gutiérrez, Joel Martinez, Alejandro Ponce and Leslie Solís

Every line is the perfect length if you don't measure it.
—Marty Rubin

Abstract This chapter provides an introduction to the framework used by the World Justice Project (WJP) to measure the rule of law in more than a hundred countries around the world. This framework was adapted to produce a subnational index within Mexico. The WJP measures the rule of law using composite indicators based on outcomes that reflect the experiences and perceptions of the general public and in-country experts. Eight factors are considered in the WJP index: (i) constraints on government powers, (ii) absence of corruption, (iii) open government, (iv) fundamental rights, (v) order and security, (vi) regulatory enforcement,

---

Camilo Gutiérrez worked at the World Justice Project from 2016 to early 2019, where he managed data analysis for the Rule of Law Index. Prior to joining the WJP, he worked as a professor and research assistant at Universidad de los Andes, in Bogotá, Colombia. He holds a B.A. and Masters in Economics from Universidad de los Andes, camilo.guti.p@gmail.com.

Joel Martinez is the Director of Engagement at the World Justice Project. Prior to joining the WJP, Mr. Martinez worked with the Massachusetts Commission Against Discrimination in its enforcement of anti-discrimination laws, focusing on outreach to low income communities. Mr. Martinez earned his B.A. in Economics and Political Science from Middlebury College, jmartinez@worldjusticeproject.org.

Dr. Alejandro Ponce is the Chief Research Officer of the World Justice Project. He joined the WJP as Senior Economist and is one of the original designers and a lead author of the WJP Rule of Law Index. Prior to joining the World Justice Project, Dr. Ponce worked as a researcher at Yale University and as an economist at the World Bank and the Mexican Banking and Securities Commission. Dr. Ponce has conducted research in the areas of behavioral economics, financial inclusion, justice indicators, and the rule of law, and has been published in collected volumes as well as top academic journals such as the *American Economic Review* and the *Journal of Law and Economics*. He holds a B.A. in Economics from ITAM in Mexico, and an M.A. and Ph.D. in Economics from Stanford University, aponce@worldjusticeproject.org.

Leslie Solís joined the World Justice Project in the fall of 2016, after spending five years as a criminal justice analyst at the prominent think tank México Evalúa in Mexico City. She was also an editorial advisor for the Justice Section at Diario Reforma, one of Mexico's largest daily newspapers, for two consecutive years. Leslie holds a B.A. in Political Science and International Relations from CIDE, lsolis@worldjusticeproject.org.

The authors extend their gratitude to Jeremy Levine-Drizin, who provided feedback and edits to this text.

© Springer Nature Switzerland AG 2020
J. A. Le Clercq and J. P. Abreu Sacramento (eds.), *Rebuilding the State Institutions*,
https://doi.org/10.1007/978-3-030-31314-2_4

(vii) civil justice, and (viii) criminal justice. This chapter explains the process through which the WJP gathers and analyzes the data necessary to measure the rule of law, and concludes with lessons learned from this exercise.

Keywords Composite indicator · Index · Rule of law · Factors · Justice · Accountability · Open government · Security · Corruption · Fundamental rights · Surveys · Outcomes · Regulation

4.1 Introduction

Across different languages and cultures there has been an agreement that the rule of law is vital for fair and functioning societies, ranging from the Code of Hammurabi to Aristotle, the Magna Carta, and the Universal Declaration of Human Rights.

The international community recognizes the rule of law as a key element for establishing peace, justice, human rights, and development (UN 2012). It affects essential aspects of everyday life, including feeling safe walking in your neighborhood; being able to protest, file petitions, profess your religion, and solve your grievances through the justice system; and enforcing contracts and property rights. Research has shown that effective rule of law helps to fight corruption, combat poverty, protect people from injustices large and small, and is correlated with economic growth and prosperity. In brief, the rule of law is considered to be "the foundation for communities of equity, opportunity, and peace" (WJP 2018).

Maintaining and improving the rule of law is, therefore, essential to societies seeking to build such communities of equity, opportunity, and peace. And, given that the rule of law is so crucial, it is important that it be measured. As the adage goes, you can't improve what you don't measure.

Yet, despite general agreement about its importance, there is currently no single, agreed-upon definition of the rule of law, let alone a consensus on how to measure it.

The World Justice Project (WJP) has worked to fill this gap by providing a comprehensive set of indicators to measure the rule of law, and thereby offering a diagnostic tool that is useful for evidence-based policy-making. To this end, the WJP designed an Index to measure the rule of law in practice, based on the experiences and perceptions of the general public and in-country experts.[1] The WJP Rule of law Index® provides scores and rankings based on eight factors: (i) constraints on government powers, (ii) absence of corruption, (iii) open government, (iv) fundamental rights, (v) order and security, (vi) regulatory enforcement,

---

[1]The World Justice Project (WJP) is an independent, multidisciplinary organization working to advance the rule of law worldwide.

(vii) civil justice, and (viii) criminal justice, which are later disaggregated into more than forty sub-factors. These factors reflect outcomes of the rule of law.

During the first eight years of the Index's development, the WJP sought to measure the rule of law on a global scale.[2] In 2018, the WJP produced its first subnational index to measure the rule of law within a single country: Mexico. The Mexico States Rule of Law Index is the most comprehensive measurement of the rule of law ever conducted in Mexico, allowing for highly detailed comparisons among all thirty-two Mexican states.

This chapter discusses the process of measuring the rule of law through the lens of WJP's experience of developing these two indices. The chapter begins by exploring two key considerations in measuring the rule of law. First, it considers the process and challenges of developing a definition for the rule of law and examines the choices made by WJP. Second, it discusses the process and challenges of measuring the rule of law and, as with the definition, considers WJP's approach. Section Four discusses the process of adapting the WJP Global Index to the Mexican context for the production of the Mexico States Rule of Law Index. Finally, the fifth section provides preliminary results from the Mexico States Rule of Law Index, and the final section presents the authors' conclusions.

4.2 The Rule of Law

In developing any measurement of the rule of law, whether global or sub-national, the process begins by determining the conceptual framework for measurement. The framework must be determined in advance in order to properly inform subsequent choices regarding the measurement methodology. Throughout this process, there are two main challenges to defining the rule of law for quantitative measurement: defining the conceptual 'thickness' of the rule of law to be measured, and designing a definition that adequately captures the multidimensional nature of the rule of law.

Regarding the first challenge, there is a debate between two different conceptions of the rule of law (Carothers 2010). The first conception, which is the least demanding and hence called the minimalist or 'thin' approach, focuses only on formal and procedural rules, which emphasizes whether rules exist, and scrutinizes whether those rules are followed by everyone, including the people in power. The second approach, called 'thick' because it is more comprehensive, focuses on substantive characteristics such as self-governance, as well as respect for fundamental rights and freedoms.

As for the second definitional challenge, the rule of law is a multidimensional concept that covers many topics and aspects of everyday life. As Rachel Kleinfeld explains, "the rule of law creates a relationship between a state and its citizens in

---

[2]The WJP Rule of law Index 2017–2018 covered 113 countries and jurisdictions, which included over 90% of the world population. Next year, the Index will include 125 countries.

which power, violence, and impunity are constrained" (2013: 2). In this way, adherence to the rule of law means the government is subject to law, citizens are equal before the law, human rights are guaranteed, citizens have access to efficient dispute resolutions, and there is a reasonable guarantee of order and security. As a multidimensional concept, the rule of law cannot be measured by focusing on one single element.

Measurements of the rule of law must wrestle with these two challenges in the construction of the conceptual framework. Determining the 'thickness' of the definition is ultimately a value judgement of the researcher, while the level of multidimensionality is, in many cases, more of a practical concern, rooted in the level of granularity that the measurement requires.

The global WJP Rule of Law Index is an effort to balance the 'thin' and 'thick' conceptions of the rule of law to enable the Index to be applied in diverse social and political systems (WJP 2018: 10). For example, it considers whether rules exist and are enforced (e.g. in regulatory enforcement), but it also considers the protection of essential fundamental rights.

To address the second challenge, the WJP Rule of Law Index relies on a multidimensional framework that encompasses all the elements of the rule of law and categorizes them into eight comprehensive factors, which are further divided into more than forty sub-factors that analyze particular aspects of everyday life. Using eight factors to conceptualize the rule of law is helpful because it translates an abstract concept into a practical measurement that is easy to dimension and understand.[3]

In crafting its definition, the WJP Rule of Law Index draws on two main principles on the relationship between the State and the citizens: the first principle measures whether the law imposes limits on the exercise of power by the State and its agents, as well as individual and private entities, while the second principle measures whether the State limits the actions of members of society and fulfills its basic duties towards its population.

The first principle is encompassed in the first four factors in the Index. In this sense, *Factor 1* measures the extent to which those who govern are bound by law. It comprises the means by which the powers of the government and its officials and agents are limited and held accountable under the law, including non-governmental checks on the government's power, arising from a free and independent press, or an active civil society. *Factor 2* measures the absence of corruption in government, with respect to government officials in the executive branch, the judiciary, the police, and the legislature. In this factor, corruption is understood as "the abuse of entrusted power for private gain" (Transparency International 2018). *Factor 3* measures the openness of government defined by the extent to which a government shares information, empowers people with tools to hold the government accountable, and fosters citizen participation in public policy deliberations. *Factor 4*

---

[3]Regarding the importance of developing a clear and practical definition of the rule of law, please consult Chemerinsky (2007: 5).

measures respect for fundamental rights, because it recognizes that a system of positive law that fails to respect core human rights established under international law is at best 'rule by law', and does not deserve to be called a rule of law system.[4]

The second principle is measured by the last four factors. *Factor 5* assesses how well a society assures the security of people and property. *Factor 6* measures the extent to which legal and administrative regulations are fairly and effectively implemented and enforced. *Factor 7* measures whether ordinary people can resolve their grievances peacefully and effectively through the civil justice system. Finally, *Factor 8* evaluates the effectiveness of the criminal justice system.

The WJP uses the eight factors described above because the rule of law is a multidimensional concept that cannot be fully captured by focusing on one single element. On the contrary, it requires a balanced basket of indicators – defined as measures to monitor progress towards a certain objective – which may lead to a more robust, reliable and comprehensive understanding of this concept. These eight factors are further disaggregated into more than forty sub-factors, and each one is measured with multiple variables that provide a comprehensive set of indicators for each topic.

4.3 Measuring the Rule of Law

Once the conceptual framework has been established, measurement methodologies may be determined. In addition to the definitional challenges noted above, any quantification of the rule of law must also address several measurement challenges. One challenge is determining the analytical focus of the measurement. The rule of law can be measured from a variety of analytical perspectives. Inputs, activities, outputs, outcomes, and long-term impacts can all be targeted for measurement, depending on the purpose of the measurement exercise. Therefore, any measurement of the rule of law must first determine its analytical focus of measurement.

To use the WJP as an example, in the course of developing the WJP Rule of Law Index, the WJP developed an approach that focuses on policy outcomes,[5] in part because the WJP recognizes that comparing the institutional means (including the legal and regulatory framework) is not an ideal way of measuring the rule of law,

---

[4]The most salient examples of 'rule by law' might be Nazi Germany or apartheid South Africa, "which were run by law but used that law as an instrument to deprive some citizens of peace and safety..." (Kleinfeld 2006: 45).

[5]Indicators can focus on inputs, activities, outputs, outcomes, or long-term impacts – depending on the goal. Input indicators include the money invested or spent to achieve a goal, and the number of people working in an institution – i.e. police officers per 100,000 inhabitants. Activities refer to actions that are designed to meet an objective, such as the amount of training provided to police officers. Outputs are the products that result from certain activities, such as generating an analytical or legislative document. Outcomes refer to short and medium-term objectives, such as increased perception of security, or a reduction in the crime rate. Impacts are long-term goals like improving transparency and accountability in a country.

given that, numerous times, a legal framework does not get translated into actual results.[6] Moreover, the links between the particular institutional means and the outcomes of the rule of law are complex and may vary depending on context.

As a result, the Index "explores the ingredients of the rule of law in terms of specific goals or outcomes that Rule of Law societies seek to achieve and that policy-makers might want to influence" (Botero/Ponce 2011: 2). Furthermore, it recognizes that societies have different rules and institutions to establish a strong adherence to the rule of law, and therefore acknowledges that strong rule of law can be pursued by different means. In this way, the WJP designed the Rule of Law Index to be applied in countries with vastly different social, cultural, economic, and political systems, so that it is culturally competent and does not force a particular viewpoint or agenda.

A second measurement challenge is determining the sources of data. Measurement may be based on various types of data, such as administrative data, expert opinion, and household survey data, to name just a few. Moreover, consideration must be given in whether to use original or pre-existing data.

The WJP is not the only institution that seeks to measure the rule of law, but its approach is unique. For example, the Worldwide Governance Indicators (WGI) of the World Bank seek to capture "perceptions of the extent to which agents have confidence in and abide by the rules of society, and in particular the quality of contract enforcement, property rights, the police, and the courts, as well as the likelihood of crime and violence" (World Bank 2018). The WGI relies on existing data sources, ranging from household surveys to expert information, and assessments from other organizations. A similar approach is taken by the Heritage Foundation, which focuses on measuring property rights and freedom from corruption to assess the rule of law as part of their Index of Economic Freedom. The Heritage Foundation also relies on expert assessments and secondary sources to assign country scores.

Freedom House, on the other hand, measures the rule of law by concentrating on questions about an independent judiciary, whether the police force is under direct civilian control, whether there is protection from political terror, unjustified imprisonment, exile, torture, and war, and whether laws, policies, and practices guarantee the equal treatment of various segments of the population. This methodology relies on information provided by analysts and expert advisers. It must be pointed out that this conception of the rule of law is only a partial component of Freedom House's measurement of Freedom in the World, instead of being a product by itself.

The WJP Rule of Law Index offers a different approach to measurement. WJP takes a user-based approach, as it draws data from both household and expert surveys (General Population Poll and Qualified Respondents' Questionnaires, respectively). This choice was driven by the intuition that strong rule of law is a system that allows citizens to thrive and enjoy the basic goods and rights necessary

---

[6]Please see the case of the "Paper Leviathan" in Acemoğlu/Robinson (2016).

to lead a prosperous life, and that an approach that does not take into account people's experiences, but focuses only on expert opinion, can lose sight of that.

Additionally, the WJP Rule of Law Index relies principally on primary data, obtained from the household and expert surveys. Building on its user-based approach, the WJP uses household surveys to focus on the perceptions and experiences of ordinary citizens, while expert surveys target academics, lawyers, and practitioners, and generate in-depth information on technical or specialized issues that may be unfamiliar to members of the general public who are not the typical users of these services (UNDP 2014: 52). To do this, the WJP developed a set of five questionnaires based on the Index's conceptual framework. One questionnaire targets the general population, while the other four target expert respondents and practitioners in the areas of public health, labor law, civil justice, and criminal justice. The questionnaires are translated into several languages and adapted to reflect commonly used terms and expressions in each country.

For the household surveys, or General Population Poll (GPP), the WJP has followed the strategy of hiring leading polling companies to conduct fieldwork among a representative sample of 1,000 people in the three largest cities of each country (before conducting full fieldwork, the polling companies also conduct a pilot exercise to test the questions and sampling methodology). These surveys are then applied face-to-face, via telephone, or online, depending on the characteristics of each country. For administrative reasons, the GPP is conducted every other year for each country included in the Index.

For the expert surveys, or Qualified Respondent's Questionnaires (QRQs), the team identifies, on average, more than 300 potential local experts per country to contribute to the surveys, and invites participants to fill out the survey instrument remotely via email. In 2017, an average of twenty-six experts completed the survey effectively in each country.

Both the household and expert surveys offer original information. The WJP designed the questionnaires in direct consultation with experts. In addition, the WJP complements the Rule of Law Index with third-party sources that measure elements of the rule of law that are not adequately captured through surveys, such as homicide rates or combat-related casualties.

Once data collection is finalized, the Index team maps the data onto more than forty sub-factors that compose the eight factors. All the indicators included by the WJP are normalized to guarantee their comparability, and scores are aggregated using simple averages. Data is cross-checked or compared against dozens of third-party sources, including quantitative data and qualitative assessments, to prevent biases and errors. Finally, the Index is tested for robustness and sensitivity via a statistical audit performed by the Econometrics and Applied Statistics Unit of the European Commission's Joint Research Centre, as well as for standard errors obtained from 100 bootstrap samples that are used to track changes over time.

As with all methodologies, WJP's approach possesses certain limitations. Some of the limitations that arise in the WJP Rule of Law Index are due to administrative constraints. For example, the Index only considers the three largest cities in each country. This has several disadvantages. Focusing primarily on urban populations may neglect the experiences of people living in rural areas, which is where the most disadvantaged people tend to be located. This limited sample frame can also affect results in important areas, such as fundamental rights, corruption, and the performance of the civil and criminal justice system, among others. Additionally, since the entire country is the fundamental unit of analysis, the WJP Index is also limited in the sense that it does not reflect differences within a particular country or jurisdiction. This can conceal particular regions with higher or lower performances.

Other limitations in the Index data arise from having a limited number of experts who answer the QRQ survey in some countries. This implies that countries with few completed QRQ surveys may have less precise estimates. It also means that having a limited number of experts, in combination with the GPP, being carried out in each country every other year, can lead to some variables not fully detecting small changes in a country's situation from one year to another.

4.4 Adjusting WJP's Definition and Measurement Approach for the Mexico States Rule of Law Index

Several of the limitations above are inherent in a globally focused index. Subnational indices offer an opportunity for WJP to adjust its definition and measurement approach for increased local precision. The Mexico States Rule of Law Index 2018 (published in October 2018) is the first subnational index to measure the rule of law in a comprehensive way. It follows the same objective as the Global Index, as it seeks to be a diagnostic tool to identify the strengths and weaknesses in each State, and to encourage policies to strengthen the rule of law across the country. In building the Mexico States Rule of Law Index, the WJP sought to apply the lessons it learned from constructing the Global Rule of Law Index while simultaneously adjusting the approach to improve the strength of its localized measurement.

In adjusting its approach for the Mexican States Index, the WJP began by contextualizing its definition. The Mexico States Rule of Law Index is built using the same eight factors that the WJP has used for the global index. The sub-factors, however, have been adapted to reflect the national context and allow comparisons at a state level. This can be seen in the following table (changes are marked in italics). These adjustments to the definition are designed to improve the local validity of the conceptual framework while simultaneously maintaining the universal nature of WJP's rule of law definition (Table 4.1).

In terms of measurement methodology, the Mexico States Rule of Law Index is built using the core methodology of the Global Index, but with some adaptations designed to improve upon several of the limitations of the Global Index. First, the Mexican Index considers the whole country, both urban and rural areas, rather than the urban-only sample of the Global Index. Likewise, it allows for comparison

4 Measuring the Rule of Law in Mexico

Table 4.1 Factors and sub-factors that compose the WJP rule of law index

Global rule of law index	Mexico states rule of law index
Factor 1: constraints on government powers 1.1 Government powers are effectively limited by the legislature 1.2 Government powers are effectively limited by the judiciary 1.3 Government powers are effectively limited by independent auditing and reviewing 1.4 Government officials are sanctioned for misconduct 1.5 Government powers are subject to non-governmental checks *1.6 Transition of power is subject to the law*	**Factor 1: constraints on government powers** 1.1 State government powers are effectively limited by the legislature 1.2 State government powers are effectively limited by the judiciary 1.3 State government powers are effectively limited by independent auditing and review 1.4 State government officials are sanctioned for misconduct 1.5 State government powers are subject to non-governmental checks from civil society, political parties, and the press *1.6 Elections are free, clean and transparent*
Factor 2: absence of corruption 2.1. Government officials in the executive branch do not use public office for private gain 2.2. Government officials in the judicial branch do not use public office for private gain *2.3. Government officials in the police and military do not use public office for private gain.* 2.4. Government officials in the legislative branch do not use public office for private gain	**Factor 2: absence of corruption** 2.1. Government officials in the state executive branch do not commit acts of corruption 2.2. Government officials in the judicial branch do not use public office for private gain *2.3. Government officials in the security and law enforcement systems do not use public office for private gain* 2.4. Government officials in the legislative branch do not use public office for private gain
Factor 3: open government *3.1. Publicized laws and government data* *3.2. Right to information* *3.3. Civic participation* *3.4. Complaint mechanisms*	**Factor 3: open government** *3.1. Civic participation in decision-making* *3.2. The right to public information is effectively guaranteed*
Factor 4: fundamental rights 4.1. Equal treatment and absence of discrimination 4.2. The right to life and security of the person is effectively guaranteed 4.3. Due process of the law and rights of the accused 4.4. Freedom of opinion and expression is effectively guaranteed 4.5. Freedom of belief and religion is effectively guaranteed 4.6. Freedom from arbitrary interference with privacy is effectively guaranteed 4.7. Freedom of assembly and association is effectively guaranteed 4.8. Fundamental labor rights are effectively guaranteed	**Factor 4: fundamental rights** 4.1. Equal treatment and absence of discrimination 4.2. The right to life and security of the person is effectively guaranteed 4.3. Due process of the law and rights of the accused are effectively guaranteed 4.4. Freedom of opinion and expression is effectively guaranteed 4.5. Freedom of belief and religion is effectively guaranteed 4.6. The right to privacy is effectively guaranteed 4.7. Freedom of assembly and association is effectively guaranteed 4.8. Fundamental labor rights are effectively guaranteed

(continued)

Table 4.1 (continued)

Global rule of law index	Mexico states rule of law index
Factor 5: order and security *5.1. Crime is effectively controlled* *5.2. Civil conflict is effectively limited* *5.3. People do not resort to violence to redress personal grievances*	**Factor 5: order and security** *5.1. Absence of homicides* *5.2. Absence of crime* *5.3. Perception of safety*
Factor 6: regulatory enforcement 6.1. Government regulations are effectively enforced 6.2. Government regulations are applied and enforced without improper influence 6.3. Administrative proceedings are conducted without unreasonable delay 6.4. Due process is respected in administrative proceedings 6.5. The government does not expropriate without lawful process and adequate compensation	**Factor 6: regulatory enforcement** 6.1. Government regulations are effectively enforced 6.2. Government regulations are applied and enforced without corruption. 6.3. Administrative proceedings are conducted effectively and efficiently 6.4. Due process is respected in administrative proceedings 6.5. The state government does not expropriate without lawful process and adequate compensation
Factor 7: civil justice *7.1. People can access and afford civil justice* *7.2. Civil justice is free of discrimination* *7.3. Civil justice is free of corruption* *7.4. Civil justice is free of improper government influence* *7.5. Civil justice is not subject to unreasonable delay* *7.6. Civil justice is effectively enforced* *7.7. Alternative dispute resolution mechanisms are accessible, impartial, and effective*	**Factor 7: civil justice** *7.1. People know their rights and trust civil justice institutions* *7.2. People have access to information and affordable quality legal counsel when facing legal problems or disputes* *7.3 People can resolve their legal problems easily and without high costs or bureaucratic procedures* *7.4 The civil justice system is impartial, independent and free from corruption* *7.5 The civil justice system guarantees a quality process* *7.6 The civil justice system is not subject to unreasonable delay* *7.7 Resolutions of civil and administrative courts are effectively enforced* *7.8 Alternative dispute resolution mechanisms are accessible, impartial and timely*
Factor 8: criminal justice *8.1. Criminal investigation system is effective* *8.2. Criminal adjudication system is timely and effective* *8.3. Correctional system is effective in reducing criminal behavior* *8.4. Criminal justice system is impartial* *8.5. Criminal justice system is free of corruption* *8.6. Criminal justice system is free of improper government influence* *8.7. Due process of the law and rights of the accused*	**Factor 8: criminal justice** *8.1. The police and the public ministry investigate crimes effectively* *8.2. The law enforcement and criminal adjudication systems are timely and effective* *8.3. Victim's rights are effectively guaranteed* *8.4. Due process of the law for the accused is effectively guaranteed* *8.5. The criminal justice system is impartial, independent, and free of corruption.* *8.6. The prison system guarantees the safety and rights of detained people*

Source The authors, using information from the Rule of Law Index 2017–2018 and the Mexico States Rule of Law Index 2018 between the thirty-two states, facilitating the identification of performance variations across the country.

The single-country focus allows for much larger respondent sample sizes than the Global Index. For the 2018 edition, the Mexican Index was calculated using first-hand data from a general population survey that was applied to 25,600 people (800 per state) using face-to-face computer-assisted personal interviewing (CAPI) surveys, and more than 14,000 experts were identified and invited to answer the surveys, resulting in more than 1,500 completed surveys in total.[7]

Furthermore, since the Mexican States Index only seeks to measure the rule of law in one country, it allowed the WJP to tailor the questionnaires to focus on the country's idiosyncrasies and include concepts that are crucial in the current Mexican policy agenda. In other words, producing a sub-national index allows for the collection of more in-depth information on the rule of law than would be possible on a worldwide basis. With this goal in mind, the WJP embarked on a thorough consultation with experts while designing the survey instruments and the framework. As a result of this consultation, the WJP adjusted three of the eight factors, and adopted more third-party sources to complement the expert and household survey data.

In this sense, Factor 5 (Order and Security) is now composed of data gathered by the Mexican statistical agency (INEGI), and includes administrative data on homicide rates, as well as data from the National Victimization Survey, which covers more than 100,000 households, and provides information to measure crime victimization rates and perceptions of safety.[8] In addition, the Mexico States Rule of Law Index removed the sub-factor on absence of civil conflict because it references casualties resulting from battles and terrorism, as defined by third-party sources,[9] which do not apply to the Mexican context.

The WJP also acknowledged the difficulties in measuring Factor 3 (Open Government) using household surveys, and decided to rely on a rigorous quantitative instrument designed by an academic institution (*Centro de Investigación y Docencia Económicas*, CIDE) alongside the National Institute on Access to Information (INAI; see Cejudo 2017). The Open Government Metric measures the levels of transparency and civic participation in Mexico at state level. The first pillar, transparency, is the equivalent of the WJP Index sub-factors of 'publicized laws and government data' and 'right to information'. The second pillar, civic participation, reflects what the WJP measures in the sub-factors of 'civic participation' and 'complaint mechanisms'. The two sub-factors included in the metric

---

[7]The global index had an average of twenty-six completed expert surveys per country, while the Mexico States Rule of Law Index had an average of forty-seven completed QRQ surveys per state. This is because the WJP team had a better network of contacts and support that allowed a greater number of experts per state to be reached.

[8]In this way, the sub-factors included in Factor 5 (Order and Security) changed from "absence of crime, absence of civil conflict, and absence of violent redress" to "absence of homicides, absence of crime, and people feel safe".

[9]See Uppsala Conflict Data Program and Center for Systemic Peace.

can be further disaggregated to assess the perspective of the government and the perspective of citizens. It is also important to point out that both in the new and old conception of this factor, the notion of accountability is not included, since there is no universal agreement as to the inclusion of this concept.

In producing a subnational index, WJP can also implement lessons learned from the exercises conducted in the past. One of these lessons comes into play in Factor 7 (Civil Justice). The WJP is one of the leading institutions, alongside multiple governments, the World Bank, the Organization for Economic Co-operation and Development (OECD) and The Hague Institute for Internationalization of the Law, among others, in measuring the burden of justiciable problems through the use of legal needs surveys.[10] Following this exercise, the WJP compared its framework with those of similar organizations, and recognized that other methodologies tend to place higher importance on effective access to justice and a fair procedure, instead of highlighting issues related to transparency. As a result of this analysis, the WJP modified Factor 7 by giving more weight to measuring access to justice,[11] as well as the procedural justice or fairness in the process, which is a fundamental component of an effective civil justice system.[12]

In addition to revising its approach to civil justice, WJP also adjusted is approach to criminal justice. For instance, the global framework does not incorporate victims' rights, but this concept was included in the Mexican Index because it was a cornerstone of the criminal justice reform that culminated in June 2016. The subnational Index reorganized Factor 8 (Criminal Justice) to encompass the perspectives of both the victims and the accused. From the victim's point of view, it measures whether the police and public prosecutor investigate crimes effectively, and whether the law enforcement and criminal adjudication systems are timely and effective, which are a proxy for measuring impunity and respect for victim's rights (8.3). From the perspective of the accused, the Index includes respect for due process of law (covering presumption of innocence, absence of discrimination, rights of the accused, right to a defense, and right to a fair and public trial), absence

---

[10]For more information, please refer to WJP's report on Global Insights on Access to Justice (2018).

[11]The WJP restructured Factor 7 to divide one sub-factor relating to access to justice into three sub-factors: 'people have trust and capability in the civil justice system', which measures the extent to which there are significant barriers of trust, legal awareness and legal knowledge that prevent people from accessing the justice system; 'the civil justice system provides effective legal aid to its users', which measures the quality and affordability or legal aid services; and 'the civil justice system doesn't have a high cost barrier for its users', which measures the monetary and procedural costs that people incur to solve their grievances through the justice system.

[12]The WJP grouped what used to be three sub-factors in the global index (absence of corruption, absence of discrimination, and absence of undue government influence) into one sub-factor relating to impartiality for the Mexican States Index. The framework now includes a sub-factor called 'the civil justice system guarantees a quality process to their users' to measure outcomes associated with the quality of the process. Finally, the outcomes that measure the timeliness, enforcement of the justice system, and the alternative dispute resolution mechanisms remain unchanged.

of corruption, and a prison system that guarantees security and respect for the rights of people deprived of liberty.

The remaining four factors of the Global Index, 'constraints on government powers' (1), 'absence of corruption' (2), 'fundamental rights' (4), and 'regulatory enforcement' (6), received some minor changes to localize the factors to a subnational context, but, all in all, the conceptual framework for these factors remains essentially the same as presented in the Global Index.

4.5 Results

The section below presents an overview of Mexico's results from both the Global Index and the Mexico States Rule of Law Index. Constructed according to the methodologies described above, the two sets of results present complementary views of the rule of law in Mexico. The Global Index provides data on specific elements of Mexico's performance in a global context and compares Mexico's performance with 112 other countries. The Mexico States Rule of Law Index, on the other hand, provides information on a state-by-state basis, highlighting in-country variations and facilitating comparisons across states.

As highlighted in the preceding section, the two indices incorporate important differences in their respective definitions and measurement methodologies. As a consequence, the results of the two measuring exercises are not comparable.[13] Nonetheless, when used as complementary sources of information, they provide a thoroughly comprehensive view of rule of law adherence in Mexico.

The Global Rule of Law Index allows users to answer broad questions about a country's rule of law performance from the global perspective. For example, how does Mexico's performance compare to other countries and among regional and income group peer countries? Data from the Global Index provides an answer to this question. From an overall perspective, Mexico ranks poorly in adherence to the rule of law, ranking 92nd out of 113 indexed countries, while the first places belong to Denmark, Norway and Finland (places 1–3, respectively), and the last places belong to Afghanistan, Cambodia and Venezuela (places 111–113). Moreover, it ranks 25th out of 30 countries evaluated in Latin American and the Caribbean and

---

[13]There are five reasons that explain why the results of the Mexico States Rule of Law Index cannot be compared with information from the Global Index: (i) differences in sub-factors (the Global Index is comprised of eight factors and forty-four sub-factors, while the Mexican Index is comprised of the same eight factors but only forty-two sub-factors); (ii) changes in surveys, (iii) use of third-party sources available only in Mexico; (iv) differences in the calculation of scores and a higher number of variables used for the Mexico Index (607 variables, compared to 389 in the global exercise), and (v) changes in the way variables are normalized (the Global Index uses the Max-Min methodology, which transforms the original variables to lie within a 0–1 interval, assigning 1 to the country with the highest score and 0 to the country with the lowest score; while the Mexico Index only transforms variables with scales other than those that range from 0 to 1, leaving all other variables intact).

34th out of 36 upper middle-income countries. From a topical viewpoint, Mexico performs particularly poorly on three specific factors, where globally it ranks in 100th place or worse: Absence of Corruption (102nd), Civil Justice (100th), and Criminal Justice (105th).

The table below presents the global rankings of rule of law adherence overall, along with the score that ranges from 0 to 1, where 1 means stronger adherence to the rule of law (Table 4.2).

In addition, the following table shows Mexico's scores for each of the factors included in the Global Rule of Law Index 2017–2018 (Table 4.3).

The results of the Global Index help set the stage for more specific questions related to Mexico's rule of law performance. For example, what variations in overall rule of law performance are observed across Mexico's states? And among Mexico's weakest topical performances – corruption, civil justice, and criminal

Table 4.2 Rule of Law around the World

	Overall score[a]	Global ranking
Denmark	0.89	1
Norway	0.89	2
Finland	0.87	3
Sweden	0.86	4
Netherlands	0.85	5
Germany	0.83	6
New Zealand	0.83	7
Austria	0.81	8
Canada	0.81	9
Australia	0.81	10
United Kingdom	0.81	11
Estonia	0.80	12
Singapore	0.80	13
Japan	0.79	14
Belgium	0.77	15
Hong Kong SAR, China	0.77	16
Czech Republic	0.74	17
France	0.74	18
United States	0.73	19
Republic of Korea	0.72	20
Portugal	0.72	21
Uruguay	0.71	22
Spain	0.70	23
Costa Rica	0.68	24
Poland	0.67	25
Slovenia	0.67	26

(continued)

Table 4.2 (continued)

	Overall score[a]	Global ranking
Chile	0.67	27
St. Kitts and Nevis	0.66	28
Romania	0.65	29
Barbados	0.65	30
Italy	0.65	31
United Arab Emirates	0.65	32
St. Lucia	0.63	33
Antigua and Barbuda	0.63	34
Croatia	0.61	35
Grenada	0.61	36
St. Vincent and the Grenadines	0.61	37
Georgia	0.61	38
Greece	0.60	39
Bahamas	0.60	40
Dominica	0.60	41
Jordan	0.60	42
Ghana	0.59	43
South Africa	0.59	44
Botswana	0.58	45
Argentina	0.58	46
Jamaica	0.58	47
Trinidad and Tobago	0.56	48
Senegal	0.55	49
Hungary	0.55	50
Mongolia	0.54	51
Brazil	0.54	52
Malaysia	0.54	53
Tunisia	0.53	54
Bulgaria	0.53	55
Bosnia and Herzegovina	0.53	56
Macedonia, FYR	0.53	57
Nepal	0.53	58
Sri Lanka	0.52	59
Peru	0.52	60
Panama	0.52	61
India	0.52	62
Indonesia	0.52	63
Kazakhstan	0.51	64
Belarus	0.51	65
Malawi	0.51	66

(continued)

Table 4.2 (continued)

	Overall score[a]	Global ranking
Morocco	0.51	67
Albania	0.51	68
Suriname	0.51	69
Burkina Faso	0.51	70
Thailand	0.50	71
Colombia	0.50	72
Guyana	0.50	73
Vietnam	0.50	74
China	0.50	75
Serbia	0.50	76
Ukraine	0.50	77
Moldova	0.49	78
El Salvador	0.48	79
Iran	0.48	80
Belize	0.47	81
Kyrgyzstan	0.47	82
Zambia	0.47	83
Cote d'Ivoire	0.47	84
Ecuador	0.47	85
Tanzania	0.47	86
Lebanon	0.47	87
Philippines	0.47	88
Russia	0.47	89
Dominican Republic	0.47	90
Uzbekistan	0.46	91
Mexico	**0.45**	**92**
Sierra Leone	0.45	93
Liberia	0.45	94
Kenya	0.45	95
Guatemala	0.44	96
Nigeria	0.44	97
Madagascar	0.44	98
Nicaragua	0.43	99
Myanmar	0.42	100
Turkey	0.42	101
Bangladesh	0.41	102
Honduras	0.40	103
Uganda	0.40	104
Pakistan	0.39	105
Bolivia	0.38	106

(continued)

Table 4.2 (continued)

	Overall score[a]	Global ranking
Ethiopia	0.38	107
Zimbabwe	0.37	108
Cameroon	0.37	109
Egypt	0.36	110
Afghanistan	0.34	111
Cambodia	0.32	112
Venezuela	0.29	113

Source WJP Rule of Law Index 2017–2018
[a]Scores are rounded to two decimal places

Table 4.3 Scores for Mexico in the WJP Rule of Law index 2017–2018

	Score (0–1)[a]
Rule of law score 2017–2018, Mexico	0.45
Factor 1: constraints on government powers	0.46
Factor 2: absence of corruption	0.31
Factor 3: open government	0.61
Factor 4: fundamental rights	0.52
Factor 5: order and security	0.59
Factor 6: regulatory enforcement	0.44
Factor 7: civil justice	0.40
Factor 8: criminal justice	0.30

Source Rule of Law Index 2017–2018
[a]Scores are rounded to two decimal places

justice – which states show the greatest need for improvement? Here data from the Mexico States Rule of Law Index provides answers.

According to the Mexican States Index, the states with the strongest adherence to the rule of law are: Yucatán, Aguascalientes, Zacatecas, Campeche, and Querétaro. The states with the weakest adherence to the rule of law are: Guerrero, Baja California Sur, Estado de México, Sonora, and Puebla.

Table 4.4 presents the state-by-state rankings for each state's overall performance, as well as scores for each of the eight factors.

The results above present only a small fraction of the total data collected by the Global Index and the Mexican States Index. And, in the context of this chapter, these results are primarily meant to illustrate the outcomes of the definitional and methodological choices outlined in the sections above regarding measurement of the rule of law. More complete data on Mexico's rule of law performance is available through other World Justice Project resources. For further information about the scores, rankings and methodologies of both indices, we warmly invite the reader to go to worldjusticeproject.org and worldjusticeproject.mx.

Table 4.4 Scores for the Mexico states rule of law Index 2018

	Rule of law score	Overall rank-ing	Factor 1: constraints on government powers	Factor 2: absence of corruption	Factor 3: open government	Factor 4: fundamental rights	Factor 5: order and security	Factor 6: regulatory enforcement	Factor 7: civil justice	Factor 8: criminal justice
Aguascalientes	0.44	2	0.46	0.41	0.43	0.56	0.46	0.40	0.39	0.43
Baja California	0.43	7	0.46	0.41	0.41	0.51	0.25	0.49	0.46	0.42
Baja California Sur	0.35	31	0.31	0.32	0.35	0.48	0.29	0.35	0.34	0.37
Campeche	0.43	4	0.47	0.38	0.37	0.49	0.53	0.41	0.41	0.36
Chiapas	0.39	14	0.39	0.32	0.35	0.47	0.59	0.30	0.36	0.35
Chihuahua	0.39	18	0.41	0.36	0.38	0.52	0.27	0.36	0.37	0.42
Ciudad de México	0.37	25	0.40	0.27	0.51	0.51	0.27	0.30	0.35	0.32
Coahuila	0.43	6	0.36	0.35	0.41	0.48	0.61	0.37	0.44	0.39
Colima	0.39	15	0.43	0.37	0.35	0.52	0.28	0.40	0.37	0.41
Durango	0.42	9	0.43	0.32	0.38	0.47	0.59	0.37	0.42	0.36
Estado de México	0.36	30	0.37	0.28	0.44	0.45	0.21	0.39	0.37	0.33
Guanajuato	0.41	12	0.40	0.42	0.48	0.51	0.28	0.38	0.40	0.41
Guerrero	0.29	32	0.28	0.28	0.37	0.35	0.19	0.29	0.28	0.30
Hidalgo	0.42	8	0.44	0.38	0.36	0.48	0.57	0.38	0.39	0.38
Jalisco	0.37	23	0.42	0.31	0.45	0.46	0.29	0.35	0.34	0.33
Michoacán	0.40	13	0.40	0.35	0.41	0.49	0.39	0.35	0.39	0.39
Morelos	0.37	26	0.42	0.36	0.38	0.51	0.23	0.27	0.33	0.42

(continued)

Table 4.4 (continued)

	Rule of law score	Overall rank-ing	Factor 1: constraints on government powers	Factor 2: absence of corruption	Factor 3: open government	Factor 4: fundamental rights	Factor 5: order and security	Factor 6: regulatory enforcement	Factor 7: civil justice	Factor 8: criminal justice
Nayarit	0.37	22	0.40	0.35	0.33	0.48	0.44	0.28	0.31	0.35
Nuevo León	0.42	10	0.48	0.39	0.38	0.54	0.39	0.41	0.39	0.36
Oaxaca	0.39	16	0.44	0.34	0.33	0.49	0.42	0.35	0.33	0.39
Puebla	0.36	28	0.38	0.33	0.34	0.44	0.37	0.40	0.32	0.31
Querétaro	0.43	5	0.43	0.42	0.27	0.53	0.51	0.43	0.36	0.46
Quintana Roo	0.36	27	0.41	0.31	0.40	0.46	0.31	0.37	0.33	0.33
San Luis Potosí	0.39	17	0.41	0.34	0.36	0.50	0.44	0.34	0.33	0.37
Sinaloa	0.41	11	0.41	0.35	0.42	0.51	0.42	0.35	0.38	0.41
Sonora	0.36	29	0.40	0.33	0.42	0.46	0.28	0.24	0.36	0.36
Tabasco	0.38	21	0.41	0.36	0.40	0.49	0.28	0.34	0.35	0.37
Tamaulipas	0.38	19	0.37	0.39	0.34	0.45	0.42	0.36	0.37	0.36
Tlaxcala	0.38	20	0.40	0.33	0.29	0.49	0.49	0.29	0.34	0.38
Veracruz	0.37	24	0.34	0.31	0.41	0.42	0.47	0.38	0.31	0.30
Yucatán	0.45	1	0.42	0.38	0.38	0.51	0.77	0.38	0.33	0.42
Zacatecas	0.44	3	0.43	0.42	0.43	0.51	0.39	0.42	0.46	0.44
National average	0.39	–	0.41	0.35	0.38	0.49	0.40	0.36	0.36	0.38

Source Mexico states rule of law index 2018
[a] Scores are rounded to two decimal places

4.6 Conclusion

In order to maintain and improve the rule of law, it must be measured and evaluated. This chapter examines the process of measuring the rule of law through the guiding examples of the global WJP Rule of Law Index and the Mexico States Rule of Law Index. In particular, it explores the choices made by the WJP in its approach to defining the rule of law and measuring the rule of law in order to offer insight into key questions regarding rule of law measurement.

Ultimately, the chapter provides the framework used by the World Justice Project to measure the rule of law based on a multidimensional, outcome-oriented and user-based approach of composite indicators. The chapter also describes the methodology behind the global Rule of Law Index, which has measured the rule of law in more than a hundred countries, as well as conceptual and methodological considerations made in producing the Mexico States Rule of Law Index.

Based on these definitional and methodological decisions, results for Mexico are presented from both the Global Index and the Mexican States Index.

Looking ahead, the WJP recognizes that even producing an index on a subnational level does not capture the full range of experiences across various demographic groups and populations. Work must be done on designing indicators that capture the experiences of vulnerable population groups. In an effort to improve the inclusion of its indicators, WJP is preparing to present thematic data products and reports that showcase the experiences of people accessing the justice system, perceptions of the criminal justice system, experiences of discrimination, knowledge of legal rights, legal awareness, and more.

Given the experiences in several countries during recent years, the importance of the rule of law cannot be overstated. And since no country has ever achieved a perfect realization of the rule of law, it is fundamental to universally promote and strengthen it. Measurement is an essential part of that process. It is our hope that the information provided in this chapter provides additional clarity and encouragement for continued measurement and evaluation of the rule of law.

References

Acemoğlu, D.; Robinson, J.A. (2016). *Paths to Inclusive Political Institutions*; at: https://economics.mit.edu/files/11338.
Botero J.C.; Ponce A. (2011). "Measuring the Rule of Law". *The World Justice Project;* at: https://worldjusticeproject.org/our-work/publications/working-papers/measuring-rule-law.
Carothers, T. (Ed.) (2010). *Promoting the Rule of law abroad: in search of knowledge* (Washington, D.C.: Brookings Institution Press).
Cejudo G. (Coord.) (2017). *Reporte de Resultados 2017: Métrica de Gobierno Abierto 2017.* CIDE, INAI; at: http://rendiciondecuentas.org.mx/wp-content/uploads/2017/03/ReportedeResultadosMetricafeb17.pdf.
Chemerinsky, E. (2007). "Toward a Practical Definition of the Rule of Law", in: *Judges' Journal*, 46, 4; at: https://scholarship.law.berkeley.edu/facpubs/2798/.

Freedom House (2018). *About Freedom in the World: An annual study of political rights and civil liberties*; at: https://freedomhouse.org/report-types/freedom-world (15 July 2018).
General Assembly resolution 67/1, *Declaration of the High-level Meeting of the General Assembly on the Rule of Law at the National and International Levels*, A/RES/67/1 (30 November 2012); at: https://www.un.org/ruleoflaw/files/A-RES-67-1.pdf.
Heritage Foundation (2018). *2018 Index of Economic Freedom: Rule of Law;* at: https://www.heritage.org/index/rule-of-law (15 July 2018).
Kaufmann, D.; Kraay, A.; Mastruzzi, M. (2011). "The Worldwide Governance Indicators: Methodology and Analytical Issues", in: *Hague Journal on the Rule of Law*, 3, 2, 220–246.
Kleinfeld R. (2006). "Competing Definitions of the Rule of Law", in: Carothers, T. (Ed.), *Promoting the Rule of Law Abroad: In Search of Knowledge* (Washington D.C.: Carnegie Endowment for International Peace).
Kleinfeld R. (2013). "How to Advance the Rule of Law Abroad", in: *Carnegie Endowment for International Peace: Policy Outlook;* at: https://carnegieendowment.org/files/Kleinfeld-PO-web.pdf.
McCubbins, M.; Rodriguez, D.; Weingast, B. (2010). *The Rule of Law Unplugged*, Public Law and Legal Theory Research Paper Series Number 158; at: https://papers.ssrn.com/sol3/papers.cfm?abstract_id=1467797.
OECD (2008). *Handbook on Constructing Composite Indicators: Methodology and User Guide*; at: http://www.oecd.org/els/soc/handbookonconstructingcompositeindicatorsmethodologyanduserguide.htm.
Tatar, M. (2002). *The Annotated Classic Fairy Tales* (New York: W.W. Norton & Company).
Transparency International (2018). What is Corruption?; at: https://www.transparency.org/what-is-corruption (15 July 2018).
United Nations Development Programme (2014). *Why, What and How to Measure? A User's Guide to Measuring Rule of Law, Justice and Security Programmes;* at: http://www.undp.org/content/dam/undp/library/crisis%20prevention/UNDP_CPR_ROLMEGuide_August2014.pdf.
United Nations Security Council, *The Rule of Law and transitional justice in conflict and post-conflict societies*, S/2004/616 (23 August 2004); at: https://www.un.org/ruleoflaw/blog/document/the-rule-of-law-and-transitional-justice-in-conflict-and-post-conflict-societies-report-of-the-secretary-general/.
Vera Institute of Justice (2003). *Measuring Progress toward Safety and Justice: A Global Guide to the Design of Performance Indicators across the Justice Sector*; at: https://www.vera.org/publications/measuring-progress-toward-safety-and-justice-a-global-guide-to-the-design-of-performance-indicators-across-the-justice-sector.
Versteeg, M.; Ginsburg T. (2017). "Measuring the Rule of Law: A Comparison of Indicators", in: *Law & Social Inquiry, Journal of the American Bar Foundation*, 42, 1: 100–137.
World Bank (2018). *Worldwide Governance Indicators;* at: http://info.worldbank.org/governance/WGI/#home (15 July 2018).
World Justice Project (2018). *Global Insights on Access to Justice*; at: https://worldjusticeproject.org/our-work/wjp-rule-law-index/special-reports/global-insights-access-justice.
World Justice Project (2018). *WJP Rule of Law Index 2017–2018*; at: https://worldjusticeproject.org/news/2017-2018-wjp-rule-law-index.
World Justice Project (2018). *Vision*; at: https://worldjusticeproject.org/about-us/overview/vision (15 July 2018).
World Justice Project (2018). Índice de Estado de Derecho en México: Perspectivas y experiencias en los 32 estados del país; at: https://worldjusticeproject.mx/indice-de-estado-de-derecho-en-mexico-2018/.

Part II
Explaining the Fragility of the Rule of Law in Mexico

Chapter 5
How Many Constitutional Reforms Produce Rule of Law?

Juan Antonio Le Clercq

Abstract The Mexican Constitution is one of the oldest constitutions compared to the average lifetime of constitutions across the world, but it also represents one of the texts with a larger degree of amendments compared to the original text. The existence of a large number of reforms can refer to high levels of flexibility, something that involves the capacity to integrate new rights and institutions to respond to political transformations and the demands of an increasingly plural society but, despite its longevity and undoubted capacity for transformation, the Constitution has been unable to constitute itself as the effective foundation for the development of a democratic rule of law in Mexico. This article focuses on two basic questions: why is the rule of law so weak in Mexico? And to what extent do the problems of design, coherence and constitutional change affect performance of the rule of law? In the Mexican case, the logic that understands the Constitution as a political instrument and the hyper-reformism that emerges from it, affecting the coherence, meaning, and effectiveness of the text, has made it impossible to transform the Constitution into exactly the coordination mechanism on which the development and quality of the rule of law partly depends.

Keywords Amendments · Constitution · Constitutional change · Hyper-reformism · Mexican constitution · Rule of law

---

Prof. Dr. Juan Antonio Le Clercq, Ph.D. in Political and Social Sciences, Department of International Relations and Political Science, UDLAP. Ex hacienda de Sta. Catarina Mártir, 72810, San Andrés Cholula, Puebla, Mexico. E-mail: juan.leclercq@udlap.mx.

© Springer Nature Switzerland AG 2020
J. A. Le Clercq and J. P. Abreu Sacramento (eds.), *Rebuilding the State Institutions*,
https://doi.org/10.1007/978-3-030-31314-2_5

5.1 Introduction

Mexico stands out for having one of the world's oldest constitutions compared to the average lifetime of constitutions across the globe, but it also represents one of the texts with a larger degree of amendments compared to the original text. In one hundred years of life, the Mexican Constitution has suffered 233 amendments affecting the content of 711 articles; such changes tend to accelerate during the democratic transition period, especially since 1997, when the ruling party lost absolute majority for the first time in at least one of the Congress's chambers.

Despite the different regime changes experienced since the end of the Mexican Revolution, constitution longevity signals political stability as well as public recognition and legitimacy. The existence of a large number of reforms can refer to high levels of flexibility, something that involves the capacity to integrate new rights and institutions to respond to political transformations and the demands of an increasingly plural society. It also reflects the willingness to modify institutions according to the agenda and interests of dominant coalitions or for the purpose of restricting rights and curbing social demands.

Despite its longevity and undoubted capacity for transformation, however, the Constitution has been unable to establish itself as an effective foundation for the development of a democratic rule of law in Mexico. Although the Mexican Constitution is regularly celebrated by political actors as the cornerstone of Mexican public life,[1] it is more an instrument of political domination that represents the ideals and aspirations of the winning groups in the different political and military disputes of national history than the supreme legal norm and starting point of the hierarchical order of the laws.

According to *The Rule of Law Index* (RLI 2018), Mexico stands out as a country with mediocre performance in measuring the quality of the rule of law. Mexico obtains a grade of 0.45 and is located in the 92nd place among 113 studied cases; which involves a setback of four places in relation to the previously occupied position. In other words, the rule of law in Mexico is very weak and its deterioration tends to increase. If we analyze each of the eight factors that make up the study, Mexico's performance is inefficient in practically all the variables, highlighting the very negative results in Criminal Justice (0.30), Absence of Corruption (0.31), Civil Justice (0.40), Regulatory Enforcement (0.44), and Constraints on Government's Powers (0.46).

The Global Impunity Index (IGI 2017) (Le Clercq/Rodríguez 2017) and the Global Impunity Index Mexico (IGI-MEX 2018) (Le Clercq/Rodríguez 2018), highlight the dysfunctions levels that characterize Mexico in terms of security, justice and respect for human rights. Such grades place Mexico in position 66 out of

---

[1]The Constitution is celebrated every February 5th, in remembrance of the date of its promulgation in 1917, as part of the regular ceremonies of Mexican politics. However, the political actors that used to celebrate the constitution with their annual speeches show no concern over its mandate's day-to-day violations.

the 69 countries studied. Up to 28 of the thirty-two states are classified as high or very high impunity cases, while just two are identified as "atypical cases" in which statistical impunity prevails due to the inconsistency of information reported by its state governments.[2] The existence of very high levels of impunity in Mexico is mainly related to problems in the structure of the justice system, inadequate functioning of the security system, and serious human rights violations.

The starting question is why is the rule of law so weak in Mexico, even when it has been subject to a large number of constitutional amendments, many of them made with the intention of updating the legal framework and national political institutions? We do not mean that a stronger rule of law is a direct function of the number of amendments in the Constitution, something that relates more to the quality of its content and the characteristics of the implementation process. Our interest is to focus precisely on the lack of correlation between reforms and the rule of law in Mexico, even when a significant number of amendments are actually meaningful and relevant for institution-building or were designed with a stronger rule of law in mind.[3]

To what extent do the problems of design, coherence and constitutional change affect the performance of the rule of law? From our perspective, the Mexican Constitution represents a case of incapability of self-imposing compliance and, therefore, failure to become an effective mechanism that coordinates interactions and exchanges with political and social actors. In other words, the existence of a large number of reforms, and especially a growing tendency to change during the period of democratic transition, has been insufficient to generate processes that effectively strengthen the rule of law, again even when congress has approved reforms with quality content. This can be explained by different kinds of factors, but especially by the interpretation and use of the Constitution as a political rather than a legal instrument.

Analyzing the "rule of law" implies distinguishing *thin* conceptual definitions, centered on "formal legality" criteria, which may include attributes of the law, legal institution fundamentals, democratic controls over government, and the protection of individual rights, from *thick* versions that additionally include qualitative

---

[2]"Statistical Impunity" refers to those cases in which the data is non-existent or insufficient due to the inability or lack of political will to report statistical information (Le Clercq/Rodríguez 2018: 169).

[3]Some of the most relevant amendments in the last decade, even when some of them were contested, are reforms on class action (29/07/2010), habeas corpus (06/06/2011), human rights (10/06/2011), education (26/02/2013), telecommunication and economic completion (11/06/2013), procedures for criminal justice (08/10/2013), energy (20/12/2013), transparency (07/02/2014), electoral politics and the independence of the general attorney's office (10/02/2014), corruption (27/05/2015), torture and forced disappearance (10/07/2015), Mexico City's political reform (29/01/2016), and crime victims (25/07/2016). The point, nonetheless, is that even when their contents are relevant to the goal of strengthening the rule of law, most reforms face implementation and compliance problems, are poorly fulfilled – especially at state level – or are strongly contested by political forces, so it's difficult to translate formal mandates into effective democratic institutions for the rule of law.

dimensions and respect for human and social welfare rights (Tamahana 2004; Bingham 2010; Skaaning 2010). Due to the characteristics of the content and scope of the Mexican Constitution, it seems more appropriate to understand the challenges involved in developing and complying with the rule of law, as well as the social expectations generated, from a thick approach.

In the first part, we discuss the role of a constitution from an institutional perspective and analyze different approaches that have emphasized its function as a coordination mechanism and understand change as an endogenous process. Secondly, we identify the distinctive characteristics of the Mexican Constitution within the framework of its centenary. Third, from a quantitative perspective we analyze the process of constitutional change in Mexico throughout its one hundred years of life, as well as the impact of its reforms in different political cycles. Fourth, we discuss the political function that has historically determined the life of the Mexican Constitution and the manner in which this has affected its proper juridical function. Lastly, we summarise our conclusions.

5.2 An Institutional Approach to the Role of the Constitution

A constitution represents the fundamental political agreement of a nation, the set of general legal norms that frame the legitimate exercise of political power. In this sense, a constitution is a specific type of institution, in fact, the institution of institutions, which establishes and structures the political order, formalizes the rights of the citizens and establishes the foundations of the rule of law. Independently of its extension or particular characteristics, it integrates guiding principles, encapsulates the values of national identity, organizes public powers and their attributions, establishes limits to public powers through checks and balances, creates mechanisms for resolving conflicts between powers, authorities and citizens, defines spaces for public deliberation, and guarantees the exercise of rights for the members of the community.

According to Grimm (2006: 33–35, 48) modern constitutions can be distinguished from fundamental laws or domination contracts by three main elements: (1) they constitute political power and do not assume it as a given fact that only needs to be modified; (2) they do not grant particular obligations, but establish the broader framework of obligations to political power; (3) their effects and scope are universal and not limited to contracting parties. Their most important element is their consensual basis, the prior consensus that allows, in principle, the constitutive act itself, but also the political and social consensus that emerges from the common norms that feed back through judicial interpretation and the legislative change.

Friedrich (1950: 27) emphasizes that the essence of constitutionalism is that it defines the basic "restraints upon the arbitrary exercise of governmental power" by means of effective democratic institutions for the division of powers and the protection of individual rights. In this sense, the content of modern constitutions usually focuses on the recognition of individual rights, the organization of political institutions, and the separation of powers. In contrast, for Sartori (2016: 233), modern constitutions should be understood as forms or procedures that "structure and discipline the decision-making processes", and in this sense, they define "the way in which the norms are created" for "ensuring a controlled exercise of power". This argument implies that the function of establishing the governance structure is more relevant than the definition of a bill of rights.

From a perspective of strategic competition, Cooter (2000: 1–2) argues that a "constitution is the state's highest law". This has three important consequences. A constitution is more general than the laws and therefore focuses on distributing powers and protection of rights, and not on implementing mandates or regulating particular behaviors. Its norms trump and prevail over any other type of laws. And, finally, it is more entrenched and harder to change than other laws. On the other hand, although the constitution establishes the basic rules and constraints for the strategic game of politics, where the coordination of individual and collective actions is central, its first objective is "to impose the rule of law and protect the liberty of citizens" (Cooter 2000: 11) – something that also implies defining the legal rules that will determine the distribution of public and private goods according to criteria such as efficiency or justice.

Also from a strategic competition perspective, Hardin (1999: 87, 103–017) points out that the constitution is wrongly understood as a kind of contract, but should rather be viewed as the institution that creates the institution of contract. The existence of a constitution provides the possibility of contracting by solving the previous coordination problem of the actions and behaviors permitted socially. That means that the costs of reform need to be higher in order to fulfil its constraining function. This perspective has been taken up by North and Weingast (1989), who understand a constitution to be an institutional equilibrium or self-imposed focal-point that allows opposing interests to be coordinated in a decentralized way, and social actors to interpret rules and mandates and to sanction non-compliance within a single legal order.

Waldron (2016) maintains a much more critical position towards liberal constitutionalism approaches centered on the negative sense of liberties and limitation of powers. He emphasizes that both the constitution and rule of law imply legal control over public powers, but also focus on the expansion or promotion of social objectives: empowerment of authorities, provision of public goods, definition of public objectives, creation of institutions to address cooperation and coordination problems, establishment of decision-making centers, facilitation of spaces for deliberation and public discussion and participation.

From a different perspective but also questioning the strictly 'negative' sense of a constitution, Bellamy (2007) claims a form of political constitutionalism in which competition, public debate and accountability through democratic processes represent more effective ways of guaranteeing the exercise of rights, controlling power, and promoting equal treatment for citizens than strictly legalistic perspectives. Meanwhile, Sunstein (2001) sees the constitution and its mechanisms of checks and balances as a structure aimed at promoting democratic deliberation, especially in societies where pluralism translates into deep disagreements in relation to common citizenship values, the provision of public goods, and different ways of understanding public affairs.

Finally, from an empirical and comparative perspective, Elkins, Ginsburg/ Melton (2009) focus their analysis on the dynamics of institutional change. While from this perspective it is important to understand constitutional functions – such as government control, the existence of rights, national goals and objectives, definitions of authority patterns and government institutions – the emphasis is on how attributes of constitutional design, such as flexibility, inclusion or specificity, can explain both performance and the way change occurs. In this sense, a constitution depends on factors such as its capacity to impose mandates or the political negotiation between elites – elements related to institutional design – rather than environmental factors or external shocks.

From this brief analysis, we can highlight four key elements of an institutional interpretation of the constitution: (1) a constitution is the institution whose principles, rules, and norms formalize political order and establish the foundations for the rule of law; (2) although guaranteeing rights, defining government institutions and controlling the exercise of power are key elements, their social objectives, decision-making capacities, and mechanisms for public deliberation are equally relevant; (3) a constitution may have its origins in or respond to exogenous or environmental factors, but its creation, interpretation, and alteration respond primarily to elements of its design that arise from political negotiations in which unequal distributive effects exist; (4) finally, it can fulfill its functions only if it is capable of endogenously self-regulating its compliance, that is, if political actors themselves have incentives to respect and fulfill their mandates and, therefore, it is reproduced as a mechanism of decentralized coordination.

5.3 The Distinctiveness of the Mexican Constitution

The Mexican Constitution has its origin in an armed conflict and, throughout its one hundred years of life, established the political bases of the social contract that governed the post-revolutionary regime. As the product of a popular revolution, one of its main attributes is the inclusion of social rights and the continuous incorporation of new rights throughout its different reforms, a trend that has increased during the first decades of the twenty-first century. The second distinctive feature is the organization of political power in a presidential regime and a federal system similar to the constitutional design of the United States. This presidential system has had to coexist first with a hegemonic party rule and later with a pluralist democracy. However, this model has also been characterized by its flexibility to absorb changes in both regime and party system design, and in recent decades, as part of a democratic transition, it has incorporated mechanisms of control over the

Executive and constitutionally autonomous organisms at both the federal and state levels.

Beyond these regime features and the rights system extension, eight characteristics are central to understanding its particularity as a political-legal instrument and the problems involved in the development of a democratic rule of law: longevity, flexibility, inclusion, specificity, institutional weakness, social character, fetishization of change, and institutional inability to establish foundations for the rule of law.

While the lifespan of constitutions is nineteen years on average (Elkins et al. 2009: 2), the Mexican Constitution has recently celebrated its first centenary. This makes it the eleventh-longest constitution in the world and the oldest in Latin America, considering the years since its enactment. In terms of duration, it is only behind the United Kingdom (1215), the United States (1789), Norway (1814), the Netherlands (1815), Belgium (1831), New Zealand (1852), Canada (1867), Luxembourg (1867), Tonga (1875) and Australia (1901).[4]

Along with its longevity, the Mexican Constitution has proved to be extraordinarily flexible and able to adapt to the various regime changes that have happened since the end of the Revolution, going through the hegemonic party presidentialism and the democratic transition.[5] As will be shown, throughout its hundred years of life, it has undergone 233 amendments, which involve the reform of 698 articles and 13 transitory articles. This translates into a modification rate of 2.33 amendments and 7.11 articles per year.

Ginsburg/Melton (2014: 4) point out that flexible and detailed constitutions, which they call "statutory constitutions", contribute to constitutional stability, as they allow design defects and unintended consequences to be remedied, and attach the constitutional text to changing political practices, thereby renewing the consent of different generations. Flexible constitutions have the additional virtue of allowing gradual instead of radical change: "The constitutions of India, Mexico, and Brazil, to take three prominent examples, are amended nearly every year. Such constitutions have the virtue of being changed through internal mechanisms, avoiding the costlier route of a total replacement".

However, several authors have noticed the existence of negative effects that the excessive amount of reforms have had on constitutional stability and coherence in the Mexican case (Casar/Marván 2014; Carbonell 2014; Fix-Fierro 2017; Fix-Fierro/Valadés 2017; Pou; 2018; Rivera León 2017; Martín Reyes 2017; Salazar Ugarte 2017; Velasco Rivera 2017). According to Caballero (2018), the constitutional reforms have taken the form of a fetish (thesis shared by Casar 2013),

---

[4]Data from the Comparative Constitution Project. This ranking considers the constitution longevity since the year of its enactment; at: http://comparativeconstitutionsproject.org/ccp-rankings/ (27 July 2018).

[5]The great quantity of reforms made to the Mexican Constitution have occurred despite the rigorous procedure established in Article 135, which requires a majority vote in both chambers of Congress and the approval of the majority of the state's legislatures. The inability of the ruling party to achieve an absolute majority in some of the chambers since 1997 did not affect the dynamic of constitutional change; in fact, the reformist tendency increased.

a practice that assumes that any type of political policy change necessarily requires modifying the Constitution, whereby elements corresponding to different legislative scope are integrated into the main text. As part of the fetish, political actors assume that everything that is integrated updates, strengthens, improves or even guarantees coherence, generating a process that reinforces itself through time.

Focusing on the same problem, Pou (2018) argues that the Mexican constitutional change takes the form of "hyper-reformism", a dynamic of continuously altering the stability, coherence, clarity and structure of the constitutional text. Hyper-reformism affects the ability of constitutions to fulfill two central functions effectively: (1) legal orientation and foundation of the rules, definition of rights, and constitutional control; (2) organization of power, distribution of functions, democratic conversation, and historical balance.

Fix-Fierro/Valadés (2017: 1–2) agree that even when the constitutional change has facilitated the inclusion of new institutions and content in response to recent political challenges, the amending dynamic has reached a limit: "it is also true that the continuous reforms and additions that it has undergone have resulted in a text that is increasingly longer and disorganized, unsystematic and neglected from a technical point of view." They propose a complete reorganization and consolidation of the constitutional text and the creation of a Constitutional Development Law as a way to guarantee its stability and viability in the long term.

The loss of order and coherence of the Constitution is also related to the excessive specificity and detail of many of its reforms, a trend that has worsened in recent years. Emilio Rabasa, one of the main critics of the constitutional project of 1917, questioned the creation of Article 27, among other things, because instead of just the addition of a specific article, it integrated an entire treatise by itself into the Constitution (Aguilar Rivera 2017: 25). This same criticism, the tendency to create extensive and detailed 'treaties', can be applied to recent constitutional reforms, such as human rights, telecommunications, economic competition, energy, electoral politics, and the struggle against corruption reforms, among many others.

The original extension of the Constitution of 1917 was approximately 21,000 words, while in 2018 its 136 articles, without counting its title and preamble, reach 66,822 words. In fact, if the transitory regime derived from the 233 amendments is considered, the Mexican Constitution reaches 121,591 words. This makes it the second most extensive constitution, only behind India's 146,385 words and ahead of Nigeria's (66,263), Brazil's (64,488), Malaysia's (64,080), and Papua New Guinea's (58,490).[6]

This extension and specificity, however, has also allowed the Constitution to be flexible, adapt to changing times and include the demands of new emerging actors, but also to promote institutional changes according to the agendas and interests of dominant groups and winning coalitions. In this sense, Ginsburg/Melton (2014) are

---

[6]Constitutions Rankings at: http://comparativeconstitutionsproject.org/ccp-rankings/ (27 July 2018). The data corresponds to information updated April 8, 2016, but for the case of Mexico, I have added the latest reforms up to September 15, 2017. In the Comparative Constitution Project, Mexico ranks in position six with 57,087 words, but this does not include five additional amendments.

right when they identify flexibility as a virtue and a mechanism to guarantee greater stability through gradual change instead of the complete replacement of the text. One way to observe the degrees of inclusion and the response to social demands is through the capacity of legislators to incorporate new rights into the Constitution. Although the Mexican Constitution stands out for its social compromise since the moment of its creation, at least 27% of the constitutional reforms had the objective of increasing or updating political, economic, social, or cultural rights (Chart 7).[7] The Mexican Constitution is in eighth position in terms of recognizing rights with a total 81 rights recognized, only surpassed by Ecuador (99), Bolivia and Serbia (88), Cape Verde and Portugal (87), Armenia and Venezuela (82).[8]

These different reforms, and especially those carried out in the context of the democratic transition, have profoundly affected the design and institutional characteristics of the regime. As mentioned earlier, several changes have been relevant and timely, with content which is meaningful for the purpose of updating national institutions, including the creation of several autonomous constitutional bodies, judicial independence and transformation of the justice system, indigenous autonomy and rights, human rights definitions, an anticorruption system, transparency mechanisms, mandates for education evaluation, new rules for private participation in the energy sector, a series of political and electoral reforms, and transformation of local-national coordination through amendments to Article 73 (see in Fig. 5.10 the articles with the most reforms).

From the perspective of institutional change, for Caballero (2018) the dependence on constitutional reform as an updating mechanism instead of judicial interpretation, secondary legislation, or public policy highlights a weak constitution with coherence problems – something exacerbated by the lack of external control over the amendment process and its content. As a result of fetishization of the reform process itself, there has been a surge in the perceived need to constantly reform the text and add elements that more properly correspond to other legal or policy areas.

Finally, despite the amount of reforms that have been carried out over the last hundred years, the extension and detail of their mandates and their capacity to incorporate new demands or adjust the institutional structure, the Mexican Constitution stands out for its inability to generate an effective rule of law. Therefore, a central problem is the profound disconnection between the norms, rules, and aspirations that the text gathers and its fulfillment in daily political and legal practice. A central theme of this chapter is precisely why a constitution that is able to reform and adapt over time does not translate into the existence of an effective and democratic rule of law.

---

[7]The fact that there has been a trend in increasing the number of rights formally recognized in the constitution does not mean that they are successfully implemented or that fundamental rights are actually respected in contemporary Mexico.

[8]Constitutions Rankings, *op cit*. Updated to April 8, 2016. Although more formal rights are added, it does not necessarily mean that they are respected or implemented. Mexico has a greater number of constitutional rights, above the international average, but with the existence of severe violations of human rights (consulted 27 July 2018).

5.4 The Dynamics of the Constitutional Reform

To understand the magnitude and scope of the constitutional change in Mexico throughout the last hundred years, and its capacity to adapt and incorporate elements and political demands, we can review the number and type of amendments that have taken place since its enactment on February 5th, 1917. Figure 5.1 shows the 233 reforms to the Constitution and their distribution per year, as well as the 711 articles altered as a result. It also highlights an increasingly reformist trend and greater impact on the modification of articles as the century of constitutional life advances. On average, the Mexican Constitution has been reformed 2.33 times, affecting 7.11 articles per year.

However, the magnitude of the constitutional change is greater than can be observed from the identification of the number of amendments and modification to its articles. Figure 5.2 incorporates into the analysis the number of transitory articles created for the implementation of the different amendments. Although the primary objective of the transitory articles is to guarantee the gradual entry into

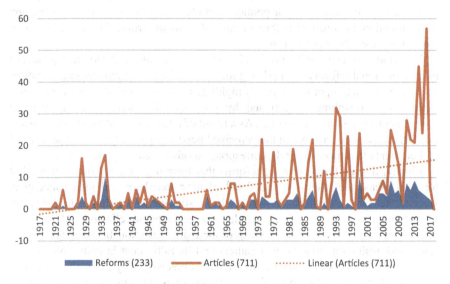

Fig. 5.1 Constitutional Reforms, 1917–2018. Graphs 1 to 9 draw upon the list of reforms per year, articles, and presidential periods elaborated by the Chamber of Deputies. However, there are no coincidences in the number of reforms and reformed articles for two main reasons: (1) the Chamber of Deputies does not take into consideration the constitutional reform to Article 22 made December 15th, 1934; (2) we detected mistakes in the listing of articles reformed during the presidencies of Plutarco Elías Calles, Aberlardo Rodríguez, Lázaro Cárdenas, Miguel de la Madrid, Ernesto Zedillo, and Felipe Calderón. See [http://www.diputados.gob.mx/LeyesBiblio/ref/cpeum.htm]. *Source* The author with information from the Chamber of Deputies of the Mexican Congress

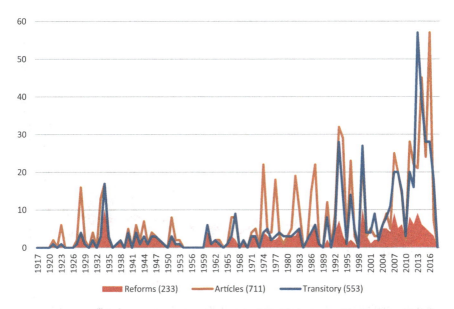

Fig. 5.2 Reforms, Articles and Transitory changes, 1917–2018. *Source* The author with information from the Chamber of Deputies of the Mexican Congress

force of the reforms, and therefore their lifespan is limited, at least since the 1990s, the number of transitory articles integrated per reform has increased. This alters their original function to become alternative mechanisms for incorporation into the constitutional text. The number of transitory articles has been added to our different charts as a complementary indicator of the real magnitude of the constitutional change in Mexico.

Figure 5.3 presents the modifications to the Constitution of each presidential period, highlighting the impact of the last two presidential terms, governed by Felipe Calderón and Enrique Peña Nieto. Although these governments together cover only twelve years of constitutional life, they made 27% of the amendments, affected 38% of the total modified articles and, highly relevant, created 48% of the total transitory articles. In fact, during the presidency of Enrique Peña Nieto, more transitory changes were created (170) than articles were modified (154). Although most of the constitutional reforms only create one (153) or two transitory articles (31), and only 23 reforms contain more than six transitory ones (with extreme cases of 17, 18 and up to 21 transitory articles), the majority of these are concentrated in the Calderón (5) and Peña Nieto (11) periods. However, it is since the presidency of Carlos Salinas de Gortari that the balance was modified in comparison with previous periods: CSG: R: (15)/A (55)/T (43); EZP: R (18)/A (80)/T (63); VFQ: R (19)/A (31)/T (40); FCH: R (36)/A (111)/T (94); EPN: R (27)/A (154)/T (170). Between 1982 and 2018 78% of the transitory articles were created, but in the

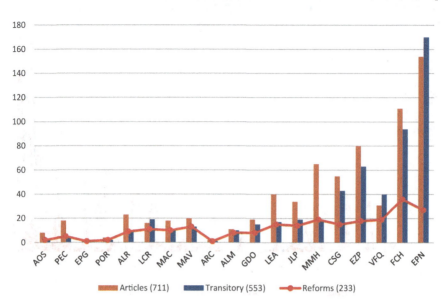

Fig. 5.3 Constitutional Reforms by Presidential Period, 1917–2018. *Source* The author with information from the Chamber of Deputies of the Mexican Congress

2000–2018 cycle, the years of presidential alternation, more transitory changes were created (304) than articles were modified (296) (Fig. 5.4).[9]

That reflects that although many of the recent reforms are increasingly complex and require a much more specific transitory frame, transitory articles were used to incorporate additional modifications to the Constitution without modifying the text itself. They tend to create mandates that correspond to secondary legislation or broader criteria to establish or limit the interpretation of the new rules. This implies the intention of containing or distorting the reach of the original constitutional reform. The increasing creation of transitory articles as part of the constitutional reforms is part of the climate of political distrust that characterizes negotiations between parties and, as its consequence, the intention of bound the design of secondary legislation directly. Chacón (2018) has analyzed the impact of the change in direction of the transitory articles in particular of the political-electoral reform of 2014.

Figures 5.4 and 5.5 show the magnitude of the constitutional change in different stages of modern Mexican history. From 1982 to 2018, 58% of the amendments were made and 70% of the articles modified, which gives a ratio of 3.72 reforms and 13.78 modified articles in this period alone, a figure much higher than the average in the hundred years of constitutional life. It is highly significant that 40%

---

[9]Carlos Salinas de Gortari (CSG), Ernesto Zedillo Ponce de León (EZP), Vicente Fox Quezada (VFQ), Felipe Calderón Hinojosa (FCH), Enrique Peña Nieto (EPN). Reforms (R), Amendments (A), Transitory Articles (T).

5 How Many Constitutional Reforms Produce Rule of Law? 93

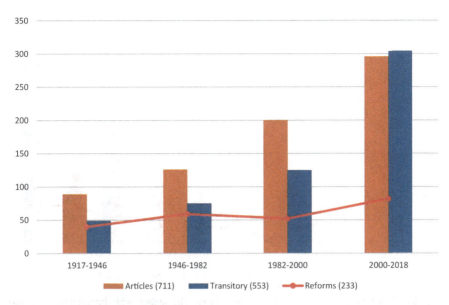

Fig. 5.4 Constitutional Reforms by Political Period, 1917–2018. *Source* The author with information from the Chamber of Deputies of the Mexican Congress

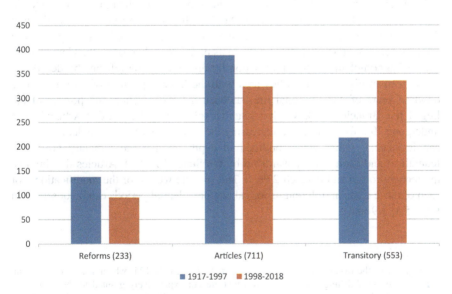

Fig. 5.5 Constitutional Reforms and Democratic Transition. *Source* The author with information from the Chamber of Deputies of the Mexican Congress

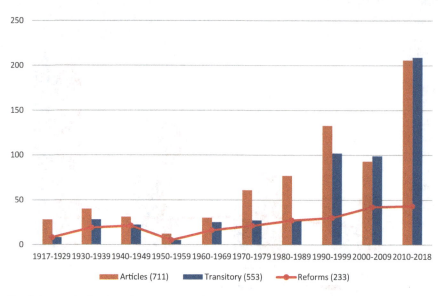

Fig. 5.6 Constitutional Reforms by Decade. *Source* The author with information from the Chamber of Deputies of the Mexican Congress

of the reforms and 45% of the modifications to articles have occurred since 1997 (a ratio of 4.5 reforms and 15.38 articles modified per year), when the ruling party did not have an absolute majority in any of the Chambers of Congress. This implies that the difficulty in building qualified majorities and the support of local congresses did not really represent an obstacle to presidents promoting changes to the Constitution. Figure 5.6 complements the information by distributing the reforms by decade.

As seen in Fig. 5.7, the policy area with the largest quantity of reforms in one hundred years of constitutional life has been the organization and powers of the Legislative Branch (27%), which is largely explained by the fact that Article 73 has undergone 79 reforms aimed at increasing the matters in which the federal congress can legislate.[10] Other areas modified in depth involve the judiciary (14.57%), federalism and economic stewardship by the State (10.42%). Articles that involve the recognition of rights reach 27%.[11] The specific weight of the modifications for each of these areas in different historical and presidential periods can be observed in Figs. 5.8, 5.9 and 5.10.

---

[10]Compared to the overall reforms involving Article 73, Article 124, which structured Mexican federalism by establishing that the faculties that are not expressively granted to the Federation correspond to the states and Mexico City, has only been modified once – as part of the political reform of Mexico City in 2016.

[11]Even when they involve the recognition of rights, Article 27, which refers to land and property rights, and Article 123, which refers to labor relations, are accounted for as part of the faculties and obligations of the economic stewardship by the State.

5 How Many Constitutional Reforms Produce Rule of Law?

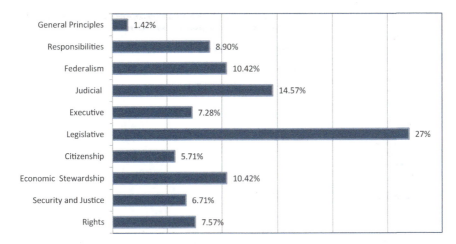

Fig. 5.7 Constitutional Reform by Selected Topics, 1917–2018. ('Rights' includes reforms to Articles 1–12, 24 and 29; Security and Justice to Articles 13–23; Economic Stewardship to Articles 25–28, 123 and 131; Citizenship to Articles 30–38 and 41; Legislative to Articles 50–78; Executive to Articles 80–93; Judicial to Articles 94–107; Federalism to Articles 42–48, 115–122, and 124; Responsibilities to Articles 79, 108–114, 125–128, and 134; and General Principles to Articles 39, 40, 49, 129, 120, 132, 133, 135, and 136). *Source* The author with information from the Chamber of Deputies of the Mexican Congress

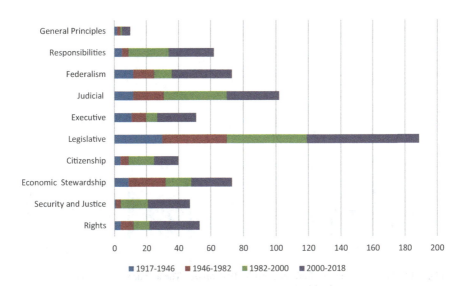

Fig. 5.8 Reforms by Selected Topic by Period, 1917–2018. *Source* The author with information from the Chamber of Deputies of the Mexican Congress

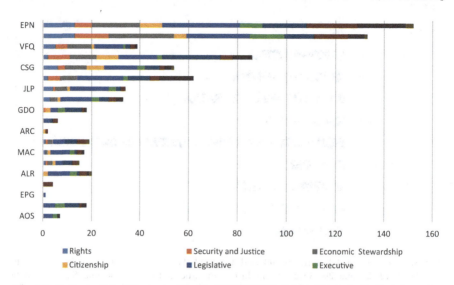

Fig. 5.9 Reforms: Select Topics by President, 1917–2018. *Source* The author with information from the Chamber of Deputies of the Mexican Congress

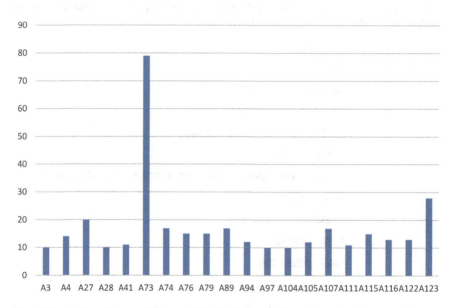

Fig. 5.10 Articles with most Reforms, 1917–2018. *Source* The author with information from the Chamber of Deputies of the Mexican Congress

5.5 Constitutional Change as Hyper-Reformism and Rule of Law Deficit

The Mexican Constitution stands out both for its longevity and its capacity to adapt and integrate changes as a response to political, economic and social transformations or as part of presidential agendas. The question is why this longevity or the magnitude of the changes made – five times the international average – has not translated into a more effective democratic rule of law, as pointed out by international indexes that measure attributes of the rule of law (Le Clercq and Rodríguez, 2017 and 2018; RLI, 2018).

The effectiveness of the rule of law does not depend exclusively on the constitutional design or the scope of its content, nor on its longevity and number of amendments. However, constitutional norms and mandates establish the foundations of the rule of law and legal mechanisms for decentralized coordination of individual and social actions. Understanding the way in which constitutional attributes foster development of the rule of law is a central political problem, especially in cases such as Mexico's, in which the Constitution is a permanent object of political negotiation and expectations of social transformation.

This analysis seeks to identify the relationship between characteristics of the Constitution and degrees of the rule of law. It reviews the potential relationship between four variables and its correlation coefficient for 114 countries (Figures 5.11, 5.12, 5.13, 5.14 and 5.15). These variables are: (1) longevity of the Constitution; (2) extension of the text according to the number of words it contains; (3) the scope of its content, understood as "the percentage of 70 major topics from the Comparative Constitutional Project that are included in any given constitution"; and (4) rule of law degrees according to the *Rule of Law Index (RLI)*.[12]

First, the data indicates a relationship between the longevity of the constitutions and a better performance in the *RLI* (Fig. 5.11), with a correlation coefficient of 0.57. We need to interpret this result carefully because there are important cases of younger constitutions with a stronger rule of law than some older constitutions, but it is relevant that constitutions with more than a forty-year lifespan tend to perform better according to the *RLI*. Even when there are cases of young constitutions with a strong rule of law, some young constitutions find it more difficult to become established as a mechanism of coordination to regulate the interactions of

---

[12] The first three variables are from the Constitution Rankings, elaborated by The Comparative Constitution Project with information updated to April 8, 2016. The seventy elements of 'scope' include characteristics from general, obligations, rights, institutional designs, elections, regulatory organs, international criteria, criminal procedures, special issues and amendment rules, [http://comparativeconstitutionsproject.org/ccp-rankings/] (Consulted 05/09/2018). The information from the *WPJ Rule of Law Index* corresponds to the 2017–2018 report, which considers forty-four indicators arranged in nine factors: constraints on government, absence of corruption, open government, fundamental rights, order and security, regulatory enforcement, civil justice, criminal justice, and informal justice, at: https://worldjusticeproject.org/our-work/wjp-rule-law-index/wjp-rule-law-index-2017%E2%80%932018 (5 September 2018).

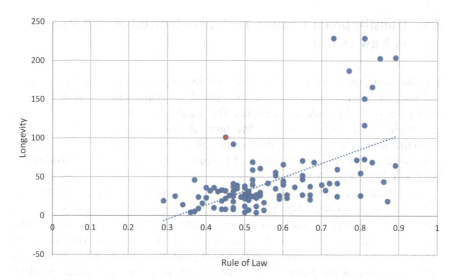

Fig. 5.11 Constitutional Longevity and Rule of Law. *Source* The author with information from the RLI and Comparative Constitutional Project. Red point locates Mexico at the chart

individuals and social groups. The Mexican case represents an exception because the Constitution is among the ten oldest analyzed, but its performance is very inefficient in terms of the development of the rule of law according to the *RLI*.

Second, a negative correlation coefficient of −0.38 is obtained when analyzing scope and degree of rule of law (Fig. 5.12). This implies that cases with more elements integrated into their constitution perform worse in the *RLI*. Again, we must take this carefully, because the majority of cases are located in a quadrant of medium scope and rule of law. Most of the cases of low scope tend to have medium and high levels of rule of law. The more ambitious a constitution is and more scopes it covers, the more complicated it is to implement its functions and turn them into an effective coordination mechanism. They also need more fiscal resources to generate the legal mechanisms and policies necessary to fulfill the constitutional objectives and mandates (Holmes/Sunstein 1999). Mexico is in a position characterized by the existence of a thematically ambitious constitution with very low degrees of rule of law.

Third, we observe a negative correlation of −0.48 between longevity and the scope and levels of rule of law (Fig. 5.13). It is possible that the oldest constitutions tend to incorporate fewer subjects than those of recent creation; in other words, older constitutions would maintain a minimal liberal design, and recent ones tend to incorporate more elements because they have to respond to increasingly plural societies during the process of constitutional creation, and therefore face greater political and social pressures. Mexico stands out as one of the oldest constitutions with the highest percentage of elements integrated, with the same percentage as

5 How Many Constitutional Reforms Produce Rule of Law? 99

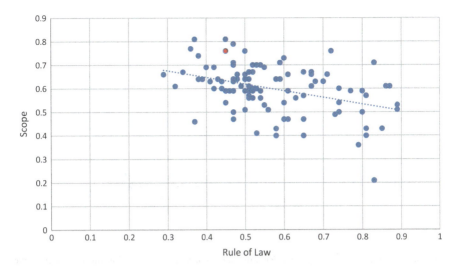

Fig. 5.12 Constitutional Scope and Rule of Law. *Source* The author with information from RLI and the Comparative Constitutional Project. Red point locates Mexico

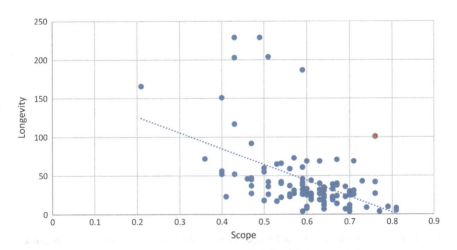

Fig. 5.13 Constitutional Longevity and Scope. *Source* The author with information from the Comparative Constitutional Project. Red point locates Mexico

Cape Verde and Portugal (.76), and only below Egypt (.77), Ecuador (.79), Angola (.80), and Kenya and Zimbabwe (.81) – cases with the highest scope level.

Finally, when integrating the extension of the text with the analysis, no relevant correlation with the other variables is obtained (Figs. 5.14 and 5.15).

These charts show the relationship between different features of constitutional change and rule of law decrees, although more comparative and qualitative research

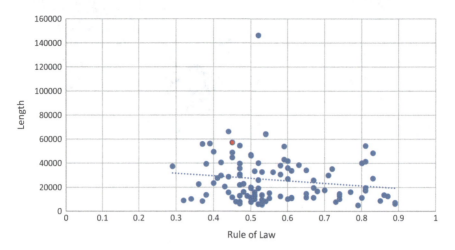

Fig. 5.14 Constitutional Length and Rule of Law. *Source* The author with information from the RLI and the Comparative Constitutional Project. Red point locates Mexico

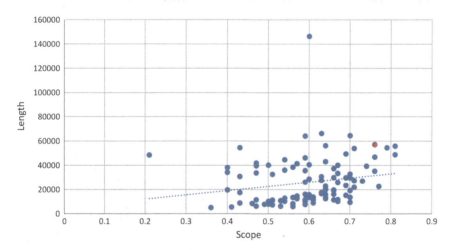

Fig. 5.15 Constitutional Length and Scope. *Source* Author with information from Comparative Constitutional Project. Red point locates Mexico

is needed. Even if factors such as longevity, scope of content, or extension can tell us much about the difficulty of converting the dynamics of constitutional change into an effective rule of law in Mexico, political variables such as the forms of control, the equilibrium generated by competition and conflict, as well as the results of partisan negotiation, become relevant as explanatory elements. In fact, political elements are key to understanding the specific characteristics that acquire the attributes of constitutional design as endogenous factors, for example, political negotiation and conflict. Several authors have correctly highlighted the importance of the national political dynamic resulting from the presidential project, partisan competition and political agreement as the main explanatory factors of constitutional change and the related problems of incoherence and weakness in ensuring compliance. Emphasis is particularly placed on the preponderance of the Constitution as a political rather than a judicial instrument, or the willingness of the actors to integrate political-social aspirations into the text as part of the broader political project (Casar/Marván 2014; Cossío 2010; Salazar 2017; Valdés Ugalde 2017; Concha 2018).

Cossío's (2010) argument is especially relevant for understanding the way in which conflict and political competition have determined the dynamics of constitutional change, establishing a process of path dependency that made development of rule of law almost impossible. In this interpretation, throughout Mexican history constitutions were not understood by political actors as the set of fundamental legal norms to regulate public life, but as instruments to make politics, exert domination, resolve distributive conflicts, and incorporate into the text the political projects of the triumphant sides in national conflicts.

During the post-revolutionary period that Cossío defines as the "long regime" (2010: 50–64), which coincides with most of the Constitution's lifespan, rather than establishing limits to the exercise of power and the fundamental legal rule, the Constitution's functions became expressing the political project of the regime, translating the political social ideology of the revolution and reflecting a popular mandate, all interpreted through the will of the incumbent president:

> (…) the Constitution did not have the character of norm, nor even of a regulatory force, since it consisted only in identifying in a general way what the prevailing social forces at a certain moment would have considered as politically relevant, without preventing it from assigning other contents the same character even without being found in the text (Cossío 2010: 51).

According to Cossío, this begins to change with the political transition and the increasing partisan competition and social plurality trend that limits the role of the president as the main interpreter and driver of constitutional change. A democratic context activates parliamentary debate and negotiation and transforms the way the Supreme Court understands its function of interpreting and responding to disputes and conflicts over the proper meaning of the Constitution. Gradually "… in a clumsy and partial manner, it began to be understood as a legal norm, as a limit to public actions, as a way of conducting social phenomena different from those that had hitherto been experienced" (2010: 72). In other words, there began to be a transition from the perception of the Constitution as a political instrument for serving the needs of the regime towards the Constitution as a juridical instrument focused on establishing the foundations of a democratic rule of law.

Undoubtedly, the democratic transition implies changes in the way political actors understand the role of the Constitution and the responsibility of political institutions to fulfill their mandates – a process that has been gradual, and in many ways embryonic, and that has resulted both from the growing partisan competitiveness and an increasing public influence of organized civil society. However, the transformation of the Constitution into a fundamental legal norm faces three problems. Firstly, the understanding of the Constitution as a mainly political instrument and the consequent logic that requires institutional change to pass through the filter of the constitutional reform has ceased to be a presidential monopoly in order to diversify itself and reflect the dynamics of conflict and negotiation between the different political parties. In other words, rather than being limited, the dispute to incorporate its own agenda and political objectives into the Constitution now extends to the different political forces.

Secondly, it is possible to identify a significant change in the way political actors understand the political significance and reach of the Constitution. A large part of the amendments made since 1997 focus on adapting the institutional framework to respond to democratic consolidation challenges, social pluralism and the complexity of international markets. However, this process is far from irreversible. The result of the 2018 presidential election shows that political actors continue to understand that the Constitution has as its primary function encapsulating the ideals, objectives and aspirations of the winning groups of national political disputes.

Finally, even when development of a democratic rule of law does not depend exclusively on constitutional coherence, a constitution that is not capable of self-imposing its compliance cannot become an effective mechanism for the coordination of political, economic and social interactions. The impossibility of translating the large number of constitutional amendments into a solid foundation for the rule of law can also be explained by the interaction of six factors: (1) problems that arise from the design, characteristics and coherence of the reforms; (2) difficulties related to the implementation of the mandates through secondary legislation (Ríos/Wood 2018); (3) weak vertical and horizontal institutional interplay, understood as a dynamic and conflictive interaction that involves institutions and actors across and between national and subnational levels; (4) inability to convert growing number of constitutional mandates into public policy as a result of scarce financial resources, social conflicts or governance problems; (5) constitutional impunity or the lack of political will to implement the mandates derived from the reforms both nationally and at state level (Díaz Sáenz 2017; Madrazo/ Méndez 2017);[13] (6) high levels of corruption, impunity and institutional capture that end up distorting the meaning and scope of the reforms, diminishing their capacity to regulate political competition, social interactions and economic exchanges (Le Clercq 2018).

---

[13]The project *Violómetro Constitucional* identifies up to twenty-eight constitutional reforms in which the Congress has not completed the corresponding adjustments to the secondary legislation. However, this reflects only legislative omissions by the national congress; an analysis of the breaches of mandates at state congress level would place this problem in a different dimension. See *Violómetro Constitucional*, CIDE, México; at: http://periodismocide.org/eventos/violometro/.

5.6 Conclusion

The analysis of constitutional change in Mexico poses significant challenges to the study of the development of the rule of law. The existence of an old constitution, accepted as a legitimate basis for political agreement between political and social actors over time, as well as an extremely flexible institution, capable of integrating political and social transformations through its multiple amendments, does not mean that the Constitution can become self-regulating as the coordination mechanism of decentralized exchanges and interactions.

Although plural debate and negotiation have involved different political forces and organized civil society has increased during recent decades, when almost throughout the twentieth century constitutional change was detached from the presidential will and party rule hegemony, the fact is that the Mexican Constitution continues to be understood by political actors as an instrument that reflects its political aspirations and projects rather than the fundamental legal norm. This implies that it is not usually assumed to be the cornerstone for the development of a democratic rule of law.

It is striking that constitutional change has become a fetish, that political actors promote and approve amendments as part of a logic that assumes that institutional change only occurs if it is incorporated into the constitutional text. Simultaneously, its implementation ends up being unequal, its compliance conditioned by political agendas, electoral times and economic interests, and its translation into new laws or public policies dependent upon the political will of federal and state authorities.

In the first decades of the twenty-first century Mexico needs to develop a democratic rule of law that allows effective institutional responses to public problems, improves access to justice, guarantees public security, reduces the very high levels of impunity, contains corruption, and protects the exercise of human rights, all within the framework of the consolidation of a more competitive, plural and inclusive democracy. One hundred years after its entry into force, the Mexican Constitution is an extraordinarily complex instrument that has managed to integrate institutional transformations, social demands and an extended system of human rights – very ambitious aspirations accompanied by the inability of the Constitution to impose compliance on political actors at the national and subnational levels.

The quality of the rule of law does not only depend on the characteristics of constitutional change, but is also related to the formulation of the laws and their content, exercise and daily respect for human rights, the design of institutions, the independence of powers, the existence of accountability, and the culture of legality – processes that acquire specific form and practice from the capacity of a constitution to become a more effective mechanism of hierarchical coordination. In the Mexican case, the logic that understands the Constitution as a political instrument and the hyper-reformism that emerges from it, affecting the coherence, meaning, and effectiveness of the text, has made it impossible to transform the Constitution into the coordination mechanism on which the development and quality of the rule of law partly depend.

References

Aguilar Rivera, José Antonio (2017). "Emilio Rabasa y la Constitución de 1917", in: Cossío, José Ramón; Silva-Herzog Márquez, Jesús (Eds.): *Lecturas de la Constitución* (Mexico City: FCE): 19–59.
Bellamy, Richard (2007). *Political Constitutionalism* (New York: Cambridge University Press).
Bingham, Tom (2010). *The Rule of Law* (London: Penguin).
Caballero, José Luis (2018). "Mitos y paradigmas sobre la Constitución mexicana y su reforma. Breve reflexión en torno al próximo Centenario y ante la necesidad de una nueva constitucionalidad", in: Serna, José María; de la Garza, Isidro: *La dinámica del cambio constitucional en México* (México: IIJ, UNAM): 23–39.
Carbonell, Miguel (2014). "¿Por qué no una nueva Constitución?", in: *Nexos* (February 2014); at: https://www.nexos.com.mx/?p=18387.
Casar, María Amparo (2013). "El fetichismo constitucional", in: *Nexos* (February 2013); at: https://www.nexos.com.mx/?p=15163.
Casar, María Amparo; Marván, Ignacio (2014). *Reformar sin Mayoría* (Mexico City: Taurus).
Chacón Rojas, Orlando (2018). "La desnaturalización de los artículos transitorios en la reforma constitucional político-electoral de 2014", in: Serna, José María; de la Garza, Isidro: *La dinámica del cambio constitucional en México* (Mexico City: IIJ, UNAM): 177–196.
Concha Cantú, Hugo (2018). "La reforma constitucional en México: disfuncionalidad del modelo democrático constitucional", in: Serna, José María; de la Garza, Isidro: *La dinámica del cambio constitucional en México* (Mexico City: IIJ, UNAM): 161–176.
Cooter, Robert C. (2000). *The Strategic Constitution* (New Jersey: Princeton).
Cossío, José Ramón (2010): "Nuestro (mal) devenir constitucional", in: Cordera, Rolando (Ed.): *Presente y perspectivas* (Mexico City: FCE): 29–80.
Díaz Saenz, Rodrigo (2017). "Impunidad Constitucional, in: Esquivel, Gerardo; Ibarra, Francisco; Salazar, Pedro: *Cien Ensayos para el Centenario*, Vol. 2 (Mexico City: IIJ, UNAM): 89–104.
Elkins, Zachary; Ginsburg, Tom; Melton, James (2009). *The Endurance of National Constitutions* (New York: Cambridge University Press).
Fix-Fierro, Héctor (2017). "Por qué se reforma tanto la Constitución Mexicana de 1917? Hacia la renovación del texto y la cultura de la Constitución", in: Esquivel, Gerardo; Ibarra, Francisco; Salazar, Pedro: *Cien Ensayos para el Centenario*, Vol. 4 (Mexico City: IIJ, UNAM): 143–162.
Fix-Fierro, Héctor; Valadés, Diego (Eds.) (2017). "Hacia la reordenación y consolidación del texto de la Constitución Política de los Estados Unidos Mexicanos de 1917. Estudio Instroductorio", in: *Constitución Política de los Estado Mexicanos. Texto reordenado y consolidado. Anteproyecto*, 2nd edn. (Mexico City: IIJ, UNAM): 1–41.
Friedrich, Carl J. (1950). *Constitutional Government and Democracy* (Boston: Ginn and Company).
Ginsburg, Tom; Melton, James (2014). "Does the Constitutional Amendment Rule Matter at All? Amendment Cultures and the Challenges of Measuring Amendment Difficulty", in: *Coase-Sandor Institute for Law and Economics Working Papers*, No. 682 (Chicago: University of Chicago): 1–29.
Grimm, Dieter (2006). *Constitucionalismo y derechos fundamentales* (Madrid: Trotta).
Hardin, Russell (1999). *Liberalism, Constitutionalism and Democracy* (New York: Oxford).
Holmes, Stephen; Sunstein, Cass R. (1999). *The Cost of Rights* (New York: Norton).
Le Clercq, Juan Antonio (2018). "El complejo impunidad", in: Loeza, Laura; Richard, Ana Lisa: *Derechos Humanos y Violencia en México* (Mexico City: CEIICH, UNAM).
Le Clercq, Juan Antonio; Rodríguez, Gerardo (2017). *Dimensiones de la impunidad global. IGI 2017* (Puebla: UDLAP).
Le Clercq, Juan Antonio; Rodríguez, Gerardo (2018). *La impunidad subnacional y sus dimensiones en México. IGI-MEX 2018* (Puebla: UDLAP).

Madrazo, Jorge; Méndez, Francisco (2017). "La Constitución Mexicana: obedézcase pero no se cumpla", in: Esquivel, Gerardo; Ibarra, Francisco; Salazar, Pedro: *Cien Ensayos para el Centenario*, Vol. 4 (Mexico City: IIJ, UNAM): 197–212.

Martin Reyes, Javier (2017). "Patologías de la Constitución de 1917", in: *Este País*, (February 2017): 9–13.

North, Douglas C.; Weingast, Barry R. (1989). "Constitutions and Commitment: The Evolution of Institutional Governing Public Choice in Seventeenth-Century England", in: *The Journal of Economic History*, 49,4 (December): 803–832.

Pou Giménez, Francisca (2018). "Las ineficacias legales y políticas del Hiper-Reformismo Constitucional mexicano", in: Serna, José María; de la Garza, Isidro: *La dinámica del cambio constitucional en México* (Mexico City: IIJ, UNAM): 397–408.

Ríos, Viridiana; Wood, Duncan (2018). *The Missing Reform: Strengthening the Rule of Law in Mexico* (Washington, D.C.: Wilson Center).

Rivera, León; Arturo, Mauro (2017). "Understanding Constitutional Amendments in Mexico: Perpetuum Mobile Constitution", in: *Mexican Law Review*, 9,2 (June-July): 3–27.

Salazar Ugarte, Pedro (2017). "El cambio constitucional como instrumento de transformación política", in: Esquivel, Gerardo; Ibarra, Francisco; Salazar, Pedro: *Cien Ensayos para el Centenario*, Vol. 2 (Mexico City: IIJ, UNAM): 379–392.

Sartori, Giovanni (2016). *Ingeniería constitucional comparada* (Mexico City: FCE).

Skaaning, Svend-Erik (2010). "Measuring the Rule of Law", in: *Political Research Quarterly*, 63,2 (June): 449–460.

Sunstein, Cass R. (2001). *Designing Democracy* (New York: Oxford University Press).

Tamanaha, Brian Z. (2004). *On the Rule of Law* (New York: Cambridge University Press).

Valdés Ugalde, Francisco (2017). "La dislocación de Sistema político y régimen constitucional en la post-transición democrática", in: Esquivel, Gerardo; Ibarra, Francisco; Salazar, Pedro: *Cien Ensayos para el Centenario*, Vol. 4 (Mexico City: IIJ, UNAM): 355–376.

Velasco Rivera, Mariana (2017). "Longevidad constitucional ¿a cambio de qué", in: *Nexos* (February); at: https://www.nexos.com.mx/?p=31364

Waldron, Jeremy (2016). *Political Political Theory* (Cambridge: Harvard University Press).

World Justice Project (2018): *Rule of Law Index 2017-2018* (Washington, D.C.: WJP); at: https://worldjusticeproject.org/news/2017-2018-wjp-rule-law-index.

Chapter 6
Security

Vidal Romero

Abstract A central task of a state is to establish order within its territory. The mere creation of the state is justified by this statement. A proper order that allows citizens to develop in all dimensions is based upon the rule of law. An insecure environment (i.e. disorder) signals a weakness in the rule of law, which is further weakened as crime and violence unfold. Mexico has been suffering an insecurity crisis since 2007 – which is not unique, or even the worst in its recent history. It is, however, the worst insecurity crisis since the country's democratization process began. The combination of a deficient rule of law, an ineffective war on drugs, a fiscal system disconnected from citizens' preferences, and the democratization process itself, has provided fertile ground for a dramatic increase in crime and violence. Under these circumstances, strengthening the rule of law is paramount, yet conditions are such that improving it will prove problematic.

Keywords Security · Violence · Rule of law · Mexico · Fiscal disconnect · war on drugs · Drug trafficking organizations · Democratization · Homicides · Drug legalization

---

Vidal Romero is Professor at the Political Science Department at ITAM and Visiting Fellow (2018–2021) at the Latin America and Caribbean Centre (LACC) at the London School of Economics and Political Science. He holds a Ph.D. in Political Science from Stanford University. He was visiting Professor at Stanford University (2012–13). Romero is Co-Director of ITAM's Center of Studies on Security, Intelligence, and Governance. His current research examines the conditions under which governments can establish (democratic) order in their territories. He has collaborated on different research projects with the World Bank, the Wilson Center, México Evalúa, the National Endowment for Democracy, and the Inter-American Development Bank. Email: vromero@itam.mx.

© Springer Nature Switzerland AG 2020
J. A. Le Clercq and J. P. Abreu Sacramento (eds.), *Rebuilding the State Institutions*,
https://doi.org/10.1007/978-3-030-31314-2_6

6.1 Security

The main task of any state is to impose order within its territory. Citizens delegate the legitimate use of force to the state, as this is a cheaper solution than every citizen, or group of citizens, attempting to impose order by themselves in a decentralized manner. Thus, it allows citizens to use their resources in a more productive manner (Bates 2001).

Those in power face competition for the position of provider of order (North 1981). In a democracy, different alternatives compete in free and fair elections. In autocracies, they must find other ways to acquire power. Citizens should prefer democratic order to autocracy since democracy it is based upon the rule of law, and it respects individual and collective rights. It provides citizens with the assurance that their property and rights will be protected by the state, and that those who break the legal norms will be prosecuted under the law.

Yet, even in democracies, there are different degrees of rule of law; sometimes it can be weak. When the rule of law is deficient – either in its definition or its enforcement – incentives for illicit behavior tend to increase. Simultaneously, high revenue generated by illicit behavior gives the beneficiaries of illegality incentives to maintain, or worsen, the deficient rule of law. A vicious circle is thus created: bad security negatively affects the rule of law, and a worsening rule of law negatively affects security. This type of dynamic is usually hard to break.

Weingast (1997: 245) defines the rule of law as "a set of stable political rules and rights applied to all citizens impartially". A society based upon the rule of law implies a state in which governments act based upon rules that are known *ex ante*. Citizens can then predict that if they do A, the state will respond by doing X, X having previously been established as a formal rule.

For instance, suppose that a citizen driving her car runs a red light and a police officer detects it. In a place in which the rule of law works effectively, the expected behavior of the police officer is to apply the penalty stated in a formal code. The citizen knows that, and has incentives to behave or face further penalties. In the opposite scenario, of a state with a deficient rule of law, there is uncertainty over whether the police officer would impose a penalty, as stated in the formal rule, or instead suggest a bribe as an alternate 'solution'. Even worse, there might be certainty that the police officer would not follow the formal norm but instead ask for a bribe.

In a democracy, the rule of law does not just provide certainty regarding the behavior of public officials; it also has another defining characteristic: it protects citizens' rights by limiting the power of the state.

Mexico is immersed in a security crisis dating back to 2007. The Mexican State already operated within a context of a deficient rule of law. Add to this the combination of a state in the process of democratic consolidation, a senseless war on drugs, and a fiscal structure whose rules are completely disconnected from citizens' preferences. Since 2007 these coexisting conditions have generated, among other calamities, over 250,000 deaths, and around 30,000 missing persons.

The purpose of this chapter is to analyze this nefarious ongoing episode of Mexico's current history and point to potential solutions, emphasizing the relationship between rule of law and insecurity as a vicious circle (as described above) that is being maintained by this country's institutions. In this chapter, I focus on two of these institutions: fiscal disconnection and drugs prohibition. To do so, I first briefly describe Mexico's current security crisis and its noxious relationship with the rule of law. I will then analyze three core determinants of insecurity in Mexico: democratization, the war on drugs, and fiscal disconnection. I conclude with a discussion on specific policies that may improve Mexico's security conditions.

6.2 Security in Mexico

To fully understand Mexico's current security crisis, it is important to contextualize it in time and space. For a start, contemporary levels of homicides are not atypical for Mexico during the last century. Current events, and the way they are reported, tend to eclipse the fact that Mexico has always been a violent country. Figure 6.1 shows the country's homicide rate from 1931 to 2017.

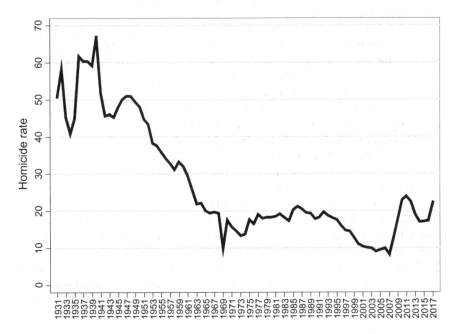

Fig. 6.1 Homicide rate per 100,000 inhabitants in Mexico (1931–2017). *Source* Anuarios Estadísticos de la República Mexicana and INEGI; at: https://goo.gl/uxrBXK

There are various relevant pieces of information in Fig. 6.1. First, if we look at the period between the 1930s to the 1980s, we can observe a steady decrease in violence which can be attributed to the formation of the Mexican state after the Revolution. Second, even as the country was being pacified, the levels of violence were still very high, especially compared with modern levels. This pacification occurred concurrently with the creation of the hegemonic party which was to dominate the Mexican government until the year 2000: the Partido Revolucionario Institucional, or PRI. Thus, the PRI can be credited with pacifying the country, but not with ruling a peaceful state. The so-called *pax priista* – i.e. the idea of a strong autocratic state under the PRI that was able to impose order in its territory – is just a myth that is not backed by empirical evidence.

Third, the average homicide rate in the previous decade (2008–2017) is almost identical to the 1980s average: 19.3 and 19.2 respectively. Thus, what Mexicans are experiencing is not new for a significant share of the population. Moreover, the current crime rate is far lower than other violent episodes in the country's history. During the Independence War (1810–1821) the rate of deaths in the conflict was around 700 per 100,000 inhabitants, during the Revolution (1910–1920) casualties amounted to around 600 deaths per 100,000 inhabitants, and during the Cristero War (1926–1929) the death rate was estimated at 400 deaths per 100,000 inhabitants – estimated by the author using the median of deaths reported by five history publications for each event.

Mexico is not even in the top tier of violent nations in the world. There are, however, specific areas in Mexico in which the rule of law has collapsed at different times in the previous decade. Specific cities within Mexico have been, or are, amongst the most violent in the world, including Acapulco, Chilpancingo, Ciudad Juarez, Culiacan, Los Cabos, Tijuana, and Reynosa.

I do not aim to minimize the gravity of Mexico's current security crisis, but we need to place it in adequate context in order to analyze it properly, and devise feasible solutions. As I have shown above, Mexico's current problem with violence lies not with the levels as such, but with the abrupt change upwards that happened as of 2008, and with the fact that the country has not been able to significantly reduce violence for the past ten years.

Along with a significant deterioration in public security, a worrisome feature in Mexico has been the failure to strengthen the rule of law after democratization. Figure 6.2 shows the Rule of Law index from the Varieties of Democracy Project from the early 1980s, when the PRI regime began losing some local elections, to 2017. The index goes from 0, low rule of law, to 1, high rule of law. The trend line does not perfectly follow the trend in homicides, because other variables have also had an impact, but it shows how rule of law has been systematically lower after the 2007 violent crime shock.

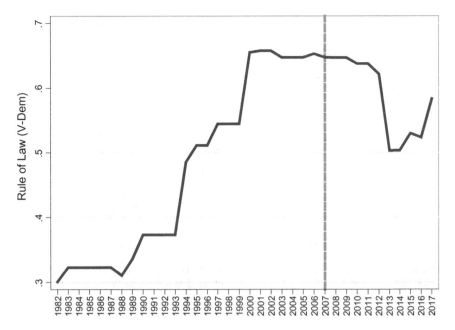

Fig. 6.2 Rule of Law in Mexico (1982–2017). *Source* Varieties of Democracy Project; at: https://goo.gl/aFRRG7

6.3 Insecurity and the Rule of Law

Mexico's (in)security circumstances are not random; they can be explained by both structural and circumstantial factors. There is a significant body of literature explaining the determinants of violence in Mexico. One strand of the literature has focused on how increasing political pluralism (unwillingly) detonated violence by weakening the monopolist structure of the Mexican State, which allowed for collusion between the government and drug cartels (Osorio 2013; Ríos 2012; Dell 2015). Other works focus on the negative effects that the specific strategy of the Mexican Government against criminal organizations has had on increasing violence (Osorio 2011; Calderon et al. 2015; Lessing 2015; Phillips 2015).[1]

In these works, structural causes such as inequality and poverty are also part of the explanation for Mexico's levels of violence since 2007. And a variable that is embedded in all explanations is Mexico's deficient rule of law.

Figure 6.3 shows the relationship between rule of law (approximated by the Rule of Law index constructed by the World Justice Project) and the homicide rate per 100,000 inhabitants (used as a proxy for insecurity), across countries for which data is available. The WJP index goes from 0, no rule of law, to 1, perfect rule of

---

[1]See Zepeda Gil (2018) for an excellent analysis of the main explanations for violence in Mexico.

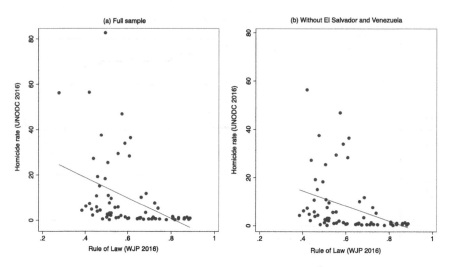

Fig. 6.3 Insecurity and Rule of Law. *Source* Homicide data is from the United Nations Office on Drugs and Crime; at: https://goo.gl/t2pH4J. Rule of law data is from the World Justice Project; at: https://goo.gl/BxJrTn

law, and, in the aggregate, a negative relationship with insecurity can be observed: as rule of law worsens, the homicide rate increases. The graph is replicated without El Salvador and Venezuela, which have extreme values on homicides, and very low levels of rule of law.

Clearly, high homicide rates are not randomly distributed across societies. No country in the high end of rule of law has a homicide rate above 2 per 100,000 inhabitants. Many of these are developed countries such as Japan, Norway, Denmark, the United Kingdom or Sweden, among others. Conversely, countries with high homicide rates are associated to low rule of law levels.

There is much more variance among countries in the middle levels of rule of law, which points to additional variables mediating the relationship between rule of law and insecurity.

A weak rule of law is fertile soil for criminal organizations to flourish. There are multiple incentives for illicit behavior since the expected probability of being caught is relatively low, given that the police are overwhelmed, incapable, and/or corrupt. In the rare event of being caught, the likelihood of being effectively prosecuted is extremely low. In Mexico, for instance, only 12.5% of intentional homicides result in a guilty verdict (Zepeda Lecuona/Jiménez Rodríguez 2018).

As illicit businesses thrive and become more profitable for both criminals and corrupt public officials, there are fewer incentives for governments to improve the rule of law. This results in further increases in crime and, consequently, there are even more incentives to weaken the rule of law. The sequelae of this vicious cycle can be observed at many levels: ordinary crime such as robbery increases, the corruption of public officials expands and escalates, organized crime strengthens its networks, and citizens become both victims and accomplices.

Note that there are societies in which insecurity does not significantly damage the rule of law; such is the case of specific localities in the United States. There are also countries with a weak rule of law that remain relatively secure, such as Ecuador or Thailand. There are distinct circumstances that trigger this vicious cycle between insecurity and a weak rule of law.

In Mexico's case, democratization, the war on drugs, and an inefficient fiscal structure account for a significant share of this deterioration in both security and of the rule of law. In the following subsections, I analyze these determinants and their effects. Note that other works in the literature, which I explicitly reference in the following paragraphs, have explored these determinants, especially democratization and the war on drugs; my contribution is on endogenously relating these variables to the rule of law and, in the next section, outlining potential policy improvements.

6.3.1 Democratization

The existing literature agrees upon the ways in which democratization processes negatively affect order (e.g. Huntington 1969; Dahl 1971; Diamond 1999). As nations democratize, individuals and groups that were not able to demand rights and resources from the State can now do so. These actors place strain upon the State's institutions, which are in charge of channeling citizen's demands. However, state institutions adapt at a much slower pace than people's claims do. A more democratic rule of law may be written, yet its effective implementation may take decades, and resources are always scarce relative to needs.

Within this context, conflict arises and, with it, multiple opportunities for criminal activities. Moreover, when there are high revenues associated with crime, as in the case of drug trafficking, there are incentives for actors both inside and outside the Government to weaken the existing rule of law, and keep their illicit business profitable. This has been the case in Mexico.

Mexico was part of a democratizing wave and, like many other nations in Latin America, it initiated a gradual transition to democracy during the late 1980s. Elections gradually became cleaner and more competitive. The ruling party's hegemonic regime slowly began losing power, until it finally lost the Presidency to the Partido Accion Nacional (PAN) in 2000 (Magaloni 2006). Yet, as the country democratized, Mexicans began to realize that freer elections do not solve all problems instantly: poverty has remained high, corruption is still a serious issue, and crime and violence have acutely worsened.

There is a significant bulk of literature explaining the recent explosion of homicides in Mexico, and a lot of this work relates it to democratization (e.g. Osorio 2013; Ríos 2012; Dell 2015). The road to democracy fragmented power across different authority levels. This made it more difficult for authorities from different political parties, and at different levels and jurisdictions, to collude. It made it harder for public officials to credibly commit to protecting drug trafficking organizations, and to enforce local monopolies. DTOs then had to compete directly for control of a specific locality, detonating bloody turf wars.

Some versions of this hypothesis are based on the previously mentioned so-called *pax priista*, which assumed a grand pact between the PRI regime and criminal organizations. This theory states that in exchange for protection from the State, criminal organizations would not fight among themselves. Yet, as shown in the previous section, the evidence does not support this hypothesis. Figure 6.2 shows how the levels of violence were much higher during the PRI hegemonic regime than they are nowadays.

As security worsens, the process of democratic consolidation is endogenously complicated. One specific point of concern is public trust in government, as trust is a key variable to consolidate the democratic regime. Insecurity erodes public trust in many dimensions (Romero et al. 2015 and 2016). Crime victimization negatively affects citizens' satisfaction with the workings of democracy, although fortunately it does not affect support for democracy itself as a form of government (Fernandez/ Kuenzi 2010; Ceobanu et al. 2010).

Public trust is also a necessary condition for success in fighting criminal organizations (Magaloni et al. 2018). More directly related to security organizations, there is strong evidence linking victimization to a decrease of public trust in the police (Pérez 2003; Ahmad et al. 2011; Blanco 2013). This creates a sort of self-fulfilling prophecy. A citizen is a victim of a crime, thus decreasing trust in the police; decreased trust further complicates the police's ability to do their job, since citizens stop cooperating with the forces of law and order; crime increases, reinforcing and increasing citizens' negative evaluation of the police, and the cycle goes on.

Negative trust in government is reflected in the reporting (or not) of crimes. In Mexico, only 6.4% of crimes were reported to authorities in 2016, the most recent year for which there is data in the National Victimization Survey (ENVIPE).[2] The figure is even more alarming with regard to specific crimes such as kidnapping, which is only reported in 2% of cases.

This is a serious issue during a process of democratic consolidation. When security worsens, citizens tend to favor combating crime with heavy-handed policies (Holland 2013; Krause 2014). This can entail serious setbacks to democratization and the rule of law.

---

[2]Available at: https://goo.gl/YM2qJY.

6.3.2 War on Drugs

In Mexico, and in many other countries, the fight against drug trafficking organizations is a key variable which simultaneously increases insecurity and damages the existing rule of law (Valdés 2013; Enciso 2015).

Prohibiting the commerce of goods with an inelastic demand[3] creates black markets with high profit margins. Thus, enforcing such prohibitions usually fails, and at a very high cost. Such has been the case with alcohol in the 1920s in the United States (Thornton 1991; Miron/Zwiebel 1995), and with the current war on drugs that is being fought by different degrees in many countries around the world (Quah et al. 2014). There are exceptions of drug prohibitions which have not generated black markets and increased crime, but these are restricted to hard autocratic regimes that harshly enforce the prohibition, such as in Afghanistan under the Taliban regime.

For Mexico, there is solid evidence that the government's attempts to enforce the drug prohibition by indiscriminately confronting all drug cartels and targeting their leaders has led to a significant increase in violence and crime (Osorio 2011; Lessing 2015). Regarding criminal organizations, or their leaders, as the enemies of the State does not solve the problem, since, in fact, the enemy is a market. Markets are not fixed by attempting to prohibit their existence; they are fixed by regulating them.

Directly fighting Drug Trafficking Organizations (DTOs) places the State, and especially a relatively weak state as the Mexican one is, in a vulnerable position. A weak state can be further debilitated not only by corruption, but also by a lack of public support because of poor performance.

Trafficking in illicit drugs is a business that is not labor-intensive. It is, however, intensive in contacts and information, especially in contacts with public officials. It takes but a few people to transport and smuggle illicit drugs, but you need the right connections to be successful. From a business viewpoint, having a close agent, or even someone from a DTO's own ranks governing a locality (or even a country), saves on transaction costs. Clearly, this setting incentivizes corruption, and opens the door for state capture by DTOs.

If DTOs expand their operations to act as retailers as well, the business model changes. It requires more labor, and also more connections with public officials. Things now become much more complicated for the State, since not only does it require more resources to fight criminal organizations, but there are many more public officials exposed to corruption, and DTOs conduct other illicit business as complements.

This seems to have been the case in Mexico. Criminal organizations were mostly occupied with trafficking illicit drugs produced in Mexico (mainly marijuana) or

---

[3] An inelastic demand is one in which a change in price will have a smaller than proportional effect upon the quantity demanded. If demand is perfectly inelastic, a change in price will have no effect whatsoever upon the quantity sought.

imported from South America (cocaine) and, to a lesser degree, from China (amphetamines). These would then predominantly flow into the United States market, to be retailed there. This circumstance changed in the mid-2000s. Mexican DTOs expanded their retail operations into Mexican cities, and diversified their activities to other crimes, such as extortion and kidnapping.

Some explanations for this phenomenon point to a change in the way that buyers in the United States paid DTOs. Payments that used to be cash only switched to part cash and part illicit drugs (Poiré 2011). This change induced Mexican cartels to hire more workers to sell the part payment in drugs in Mexico's main cities, where the demand is. It significantly increased the size of DTOs, which meant a more expensive payroll.

To take advantage of a bigger workforce, and the bribes to public officials (which are a sort of sunken cost), a natural step was to diversify into other illicit activities. This in turn required bribes to further authorities, specifically at the municipal level: those who oversee the local streets. Rule of law further deteriorated as corruption reached deeper and deeper into government structures, at all levels.

It is clear now that the war on drugs has failed, not only in Mexico, but around the world. It has not achieved its initial goal of keeping illicit drugs away from consumers, making countries safer or cleaning police forces. On the contrary, things have seriously worsened.

6.4 Fiscal Disconnect

A third ingredient deteriorating both security and the rule of law in Mexico is the existing disconnect between the authority collecting taxes, and the authority spending public monies. This divergence generates incentives for the misallocation of resources – corruption and pork projects mainly – that affect the incentives and capabilities of local governments to fight crime effectively.

To the degree that citizens are not able to estimate how their share of the taxes they pay is linked to public spending, public officials become relatively unaccountable. Citizens mostly look at public spending and are unable to connect it to their tax payments; governments have incentives to invest in projects which are politically profitable, but not necessarily efficient. There is evidence to show that this disconnect between central tax collection and local spending creates perverse incentives for both inefficient spending and corruption (Weingast et al. 1981; Díaz-Cayeros et al. 2010; Romero 2015).

In Mexico, around 86% of the public funds spent by subnational governments are collected by the central government (Herrera González et al. 2017). Funds flow outwards from the center, and officials at all the different subunits (state and municipal) are faced with this peculiar incentive to undertake as many projects as they can with money that is transferred by the central government. Thus, the aggregate spending of the country is bigger than it should be and it would tend to be inefficiently spent.

The 86% proportion is replicated in security spending, creating multiple wrong incentives for efficacy and efficiency in security policy-making, and deteriorating the existing rule of law.

In this context, the divergence of interests between national and subnational authorities regarding public security policies complicates effective crime-fighting. Let us assume that in a democracy, policy preferences are, at least partially, determined by citizens' demands. Thus, we can plausibly assume that public officials at the municipal level would follow the preferences of local citizens, who would rather invest public monies in fighting ordinary crime (e.g. thefts, break-ins or simple assaults) than crime related to DTOs. It is precisely their jurisdiction, and just by the incidence of each type of crime, that this should be the case: in 2017 the robbery rate was around 20,000 per 100,000 inhabitants,[4] whereas the homicide rate was 25 per 100,000 inhabitants.[5]

However, federal authorities clearly prefer fighting organized crime related to illicit drugs. This tier of government is formally in charge of this type of crime, and it is the one facing pressure from the United States government and other international organizations to do so.

Since, as stated, 86% of security funds spent by local governments in Mexico come from federal monies, the federal government has multiple tools to induce local governments to spend much of their funding fighting organized crime and drug-related crimes. And because resources are scarce, every peso spent on capturing a small drug dealer implies a peso not spent on other more pressing crimes, such as robbery.

Further compounding the problem is the fact that local police corporations are the ones fighting DTOs, making public posts at local level quite attractive to criminal organizations. This has placed local governments in a vulnerable situation, opening opportunities for corruption and local government capture by drug traffickers. Thus, rule of law has further weakened at the local level.

In the 2018 Mexican elections, more than a hundred candidates and public officials were assassinated during the political campaigns.[6] It is very likely the murdered politicians were inconvenient to drug trafficking organizations wanting to keep or gain power in a particular municipality.

Local governments just do not have the right incentives to fight DTOs, and they should not do it, if we consider constituents' preferences. Money laundering illustrates this issue well. Romero (2017) explains how, regarding money laundering, the divergence in interests between local and federal governments results in poor local government performance, and an explosion in homicides as a negative

---

[4]Data from to the National Survey on Victimization and Security Perception (ENVIPE). Available at: https://goo.gl/htQTuy.
[5]Data from INEGI. Available at: https://goo.gl/uxrBXK.
[6]As reported by Etellekt Consulting to CNN in Spanish https://goo.gl/Ki7J3p. Other media outlets have reported similar figures.

externality. The study shows that atypical increases in local economic activity result in a significant increase in homicides three years afterwards, on average.

The explanation runs as follows: suppose a criminal organization decides to launder money at a given locality. Local governments are the best equipped to detect it as they have more information on who is who, and what businesses they are up to. However, they also have incentives not to denounce it because the laundering operation also implies more local jobs, more local taxes, and more money flowing into the pockets of compliant local officials. On the other hand, the federal government is formally in charge of fighting money laundering, but does not have details of local economic activity, relying instead on tax returns and formal financial statements to detect illicit operations. Local economic bonanzas create incentives for other criminal organizations to enter the same locality, creating turf wars that increase violence.

In a nutshell, Mexico's fiscal institutional setting deters local governments from fighting the crime that citizens most care about, and fighting organized crime by local police has proven ineffective, contributing to corruption within this most basic tier of government. Thus, most efforts by the national government to induce local governments to fight organized crime would prove ineffective.

6.5 Improving Security and the Rule of Law

In this chapter, I have analyzed Mexico's security conditions and its rule of law. I have discussed the current nature of the relationship between these two variables as a vicious circle in which weak rule of law leads to insecurity, and insecurity engenders further deterioration of the rule of law.

Looking at the cases of developed countries, two points become clear: first, improving public security takes time and, second, the level of crime and violence in any given society is not random. As long as the underlying conditions incentivize criminal behavior, insecurity will be the outcome.

The challenge Mexico faces is to design and enforce a set of institutions that creates the right incentives for individuals and officials to behave in accordance with the rule of law. Two significant institutional changes are necessary in Mexico for the security situation to improve: legalizing and regulating all drugs that are now illicit, and fixing the fiscal disconnect.

Regarding legalization, we must begin by recognizing that the magnitude of the problem is much bigger than the available resources that the Mexican State possesses to fight it. Even if the State had such resources, it would be socially inefficient to spend them on this issue.

For Mexico, a potential solution is to shrink the problem to a manageable size, given the existing resources. Legalizing and regulating the whole market for drugs that are now illicit would achieve this. A regulated market for drugs creates fewer incentives for corruption and violence. It would also free many resources that can be utilized to fight the crimes that truly hurt society, such as robbery, kidnapping and extortion, thus creating a more adequate alignment between citizens' preferences and public policies.

Legalizing and regulating will not magically fix violence or corruption, but it will shrink the size of the problem, making it more solvable. Enforcement of a regulated market would, of course, be an issue, given the weakness of the Mexican State, yet market mechanisms would kick in to help. Additionally, it is much cheaper, and much less violent, to enforce regulation than to fight the production, transportation and commerce of illicit drugs in a country of Mexico's size and complicated geography.

Note, however, that how illicit drugs are legalized is not straightforward (LSE Ideas 2014; LSE Ideas 2016; Global Commission on Drug Policy 2018), and fully discussing it would require more space than is available in this chapter. However, it is worth including here a few relevant points that would frame this issue and that have been analyzed in multiple other works. First, there is no conclusive evidence that legalizing drugs would increase their consumption (Eastwood 2016; Global Commission on Drug Policy 2018). Second, drugs legalization may generate significant spillovers (UNODC 2015), which could be invested in other topics that are more socially beneficial. And, third, there are strong actors against legalization, most notably the United States (Enciso 2015; Valdes Castellanos 2013) and different international organizations (McAllister 2012).

Regarding the fiscal disconnect: fixing Mexico's fiscal structure is a necessary change which would also contribute towards improving security and the rule of law. To the degree that municipalities collect a higher share of what they spend, they become more accountable to their citizens. This would induce governments to spend more on what citizens actually prefer to fight, which is ordinary crime, not DTOs.

Both institutional changes, unfortunately, seem unlikely in the short-term. As is common in many other policy areas, many of those with the formal power to change the status quo are also those with the greatest interest in maintaining it. Despite the preferences of Mexican politicians, who may agree or not with drug legalization, the Mexican government faces strong pressure from the United States' federal government to keep things as they are now.

As I have pointed out in this paper, we are trapped in a vicious cycle. The obvious question regarding a vicious cycle is where and how we start to break it. In the relationship between insecurity and a deficient rule of law, it is not trivial to assess whether we should first combat insecurity, strengthen the rule of law, or tackle both simultaneously.

Solving this type of problem sometimes requires some sort of shock. It may be a shock endogenous to the issue. For instance, the fight against kidnapping in the United States was significantly propelled by the infamous case of the Lindbergh baby, and the tightening of airport security was only implemented after the 9/11 tragedy in New York.

Alternatively, it could be an exogenous shock, such as a government change. Democracy provides this opportunity periodically (in the case of Mexico, every six years). It may create a sort of focal point that allows citizen coordination to demand policy solutions (Weingast 1997). New governments are windows of opportunity for significant policy changes. In this alternative, public opinion is the force behind politicians' incentives to change the status quo.

Regretfully, new federal administrations in Mexico have not historically sought to implement fresh alternatives. Instead, they have implemented traditional punitive approaches that implicitly assume that the solution to violence is to combat it with sheer physical force. It is presumed that somewhere in the policy universe there is an alternative in which a large enough number of police officials, or of weaponry, or display of brute force, would solve the problem. But the evidence has clearly shown that this is not the case. This chapter outlines two possible policy choices to break the vicious cycle of violence Mexico finds itself in, and to help build the rule of law it so desperately needs.

References

Ahmad, N.; Hubickey, V.; McNamara, F. (2011). "La confianza en la Policía Nacional", in: *Perspectivas desde el Barómetro de las Américas*, 59: 1–11.
Bates, R.H. (2001). *Prosperity and Violence: The political economy of development* (New York: W.W. Norton).
Blanco, L.R. (2013). "The impact of crime on trust in institutions in Mexico" in: *European Journal of Political Economy*, 32: 38–55.
Calderón, G.; Robles, G.; Díaz-Cayeros, A.; Magaloni, B. (2015). "The Beheading of Criminal Organizations and the Dynamics of Violence in Mexico", in: *Journal of Conflict Resolution*, 59, 8: 1455–1485.
Ceobanu, A.M.; Wood, C.H.; Ribeiro, L. (2010). "Crime victimization and public support for democracy: Evidence from Latin America", in: *International Journal of Public Opinion Research*, 23, 1: 56–78.
Dahl, R. (1971). *Poliarchy* (New Haven: Yale University Press).
Dell, M. (2015). "Trafficking networks and the Mexican drug war", in: *American Economic Review*, 105, 6, 1, 738–79.
Diamond, L. (1999). *Developing Democracy: Toward Consolidation* (Baltimore and London: The John Hopkins University Press).
Diaz-Cayeros, A.; McElwain, K.M.; Romero, V. (2010). *Fiscal Decentralization and Particularistic Spending across Countries* (Manuscript in preparation).
Eastwood, N.; Fox, E.; Rosmarin, A. (2016). *A quiet revolution: Drug decriminalisation across the globe* (London: Release).
Enciso, F. (2015). *Nuestra historia narcótica* (Mexico City: Editorial Debate).
Expert Group on the economics of drug policy (London: London School of Economics and Political Science).
Fernandez, K.E.; Kuenzi, M. (2010). "Crime and support for democracy in Africa and Latin America", in: *Political Studies*, 58: 450–471.
Global Commission on Drug Policy (2018). "Regulation: The Responsible Control of Drugs" (Geneva: GCDP); at: https://goo.gl/7RvpFC.
Herrera González, V.; Hernández, M.; Oralia, S. (2017). *Diagnóstico de las Haciendas Públicas Locales en México* (Mexico City: Instituto Belisario Domínguez del Senado de la República).
Holland, A.C. (2013). "Right on crime? Conservative party politics and *mano dura* policies in El Salvador", in: *Latin American Research Review*: 44–67.
Huntington, S. (1969). *Political Order in Changing Societies* (New Haven: Yale University Press).
Krause, K. (2014). "Supporting the iron fist: Crime news, public opinion, and authoritarian crime control in Guatemala", in: *Latin American Politics and Society*, 56, 1: 98–119.

Lessing, B. (2015). "Logics of violence in criminal war", in: *Journal of Conflict Resolution* 59, 8: 1, 486–1,516.
LSE IDEAS. (2014). *Ending the Drug Wars* (London: London School of Economics and Political Science).
LSE IDEAS. (2016). *After the Drug Wars* (London: London School of Economics and Political Science).
Magaloni, B. (2006). *Voting for Autocracy: Hegemonic party survival and its demise in Mexico* (Cambridge: Cambridge University Press).
Magaloni, B.; Díaz-Cayeros, A.; Matanock, A.; Robles, G.; Romero, V. (2018). *Living in Fear: The dynamics of extortion in Mexico's drug war* (Manuscript in preparation).
McAllister, W.B. (2012). *Reflections on a Century of International Drug Control: Governing the global drug wars* (London: London School of Economics and Political Science).
Miron, J.A.; Zwiebel, J. (1995). "The economic case against drug prohibition", in: *Journal of Economic Perspectives*, 9, 4: 175–192.
North, D.C. (1981). *Structure and Change in Economic History* (New York: W.W. Norton and Company).
Osorio, J. (2011). *Dynamic and structural determinants of drug violence in Mexico*. Working paper; at: https://fsi-live.s3.us-west-1.amazonaws.com/s3fs-public/evnts/media/OSORIO_Drug_Violence_111102.pdf.
Osorio, J. (2013). *Democratization and Drug Violence in Mexico*. Working paper, at: https://eventos.itam.mx/sites/default/files/eventositammx/eventos/aadjuntos/2014/01/democratizacion_and_drug_violence_osorio_appendix_1.pdf.
Pérez, O.J. (2003). "Democratic legitimacy and public insecurity: Crime and democracy in El Salvador and Guatemala", in: *Political Science Quarterly*, 118, 4: 627–644.
Phillips, B. (2015). "How does leadership decapitation affect violence? The case of drug trafficking organizations in Mexico", in: *Journal of Politics*, 77, 2: 324–336.
Poiré, A. (2011). "Los homicidios y la violencia del crimen organizado", in: *Nexos*; at: https://goo.gl/VLpnds.
Quah, D.; Collins, J.; Atuesta Becerra, L.; Caulkins, J.; Csete, J.; Drucker, E.; Restrepo, P. (2014). Ending the Drug Wars: report of the LSE.
Rios, V. (2012). "How Government Structure Encourages Criminal Violence: The causes of Mexico's drug war" (PhD dissertation, Harvard University).
Romero, V. (2015). "The political economy of progressive tax reforms in Mexico", in: Mahon, J. E.; Bergman, M.; Arnson, C. (Eds.), *Progressive Tax Reform and Equality in Latin America* (Washington D.C.: Woodrow Wilson Center).
Romero, V. (2017). *Money Laundering, Misaligned Incentives, and Violence*. Working Paper Series 2017-002 (Mexico: ITAM).
Romero, V.; Magaloni, B.; Díaz-Cayeros, A. (2015). "The Mexican war on drugs: Crime and the limits of government persuasion", in: *International Journal of Public Opinion Research*, 27, 1: 125–137.
Romero, V.; Magaloni, B.; Díaz-Cayeros, A. (2016). "Presidential approval in hard times: Mexico's war on crime", in: *Latin American Politics and Society*, 58, 2: 100–123.
Thornton, M. (1991). "Alcohol prohibition was a failure", in: *Cato Institute Policy Analysis*, 157; at: https://goo.gl/sieKxh.
United Nations Office on Drugs and Crime (UNODC) (2015). *World Drug Report 2015*. (New York: United Nations).
Valdés Castellanos, G. (2013). *Historia del narcotráfico en México* (Mexico City: Aguilar).
Weingast, B.R. (1997). "The political foundation of democracy and the Rule of Law", in: *American Political Science Review*, 91, 2: 245–263.
Weingast, B.R.; Shepsle, K.A.; Johnsen, C.H. (1981). "The political economy of benefits and costs: A neoclassical approach to distributive politics", in: *Journal of Political Economy* 89, 4: 642–664.

Zepeda Gil, R. (2018). "Siete tesis explicativas sobre el aumento de la violencia en México", in: *Política y Gobierno*, 25, 1: 185–211.
Zepeda Lecuona, G.; Jiménez Rodríguez, P. (2018). "Impunidad en homicidio doloso en México: Reporte 2018", in: *Este País* (November); at: https://www.impunidadcero.org/uploads/app/articulo/87/contenido/1541455707N85.pdf.

Chapter 7
Human Rights and Unreliable Institutions in a Globalized World: The Case of Irregular Migrants in Mexico

Mauricio Olivares-Méndez and Radu-Mihai Triculescu

Abstract State sovereignty, it has been argued, is starting to be found more and more in a multiplicity of arenas, but the State no longer plays the only role in the reallocation of this sovereignty. Globalization has pushed states to accept giving up some powers, and it seems that as a result they strongly assert others that are mostly uncontested. Immigration law seems to have become the last bastion of a state's ability to unilaterally impose its sovereign powers, this much more so when it comes to its response to irregular migration. The dynamic between the forces of globalization and the reaction of the State to those forces pushes irregular migrants into a grey area where their claim to fundamental rights is not met with the proper protections expected from a state with a strong rule of law. Mexico, as this book has made clear, faces significant challenges in rethinking and rebuilding its relationship with citizens and non-citizens alike. Shining a light on the experiences of the latter group is a key aspect of designing a better institutional framework that guarantees the access and protection of human rights. This chapter provides a review of the interlinked understandings of sovereignty, globalization and the rule of law, then uses data collected through the Documentation Network of Migrant Advocacy Organizations (REDODEM) and other civil society organizations to illustrate the difficulties migrants encounter in their transit and stay in Mexico, and ends with a series of reflections for the long journey ahead.

Keywords Rule of law · Sovereignty · Globalization · Irregular migration · Human rights

---

M. Olivares-Méndez, Universidad Autónoma de Querétaro, Querétaro, Mexico. Email: mauricio.olivares@uaq.mx; R. M. Triculescu, Early Stage Researcher under the Marie Skłodowska-Curie actions, Horizon 2020 of the E.U., University of Twente, Enschede, The Netherlands. Email: r.triculescu@utwente.nl.

© Springer Nature Switzerland AG 2020
J. A. Le Clercq and J. P. Abreu Sacramento (eds.), *Rebuilding the State Institutions*,
https://doi.org/10.1007/978-3-030-31314-2_7

Understanding the state of human rights protections in Mexico cannot be done independently of the effectiveness of the country's rule of law apparatus. As May argues, "human rights cannot be operationalized outside of the context of a functioning state that establishes and enforces a rule of law that is based on a certain set of universal principles" (2007: 9). The institutional strength needed to achieve an effective rule of law can be challenged and undermined by the forces of globalization and the State's response to these forces.

The following chapter will attempt to bring these concepts together by exploring the links that exist between human rights, globalization, and state sovereignty. Specifically, by analyzing reports and analysis of non-governmental organizations working on the ground in Mexico, we will argue that the reaction of the Mexican State to globalization has led it to assert its sovereignty in the field of border protection in a way that leaves irregular migrants at great risk of suffering violations of their basic human rights. By analyzing how rule of law in the area of migration is caught at the intersection of sovereignty and globalization, and how this dynamic pushes irregular migrants into a grey area where their claim to fundamental rights is not met with the proper protections expected from a state with a strong rule of law, this chapter will offer an understanding of the plight that this vulnerable group faces.

This chapter is organized as follows: in the first two sections, the dynamic between sovereignty, globalization and rule of law will be analyzed based on existing literature. Section 7.3 will then offer some conclusions regarding what this means specifically when it comes to policies regulating irregular migration. Section 7.4 will explore human rights protections specifically in the Mexican context, while Sect. 7.5 will analyze the data provided by NGOs that work directly with irregular migrants in the country. Lastly, there will be a discussion of the current state of affairs in the context of a push for more and better governance, paving a way forward to secure human rights protections in Mexico.

7.1 Sovereignty and Globalization: Zero-sum or Complementary?

There is little to argue against the forces of globalization and their effect on national political landscapes. Whether it is in economic policies, defense spending, education standards, or any number of other policy areas, globalization has deeply affected a state's ability to retain full control over decision-making processes. This is not something happening overnight, and neither is it something that has caught states by surprise. Be it forces that have pushed a government to adopt certain macroeconomic measures, or alliances that have pushed defense institutions to behave in certain ways, states that take part in the current international order generally gain as much, if not more, than they pay into this regime. Despite this, however, there is little argument over the fact that trends in globalization have drastically changed the way sovereignty has come to be understood, defined, or conceptualized.

Initially, sovereignty was intricately linked to the territoriality of state. Be it a democratic claim to legitimacy to rule over said territory, or a more violent representation of the responsibility to defend it, sovereignty was imbedded with a geographic characteristic that made the concept, if not tangible, at least pinned to a physical location. The sovereignty of a state could be defined based on cartographic characteristics (Sassen 1996). It is on the basis of these definitions that, once globalization became not just a topic for discussion but a reality of the international order, the perceived conflict between international and national political forces could be rationalized as a zero-sum game: if decision-making powers now transcend national borders, sovereignty would stand to lose. Based on all expatiations, the power of the State to regulate and enforce policy should diminish.

It should be noted that the association between sovereignty and territory is not one without its critics. States, these critics will argue, never actually exerted full autonomy over their territories, thus meaning that globalization is not eroding sovereignty, but rather adding a new layer of complexity to it (Agnew 2009). Sovereignty, Agnew argues, is not fundamentally being altered by its unmooring from territorial ties, because such ties were never rigid to begin with. Even if this is the case, however, the fact is that the forces of globalization are changing the way we think about the State's ability to exercise its power in different fields.

Agnew could very well be right in his assertion, and it is not the intention of this work to challenge his claim. But in practice, governments behaved throughout the twentieth century in ways that put the (territorial) state at the center. "Political geographers believe that power is firmly rooted in the physical nature of the world itself" (Parker 1985). Even if governments have never exerted full control over their territory, this has always been taken as a metric of political strength and sovereignty.

So the question is: where does this leave the discussion on sovereignty today? Even those who, like Agnew, challenge the original conceptualization of the term, cannot deny that critical shifts are taking place in our thinking about sovereignty, from both an academic perspective and a practical one (Beeson 2003). Firstly, as part of the process of being shaped by globalization, the international system is moving toward a world polity of shared norms and models. Without any state that controls this system, we can imagine certain national (or corporate) interests being reflected, but no one establishing authority over these, and they are very much organic. As climate change becomes an issue of concern, for example, these concerns are challenged toward the building of common models, but not over the creation of a bureaucratic authority to oversee these (Meyer 2000). It is the same thought that Cohen (2012) promotes: the move toward a world governed with nobody ruling. While globalization, therefore, may not be the source of national policies, it surely shapes how those policies are created. At the very least, a curtailment of powers exists (Dale 1999: 2).

7.2 Sovereignty and Rule of Law in an Interconnected World

So far, globalization has been largely treated as an economic issue, with its impact being measured in terms of trade, investment, treaties, etc. Blanton/Blanton (2016) prove that this approach is incomplete by showing the multifaceted effects of globalization in the area of labor rights, a field which, at first glance, seems overwhelmingly economics-centered, and by showing the effects of globalization in political and social dimensions of this issue as well. Explorations of the effects of globalization, as they point out, must go beyond economics. Rule of law and the equality of government resulting from the pressures applied by globalization have tremendous societal impact that cannot always be measured through the use of economic indicators (Khan 2016).

Rule of law, in particular, can be greatly impacted by the international forces that promote globalization worldwide. But what exactly does one mean by "rule of law", and what is there about this definition that would make it malleable by international (f)actors? Indeed, pinpointing exactly what is meant by "rule of law" can be difficult, especially when considering the saturation of the concept in public and academic discourse (Stein 2009: 296). Nevertheless, it is precisely because of this (some would say) overuse of the term that defining it is crucial. Stein (2009) claims that the best way to address it is through a definition which encompasses the idea that, first and foremost, the law must be above all members of society, including those who hold political power. This means that, in the old cliché often cited on television and in movies, no one can be above the law. Secondly, the law must be stable, predictable and known. In other words, similar situations under the law must yield similar results, and legal principles must be applied in a non-arbitrary fashion. Lastly, members of society must have the right to participate in creating and revisiting laws, legal frameworks must protect human rights and dignity, and judicial power must be completely independent from any branches of power. For there to be adequate rule of law the process of developing and enforcing laws must be sufficiently strong to ensure complete independence and accessibility to all members of society (2009: 302).

The general tenets of this definition, it needs to be pointed out, make rule of law susceptible to the forces of globalization. Undeniably, the law must be superior to all members of society, regardless of positions, but can it be above an international system that governs, but does not have a ruler? Laws, according to the above definition, cannot be subordinated to any ruling power. How, then, can the independence from a ruler-less institution be assessed? Similarly, if the norms and ideologies that dictate the values that drive the forces of globalization are organic, and the issues of concern are constantly shifting, the predictability of the applicability of rule of law cannot be claimed. This, of course, leads itself to a flexibility of rule of law in the age of globalization. This is not to say that the latter renders the former powerless, but rather that the aspect of predictability, stability, and rigidity of rule of law are no longer a given. In other words, the challenges that globalization poses to state sovereignty have a direct effect on how rule of law is not only conceptually interpreted, but also how it is applied in practice. Given the multiplicity of arenas in which these terms interact, it stands to reason that different policy areas within a state will be affected differently by these disputations.

Sovereignty, then, can no longer be considered to be unconditional because, in a globalized system, states cannot be treated as possessors of any intrinsic value. Their worth comes from the ability to protect and benefit the individuals within, and these standards of protection are defined internationally (Nijman/Werner 2013; Dunoff 2013). In other words, sovereignty cannot exist just for the sake of sovereignty. The paradox, however, is that the international governance structures that define the standards of protection are not able in themselves to create binding laws. Ultimately, it is a state's ability to enforce its rule of law that defines how well it carries out the tasks of protecting those within. The following section will focus on one specific aspect within rule of law, namely the regulation of irregular migration. In this area, the argument will be made, states are making a strong stand on sovereignty, as a show of force against all other powers lost to the forces of globalization.

7.3 Irregular Migration: The Last Bastion of State Sovereignty

The regulation of migratory flows provides an image of the tug-of-war between traditional state sovereignty and the effects that globalization has on this. Migration, by definition, is bound to geography: the relocation from one physical location to another. Regulating this movement, therefore, fits well into the paradigm of sovereignty that defines it as the State's ability to protect and manage the territorial integrity of its territory. On the other hand, the movement of people and capital across borders is a staple of globalization "as it cannot be managed unilaterally by national policies" (Crépeau/Atak 2006: 114). While regulating movements across borders is a signal of traditional sovereignty, the existence of those very movements is indicative of forces of globalization at work.

Irregular migration, however, falls slightly outside this paradigm. It does so, in fact, in such a way that the regulation of this particular type of movement has been branded, much more than any other form of migration, the last bastion of state sovereignty (Dauvergne 2004: 600). The argument in this case can be quite clear-cut: irregular migrants intrinsically undermine the power of the State to control its border, therefore providing incentives for a fierce crack-down. While legal mechanisms are influenced by globalization, irregular migrants can be easily categorized as 'illegal', and placed in an us-vs-them narrative which, in turn, allows the state to reassert its nationhood – in essence, they provide the tool necessary for establishing complete sovereignty in an age when such opportunities are less and less frequent.

Dauvergne (2004) further makes the argument that by creating this framework, essentially one where this category of immigrant is placed outside the scope of the law, justifications exist for not giving them the benefits of human rights and/or due process, benefits that international institutions are trying to ensure that all people have access to. Otherwise put, irregular immigrants, serving as a great tool for asserting full sovereignty by the State, have no recourse for claiming the rights which they would otherwise be granted if not for the label of 'illegal'. Even in countries such as Mexico, as we will see below, where the Constitution explicitly states that the rights granted are meant for everyone, not just citizens, this group is constantly left at the periphery of rule of law mechanisms that should grant them said rights.

Returning to the discussion regarding the principle of rule of law "the core of the existing principle is that all persons and authorities within the state, whether public or private, should be bound by and entitled to the benefit of laws publicly and prospectively promulgated and publicly administered in the courts" (Bingham 2007: 69). There is little doubt that migration law has, from an international perspective, entered the stage of being part of the concept of rule of law (Foster 2015). What, then, can be deduced from any country where the laws applied to a certain group, regardless of their status, do not meet the standards for benefits granted generally? Furthermore, what can be said of states which purposely curtail benefits available through the law to a certain group? A vicious circle of deficiency seems to be created, where a weak application in the rule of law creates uneven distribution of benefits in the area of irregular migration, which in turn feeds back into perpetuating the weak application of rule of law.[1]

The globalization of standards for human rights and procedures for dealing with vulnerable people seem to hit an impasse when these applications reach a state's determination to reassert its sovereignty where this can still be done. Through the construction of illegality, irregular migrants are being kept outside the range of responsibilities that a state has in ensuring equal protection under the law, in conformity with the demands of international institutions. The grey area in which these people find themselves, therefore, leaves them vulnerable to a vast number of abuses, many of which are well documented and publicized. While, as argued earlier, international migration law (and therefore national transposition) is clearly part of the system of rule of law, the only conclusion can be drawn is that in some aspects rule of law falls short. The case of Mexico, detailed below, shows how this can be the case, and how irregular migrants here have been subject to conditions that would not be accepted by any other group under the standards and requirements of human rights protection and promotion of human dignity.

---

[1]This is not to say that irregular migrants are the only victims of weak rule of law application in Mexico. According to the World Justice Project Rule of Law Index (2018), Mexico is ranked 92nd out of 113 countries in terms of rule of law application. The country scores below average in all categories, including security, fundamental rights, and criminal justice.

7.4 Human Rights in Mexico: Between Innovation and Contradiction

For over a quarter of a century, Mexico's legal system has gone through an extensive process of reform that has touched almost every corner of the judiciary in search of improvements to the country's rule of law (Narváez Medécigo 2015). During the first semester of 2011, the Mexican Congress enacted a constitutional reform that would alter how citizens and non-citizens could demand their rights and how decision-makers should design law and policy for the benefit of all. As Andrea Pozas-Loyo and Julio Ríos Figueroa explain, "the first reform transforme[d] the catalogue of justiciable rights" (2017: 32), changing the name of Title One of the constitution from "Individual Guarantees" to "Human Rights and their guarantees", equating the language – and, with it, the meaning – of those rights recognized by the Constitution to the one used in the literature and international system of protections.

Along with the change in language, an amendment to Article 1 gave constitutional rank to the international treaties and conventions signed by Mexico, making the rights recognized in them as exigible as any other that appears in the Constitution and, with this, giving the judiciary a significant new arsenal for its rulings (Ginsburg 2017: 4). Furthermore, the human rights principle of *pro personae* made clear that in any given case the judicial interpretation that better protects the person is the one that ought to be used. The first two paragraphs read as follows:

> In the United Mexican States, all individuals shall be entitled to the Human Rights granted by this Constitution and the international treaties signed by the Mexican State, as well as to the guarantees for the protection of these rights. Such Human Rights shall not be restricted or suspended, except for the cases and under the conditions established by this Constitution itself.

> The provisions relating to human rights shall be interpreted according to this Constitution and the international treaties on the subject, working in favor of the broader protection of people at all times.

In 2013, however, the Mexican Supreme Court of Justice (MSCJ) struck a blow to the *pro personae* principle. In a ten-to-one decision, the MSCJ ruled that international treaties would apply to any case wherein that rule provided an ampler protection to the claimant unless it contradicts any specific exception contained in the Constitution itself.[2] This ruling – we posit in agreement with dissenting justice, Cossío Díaz – violates the principle *pro personae* itself, effectively producing a

---

[2]Mexican Supreme Court of Justice, 2011: *Contradicción de Tesis 293/2011*; at: http://www2.scjn.gob.mx/asuntosrelevantes/pagina/seguimientoasuntosrelevantespub.aspx?id=129659&seguimientoid=556.

hierarchical relation between the human rights of constitutional origin and those of conventional origin.[3]

With this caveat, it is well understood that since the Constitution states that 'all individuals shall be entitled to [...] Human Rights' whether those come from the Constitution or international treaties, the protection of rights also extend to all non-citizens in the country.[4] The right to freedom of expression, the right to live free from discrimination or to choose one's religion, among many others, are protected by the law.

According to the Migration Act of 2011,[5] regardless of their migratory status, migrants have the right to seek medical attention and to receive an education[6]; the right to access justice and due process; the right to denounce the infringement of their rights; the right to receive information about their rights and obligations, the requisites for admission, permanence and exit from the country, and the possibility of seeking asylum; and the right to complementary protection or the recognition of their statelessness. The Act recognizes the inalienable rights at the same time that it defines the sanctions on officials and citizens who endanger the migrant's stay or transit through the country.

So far it seems that the 'Human Rights Reform' of 2011 and the cascade of amendments to other acts and provisions not only gave the judiciary a new set of tools to judge cases with a human rights perspective, but also empowered citizens and organizations to demand the protection of the State through writs of *amparo* founded upon international instruments. The first article continues:

> All authorities, in their areas of competence, are obliged to promote, respect, protect and guarantee Human Rights, in accordance with the principles of universality, interdependence, indivisibility and progressiveness. As a consequence, the State must prevent, investigate, penalize and rectify violations to Human Rights, according to the law.

---

[3]The importance of this opinion is that, on interpretation, a judge may find that a person – especially one belonging to a group in a situation of vulnerability – falls within one of the constitutional exceptions, preventing them from receiving the protection of international instruments and curtailing their right to access justice.

[4]This interpretation was added in the same amendment process to the article that defines who is a foreign national, the controversial Article 33. This article has been the basis for extra-judicial detentions and deportations since its origins in Mexico's post-revolutionary panic and xenophobia. It says in its third paragraph: "Foreigners may not in any way participate in the political affairs of the country", causing a sense of alienation and uncertainty in some migrants. For a detailed historical study on this matter, see Yankelevich (2011).

[5]Before 2011, Mexico didn't have a Migration Law but had migratory dispositions within the General Population Law of 1974 whereby entering and leaving the country without proper documentation was considered a felony. The 2008 reform to this statute made it possible to treat irregular migration as a misdemeanor.

[6]On the right to a free education the Mexican government has published the "Standards of School Control related to Registration, Re-enrollment, Accreditation, Promotion, Regularization and Certification in Basic Education" that define the procedures for the incorporation of migrant children and teenagers into the national school system regardless of their migratory status.

The reform and the new Migration Act have been undeniable steps forward in developing a solid framework that would assure migrants' rights and the effective prosecution of those who infringe them regardless of their immigration status.[7] However, as is the case with other laws and regulations in states with weak institutional capacities, the spirit of the reform hasn't been properly translated into action by government officials, nor has there been proper allocation of training and resources for those officials' sanctioned activities. Furthermore, the judiciary has to undertake more discussions to scrutinise the constitutional implications of the rights approach of the first title when the enjoyment and access to those rights is regulated by the Migration Act without giving sufficient clarity on the government's motives for exceptions beyond national security and, of course, the preservation of the State's sovereignty.[8]

In 2015 the *Auditoría Superior de la Federación* (Superior Audit Office) carried out a performance audit of the National Institute of Migration (abbreviated to INM in Spanish), the institute in charge of the implementation of most of the policies whose origins lie in the Migration Act. This audit produced a scathing report that was clear on the fact that the deficiencies identified in the processes of regulation, control, verification, surveillance and protection, coupled with the lack of action protocols for the operation of processes to manage the regular and irregular migratory flows, place foreigners who enter, transit, remain or intend to leave the national territory in a situation of vulnerability, and put their human rights at risk, regardless of their immigration status.[9]

It seems that after the implementation of what was called '*Programa Frontera Sur*' (Southern Border Program), the tasks of the Institute revolved around security and the management of migration flows other than promoting and protecting migrants' rights. This program was set in motion after the government of the United States transferred resources under the Merida Initiative to Mexico for it to fortify its own southern border due to the number of Central American migrants reaching the US-Mexico border, especially unaccompanied migrant children. This, advocates argue, accelerated a process of externalization of the US southern border to Mexico's southern border. The press release from the Mexican Executive stated that the program had the purpose of protecting and safeguarding the human rights of

---

[7]In addition to these changes, other advancements were possible due to the publication of the Law on Refugees and Complementary Protection (2011), the General Law to prevent, sanction and eradicate crimes related to trafficking in persons and for the protection and assistance of victims of these crimes (2012), the General Law on the rights of children and adolescents (2014), and the creation of the Investigation Unit for Crimes Against Migrants (2015) (Claderón Chelius 2012).

[8]For an in-depth review on the constitutionality of the Migration Act see Castilla Juárez (2014).

[9]Auditoría Superior de la Federación (2014) Auditoría de Desempeño: 14-0-04K00-07-0060; at: https://www.asf.gob.mx/Trans/Informes/IR2014i/Documentos/Auditorias/2014_0060_a.pdf.

migrants who enter and transit through Mexico, and of ordering the international crossing points to shore up development and security in the region.[10]

Tellingly, a little over a year later, the Undersecretary of Population, Migration and Religious Affairs, Humberto Roque Villanueva, stated that the subject was being carefully handled and the expected results were being reached to the extent that migrants were not getting through, achieving a containment effect.[11] In that same interview, the Undersecretary made clear that one of the things he regarded as positive was that the United States government wouldn't put so much pressure on Mexico due to the reduction in the number of Central American migrants reaching the US.[12] This illustrates clearly how the international dynamics of globalization and securitization shape the national 'politics of policy-making'.

Pillar Three of the Merida Initiative provided funds for what was labeled a "21st century border". Over 2.5 billion US dollars have been allocated to the program, which focuses on preventing 'spill-overs' of organized crime by securing the border through investments in infrastructure and the training of Mexican officials by US Immigration and Customs Enforcement (ICE) and Customs and Border Protection (CBP) agents. As Sarabia (2018) has made clear, the pressure from the United States for Mexico to achieve the goals of the program, including the interception of Central American migrants, has 'thickened' the border. The dynamics of securitization and the externalization of borders – and responsibilities – can be clearly seen in both the Merida Initiative and the Central America Regional Security Initiative, driving much-needed reforms to the justice systems but also effectively criminalizing and endangering unauthorized migrants within Mexico. It's clear to most that globalization has a severe impact on the reasons why residents of certain places become migrants; neoliberal policies pushed by international agencies and the transnational dynamics of capitalism, crime, violence and exploitation push people out of their places of origin and then those same forces of globalization shape the way transit and arrival countries outline their justice system, attempt to govern migration flows and respect the human rights of unauthorized migrants.[13]

---

[10]Presidencia de la República (2014): "Pone en marcha el Presidente Enrique Peña Nieto el Programa Frontera Sur"; at: https://www.gob.mx/presidencia/prensa/pone-en-marcha-el-presidente-enrique-pena-nieto-el-programa-frontera-sur.

[11]"Resalta la Segob contención migratoria", in: *Reforma* (2 November 2015).

[12]In fact, Mr. Johnson, then Secretary of the Department of Homeland Security, released a statement that in part read: "We are also pleased that the Mexican government has itself taken a number of important steps to interdict the flow of illegal migrants from Central America bound for the United States." Department of Homeland Security (2014): "Statement by Secretary Johnson About the Situation Along the Southwest Border". Available at: https://www.dhs.gov/news/2014/09/08/statement-secretary-johnson-about-situation-along-southwest-border.

[13]Kovic/Kelly (2017) posit that "the violations of economic rights of transmigrants within their sending communities are practically invisible as they attempt to make the journey north. These violations – created by global capitalism and neoliberal reforms promoted by international financial agencies – are the very reasons that migrants leave their homes and communities."

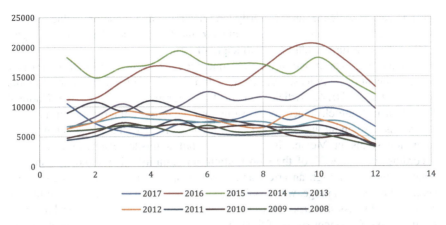

Fig. 7.1 Foreign nationals detained and presented to the National Migration Institute, 2008–2017. *Source* SEGOB, Unidad de Política Migratoria; at: http://www.politicamigratoria.gob.mx/

7.5 Migrants in Transit Through Mexico

Just in the first semester of 2018, according to official figures, 64,222 migrants have been detained and presented to the authorities, an increase compared with the same period in 2017, which amounted to 43,518 detained migrants.[14] 51,748 migrants with an irregular status have been deported in this same period, an overwhelming majority of them being nationals of the countries of Central America's Northern Triangle: Honduras, El Salvador and Guatemala (Fig 7.1).[15]

In 2016, a petition identified as Case P-652-16[16] was filed in front of the Inter-American Human Rights Commission (IAHRC) by almost forty organizations against the United States and Mexico for the amount and procedures for deporting tens of thousands of migrants from Guatemala, Honduras and El Salvador. At one point, Mexico deported more Central American nationals than the United States did.[17] The petition stated that most of these people were being sent back to dangerous places where they ran a risk of persecution and death, and these states,

---

[14] 2017 saw 93,846 migrants with an irregular status detained and processed through the INM.

[15] Another 38,000 people from those countries have been subject to 'voluntary return' policies between January and June 2018. In addition to these numbers, another 3,000 non-nationals were given a letter of exit that allows them to leave the detention facilities to start their regularization process or leave the country without being deported (Unidad de Política Migratoria).

[16] Adolescentes en el camino et al. (2016): "Petition for interim and permanent measures regarding systematic violations of the American Convention on Human Rights and other international covenants against Central American migrants in Mexico"; at: https://www.centerforhumanrights.org/PDFs/IACHR_PFS_Petition.pdf.

[17] The Washington Office on Latin America (WOLA) (2015): "Mexico Now Detains More Central American Migrants than the United States"; at: https://www.wola.org/2015/06/mexico-now-detains-more-central-american-migrants-than-the-united-states/.

through acts of violence, unnecessarily long detention and violation of due process, were preventing migrants from applying for and being granted international protection. This, in turn, violates the principle of non-refoulement.

Holding migrants in one of the fifty-nine detention centers in Mexican territory seems to be, at the very least, questionable, if not outright illegal or unconstitutional (Castilla Juárez 2014). Article 111 of the Migration Act gives the National Migration Institute clearance for arresting and detaining[18] migrants with an irregular status throughout the country. The issues here are, first, that having an irregular migration status in Mexico is not a crime but a misdemeanor; and secondly, according to Article 21 of the Constitution, an administrative authority can only detain someone through an arrest and only for up to thirty-six hours before presenting the case to a judge, who would then be able to set a sentence, set conditional release, or dismiss the case. However, immigration officers have been known to detain people for longer spans of time than the rules allow. Article 111 itself allows the immigration authorities to keep someone in their custody for up to fifteen days, and if the detainee demands a judicial review of his or her case or a writ of *amparo*, the time spent in the detention facility can be longer. This provision in particular goes further to violate another set of human rights – access to justice, the right to consular assistance and the right to due process, to name just a handful. These long stays in detention facilities are particularly difficult for unaccompanied children, victims of sexual assault and abuse, members of the LGBTTTIQ community and those who live with other intersecting vulnerabilities (CCINM 2017).

The United Nations Subcommittee on Prevention of Torture and other Cruel, Inhuman or Degrading Treatment or Punishment (SPT 2017) wrote a report about its visit to Mexico in 2016 in which it registered conditions of overcrowding in migratory stations and noted that information is not consistently provided to migrants about their detention and other proceedings. The Subcommittee also pointed out that migration officials do not help migrants contact their families or reach consular assistance, that the detainees claim to have been victims of beatings, torture (e.g. waterboarding, use of *picanas* or other electrical prods) and were themselves witnesses to inhumane treatment in detention facilities with deplorable conditions. One of the now-famous concluding remarks of the Subcommittee stated that "torture in Mexico is generalized". Testimony on this type of treatment has been documented by several civil society organizations.

Data from the Documentation Network of Migrant Advocacy Organizations (REDODEM 2018), a network which collects data in a systematic way from shelters, community kitchens and other organizations that work with migrants, shows that out of the 28,288 migrants interviewed at these places from January to December 2017, 2,724 were victims of a crime and an additional 425 migrants were

---

[18]The INM uses the word '*alojar*', which means 'host' or 'accommodate', a word legislators decided would describe their policies better than detaining or incarcerating. It doesn't.

Table 7.1 Perpetrators of crimes against migrants

Origin of victimizer		2014 (%)	2015 (%)	2016 (%)	2017 (%)
Government agents		20.16	41.51	17.39	25
Non-government actors	Private individuals	25.56	12.72	62	75
	Organized crime	54.27	45.72	11.49	N/A
	Private train guards	N/A	N/A	6.05	N/A
	Other	N/A	N/A	3.07	N/A

Source Data from the Documentation Network of Migrant Advocacy Organizations 2017 report (REDODEM 2018)

witnesses to a crime.[19] Most of these were committed in the states of Chiapas, Oaxaca and Veracruz.

Table 7.1 shows the relative amount of times that migrants singled out different types of victimizers when interviewed at the REDODEM-affiliated centers. The categories have been changing with every report, but the amount of government agents identified as perpetrators of crimes against migrants seems to hold constant at around 20% except for 2015, the first full year where the *Frontera Sur* Program was implemented. The data presented relies on the recollection of migrants who arrive at these shelters, and the routes they take each time are affected by the knowledge of government raids or checkpoints, criminal activity in specific hot spots or the availability of transport and other resources. The restrictive migration policy that comes with the *Frontera Sur* program is supported on the argument of safeguarding national security, producing not only a surge in arrests, detentions and deportations, but also in crimes, including torture, kidnapping, extortion and murder.

The same report states that the dangers and threats to migrants and refugees within the known routes have risen in part due to the culture of illegality that permeates Mexico, a problem that will undoubtedly continue if no action is taken to reform not only the courts, but also the way law-enforcement officials operate to stop 'regime policing' (see Neild 2001) and develop accountable and trustworthy practices (Davis 2006; Uildriks 2010). Having said this, government officials are only some of the actors involved in endangering migrants' transit through Mexico. As other research shows, migrants can also fall prey to gang violence and organized

---

[19]It is important to note that the data collected by the REDODEM has limitations. The information collected conveys the experiences of migrants who actually get to one of the twenty-three different affiliates, naturally leaving outside of its scope migrants who are apprehended or deported before reaching a shelter or those who use different routes or means of transportation that would make them undetectable to the centers participating in the network. It is a reality that migrants are looking for new paths to make their way through Mexico, but it is also known by them that aid is provided throughout the usual routes, providing incentives for migrants to use them and hence making the network's database more relevant.

crime (Anaya Muñoz/Díaz de León 2012; Correa-Cabrera 2014). Migrant advocates constantly denounce the strong relationship between crimes by private individuals and the participation of agents of the Mexican State. In many cases, stretches of migratory routes have been documented in which massive kidnappings are carried out (REDODEM 2018).

The San Fernando massacre of 2010 is one of the most horrific examples of the dangers that migrants face without proper protection by the State. In the border state of Tamaulipas, at least seventy-two migrants from Central and South America were kidnapped and then murdered by Los Zetas drug cartel, either because of their refusal to work for the criminal organization or their inability to pay a ransom. Diamond (1999: 91) pointed out that "in the context of weak states and inefficient, poorly disciplined police, crime may inspire drastic, illegal, unconstitutional and grotesquely sadistic responses to try to control it". The crack-down by Mexican state officials has led many people with an irregular migration status to find new and more dangerous routes through the country, risking their lives in the hope that they can make it to the United States. Mexico, then, is falling short of its obligations to safeguard human rights not only by not having a standardized framework to protect migrants – even from the action of its own government agents – but also by its omissions in confronting criminal activity and by its apparent tolerance of illegality and corruption, thus further endangering a group that was already in a position of vulnerability.

7.6 Asking for Directions: A Move Towards Migration Governance at the Local and Global Level

The IAHRC case described above stated that the governments of Mexico and the United States create and condone an environment of hyper-violence and impunity, that the detention of asylum seekers is itself a clear violation of international law – let alone the conditions of the detention facilities – and that migrants seldom receive anything similar to a fair procedure to be granted asylum. The failures in protecting migrant rights are related to the lack of implementation of international law standards at national level (Martin/Abimourched 2009) in defense of the State's right to sovereignty; the lack of an "authoritative global monitoring and oversight mechanism" (Atak 2018: 34) means that states are not held accountable for their inaction or outright human rights violations.

The infringement of migrants' rights and the people seeking international protection is a result of the contradictory nature of different international standards and local rules that govern migration flows in Mexico. These contradictions are themselves a result of the interplay between the forces of globalization, the resistance of sovereignty claims and, in the middle, a weak institutional set-up that won't respond to the needs of the most vulnerable due to its poor design or the lack of willingness to implement a transversal human rights approach to migration management. These conclusions had already been reached over five years ago in a report by the IACHR (2013) on the human rights of migrants and other persons in the context of human mobility in Mexico, stating that:

> immigration policies, laws and practices that criminalize migration, or those that take a dual approach – on the one hand recognizing that migrants have human rights, but at the same time regarding them as a threat to national sovereignty or security – contain an inherent contradiction and are at odds with what a human-rights-based immigration policy should be.

Without re-thinking migratory flows as a governance issue that requires the full cooperation of states instead of regulating only through the perspective of national security, trade, jobs or other market factors, the assertion of sovereignty will continue to push people with an irregular migration status into the shadows. In a globalized world, migration governance with a solid institutional framework based on a human rights perspective that also disincentives non-compliance or the formation of competing informal institutions is the only avenue to assure complete respect for and promotion of the rights of those in the margins, in the dangerous routes, in the desert and on the trains. The Special Rapporteur pointed out that migration governance would not hinder sovereignty, it would provide the means for coordination and cooperation between states and it would lead to a more robust system for the protection of migrants against human rights abuses by states, organized crime and the private sector (UNHRC 2013). If states are able to ascertain their domain over the territory with strong institutions and protections that work within an international cooperation framework, criminal organizations, human traffickers, *coyotes* and other actors that take advantage of migrants would find a less fertile ground for their operations.

After the UN General Assembly's New York Declaration for Refugees and Migrants, some new avenues have opened in this direction. The Global Compact for Safe, Orderly and Regular Migration (GCM) is the first international instrument to set specific goals and commitments in migration governance involving states, civil society and the private sector to achieve them. It compels states to produce data for evidence-based policy, to define more and clearer paths for regular migration, to strengthen certainty and predictability in migration procedures, and to work towards the full incorporation of migrants and diasporas into host countries with the complete protection of national and international law. The Compact recognizes states' rights to self-determination and sovereignty, leaving most countries willing to get on board. The problem is that, again, the instrument is not binding.

Other agreements and frameworks have missed their mark in the past, producing suboptimal results, or even strengthening border control without improving human rights protection, oversight or accountability. Money, Lockhart/Western (2016) have shown that the status quo privileges receiving states, but provides no incentives for them to bargain with sending states to achieve a more comprehensive mobility system. For this reason, countries have to push for a set of international standards that assure compliance with human rights law, and at the same time they also have to push their own legislative bodies and their own judiciary towards the strengthening of their institutions, towards the capacity-building of civil society and advocacy groups, and towards opening more channels for legal migration and the regularization of migrants. States have to produce better data and base their legislation and policies on this rather than toxic discourses. Investment in new avenues that assure the protection of rights can prove to be a more effective way to foster local and regional development than the current approach. Migration governance, then, can only work if the cooperative partners can individually be relied upon to respect and apply the law in a consistent and predictable way, if they have oversight mechanisms to assure accountability and transparency, if they have well-proportioned sentencing, and if their actors, policy and laws are gender-sensitive and human-rights sensitive. "Good governance at the national level is a basis for more effective cooperation at the regional and global levels" (Crépeau/Atak 2006: 143).

Mexico being at same time a sending and receiving country and also a country of transit is in a unique position to understand both the push and pull factors that are in play when people migrate in a globalized arena. The country has taken a central voice in shaping the international agenda on this matter, but it still has a major debt to pay to migrants in its territory. The transformation that Mexico has to go through to strengthen its rule of law has to take into account a human rights perspective which has to be mainstreamed in the actions of everyone from the police to the Mexican Supreme Court of Justice, from every public servant to all private sector actors. The treatment of the most vulnerable in society is a litmus test for a state's institutions. The basic tenet of the rule of law is that everyone is equal before the law; Mexico's institutional framework has to assure the enfranchisement of its denizens, providing a clear and predictable path to access justice regardless of their citizenship or migratory status.

References

Agnew, J. (2009). *Globalization and Sovereignty* (Lanham, MD: Rowman & Littlefield).
Anaya Muñoz, A.; Díaz de León, A. (2012). "El activismo transnacional alrededor de los derechos humanos de los migrantes en tránsito por México", in: Heredia Zubieta, C.; Velázquez Flores, R. (Eds.), *Perspectivas migratorias II: La agenda pendiente de la migración* (Mexico City: CIDE).
Atak, I. (2018). "An international human rights framework for migration in a globalizing world", in: Triandafyllidou, A, *Handbook of Migration and Globalization* (Cheltenham, UK and Northampton, MA: Edward Elgar Publishing).
Beeson, M. (2003). "Sovereignty under siege: Globalization and the State in Southeast Asia", in: *Third World Quarterly*, 24,2: 357–374.
Bingham, T. (2007). "The Rule of Law", in: *The Cambridge Law Journal*, 66,1: 67–85.
Blanton, R.; Blanton, S.L. (2016). "Globalization and Collective Labor Rights", in: *Sociological Forum*, 31,1: 181–202.
Calderón Chelius, L. (2012). "Cambios en la agenda migratoria: entre el nuevo marco jurídico y las nuevas formas de migración en México", in: Ramírez, T.; Castillo, M.A. (Eds.), *El estado de la migración: México ante los recientes desafíos de la migración internacional* (Mexico City: CONAPO).

Castilla Juárez, K.A. (2014). "Ley de Migración mexicana: Algunas de sus inconstitucionalidades", in: *Migración y desarrollo* 11,23: 151–183.
CCINM (Consejo Ciudadano del Instituto Nacional de Migración). (2017). *Personas en detención migratoria en México: Misión de Monitoreo de Estaciones Migratorias y Estancias Provisionales del Instituto Nacional de Migración* (Mexico City: INM).
Cohen, J.L. (2012). *Globalization and Sovereignty: Rethinking Legality, Legitimacy, and Constitutionalism* (Cambridge: Cambridge University Press).
Correa Cabrera, G. (2014). "Seguridad y migración en las fronteras de México: diagnóstico y recomendaciones de política y cooperación regional", in: *Migración y desarrollo*, 12,22: 147–171.
Crépeau, F.; Atak, I. (2006). "Global migration governance: Avoiding commitments on Human Rights, yet tracing a course for cooperation", in: *Netherlands Quarterly of Human Rights*, 34,2: 113–146.
Dale, R. (1999). "Specifying globalization effects on national policy: a focus on the mechanisms", in: *Journal of Education Policy,* 14,1: 1–17.
Dauvergne, C. (2004). "Sovereignty, Migration and the Rule of Law in Global Times", in: *The Modern Law Review*, 67,4: 588–615.
Davis, D.E. (2006). "Undermining the Rule of Law: Democratization and the Dark Side of Police Reform in Mexico", in: *Latin American Politics and Society*, 48,1: 55–86.
Diamond, L. (1999). *Developing Democracy: Toward Consolidation* (Baltimore, MD: The Johns Hopkins University Press).
Dunoff, J. (2013). "Is Sovereign Equality Obsolete? Understanding Twenty-First Century International Organizations", in: Nijman, J.; Werner, W. (Eds.), *Netherlands Yearbook of International Law 2012: Legal Equality and the International Rule of Law: Essays in Honour of P.H. Kooijmans* (The Hague: Springer).
Foster, M. (2015). "Research Handbook on International Law and Migration" (Book Review), in: *International Journal of Refugee Law*, 27,2: 392–394.
Ginsburg, T. (2017). "Introduction", in: Castagnola, A.; López-Noriega, S. (Eds.), *Judicial Politics in Mexico: The Supreme Court and the Transition to Democracy* (New York: Routledge): 1–7.
Khan, H.A. (2016). "Globalization and the Quality of Government: an Analysis of the Relationship", in: *Public Organization Review*, 17: 209–224.
Kovic, C.; Kelly, P. (2017). "Migrant bodies as targets of security policies: Central Americans crossing Mexico's vertical border", in: *Dialectical Anthropology*, 41,1: 1–11.
Martin, S.; Abimourched, R. (2009). "Migrant rights: International law and national action", in: *International Migration*, 47,5: 115–138.
May, R.A. (2007). "Human Rights NGOs and the role of civil society in democratization", in: May, R.A; Milton, A.K. (Eds.), *Uncivil Societies: Human Rights and Democratic Transitions in Eastern Europe and Latin America* (Lanham, MD: Lexington Books): 1–10.
Meyer, J.W. (2000). "Globalization: Sources and Effects on National States and Societies", in: *International Sociology*, 15,2: 233–248.
Money, J.; Lockhart, S.; Western, S. (2016). "Why migrant rights are different than human rights", in Freeman, G.P.; Mirilovic, N. (Eds.), *Handbook on Migration and Social Policy* (Cheltenham, UK and Northampton, MA: Edward Elgar Publishing).
Narváez Medécigo, A. (2015). *Rule of Law and Fundamental Rights: Critical comparative analysis of constitutional review in the United States, Germany and Mexico* (Berlin: Springer).
Neild, R. (2001). "Democratic policing", in: Reychler, L; Paffenholz, T. (Eds.), *Peacebuilding: A field guide* (Boulder, CO: Lynne Rienner Publishers): 416–427.
Nijman, J.; Werner, W. (2013). "Legal Equality and the International Rule of Law", in: Nijman, J.; Werner, W. (Eds.), *Netherlands Yearbook of International Law 2012: Legal Equality and the International Rule of Law: Essays in Honour of P.H. Kooijmans* (The Hague: Springer).
Parker, G. (1985). *Western Geopolitical Thought in the Twentieth Century* (Abingdon: Routledge).
Pozas-Loyo, A.; Ríos-Figueroa, J. (2017). "The transformations of the role of the Mexican Supreme Court), in: Castagnola, Andrea; López-Noriega", Saul, *Judicial Politics in Mexico: The Supreme Court and the Transition to Democracy* (New York: Routledge): 8–40.

REDODEM (Red de Documentación de las Organizaciones Defensoras de Migrantes). (2018). *El estado indolente: recuento de la violencia en las rutas migratorias y perfiles de movilidad en México* (Mexico City: REDODEM).
Sarabia, H. (2018). "Citizenship in the Global South Policing Irregular Migrants and Eroding Citizenship Rights in Mexico", in: *Latin American Perspectives*: 1–14.
Sassen, S. (1996). *Losing Control? Sovereignty in the Age of Globalization* (New York: Columbia University Press).
SPT (United Nations Subcommittee on Prevention of Torture and other Cruel Inhuman or Degrading Treatment or Punishment). (2017). *Visita a México del 12 al 21 de diciembre de 2016 observaciones y recomendaciones dirigidas al Estado parte. CAT/OP/MEX/R.2.*
Stein, R. (2009). "Rule of Law: What Does It Mean?", in: *Minnesota Journal of International Law*, 18,2: 293–303.
Uildriks, N. (2010). *Mexico's UnRule of Law: Implementing Human Rights in Police and Judicial Reform under Democratization* (Lanham: Lexington Books).
UN Human Rights Council (2013). *Report of the Special Rapporteur on the human rights of migrants: Note of the Secretary General, A/68/283*; at: https://www.ohchr.org/Documents/Issues/SRMigrants/A-68-283.pdf.
World Justice Project (2018). *Rule of Law Index 2017–2018* (Washington, D.C.: WJP); at: https://worldjusticeproject.org/sites/default/files/documents/WJP_ROLI_2017-18_Online-Edition.pdf.
Yankelevich, P. (2011). *¿Deseables o inconvenientes? Las fronteras de la extranjería en el México posrevolucionario* (Mexico: Bonilla Artigas Editores).

Chapter 8
Amparo and Administrative Trials as Accountability Mechanisms in Mexico

Ana E. Fierro

Abstract This paper explores constitutional and administrative trials as accountability mechanisms provided by the Mexican legal system. Following Kitrosser (2015), we understand accountability as the substantive dimension of the rule of law and part of the overall control of power by Congress and the judicial branch. We define accountability as the legal norms that establish control mechanisms whereby a state agency is obliged to inform and justify its action to an authority which judges and sanctions its performance in order to guarantee its compliance with state goals, including the protection of human rights, and to demand certain results (Fierro 2017), We suggest that *amparo* and administrative trials are powerful procedures in the hands of citizens for demanding government accountability. We show how, in the Mexican legal system, nullity trials, state liability trials and *amparo* not only protect the rule of law but also serve as tools for bringing the authorities to account and ordering measures for their improvement. We attempt to show the challenges these procedures still encounter and suggest ways of overcoming them.

Keywords Accountability · *amparo* · Administrative courts · Constitution · Human rights · Rule of law · Nullity trial · State liability trial · Judicial control · Governance

8.1 Introduction

For most of the twentieth century, Mexico was ruled by a single party, the PRI. It was only in 2000 that Vicente Fox from the PAN, the main opposition party at the time, became President. This democratization process developed into a significant

---

Doctorate in Law from the Instituto de Investigaciones Jurídicas de la UNAM. LLM from the Georgia University and Master in Philosophy from the Universidad Anáhuac, campus Mayab. Bachelor in Law from ITAM. Nowadays, Ana E. Fierro is Coordinator of the Master in Management and Public Policy and research professor at the CIDE. Her interests are transparency, accountability and responsibility of civil servants. Email: ana.fierro@cide.edu.

effort to strengthen the rule of law by demanding a more transparent, accountable government, establishing a civil service and implementing constitutional reforms to protect human rights. Nevertheless, today we still face significant challenges regarding full respect for the rule of law. This paper explores the accountability mechanism offered by the Mexican legal system. Following Kitrosser (2015), we regard accountability as the substantive dimension of the rule of law, and part of the overall control of power by Congress and the judicial branch. We suggest that administrative trials and *amparo* are powerful tools in the hands of citizens for making the government accountable. We show how nullity trials; state liability trials and *amparo* not only protect the rule of law but also serve as tools for bringing the authorities to account and ordering measures for their improvement. We seek to show the challenges these procedures still encounter and suggest ways of overcoming them.

8.2 Rule of Law

Although the rule of law is a commonly used term, its meaning varies from one legal system to another. In the common law tradition, the main purpose of the rule of law is to extend the law to all people, thereby guaranteeing equal treatment for everyone. The German concept *Rechtsstaat* emphasizes public power as the means of achieving the State's goals. In the French case, the rule of law is a way of limiting state power to guarantee human freedoms through the division of power and recognition of the universal value of human rights (Cossío 2004). A common feature of these concepts is the idea that the rule of law serves as a means of controlling power to prevent its abuse.

As states become more sophisticated by regulating the market, preserving the environment and providing public services, forms of control must also evolve to be able to address new challenges. Nowadays, it is not enough to have a division of power into three main branches and regular elections. We require mechanisms that guarantee the transparency of public decisions, and state accountability for the results of its actions (Cossío 2004). Therefore, today accountability mechanisms should be considered part of the rule of law as a means of guaranteeing state goals by strengthening our capacities to control public power and demand certain results.

In the Mexican legal system, the rule of law is understood, as in the French tradition, as a way of controlling power and guaranteeing human rights. Since our beginning as an independent nation, the division of power and the recognition of certain rights have been part of our legal system. Nevertheless, our recent history has shown that these controls are not enough on their own. In the twenty-first century, the Mexican legal system has undergone major reforms to strengthen the rule of law, such as the 2011 constitutional amendment of Article 1 to recognize human rights not only as enshrined in the Constitution but also in human rights treaties, and the renovation in 2013 of the *Ley de Amparo*, the process for controlling the constitutionality of public acts by the federal judiciary where the citizens have standing. Accountability mechanisms have also acquired importance in the Mexican legal system. The following sections will explore these judicial procedures in the hands of citizens as accountability mechanisms, as well as their results and limitations.

8.3 Accountability

Accountability has gained prominence since the beginning of this century as a fundamental concept in the rule of law. Nevertheless, as Mulgan (2002), Schedler (2010) and Bovens (2010) have pointed out, it is used with various meanings and objectives. Accountability refers to good governance, transparency, efficiency and sanctions in the event of corruption (Bovens 2010). Unfortunately, accountability has been also used as an instrument of rhetoric, making it ambiguous at times (Kitrosser 2015). It is therefore necessary to have a clear definition of the concept in order to analyse its role in a particular legal system.

Professor Boven distinguishes two main ways in which the concept of accountability is used. The first is accountability as a quality of responsible people, an ideal to which public servants should aspire. *Black's Law Dictionary* (2017) defines accountability as "the state of being responsible or answerable". It is the way in which public servants should act, and involves behaving in a rational, prudent manner. Accountability in this sense is used to determine whether the actions of a person, such as a public servant, comply with the qualities expected of them. It refers to the state of being responsible for your own actions. The second meaning of accountability is as a mechanism. It is an institutional arrangement whereby an actor may be held to account by an agency. Here, the focus of accountability studies is not the behaviour of individuals in the public service, but the way these institutional arrangements work (Bovens 2010). This second meaning is useful for guaranteeing the rule of law by strengthening the capacity to control public power and demand certain results.

In keeping with these distinctions, accountability as part of the rule of law should be understood as a mechanism that requires formal procedures in which the actions of public agencies are judged and sanctioned. Ackerman (2008) states that these mechanisms are proactive controls of power, whereby an authority is entitled to analyse another person's actions and determine the consequences they warrant. O'Donnell (2008) notes that accountability should be understood as a means of control of the State's activity in two dimensions: a vertical one through periodic elections and a horizontal one through a system of checks and balances. These are bilateral mechanisms designed to ensure the evaluation of actions of public agencies by an authority not only to sanction their possible departure from the law but also to improve their performance (Argyris/Shon 1997). Lapsely (1995) explains that in any public administration procedure, accountability is an essential element for evaluating the results of a public agency and its efficiency and for finding ways of improving its outcomes. In this respect, accountability, as Kitrosser (2015) points out, is the substantive dimension of the rule of law and part of the overall control of power by Congress and the judicial branch. Thus, accountability as a dimension of the rule of law can be defined as the legal norms that establish control mechanisms whereby a state agency is obliged to inform and justify its action to a different authority, which judges and sanctions its performance in order to guarantee its compliance with state goals, including the protection of human rights, and to demand certain results (Fierro 2017).

If accountability is a legal process, then a judicial review of agencies' performance can be regarded as an accountability mechanism whereby the judiciary uses legal guidelines to analyse the actions of a given authority to determine its compliance with the rule of law, evaluates the outcomes of its action and provides solutions and institutional corrections if required (Fox 2008). The other main accountability mechanism is congress budgetary controls. These controls focus on the agencies' performance, their outcomes and efficiency (Behn 2001), and are usually considered accountability measures. Both mechanisms constitute checks for branches of government in which independence from either Congress or judges is an essential feature.

Accountability mechanisms are important elements of the rule of law. How they work and how frequently they are used are key indicators of the strength of the rule of law itself. Accordingly, the following sections focus on how judicial procedures operate as accountability mechanisms in the Mexican legal system, exploring their strengths and challenges. Although we recognize that Congress budgetary control is an important accountability mechanism, in this paper we concentrate on those mechanisms that aim to ensure the rule of law, therefore we analyze the administrative and constitutional trials in the Mexican legal system that fulfil the characteristic of our definition of accountability; both are procedures where citizens have standing and the authority that judges is from a different branch of government from the agency being judged.

8.4 Constitutional and Administrative Courts as Accountability Mechanisms

We defined accountability as the substantive dimension of the rule of law and the legal norms that establish control mechanisms whereby a state agency is obliged to report and justify its actions to a different authority which judges and sanctions its performance to guarantee its compliance with state goals, including the protection of human rights, and to demand certain results. Since state goals and human rights are usually part of the Constitution, accountability mechanisms are therefore procedures which enable citizens to demand that government actions comply with the constitutional mandate as the supreme law of the land. To ensure the effectiveness of this compliance, the legal system requires mechanisms to determine the validity of the authorities' actions. Constitutional and administrative procedures which provide these accountability mechanisms guarantee the independence of the agent that judges from the authorities whose actions are being reviewed.

Ginsburg points out that the evolution from authoritarian regimes to democratic ones governed by the rule of law is characterized by the transition from the political control of government actions by ideology and hierarchy to the institutionalization of legal procedures governed by law, in charge of independent bodies and respectful of due process. Accordingly, constitutional and administrative courts gain importance as accountability mechanisms in democratic regimes (Ginsburg/Tamir 2008). This type of mechanism has the virtue of empowering citizens by granting them standing in the judicial process in which government actions are called to account. In this respect, citizens play an essential role in accountability mechanisms by bringing authorities whose performance is unsatisfactory to court. These actions not only protect the plaintiffs' rights but are also a means of controlling agencies' performances. They function as alarms triggered by citizens when governments' actions fail to comply with the law or the Constitution (McCubbins 2011). Involving citizens in these accountability mechanisms also has the virtue of not requiring ad hoc institutions for the control of agencies' actions. Moreover, because it is an adversarial procedure, its quality can be assessed based on the complaint and the defendant's response, making it also an efficient, democratic option (Ginsburg/Tamir 2008). In this respect, constitutional and administrative courts grant sovereign citizens control of their government, making them democratic accountability mechanisms (Nohlen 2007).

Administrative courts as an accountability mechanism are the authorities responsible for ensuring the rule of law. They revise the legality of government actions through a judicial procedure. They serve as the guarantors of correct government performance through what García Enterría (2007) defines as the protection of the right to a good administration. Asimov (2015) distinguishes four types of administrative courts in the various legal systems. These courts vary, depending on how they function as independent agencies or separate tribunals, in either adversarial or inquisitorial procedures, and according to the scope of the judicial review that is open or closed to the introduction of new evidence, and whether the judicial review is conducted by general or specialized courts. The Mexican case follows the French model by having special independent courts with an inquisitorial system, open to new evidence.[1]

---

[1]With the Anti-corruption constitutional reform of 2015, the federal and all the state-level administrative courts became independent. See Diagnóstico de Justicia Administrativa; at: http://repositorio-digital.cide.edu/handle/11651/1496.

The procedures by which the adherence of performance to constitutional norms is evaluated are known as constitutionality controls and constitute accountability procedures. The analysis is conducted by a diverse, autonomous reviewing body. Its purpose is to analyse the performance of an agency to determine whether its actions comply with the rights and principles contained in the Constitution and sanction them accordingly. Constitutional courts are responsible for the effectiveness of human rights by empowering citizens to demand from their authorities their complete fulfilment (Ferrajoli 2000). The court reviews all acts of government to determine their compliance with the observance of human rights and regards the goals contained in the Constitution as the supreme law of the land. It is therefore an accountability mechanism that guarantees the adherence of the exercise of power to the Constitution. There are two main models of constitutional control: the European model, with specialized Constitutional courts, and abstract control, where decisions have *erga omnes* effects. In the common-law model, constitutional control may be exercised by any judge within the ordinary judicial procedure, and the decision only has an *inter partes* effect (Cossío 2011).

In the Mexican case, the main constitutional control in the hands of citizens is the *amparo*, which is a combination of the two models. The Mexican case is paradigmatic, with some authors such as Burgoa (2010) and Tena (1984) considering it unique. Since it is a specialized procedure undertaken in federal courts, the decision only affects the parties being tried, except for some cases in which there is a declaration of general effects by the Supreme Court of Justice of the Nation (SCJN).

8.4.1 Administrative Courts as Accountability Mechanisms

In Mexico, there are two main ways of controlling administrative agencies: nullity trials and state liability trials. Both are designed to ensure that administrative agencies comply with the law. The Constitution regulates these procedures differently for each level of government. For the Federation, the Mexican Constitution (Article 73, XXIX, H) empowers Federal Congress to issue laws that create administrative courts, which are responsible for both nullity and liability proceedings. Through these lawsuits, individuals may sue agencies whose actions they regard as unlawful. At the state level, in accordance with the provisions of the Mexican Constitution (Article 116, Section V and 122, 5), local administrative courts are authorized to resolve this type of controversy. In turn, the Mexican Constitution (Article 115) also empowers local congresses to establish procedures for the resolution of disputes with municipal authorities. These are procedures in which, based on a request by an individual, a judge sanctions a government action. Since this accountability procedure takes the form of a trial, individuals play an important role as plaintiffs. A citizen's complaint serves as an alarm, indicating that they have been affected by an action that departs from legality. The type of cases commonly taken to these courts are administrative decisions, such as government purchases, permits, licenses, or fines. The decision of the Court may:

- declare the validity of the contested action with respect to the powers conferred by the legal order. as a result of which the action remains;
- declare that the contested action departs from the normativity, in which case it proceeds to:
  - decree the full nullity of the action, since the problems cannot be corrected;
  - or decree partial nullity, since it is possible to correct the problems of the contested action;
  - and/or request redress or payment of damages where appropriate.

The purpose of the nullity trial is therefore to verify the compliance of government actions with the law and, in the event of a mistake, to order it to be corrected, which constitutes an accountability procedure as defined earlier.

The second trial in administrative courts operating as an accountability mechanism is the state liability procedure. This procedure focuses on repairing the damage caused by the acts or omissions of public administration, at the federal and local levels. Article 109 of the Mexican Constitution states that irregular administrative activity makes the State liable. The Supreme Court of Justice of the Nation (SCJN) has declared that the Constitution establishes the substantive right of individuals to receive compensation when irregular administrative activity has caused damage. The purpose of this right is "to redress damage, through financial compensation, as well as to ensure, through legislation and the corresponding ordinary channels, a procedural vehicle to secure compliance.[2] Article 109 of the Mexican Constitution establishes a substantive right in favor of the people. The SCJN concluded that irregular administrative activity alone constitutes the object of this procedure, which excludes judicial error or failures in Congress, and that it should be understood as state action undertaken without meeting the legal requirements for the undertaking of this administrative act. Its purpose is to repair the damage caused to individuals by irregular administrative activity – in other words, activity which, by action or omission, fails to comply with established legal obligations – or by a performance failure on the part of the public sector.[3] State liability can therefore be understood as an accountability mechanism whereby administrative courts judge the acts of state agencies as well as the damage caused and the way the latter can be redressed. Redress can create a system of incentives to prevent the repetition of certain actions and, in the long run, improve agencies' performance, since it causes the internalization of the costs caused by irregular actions (López/García 2017), which in turn makes them effective accountability mechanisms, since they foster the improvement of government actions.

---

[2]Semanario Judicial de la Federación and Gaceta, Vol. XXIX. 167386. 1a. LIV/2009. Primera Sala. Novena Época (April 2009): 590.
[3]SCJN[TA]; 10a. Época; T.C.C.; S.J.F. and Gaceta; Book XVIII, Vol. 3 (March 2013): 2077.

Once again, the citizen as plaintiff plays a key role in this procedure by highlighting the irregular performance of public administration. The SCJN has pointed out that the Constitution establishes the substantive right of citizens to receive compensation when the irregular administrative activity of the State has caused them harm. The aim is to provide proper redress, as well as a vehicle to secure compliance.[4] Regarding the purpose of this procedure, and in keeping with the concept of accountability, the SCJN has established that state liability procedures have four main purposes:

(i) to compensate damage;
(ii) to create incentives designed to prevent damage and accidents;
(iii) to guarantee the proper functioning of government,
(iv) to ensure that administrative actions are free from liability.

State liability trials are therefore important accountability mechanisms that create a direct system of incentives to correct illegal actions by agencies. They are a powerful tool for improving government. Even the SCJN has established that the reason for the existence of state liability procedures is to guarantee that administrative activity complies with the law and that public services are delivered in accordance with certain quality standards, which constitutes a fundamental right to an efficient public administration, because if these standards are not met, the right to compensation is guaranteed.[5] Accordingly, the SCJN considers that it is a form of control designed to ensure that public administration functions efficiently, noting that an efficient public administration is a fundamental right. The state liability procedure is one of the procedures in the accountability system with the clearest corrective purpose.

8.4.2 Weakness and Challenges

As established by Ginsburg/Tamir (2008), in authoritarian regimes, conflicts with the administration are not resolved through legal channels such as trials but by informal means. This was true of Mexican administrative courts in the twentieth century. These courts were not very well known, and their use was limited mainly to federal tax conflicts; only twenty-nine states had administrative courts (López et al. 2010). By the end of the twentieth and the beginning of the twenty-first century, the coming to power at the state and federal level of parties other than the PRI (the state party) led to the creation of more administrative courts, and today all thirty-two states have one. Nowadays these courts play a greater role in the control of the administration and preservation of the rule of law. A recent paradigmatic case, popularly known as *Teresa y Jacinta*, involved two indigenous women who

---

[4]SCJN[TA]; 9a. Época; 1a. Sala; S.J.F. and Gaceta; Vol. XXIX (April 2009): 592.
[5][TA]; 9a. Época; 1a. Sala; S.J.F. and Gaceta; Vol. XXIX, (April 2009): 592.

were accused of kidnapping soldiers and were wrongfully imprisoned. They sued the federal prosecutor in a state liability trial at which the court ordered not only redress but also a public apology, thereby showing its effectiveness as an accountability mechanism.[6] Nevertheless, access to justice in these courts is still far from simple. The process is extremely formal and sometimes lengthy. These courts at the state level are still underfunded and the personnel require better training. (López et al. 2010). This is especially true of state liability trials: a recent study shows that, even at the federal level, between 2005 and 2017 only 398 cases were taken to Court (Morsi 2007).

Judicial independence is another challenge these courts must overcome. The judge's appointment by the legislative branch from candidates suggested by the President or governor without a clear profile or justification lacks the necessary transparency to guarantee the autonomy of judges. The SCJN has stated that for the appointment of administrative judges, the proposals must contain elements related to their performance. Those reviewing the candidates must determine whether they comply with the constitutional principles of efficiency, probity, honesty, good reputation, proven ethics and professionalism which all public servants should follow (*Amparo*, AR 753/2015). Nevertheless, these criteria are seldom met.

Limiting state liability trials to administrative irregular activity undermines the potential of these procedures to operate as comprehensive accountability mechanisms. In other legal systems, such as the Colombian or Spanish, state liability procedures encompass actions from the three branches of government (Gil Botero 2013). This strengthens the capacity of citizens to bring all authorities to account. In this sense, the Mexican legal system should expand the competence of state liability trials to judicial and legislative errors.

To ensure that authorities abide by the rule of law, greater efforts must be made to guarantee access to these courts and to make their procedures and decisions comprehensible to everyone. Moreover, the professionalization of the Court and the guarantee of its independence through autonomous appointment procedures and adequate funding are required for this accountability mechanism to work fully as part of a democratic state governed by the rule of law.

8.4.3 The Amparo Trial as an Accountability Mechanism

Within the Mexican legal system, the *Amparo* Trial constitutes the main procedure for ensuring constitutionality. Because of the democratization movement at the beginning of the twenty-first century, a series of constitutional reforms were undertaken to strengthen the rule of law, including the 2010 Human Rights Reform (National Human Rights Commission 2012) and the 2011 *Amparo* Reform (Official

---

[6]See at: http://centroprodh.org.mx/?option=com_content&view=%20article&id=2250%3A2017-02-18-06-00-48&catid=278%3Ainfografias&Itemid=220.

Journal of the Federation 2011) The Constitution regulates this trial in Articles 1, 103, and 107. In accordance with Paragraph 3 of Article 1 of the Constitution, all acts of government must promote, respect, protect and guarantee human rights, and constitutional control procedures are a way of ensuring that this in fact happens. The *amparo* is the jurisdictional procedure whereby individuals can challenge any action they consider contrary to the Constitution, regardless of the level or branch of government by which it was undertaken. Given this range of subjects, the *amparo* is the most powerful accountability mechanism in the Mexican legal system. Moreover, as a result of the *amparo* law reform of June 2011, its scope for protection was expanded in line with the constitutional reform of Article 1, known as the Human Rights Reform. This reform stipulates that in Mexico human rights will be recognized not only as expressly stated in the Constitution but also in international treaties. Subsequently, the SCJN, in decision 293/2011,[7] reinforced this new mandate, stating that both the constitutional norms and the human rights norms contained in international treaties signed by Mexico should be considered part of the Constitution. In addition, the SCJN ruled that all precedents of the Inter-American Court of Human Rights (CIDH) will be mandatory within the Mexican legal system. Consequently, all judges must observe both the human rights mandates contained in the Constitution, the treaties, and the decisions issued by the SCJN and the CIDH. Accordingly, *amparo* should now be used in violations of constitutional articles and the international treaties signed by Mexico concerning human rights. Thus, *amparo* exercises both constitutional and conventional control.[8]

Moreover, the 2010 and 2011 reforms not only broaden the scope of the review of actions involving human rights and constitutional principles, but also make the requirements for beginning an *amparo* more flexible, thereby giving people greater access to it. Nowadays, it suffices to prove that an act or ruling has caused or could cause unlawful damage and that the person coming to court has a legitimate interest in preventing it, without necessarily having to prove the infringement of a subjective right. Citizens can now also present a class action. Since the 2011 reform, it has been possible to use *amparo* to sue not only traditional government agencies but also private entities if they provide a public service. Moreover, in the case of administrative activity, the Constitution expressly allows a citizen to protest against omissions, as indicated in Section IV of Article 107 of the Constitution. On a number of occasions, the SCJN has emphasized that the timely exercise of the powers of state bodies is part of individual guarantees, and therefore that the omission of this exercise constitutes a violation of the Constitution. This flexibility in *amparo* procedure has strengthened it as an accountability mechanism enabling people to sound the alarm when an action of any authority threatens the Constitution.

---

[7]See at: https://sjf.scjn.gob.mx/sjfsist/Paginas/DetalleGeneralScroll.aspx?id=24985&Clase=DetalleTesisEjecutorias.

[8]In the SCJN decision A.R. 293/2011 conventional control was limited. This decision determines that when the Mexican Constitution establishes a restriction to a human right it should be upheld regardless of what human rights treatises mandate.

When opposition to an administrative act or a law is brought before a district judge, it is called *amparo indirecto*. In this case, after a procedure with the appropriate procedural stages of merit (claim, response, hearing, and allegations), its outcome may be:

- to grant an *amparo*, in which case the sanction consists of determining that the action opposed contradicts the Constitution and must be corrected;
- to refuse an *amparo*, in which case the judge considers that the action complies with the Constitution or that the defendant has not engaged in an omission;
- that the judge deems it inappropriate to try the case due to its failure to comply with the legal requirements.

The decision may be appealed. The Courts of Appeals or in some cases the SCJN may confirm, modify or revoke the decision.

Amparo is also a mechanism to control judges. This is called *amparo directo*. In this case, if a citizen deems that a decision contravenes the Constitution he or she comes to *amparo* before a *Tribunal Colegiado* federal court with three judges. The decision has the same outcomes as an *amparo indirecto* but without an appeal in general, though exceptionally the SCJN can grant a review in these cases.

Regarding sanctions, Section XVI of Article 107 of the Constitution establishes measures to guarantee compliance with the judgment and therefore the achievement of the purpose of the accountability procedure. At the same time, it provides deadlines for the agency to comply with the resolution or request more time to achieve it and establishes forms of substitute compliance for cases in which it is impossible or extremely burdensome to comply with it. In this last case, it is essential for the violation to be redressed through the payment of damages.

Recent cases where an *amparo* has been granted due to an omission on the part of the government include *Ward 13* (AR378/2014), in which HIVS patients sued a public hospital for failing to build a special ward to prevent them from becoming sicker after the funds for doing so were granted, thereby undermining their right to health. In the *Acueducto Independencia* (AR 323/2014, www.scjn.gob.mx) case, an *amparo* was granted to an indigenous community because the aqueduct was approved without the prior consultation which should have taken place in compliance with the ILO Convention 169. These are good examples of the way the *amparo* is used as an accountability mechanism that ensures what Kristosser calls the substantive dimension of the rule of law, in other words, the effectiveness of human rights.

8.4.4 Weakness and Challenges

The *amparo* is the main procedure under Mexican law for the protection of human rights and a means of bringing any part of government to account. The 2010 and 2011 constitutional reforms not only strengthened the rule of law in Mexico but also sought to guarantee an efficient way to ensure this. Nevertheless, access to justice is still an issue in *amparo* cases. The number of formalities it involves still causes over 60% of cases to be dismissed. Only 9.6% are granted an *amparo* and only 16% of the appeals reverse the judge's decision. The reason for the high rate of dismissal is usually case overload in courts (Soberanes 2018). Experts such as Magaloni consider that this situation makes the *amparo* only available to rich people who can afford a sophisticated lawyer from a firm that is able to overcome the formalistic barriers (Magaloni 2017). Efforts must therefore be made to make the *amparo* accessible to everyone.

Another aspect of the *amparo* that is deemed to be one of its weaknesses as an accountability mechanism is its limited ability to guarantee full redress for human rights violations. Since its inception, the *amparo* has been regarded as an effective means of protecting human rights and was even used as a model at the American Convention of Human Rights, (Quintana 2016). Particularly in health matters, the SCJN has upheld the right to a solution and even the obligation to oversee the changes required to prevent future violations (AR152/2013). Nevertheless, authors such as Quintana (2016) have pointed out that the *amparo* has often fallen short of fully redressing violations. Moreover, the SCJN declared that the *amparo* is limited with regard to the remedies it can provide and, in general, these should only take the form of financial compensation.[9] This decision undermines the *amparo* as an accountability mechanism. Limiting redress to payment reduces the scope for improving government actions. Moreover, democratic exercises such as the recognition of wrongdoing by ordering public apologies are denied. Hopefully, the SCJN will reconsider this decision since the lower courts seem to continue to consider the *amparo* an important tool for countering arbitrary government actions. For example, following the disappearance of forty-three students in *Ayotzinapa*, the Court of Appeals decided, given the gross violations of the prosecution in the investigation of this case, to establish a Truth Commission overseen by the national ombudsman and with the participation of the victims (Medellín 2018).

8.5 Final Thoughts

In the past twenty years, Mexico has undergone a process of democratization whereby political control of power has lessened and transparency and accountability mechanisms have become more common. Today, administrative and constitutional courts have become key actors in the protection of the rule of law by bringing government to account in significant matters regarding human rights. Nevertheless, these courts still have major challenges that must be met for them to fulfil their role as accountability mechanisms.

---

[9]Gaceta del Semanario Judicial de la Federación. Medidas de reparación integral por regla general, 2014342. 1a. LIII/2017 (10a.). Primera Sala. Décima Época Libro 42 (May 2017): 469.

Judicial independence, particularly in administrative courts, must be reinforced. At the state level, the influence of the incumbent governor in the appointment of judges as well as the control over the courts' budgets is undermining the efficacy of administrative courts as accountability mechanisms. In this area, the recent involvement of civil society pushing for open appointment procedures where decisions must be deliberated has helped.

Access to justice should also be facilitated. The public´s lack of awareness of the existence of administrative trials and their purpose as well as excessively formal procedures have resulted in their underuse (López/García 2017). Regarding state liability trials, their scope should be broadened to include not only administrative agencies' actions but also judicial error. In the case of the *amparo*, although it is better known, universal access to it is far from guaranteed. Efforts must be made to ensure that every citizen has access to these accountability mechanisms and only then will the Mexican legal system fully comply with the rule of law.

The 2018 elections have resulted in a significant concentration of power by the elected President Andres Manuel Lopez Obrador. His party Morena has the majority of both houses of Congress, therefore traditional checks and balances might be weakened. To minimise the danger of going back to a government that concentrates all power in one party and where loyalty to the President is more important than the law, it is essential that people learn about the accountability mechanisms explained in this chapter and use them to guarantee their rights and the compliance of authority to the rule of law.

References

Ackerman, J. (2008). *Más allá del acceso a la información: transparencia, rendición de cuentas y estado de derecho* (Mexico City: Siglo XXI).
Argyris, C.; Shon, D. (1997). "Organizational learning: a theory of action perspective", in: *Revista Española de investigaciones sociológicas*, 77/78: 345–348.
Asimow, M. (2015). "Five Models of Administrative Adjudication", in: *Stanford Public Law Working Paper* No. 2632711; at: https://ssrn.com/abstract=2632711 or http://dx.doi.org/10.2139/ssrn.2632711.
Behn, R. (2001). *Rethinking Democratic Accountability* (Washington D.C.: Brookings Institution Press).
Bovens, M. (2010). "Two Concepts of Accountability: Accountability as a Virtue and as a Mechanism", in: *West European Politics*, 33,5: 52.
Black's Law Dictionary (Free Online Legal Dictionary), 2nd Edn.; at: https://blognisaba.wordpress.com/2011/04/24/apa-cmo-citar-el-diccionario-de-la-real-academia-en-lnea/.
Burgoa, I. (2010). *Derecho constitucional mexicano* (Mexico City: Porrúa).
Cossío, J. (2004). *Bosquejos constitucionales* (Mexico City: Porrúa).
Ferrajoli, L. (2000). *Derecho y razón* (Madrid: Trotta).
Fierro, A. (2017). *El sistema normativo de rendición de cuentas y el ciclo del uso de los recursos públicos en el orden jurídico mexicano, doctoral dissertation* (Mexico City: IIJ UNAM).
García Enterría, E. (2007). *La transformación de la justicia administrativa de excepción singular a la plenitud de jurisdiccional* (Madrid: Thomson Civitas).
Gil Botero, E. (2013). *Responsabilidad Extracontractual del Estado* (Bogotá: Temis).

Ginsburg, T.; Tamir, M. (2008). *Administrative Law and the Judicial Control of Agents in Authoritarian Regimes* (Cambridge: Cambridge University Press).
Kitrosser, H. (2015). *Reclaiming Accountability* (Chicago: University of Chicago Press).
Lapsley, I. (1995). "Audit and accountability in the public sector: problems and perspectives", in: *Financial Accountability & Management*, 11,2 (May): 107–110.
López, S.; Fierro, A.; García, A.; Zavala, D. (2010). *Diagnóstico del funcionamiento del sistema de impartición de justicia en materia administrativa a nivel nacional* (Mexico City: CIDE).
López, S.; García, A. (2017). *Perspectivas comparadas de la justicia administrativa* (Mexico City: CIDE).
Magaloni, A. (2017). *Diálogos por la Justicia Cotidiana: Diagnósticos conjuntos y soluciones*; at: https://www.gob.mx/cms/uploads/attachment/file/79028/Di_logos_Justicia_Cotidiana.pdf.
Mccubbins, D.; Schwartz, T. (2008). "Overlooked: congressional oversight police patrols versus fire alarms", in: *American Journal of Political Science*, 28 (25 August): 165–179.
Mulgan, R. (2002). "Accountability: an ever-expanding concept?", in: *Public Administration*, 78: 555–573.
Morsi, Z. (2007). "Fundamento de una teoría sobre responsabilidad del estado y su remediación" (Ph.D. dissertation, Mexico: UNAM).
Medellín, X. (2018). "Caso Iguala: Los claroscuros de una polémica sentencia de amparo", in: *Derecho en Acción* (Mexico City: CIDE); at: http://derechoenaccion.cide.edu/author/ximena-medellin-urquiaga.
Nohlen, D. (2007). "Jurisdicción constitucional y consolidación de la democracia", in: *Tribunales constitucionales y consolidación de la democracia* (Mexico City: Suprema Corte de Justicia), 3: 53.
O'Donnell, G. (2008). *Democracia y estado de Derecho. In Más allá del acceso a la información: transparencia, rendición de cuentas y estado de derecho* (Mexico City: Siglo XXI): 89–99.
Quintana, K. (2016). "La obligación de reparar violaciones de derechos humanos: el papel del amparo mexicano", in: *¿Cómo ha entendido la Suprema Corte de Justicia de la Nación los derechos en la historia y hoy en día? Estudios del desarrollo interpretativo de los derechos* (SCJN); at: https://www.academia.edu/30840208/La_obligaci%C3%B3n_de_reparar_violaciones_de_derechos_humanos_el_papel_del_amparo_mexicano.
Schedler, A. (2010). *¿Qué es la rendición de cuentas?*, Vol. 3 (Mexico City: IFAI).
Soberanes, J. (2018). "El amparo está diseñado para que los ciudadanos pierdan", in: *El Universal*; at: http://www.eluniversal.com.mx/articulo/jose-maria-soberanes-diez/nacion/el-amparo-esta-disenado-para-que-los-ciudadanos-pierdan (26 June 2018).
Suprema Corte de Justicia de la Nación (June 2011); at: https://www.scjn.gob.mx (2 July 2018).
Suprema Corte de Justicia de la Nación (September 2013); at: https://www.scjn.gob.mx (2 July 2018).
Tena, F. (1984). *Derecho constitucional mexicano* (Mexico City: Porrúa).

Chapter 9
Citizenry, Civic Education and Rule of Law

Jose Pablo Abreu Sacramento

Abstract This chapter argues that living under the rule of law requires not only efficient and effective government agencies but also the extensive and responsible cooperation of ordinary people. This argument relies on a thick perspective of the rule of law (see Chaps. 2 and 4), implying a democratic life where people can exercise their human rights, among other things. Moreover, based on a reviewed version of the Principle of Fairness, the author maintains that individuals have to actively participate in public affairs and cooperate in community life as a moral implication of living together under the rule of law. And, in order to meet this goal, he contends that it is necessary to strengthen a public policy of civic education. Finally, the author argues in favor of that public policy because it helps to develop the virtue of reciprocity, a quality that is conducive to human flourishing and living together, taking into account that our social nature coexists with a liberal self-centred culture nowadays.

Keywords Rule of law · Civic education · Citizenry · Moral obligation · Principle of fairness · Reciprocity

9.1 Introduction

The human being is social. We live in society. Moreover, we see ourselves as part of a community (Sandel 1981). 86% of people[1] agree with this statement on a local level, and 93% see themselves as part of a country (WVS 2018). But human relationships are also complicated by nature. Individuals care about multiple things; we have different priorities, which are frequently in conflict or competition.

---

[1] Data from the World Value Survey Wave 6, based on the views of people from countries within the European Union, America and Oceania.

Prof. Dr. Jose Pablo Abreu Sacramento, Ph.D. in Law. Department of Law, Tecnológico de Monterrey, Campus Santa Fe, Mexico City. E-mail: jpabreu@tec.mx.

Disagreements of that kind, combined with other elements that are part of the increasing complexity of societies where scarce resources are one of the realities, have made some philosophers propose a structural order for living together, pointing out which institutions are justified and how they should work.

In addition to the institutional structure, there has been permanent concern and discussion about people's behavior and the moral implications for each of us since we, in fact, live together. In this sense, the three main approaches to normative ethics use different criteria to define what is right and wrong: virtue ethics defends how one ought to be, deontology emphasizes one's duties or binding rules, and consequentialism the outcome of one's actions. However, it is recognized that each approach accepts features of the rest (Hursthouse/Pettigrove 2016) – as you will notice I do when expounding my arguments.

This book analyses where Mexico stands in relation to the rule of law and why this occurs. In accordance with this, this chapter focuses on how members of a community should behave because of this membership, if they aspire to live under the rule of law. And I assume in this chapter that we aspire to accomplish that, because it is the starting point to bring about the equity, prosperity and peace to communities that Gutiérrez, Martinez, Ponce and Solís highlight in Chap. 4.

In order to support my arguments, I base them on a thick conception of the rule of law – a conception that includes some of the attributes that Sarsfield describes in Chap. 2 of this book, such as the necessity for institutional equilibrium, where civil servants and social actors obey the law and this law is neutral and independent of any power; a conception that also includes a democratic life where people can exercise their individual rights.

This chapter therefore argues that if democracy and the exercise of human rights are necessary conditions to ensure the rule of law, efficient and effective government agencies are not sufficient to grant democratic life and personal liberty.

According to political theory, the basic elements of a state are a territory, a government, a legal order and a population. But when people try to analyze the way a particular state functions they usually focus on the government design or the legal content.

In this chapter it is argued that people should be required to participate in public affairs and to contribute towards the life of the community; and I strongly believe that there is an individual moral obligation to have this attitude, beyond a legal one.

I therefore advocate a wider civic education policy to generate a civic culture and foster an autonomous, cooperative and responsible citizenry that strengthens the rule of law.

To be clear, in this chapter civic education is viewed as a formative process that cultivates the knowledge, attitudes, values and skills to dispose individuals to participate in public affairs and cooperate in community life (Conde 2016).

In this sense, this chapter answers two questions: Where, if anywhere, does a moral obligation to participate in public affairs and cooperate with the community originate? Why is it relevant to strengthen civic education in Mexico?

Section 9.2 recommends fostering in individuals a moral obligation to collaborate with the community based on the Principle of Fairness, considering that this collaboration indirectly ensures the existence of some essential and necessary measures for the public good (i.e. the rule of law).

Section 9.3 contends that a wider policy of civic education in Mexico would build up the disposition to collaborate in an autonomous and responsible way.

9.2 Citizenry, Rule of Law and the Principle of Fairness

In this section the individual moral obligation to participate in public affairs and cooperate in a community is advocated on the Principle of Fairness. Thus, first the section shows how people in Mexico are not participating in public affairs or cooperating within community life, thereby affecting the status of the rule of law. Then Hart's concept of the Principle of Fairness (1955) is analyzed and some objections and adjustments proposed by Nozick (1974), Otsuka (2017) and Klosko (2004) are discussed, before reaching the conclusion that, based on this principle, there is a moral obligation to collaborate with the State and the community, even if the received benefit – which in this particular case is related indirectly to the aforementioned attributes of the rule of law – is neither requested nor essential.

9.2.1 How People Participate in Public Affairs and Cooperate in Community Life in Mexico

In this chapter the concept of democracy accords with the definition provided in Article 3 of the Mexican Constitution: "a life system founded on the constant economic, social and cultural improvement of the people". This conception of democracy also agrees with Article 2 of the Inter-American Democratic Charter when it mentions that "(r)epresentative democracy is strengthened and deepened by permanent, ethical, and responsible participation of the citizenry…". In fact, people in the occidental world have the vision that individuals must be politically involved (Almond/Verba 1989).

Moreover, it is assumed that we value the deliberative character of democracy outlined by Elster: "All agree, I think, that the notion includes collective decision-making with the participation of all who will be affected by the decision or their representatives: this is the democratic part. Also, all agree that it includes decision-making by means of arguments offered by and to participants who are committed to the values of rationality and impartiality: this is the deliberative part." (1998: 8).

In other words, in a democracy it is not enough to have free and periodic elections; the relevant participation of the people in public affairs is also necessary. And this requirement of civic – not only political – participation is even more urgent since representative democracy has been in crisis for the last few decades, with people usually distrusting and rejecting politicians and parties. Additionally, for a democracy to be truly deliberative, there is a belief that people participation has to incorporate some degree of epistemic autonomy at the moment of discussing and making collective decisions.[2]

But in this chapter it is also held that cooperation between people is necessary to bring about a system of life whereby people's economic, social and cultural conditions are improved. We will not succeed in creating such a system by the performance of effective and efficient government agencies alone.[3] Moreover, it is arguable that this effectiveness and efficiency is unattainable without the cooperation of the people.[4]

However, it looks as though not all people are playing their part in Mexico.

In the electoral field (INE-COLMEX 2015), the participation of Mexicans is acceptable on election day (62%), compared with countries like Germany (72%), Spain (69%), USA (68%), Canada (61%), France (55%) and Chile (49%). But if we extend this field to other areas where people can express their political opinion, that participation plummets.

Even though Mexicans have been able to propose legislative initiatives since 2012, they have exercised this right just ten times (Murillo 2017). Also, for the last six years they have been entitled to ask for a popular consultation on topics of national concern, but they have never requested one.[5]

People can additionally choose what kind of projects should receive public funds in some federal entities. But just a small percentage of them participate in these

---

[2]It is accepted that the ideal of epistemic autonomy in all citizens is just that – an ideal; but there is a belief that any democracy needs a balance among its population, whereby some of them would come closer than others this ideal.

[3]This chapter is not suggesting that institutions don't matter. They do, but even from the institutionalism perspective, political scientists and philosophers have dropped the classic treatment of political institutions and now they admit that it is necessary to look beyond arrangements of representation and government and to expand the analysis to social organization (Lowndes/ Roberts 2013; March/Olsen 1989).

[4]See Chap. 2 to explore some arguments on this topic.

[5]Political parties have tried to use the constitutional consultation, and President Lopez Obrador sounded out public opinion to define some of his projects before beginning his term in office.

civic exercises – for example, just 3.82% of the voters in Mexico City showed up in 2016 (IEDF 2017).

Also, only 10% have shared political information on social media, 9% have signed a protest document and 6% have been part of a public demonstration (INE-COLMEX 2015).

Moving on from the political field to other public affairs, the result is no better.

The prosecution of crimes sometimes requires people's reports, and even if their evidence is not essential it strongly helps to clarify the investigation. However, Mexican victims report just 6.8% of the crimes they have suffered (INEGI 2018a).

Mexico is in 135th place out of 180 countries on the Corruption Perceptions Index 2017 (International Transparency), and 62% of Mexicans have had contact with or heard about a corruption act. However, only 5% denounced it (INEGI 2017).

Public policies depend on tax collection. Nevertheless, 57% of the Mexican population works informally, avoiding taxes (INEGI 2018b).

Earlier I stated that we need not only people's participation in public affairs, but also individuals' cooperation in community life.

However, it appears that a large group of Mexicans are not interested in this sort of exchange. For example, 46% of people have never been a member of any kind of social organization (INE-COLMEX 2014). Maybe this correlates with 87% of Mexicans believing that you have to be careful before trusting people, 40% thinking people will try to take advantage of you if they get a chance and 18% feeling you should not trust your neighbor at all – this last percentage is double the distrust percentage of the world percentage (WVS 2018).

Furthermore, 20% of Mexicans have been discriminated against and 23% have been denied the exercise of a human right (CONAPRED 2017) because of a personal condition or preference. For example, it is estimated that women earn 34% less than men for identical jobs (Solís 2017).

This data shows how Mexicans are not actively participating in public affairs – neither electoral nor other sorts. It is difficult to affirm that our electoral democracy is doing well when this data is contrasted with the deliberative democracy conception.

It also demonstrates that a huge group of Mexicans are not cooperating with public agencies, which is affecting crime prosecution and therefore security; tax revenues and thus public budget; and the labor market and hence social security. It also reveals that there is considerable indifference to cooperating in community life, and there is a worrying level of distrust and discrimination, which impacts on people's economic, social and cultural life.

Therefore, if you agree that this participation and cooperation are essential for the rule of law, you will think that some kind of obligation should exist. In the next section I will argue for a moral obligation to participate and cooperate, beyond a concrete legal obligation that could apply in some of the aforementioned cases.

9.2.2 The Extent of the Principle of Fairness

This section will explain the moral obligation to participate in public affairs and cooperate in community life, derived from the Principle of Fairness. But first it is important to clarify what an obligation implies.

An obligation (Brandt 1964) generally involves (a) an action from one individual; (b) two parties – the aforementioned who has to perform the action and another person for whom the action has to be done; (c) a previous action – promise or transaction – that generates the obligation. For example, if *I promise* to *take you to the airport* if *you leave on a Sunday*, I will have an obligation to take you to the airport next time you travel on a Sunday. And this also implies that you have a right to require me to take you to the airport when you travel on a Sunday.

In that sense, when Hart held that those persons who have jointly made an individual effort to bring about a collective good "have a right to a similar" effort from anybody else who has enjoyed the benefits of that good (1955: 185), he also meant that the latter has *an obligation* to make a similar effort for the persons who acted jointly to bring about the collective good. For example, suppose you and a colleague agree to buy a coffee machine for the office and to split the cost of any repairs. According to the Principle of Fairness, if I want to drink coffee from that machine, I will have an obligation to pay you a proportional fee. It will be unfair if I enjoy coffee for free from your machine. The Principle of Fairness appeals to "the just distribution of benefits and burdens" (Lyons 1965: 164).

However, to maintain a fair balance it is not always necessary to limit your liberty by encumbering you with an obligation. There are different possible movements to assure fairness (Klsoko 2004): (a) restructuring things in such a way that you don't enjoy the benefits of the collective good; (b) liberating the rest of the group from their mutual restrictions; or (c) sharing the restrictions that are required from the group to bring about that collective good. Returning to the case of the coffee machine, you and your colleague can lock it up every time you finish using it so that I won't be able to enjoy your coffee unless you invite me. Or, imagine that before you buy the machine, your boss decides to offer the employees free coffee, avoiding your sacrifice. Only if it is impossible to apply (a) or (b) will one have an obligation of the kind of (c).

It is this logic that is used to support the argument that members of a specific community acquire a moral obligation to perform some participation and cooperation that generates and maintains the rule of law. However, the argument is not straightforward since public goods are not strictly equivalent to collective goods because there are different categories of them and multiple ways to generate them.

Collective goods are goods generated jointly by two or more individuals. In contrast, public goods (Olson 1965) are collective goods that have two main features: (i) enjoying the benefits of a public good doesn't threaten consumption for other members of the community; and (ii) if the good is available to one, it is available to all the members of the community. For example, if we talk about national border security, it doesn't make a difference if you or a thousand more people enjoy its benefits. Securing national borders will have the same effect – no one without a passport is entitled to cross the border. But also, if the government offers national security by policing the borders, it will be impossible to exclude you or more people from the benefits of that action.

It has been mentioned that participating and cooperating in community life is a moral obligation derived from the Principle of Fairness for bringing about the rule of law and its benefits. In this way, the Principle of Fairness would avoid free-riders of a public good.[6] Nevertheless, it is necessary to justify why some public good derived from the rule of law should be included, since, for some authors, it makes no sense to argue for an obligation of this kind if the collective good is non-excludable – such as public goods – and one has received it without asking for it.

In this sense, Nozick (1974), in his argument for a minimal state, has rejected an obligation to perform specific actions inside a community to bring about not-requested public goods. He presents the case of a coordinated neighborhood where 364 of its 365 members (you are the last member) sweep the street during the year – one per day – in order to have a clean street. He criticizes those who try to apply the Principle of Fairness to justify your obligation to sweep the street on the 365th day. Even if members of a community have restricted their liberty to jointly generate the public good and you have been enjoying the benefits of that clean street while living there, it doesn't follow that you should have that kind of obligation. Maybe you would prefer not to enjoy that benefit. Therefore, the impossibility of avoiding the benefits of that clean street shouldn't justify that kind of obligation against your liberty – it would be ridiculous to close your eyes or imagine a dirty street to avoid the benefit.

Otsuka (2017) offers a revised version of the Principle of Fairness to beat this Nozickean objection. To do so, he presents the case of members of a community living on a little shelf by a riverbank who have to raise a wall of sandbags to avoid a flood that would otherwise cause their death. Therefore, they decide to raise the wall. He argues that this public good, even if passively received by one of the members of the community – received without that member's consent – generates an obligation on the basis of the Principle of Fairness. And this is because of the urgency and essentiality of the good. Unlike a clean street, which can be considered non-essential, it is vital that no inhabitants die from the flood, and it would therefore be unfair to take advantage of the hard work of others without sharing the effort to secure the benefit of that wall.

Klosko apparently agrees with that limit of the Principle of Fairness for public goods. Such benefits should be indispensable to the individuals who have passively received them. He also specifies, and in these next two points concurs with Arneson (1982), that the balance between the received benefits and the required effort should

---

[6]A free-rider is an individual who deliberately receives the benefits from a collective good without doing their fair share to bring about that good (Arneson 1982). For a thorough explanation of the free-rider concept, see Hardin (2013).

be positive – i.e. it would not be fair to require help to build the wall if it were known that the wall wouldn't stop the flood. And, at the same time, there must be a balance of burdens and benefits among members of the group. Finally, we have to consider that even if the benefits have been reached at one point, it is necessary to maintain the fair share of them, since achieving things for the public good generally requires an unbroken chain of coordinated actions.

At this point, it becomes clear why the Principle of Fairness also entails an obligation to cooperate and bring about indispensable public goods. In the contractualist view, someone who is properly informed will sound unreasonable by rejecting a rule of this kind that represents some cost – one's fair share – when other alternatives impose more cost – death or putting oneself at risk of a deadly threat (Scanlon 1982).

Klosko appears to agree with Otsuka's limitation of public goods, because he relates the qualification of essential goods with their indispensability. However, Klosko's idea is less restricted than Otsuka's. Otsuka's description of the flood case is clear: the benefits of the wall are "vital and urgent" (2017: 12). If they don't build that wall, they will die. In contrast, Klosko widens the criterion a little and starts including goods required by all individuals to enjoy a satisfactory life. Because of their need to enjoy a satisfactory life, every member of the community will want, as a rational being, to have those goods (Rawls 1999). But even if Klosko reduces the list to public and not private goods, and later to "physical security… and provisions for satisfying basic bodily needs", he leaves the door open when he considers the possibility of including "others as well" (2004: 40).

9.2.3 Citizenry, Democratic Life and the Principle of Fairness

These positions have been recapitulated because they could be clear objections to applying the Principle of Fairness to some public good that can be achieved through citizenry participation in public affairs and cooperation in community life, like sharing political opinions, reporting crimes or joining social organizations.

Nozick's own example of the clean street will now be used to argue against the limits he places on the Principle of Fairness. Maybe you agree with Nozick that it is not vital or indispensable to sweep your street daily or periodically. But remember that Nozick is thinking in terms of a minimalist state, in which case there wouldn't be any public cleaning services. Therefore, if you and your neighbors don't clean your street, nobody else will. Litter will accumulate and flies, cockroaches, and rats will proliferate, bringing diseases. In a neighborhood with no public cleaning services, residents need to cooperate in order to keep the street clean. One can object, "Well, no cleaning will be necessary if neighbors don't litter". But even then, cooperation to clean the street will be necessary because animals in the vicinity – e.g. birds and foxes – die, tourists litter and other scenarios could threaten the health and well-being protected by clean streets. The relevant benefit to justify the application of the Principle of Fairness is the impact of that clean street on neighbors' health, not on how it looks.

Now let's take the case of a community with more than a minimal state. Some people, using Otsuka's criterion, could object that there is no need to involve neighbors in keeping the street clean in order to secure healthiness. Moreover, there is no urgency. Well, somebody could disagree again because this may be true for a regular European city, but not necessarily for other kinds of cities or towns. Let's look at a small town where the public budget is reduced and government employees are few – just enough to maintain security, the medical center, the school and the construction/renovation of one public space every year. This political community will require the cooperation of neighbors to ensure healthiness. And even if not urgent now, it will become urgent at some point, and that point will be cyclical.

Let me introduce a real-life example related to health. In tropical countries, during the rainy season, the threat of mosquitoes and mortal diseases such as dengue is commonplace. It is therefore necessary to avoid leaving water storage containers in backyards as they are mosquito breeding grounds. Even if the government supplies medicines or fumigates towns, this standing water will be a threat to neighbors' health. A coordinated action of the neighbors is necessary to avoid such threats, and it is fair that each neighbor does his or her share – removing items that can harbor eggs – to enjoy the benefit of healthiness.

In sum, the problem with Nozick's rejection of the obligation to maintain a clean street is that he takes only the simplest benefit from it. The problem of Otsuka's case to develop a criterion of vitality and urgency is that he presents an extreme case where nobody will refuse the vitality and urgency of the good and he overlooks the unbroken chain of coordinated actions that are necessary to sustain goods of this kind, and that could mislead people to reject public goods like a clean street from their classification.

A similar objection can be made to Klosko's analysis of the Principle of Fairness's application using cases that involve physical security. In extreme cases, nobody will reject the indispensability of the public good, but I have just demonstrated that cases with more nuances can challenge the limited application of the Principle of Fairness and that there are more than extremes or catastrophic cases in real life.

It could be said that Klosko accepts the application of the Principle of Fairness beyond essential public goods. He agrees that there could be an obligation to cooperate in the generation of other 'discretionary' public goods (2004: 86) when they are necessary to provide an essential one. I will not reject this argument, but I think he has other kinds of goods in mind with his indirect argument defending the application of the Principle of Fairness when it is practically indispensable to provide some discretionary public goods in order to generate the essential one. For example, he mentions that national security will require a transportation and communication infrastructure. In this way, he is thinking about an interdisciplinary cluster of public goods, but in this part of the presented argument, this particular chapter is not.

I believe that some public goods are directly related to the essential public good. They could be called "quasi-essential" public goods; i.e. goods that are a necessary but not sufficient condition to ensure the essential public good.[7] In the aforementioned examples, the clean street and the avoidance of breeding grounds are those quasi-essential public goods. They don't guarantee the healthiness of a neighborhood, but they are necessary to guarantee it, because of the direct relation that exists with the healthiness.

Practical objections could be presented against my argument. It could be held that opening the list would demand us to consider as essential or quasi-essential dozens of public goods, a number too demanding to sustain. Requiring people to cooperate to pay taxes for essential public services such as the armed forces, and to develop an attitude to participate and cooperate for quasi-essential public goods such as clean streets, would diminish their liberty to decide their plan of life. "And surely you don't want that." And indeed, that is not the purport of this paper. My point here is only to show that more than those extreme essential goods are necessary to have a satisfactory life. And even those extreme essential goods can appear not that essential for some communities. For example, Costa Rica is a country without an army, a national public good that I am sure is seen as vital and urgent for countries such as the USA and Russia.

People's cooperation in community life is also a necessary obligation to bring about some discretionary goods that are indirectly connected to essential public goods: those goods that are part of the "basic societal infrastructure" (Klosko 2004: 88). For example, Klosko views as discretionary goods a basic level of public education and a policy that maintains a stable economy. In the same way, people's cooperation can generate social capital through habits that reinforce the network among members of different communities. The custom of students sharing relevant information about previous experiences at a university could develop into an alumni society. The habit of reporting crimes could lead to a victims' association. It has been said that social capital is a necessary good to sustain the democratic system (Putnam 2000) – and if you accept a thick conception of the rule of law, you will agree that democracy is vital for our liberties, including personal freedom. This example demonstrates the diverse nature of the cluster of interdisciplinary discretionary public goods that are necessary to bring about an essential public good.

An objection to my application of the indirect argument is that I could be forcing the necessity of those discretionary public goods to bring about essential public goods. Some could say that periodic and authentic elections guarantee democracy, period. But even Klosko recognizes the 'fraught' area that we enter when analyzing the connection between essential and discretionary goods, the multiple ways to bring about essential goods and the deliberative process that every community should follow to define them (2004: 89). Therefore, it is valid to consider discretionary goods such as social capital.

---

[7]To examine further the difference between conditions that are necessary, but not on their own sufficient to bring about the desired results, see Mackie (1965).

It could be argued that including all these public goods justifies perfectionism,[8] a mindset which this chapter is not proposing to endorse. However, as Klosko mentions (2004), we value different public goods in different ways, qualifying violations of them to different degrees. The law considers not paying taxes to be worse than ignoring a traffic sign, even if disregarding the sign could be more dangerous and obeying it more crucial for an essential good such as personal physical safety. In the same way, I am convinced that some ways of cooperating with community life have to be protected by the political structure and others should not be. Moral – not legal – obligations are sometimes enough.

Another objection that could be raised in response to my argument in favor of moral obligations is that such an obligation might successfully bind people where the rule of law is actually ruling, but why should it bind people where impunity, crime and violation of human rights are a constant? There are people who are not enjoying the benefits of a public good such as the rule of law. However, the argument for a moral obligation still stands because I started this chapter assuming that we aspire to establish a general rule of law in Mexico and I have used cases where members of a community have to do their fair share to bring about a public good, just as Mexicans need to do.

Commensurate with my arguments is a revised version of the Principle of Fairness: when an individual enjoys a benefit available to everybody and this benefit exists just because of the sacrifice of others, that person has an obligation to do his or her fair share to maintain that benefit, if that benefit is necessary and directly connected to an essential benefit, even if this benefit is received passively.

That means that we are morally obliged to participate and cooperate to guarantee those public goods related to democratic life when that collaboration with the State and community is necessary to accomplish the rule of law.

9.3 A Starting Point: Strengthen Civic Education Policy

The individual moral obligation to participate in public affairs and cooperate in community life finds its base in the Principle of Fairness: if people value the rule of law, democratic life and their human rights, it is necessary to do their fair share to sustain that regime. Participating in public affairs (voting, paying taxes, reporting crimes, getting involved in public debates, etc.) and cooperating in community life (not discriminating, being part of organizations, collaborating with neighbors) is that fair share. In John Stuart Mill's words (1861):

> ... that political machinery does not act of itself... The people for whom the form of government is intended... must be willing and able to do what is necessary to keep it standing. And they must be willing and able to do what it requires of them to enable it to fulfill its purposes. The word "do" is to be understood as including forbearances as well as acts.

---

[8]Perfectionism as a moral theory demands us to take care of perfection in human life. For a general review of perfectionism, see Wall (2012).

However, it has been shown that people in Mexico are not doing their fair share and this has negatively affected the rule of law, democratic life and the exercise of human rights.

Collaboration is insufficient to produce a State where the law rules, people enjoy their liberties, and economic, social and cultural life continuously improves.[9] It is necessary for individuals to do more to achieve that goal.

Thus, if Mexicans have a moral obligation to participate in public affairs and cooperate in community life as members of a State aspiring to ensure the rule of law, but we as members of the community are not recognizing that obligation, wide civic education programs will be necessary to generate the required mass culture. There is a necessity for a social ethos that "informs individual choices" (Cohen 2008: 16).

A wide conception of rule of law demands a series of values, beliefs, attitudes and orientations from citizenry. To consolidate and maintain democracy, it is necessary to develop a mass political culture, and its development cannot be assumed (Diamond 1994a). Citizens need to be aware of their political system, their rights and obligations and how they could affect political processes, public policies and outcomes. If they live in a representative democracy, they must select their representatives and state their needs and preferences. Individuals should be able to access information that relates to public affairs and should have the capacity to analyze that information.

But that culture also requires a broader culture, a civic one, that nudges individuals to cooperate and fosters social trust.

This conception of civic culture is closely related to what Almond/Verba (1989) understand as a set of norms and attitudes of the political elites, but also of the ordinary people who live in a political society. They describe their conception of civic culture as the required political culture "plus something else" (Almond/Verba 1989: 29), underlining the relevance of trust, cooperation, solidarity and compromise among members of the community in general, and adding from Lasswell's communication model (1948) an inclusive attitude toward individuals and values.

My concern to highlight that kind of program takes into account the fact that for the last twelve years the Mexican Government has concentrated its efforts on a security and criminal justice strategy. Congress has approved different reforms, Executive has spent millions of pesos, Judicial has trained thousands of people – yet crime, corruption and impunity are still in the news every day.

But security and criminal justice are only two of the many elements of the institutional areas that validate the rule of law. In the World Justice Project measurements, for example, they constitute just two of the eight factors (see Chap. 2).

---

[9]There are other factors which affect the status of the rule of law in a nation, such as historical experience, international influence, socio-economic changes and a strong migratory flow.

Therefore, it is time to invest more in those who have to take part in the deliberative process of public affairs and who could affect other people's rights and life: Us.

Decades ago, Almond and Verba identified a large gap between what people from non-stable democracies – including Mexico – believed they should do, they could do and they actually do. Moreover, they underline this gap in the country as the "most interesting imbalanced pattern of commitment and involvement" (1989: 363).

This gap is still present in the country. For instance, even though 71% of the population thinks cheating on taxes is never justified, only 43% pay their taxes. Although 73% of Mexicans strongly believe it is wrong for someone to receive a bribe in the course of their duties, 62% have experienced or heard about a corruption act but not denounced it. Additionally, 68% of Mexicans think it is important to do something for other people, but only 48% believe unselfishness is an important aspect of children's education, and just 18% mention that the Government should care about progressing toward a less impersonal and more humane society (WVS 2014).

That gap is also present in the political field: 75% of the population thinks it is important to develop in children the feeling of responsibility, 64% believes democracy is essential to protect people's liberties and one in every four Mexicans believes that the Government should give people more say in important public decisions, but just 8% of the citizenry it is very interested in politics, only 10% has shared political information on social media, 9% has signed a protest document and 6% has been part of a public demonstration (WVS 2014).

Civic culture helps to maintain a balanced and responsible government. Once again, a State doesn't need people to participate in politics all the time, but when its government is not working properly, if people don't believe they should do something, they won't do it, and without accountability that government that is working poorly, inefficiently or against people's interest, will continue on that path.

Almond and Verba (1989) also linked political participation with social participation and attitudes toward fellow citizens. If individuals don't trust other people, how would they participate in political actions? How would they stand together in front of the Government?

In ordinary circumstances, these people would trust their government and focus their attention on their personal business. But when public agencies are threatening the public common good, people will demand a change in public policies.

Mexico's civic education policy has been through seven stages during the twentieth and twenty-first centuries (INEE 2018): as a nationalist course (1908–1971), as part of the Social Science course (1971–1993), as a citizenship course (1993–1999), as a civility and ethics course (1999–2006), as a comprehensive program focused on the development of competences (2006–2011), as a reloaded version of that program directed to the individual, ethics and citizenship (2011–2017), and finally, with the new model of education approved in 2017, as a formative process that starts in preschool and finishes in high school. Before this last stage, this policy only focused on elementary and secondary school.

Despite this, that policy has been qualified as ineffective (Morales/Martínez 2012) or insufficient to develop the required cultural path (Booth/Seligson 1994). Mexico is one of the bottom three countries out of twenty-two states evaluated on civic knowledge, and this poor performance could be related to a higher approval of antidemocratic attitudes and illegal behaviors (INEE 2016).

Mexico needs to change that pattern of behavior, and it looks as though what the Government has done is not enough.

At a time when the President of Mexico is announcing a Moral Constitution, Mexicans feel part of a community, but we don't trust that community. As a consequence, we don't invest our time and money in that community. And, without the cooperation of the people, a government cannot raise the rule of law.

Silvia Conde stands for a policy of "pertinent, critical, practical, relevant and humanist formation" for the Mexican population (2017: 54).

Schools and universities have a transcendental role to play in this task by internalizing norms and values, generating identity and beliefs, and developing social and political participation skills through new ideas, knowledge and innovative curricula. For example, in the United States, the Stone Brook University School runs a project on news literacy to develop in students the required skills to analyze the information they constantly receive through social media and traditional media (Klurfeld/Schneider 2014). These skills are required to counteract fake news and the radicalization of people's perspectives. If individuals are able to acquire these skills it could diminish some of the distrust in fellow citizens that is generated nowadays, and empower them to participate in political and social processes.

The task of equipping people with these skills should not be confined to the education system, because the civic culture we should foster includes attitudes and feelings that are harder to learn in the classroom and best developed through regular social experience.

Therefore, a strategy of this kind should involve institutions like autonomous organizations from society, independent agents of cultural change related to social education and the promotion of legality, democratic and human rights culture, and government agencies like the National Electoral Institute (INE), the National Council Against Discrimination (CONAPRED) and the Ministry of National Affairs (SEGOB).

People need experiences more than knowledge to develop a culture of civility. Therefore, different institutions need to be involved: family, workplace, social groups and associations, churches, labor unions, neighborhood committees. Institutions where people live their daily lives and can learn about support and solidarity. Social spaces where children, youths and adults can get used to listening to discussions about politics and government.

In Germany, for example, labor unions, churches and political parties receive public funding to develop programs related to civic culture. These three institutions offer diverse circles of community life where people seek and find professional, spiritual and political experiences.

Maybe these institutions are not the best options in Mexico, but we could call on business associations, neighborhood committees and community centres to cooperate in this task.

Reich (2016) describes how foundations working with private or public funds can support democracy, using pluralist and innovative arguments, and Lamarche (2014) adds the criteria of transparency, effectiveness, integrity, and inclusion. There are also good examples of society working on matters such as neighborhood design (RESIDential Environment Study 2018), the promotion of groups for mutual support (Society for Community, Research and Action 2018), and multicultural integration (9 Barris Accul neighbors' association 2018).

The role of autonomous social groups in fostering a civic culture and supporting democracy has already been explained in recent decades (Diamond 1994a, b; Sadowski 1994; Putnam 2000); however, in Mexico, these kinds of organizations need to strengthen their institutional design and cover other cities in addition to the capital.

Government agencies should build up a strong partnership with social groups, as the INE tried to do a couple of years ago via the National Strategy of Civic Culture (2016). Sadly, this document didn't become a fundamental public policy because of the lack of budget to develop it, among other reasons.

This is not the place to delineate the contents of that policy,[10] but the diversity of subcultures that exist in Mexico should be underlined, and this requires recognition of political subcultures as well. Therefore, it will be necessary to involve regions and local communities in the process of defining the values, attitudes, beliefs and orientations that should be reinforced or discouraged without losing the desired balance in the country.

Another benefit of civic education for individuals and community life is that this kind of formative policy could develop the virtue of reciprocity, a virtue that is relevant for human flourishing and living together, taking into account that our social nature coexists with a liberal self-centred culture nowadays.

Aristotle appealed to virtues as a necessary, but not sufficient, condition to reach happiness (Hursthouse/Pettigrove 2016). In this sense, there is a relationship between the sociopolitical structure, the individual's behavior, the common good and individual happiness. What I mean, in a nutshell, is that even the best basic sociopolitical structure requires people's help, and virtuous people are the kind of help I imagine – people who show their excellent character traits through their attitudes and actions (Foot 2002).

Specifically, reciprocity has been identified as one of the virtues required to sustain a balance of spontaneous social exchange that will help to foster the common good (including the rule of law) and individual happiness. In this chapter

---

[10]Just to illustrate, Diamond (1994a: 12) takes from Inkeles a list of components for a democratic culture: "flexibility, trust, efficacy, openness to new ideas and experiences, tolerance of differences and ambiguities, acceptance of others, and an attitude toward authority that is neither *blindly submissive* nor *hostilely rejecting* but rather *responsible... even though always watchful.*" But I have said that civic culture is broader than a political culture; so we will need to add other attitudes.

Becker's conception of reciprocity is used (1986), which, following Anscombe's requirement to describe a virtue through types of characteristics (1958), is based on these maxims: One should return good for good and not return evil for evil. One should resist evil received and restore evil done with good. The recipient of good should return the favor and the doer of evil should make restitution. One's returns and restitutions should fit and be commensurate with the good or evil. One's returns should be made for any good received, even if it wasn't requested. And one should be willing to reciprocate because it is a moral obligation.[11]

When considering the relevance of this virtue for social balance, we must note that there are some psychological states of mind related to this virtue. Virtues work as correctives of our desires (Foot 2002); by maintaining a general reciprocal attitude, an individual collaborates to sustain a social equilibrium, since people grow up expecting to receive a proportionate good for what they have done. In the same way, this disposition to return the good one receives and restore the evil one does is related to self-esteem. Since people expect from others a general attitude to reciprocate, when an individual fails to perform in this way, others start to see that person as worthless for social interaction, and because individuals value their self-worthiness, even if it is not the only factor, this can decrease self-esteem. Conversely, behaving with a reciprocal attitude can strengthen a person's self-esteem (Becker 1986). Consequently, reciprocity as a virtue will reinforce a social condition of self-respect, a very important primary good – the most important for Rawls (1999) – because it reflects an individual's value and boosts confidence, making it easier to achieve life goals.

This is not an observation about the necessity of being altruistic. It is a call for a self-interested attitude that recognizes the needs and interests of other people, especially those who live in the same community. This civic virtue requires us to have a helpful, respectful and trustful attitude towards each another (Putnam 1993).

Moreover, in the political arena, this attitude is perfectly aligned with the "orientation to action" that Diamond (1994a: 8) describes as a component of political culture, and the engagement in cooperative activity that Almond/Verba (1989) identify as a fundamental mindset for sustaining democratic culture.

A culture of reciprocity is an essential component of harmonious community life, and civic education is a good way to learn about citizenship and help people develop the character traits that foster reciprocity and other civic virtues. It therefore follows that civic education should be promoted in every community as a vital tool in the process of understanding the moral implications of living together and inculcating a spirit of public mindedness.

---

[11]This kind of disposition relates to the communal reciprocity presented by Cohen (2009). Recognizing that we live in a world where everybody needs help from other people, you choose to have the disposition to maintain the social balance of exchanges because of another individual's needs and, at the same time, because of your own need of their help. Returning good for good in this form of reciprocity implies recognition of human social nature, whereby I notice your – and my – limits and decide to continue with this virtuous social balance that you need to reach your happiness and that will allow you to help me reach mine.

The aim of the rule of law is to expand the enjoyment of human rights. This is how political authorities and structures justify their existence. The more liberties a society can exercise, the more legitimacy the State has. The fewer opportunities, essential goods and security individuals have in a society, to the detriment of people's rights, the more complaints will arise in the State, generating instability and affecting the State's legitimacy (Abreu/Le Clercq 2011).

However, the political structure cannot guarantee the common good or enable everybody to flourish without the cooperation of society. A constitution secures liberties, but does not secure the best use of individuals' liberties. Moreover, it does not secure adequate exercise of those liberties in favor of the community; rather, it encourages selfishness (Isensee 2011). This individualism should be balanced by a public spirit that ensures the common good (Diamond 1994a) through the cooperation of a civic community (Putnam 1993).

Even the best political structure is insufficient to assure well-being and happiness. The attitudes and behavior of individuals can have a profound effect on other people's well-being and happiness, making cooperation, collaboration and reciprocity essential aspects of community life. People need to cultivate a much greater willingness to participate in community endeavors, and promoting a wider civic education policy for living together under the rule of law is the starting point.

References

9 Barris Accul, Asociación vecinal; at: https://9bacull.org/es/ (28 December 2018).
Abreu, Jose P.; Le Clercq, Juan A. (2011). "Introducción", in: Abreu, Jose P.; Le Clercq, Juan A. (Eds.), *La reforma humanista* (Mexico City: Porrúa): 9–31.
Almond, Gabriel; Verba, Sidney (1989). *The Civic Culture: Political Attitudes and Democracy in Five Nations* (Newbury Park: SAGE Publications).
Anscombe, G.E.M. (1958). "Modern Moral Philosophy", in: *Philosophy* (Cambridge University Press), 33,124: 1–19.
Arneson, Richard (1982). "The Principle of Fairness and Free-Rider Problems", in: *Ethics*, 92,4 (July): 616–633.
Becker, Lawrence (1986), *Reciprocity* (New York: Routledge).
Booth, John A.; Seligson, Mitchell A. (1994). "Paths to Democracy and the Political Culture of Costa Rica, Mexico, and Nicaragua", in: *Political Culture & Democracy in Developing Countries* (Boulder, CO: Lynne Rienner Publishers).
Brandt, Richard B. (1964). "The Concepts of Obligation and Duty", *Mind*, New Series, 73,291 (July): 374–393.
Cohen, G.A. (2008). *Rescuing Justice and Equality.* (Cambridge, MA: Harvard University Press).
Cohen, G.A. (2009). *Why not Socialism?* (Princeton, NJ: Princeton University Press).
CONAPRED, Consejo Nacional para Prevenir de la Discriminación (2017). *Encuesta Nacional sobre Discriminación 2017* (Mexico City: CONAPRED); at: https://www.conapred.org.mx/index.php?contenido=pagina&id=604 (31 August 2018).
Conde, Silvia L. (2016). *Formacion ciudadana en Mexico* (Mexico City: INE); at: https://www.ine.mx/wp-content/uploads/2019/04/cuaderno_32.pdf (31 August 2018).
Diamond, Larry (1994a). "Introduction: Political Culture and Democracy", in *Political Culture & Democracy in Developing Countries* (Boulder, CO: Lynne Rienner Publishers).

Diamond, Larry (1994b). "Causes and Effects", in: *Political Culture & Democracy in Developing Countries* (Boulder, CO: Lynne Rienner Publishers).

Elster, Jon (Ed.) (1998). *Deliberative Democracy* (Cambridge: Cambridge University Press).

Foot, P. (2002). "Virtues and Vices", in: *Virtues and Vices: and other essays in moral philosophy* (Oxford: Oxford University Press); at: https://doi.org/10.1093/0199252866.003.0001 (22 August 2017).

Hardin, Russell (2013). "The Free Rider Problem", in: Zalta, Edward N. (Ed.), *The Stanford Encyclopedia of Philosophy* (Spring); at: https://plato.stanford.edu/archives/spr2013/entries/free-rider/ (22 August 2017).

Hart, J. (1955). "Are there any natural rights?", in: *The Philosophical Review*, 64,2 (April): 175–191.

Hursthouse, Rosalind; Pettigrove, Glen (2016). "Virtue Ethics", in: Zalta, Edward N. (Ed.), *The Stanford Encyclopedia of Philosophy* (Winter); at: https://plato.stanford.edu/archives/win2016/entries/ethics-virtue/ (22 August 2017).

INEGI (2017). *Encuesta Nacional de Calidad e Impacto Gubernamental*; at: https://www.inegi.org.mx/contenidos/programas/encig/2017/doc/encig2017_principales_resultados.pdf (31 August 2018).

INEGI (2018b). *Encuesta Nacional de Empleo y Ocupación*); at: https://www.inegi.org.mx/contenidos/saladeprensa/boletines/2018/enoe_ie/enoe_ie2018_08.pdf (31 August 2018).

Instituto Electoral del Distrito Federal (IEDF) (2017). *Estadística de Participación de la Consulta Ciudadana sobre Presupuesto Participativo 2016*; at: http://portal.iedf.org.mx/biblioteca/estudioselect/estadistica_participacion_ccpp_2016.pdf (31 August 2018).

Instituto Nacional de Estadística y Geografía (INEGI) (2018a). Press release: *Encuesta Nacional de Victimización y Percepción sobre Seguridad Pública*; at: http://www.beta.inegi.org.mx/contenidos/saladeprensa/boletines/2018/EstSegPub/envipe2018_09.pdf (25 September 2018).

Instituto Nacional Electoral (INE) (2016). *Estrategia Nacional de Cultura Cívica 2017–2023*; at: https://portalanterior.ine.mx/archivos2/portal/historico/contenido/recursos/IFE-v2/DECEYEC/DECEYEC-Varios/2016/ENCCIVICA-Resumen-Ejecutivo.pdf (31 August 2018).

Instituto Nacional Electoral and El Colegio de México (INE-COLMEX) (2015). *Informe país sobre la calidad de ciudadanía en México*; at: https://portalanterior.ine.mx/archivos2/s/DECEYEC/EducacionCivica/Resumen_Ejecutivo_23nov.pdf (31 August 2018).

Instituto Nacional para la Evaluación Educativa (INEE) (2018). *Estudio Internacional de Educación Cívica y Ciudadana, CIVICA 2016*; at: https://www.inee.edu.mx/index.php/evaluaciones-internacionales/civica-2016 (31 August 2018).

International Transparency (2017). *Corruption Perception Index 2017*; at: https://www.transparency.org/news/feature/corruption_perceptions_index_2017 (31 August 2017).

Isensee, Josef (2011). "Libertad ciudadana y virtud ciudadana. La necesidad vital de la comunidad liberal", in: Abreu Sacramento, Jose Pablo; Le Clercq, Juan Antonio (Eds.), *La reforma humanista* (Mexico City: M.A. Porrúa): 51–64.

Klosko, Georges (2004). *The Principle of Fairness and Political Obligation* (Lanham and Oxford: Rowman & Littlefield Publishers).

Klurfeld, James; Schneider, Howard (2014). *News Literacy: Teaching the Internet Generation to Make Reliable Information Choices*; at: https://www.brookings.edu/wp-content/uploads/2016/06/KlurfeldSchneiderNews-Literacyupdated-7814.pdf (25 September 2018).

Lamarche, Gara (2014). "Is Philanthropy Bad for Democracy?", in: *The Atlantic*; at: https://www.theatlantic.com/politics/archive/2014/10/is-philanthropy-good-for-democracy/381996/ (28 December 2018).

Lasswell, Harold D. (1948). "The Structure and Function of Communication in Society", in: Bryson, Lyman (Ed.), *The Communication of Ideas* (New York: Institute for Religious and Social Studies).

Lowndes, Vivien; Roberts, Mark (2013). *Why Institutions Matter: The New Institutionalism in Political Science* (Basingstoke; New York: Palgrave Macmillan).

Lyons, David (1965). *Forms and Limits of Utilitarianism* (Oxford: Oxford University Press); at: doi: https://doi.org/10.1093/acprof:oso/9780198241973.001.0001 (28 December 2018).

Mackie, J.L. (1965). "Causes and conditions", *American Philosophical Quarterly*, 2,4 (October, 1965): 245–264.
March, James G.; Olsen, Johan P. (1989). *Rediscovering Institutions: The organizational basis of politics* (New York: The Free Press).
Mill, John Stuart (1861). *Considerations on representative government* (Kitchener: Batoche Books/The Gutenberg Project Ebook) (29 December 2018).
Morales, Víctor; Martínez, Jorge (2012). "La educación cívica en México. Una nueva oportunidad", for Association Francophone Internationale de Recherche Scientifique en Education (AFIRSE); at: https://www.researchgate.net/publication/315717238_LA_EDUCACION_CIVICA_EN_MEXICO_UNA_NUEVA_OPORTUNIDAD_LAS_RECIENTES_REFORMAS_CONSTITUCIONALES_ELECTORALES (31 August 2018).
Murillo, Stefana (2017). "Las 9 iniciativas ciudadanas que el Congreso desdeñó", in: *La Silla Rota* (20 December); at: https://lasillarota.com/especialeslsr/las-9-iniciativas-ciudadanas-que-el-congreso-desdeno-congreso-ley-3de3-camara-de-diputados-senado/195414 (31 August 2018).
Nozick, Robert, (1974). *Anarchy, State, and Utopia* (New York: Blackwell Publishing).
Olson, Mancur (1965). *The logic of collective action* (Cambridge, MA; London: Harvard University Press).
Otsuka, Michael (2017). "The principle of fairness (PF), public goods and political obligation", *Philosophy, Moral and Politics*; lecture slides week 17, London School of Economics and Political Science, London.
Putnam, Robert D. (1993). *Making Democracy Work* (Princeton: Princeton University Press).
Putnam, Robert D. (2000). *Bowling Alone* (New York: Simon & Schuster).
Rawls, John, (1999). *A Theory of Justice*, revised edn. (Cambridge, MA: Harvard University Press).
Reich, Rob (2016). "On the Role of Foundations in Democracies", in: Reich, Rob; Cordelli, Chiara; Bernholz, Lucy (Eds.), *Philanthropy in Democratic Societies* (Chicago: The University of Chicago Press): 64–85.
RESIDEntial Environment Study (RESIDE), The University of Western Australia; at: http://www.science.uwa.edu.au/__data/assets/pdf_file/0009/2805543/CBEH_Reside_Brochure_.pdf (28 December 2018).
Sadowski, Christine M. (1994). "Autonomous Groups as Agents of Democratic Change in Communist and Post-Communist Eastern Europe", in: *Political Culture & Democracy in Developing Countries* (Boulder, CO: Lynne Rienner Publishers).
Sandel, Michael (1981). *Liberalism and the Limits of Justice* (Cambridge: Cambridge University Press).
Scanlon, T.M. (1982). "Contractualism and Utilitarianism", in *Utilitarianism and Beyond* (Cambridge: Cambridge University Press).
Solís, Patricio (2017). *Discriminación structural y desigualdad social* (Mexico City: CONAPRED; at: https://www.conapred.org.mx/documentos_cedoc/Discriminacionestructural%20accs.pdf (31 August 2017).
The Society for Community Research and Action (SCRA), Community Psychology, Division 27 of the American Psychological Association, at: http://www.scra27.org/resources/document-library/ (28 December 2018).
Wall, Steven (2012). "Perfectionism in Moral and Political Philosophy", in: Zalta, Edward N. (Ed.), *The Stanford Encyclopedia of Philosophy* (Winter 2012); at: https://plato.stanford.edu/archives/win2012/entries/perfectionism-moral/ (22 August 2017).
World Value Survey Association (2018). World Value Survey Wave 6, 2010–2014, Official Aggregate v.20150418 (Madrid: Asep/JDS); at: http://www.worldvaluessurvey.org/wvs.jsp (31 August 2018).

Chapter 10
The Challenge of Developing a New Human Rights Culture in Future Mexican Lawyers

Eduardo Román González

Abstract The 2011 constitutional amendment on human rights had a profound impact on the Mexican legal system. This impact needs to be reflected in the legal education that future lawyers receive. This paper analyzes the main challenges posed by the reform for Mexican law schools to provide a new generation of lawyers with a greater culture of human rights awareness, who are more sensitive and better prepared, both in knowledge and skills, to advocate human rights cases.

Keywords Culture · Human rights · Challenges · Legal education · Lawyers · Mexico · Constitutional amendment · Law schools · Teaching · Rule of law

10.1 Introduction

In 2014 the First Chamber of the Mexican Supreme Court ratified the *amparo en revision* 4102/2013 – two years after the constitutional amendment of human rights of 2011, in which the incompatibility of national law with the Universal Declaration of Human Rights was alleged. The First Chamber ruled that the provisions of the Declaration "invoked in isolation, cannot serve as a parameter to determine the validity of Mexican legal norms, as it does not constitute an international treaty signed by the Federal Executive and approved by the Senate." (SCJN, T.A. 1a. CCXVI/2014 (10a.)).

Doctor in Law, Government and Public Policy from Universidad Autónoma de Madrid, Spain; Coordinator of Research at CEEAD, a Mexican independent research center focused on legal education; Professor of Constitutional Law, Human Rights and Public International Law at Facultad Libre de Derecho de Monterrey and Tecnológico de Monterrey, Monterrey Campus; Member of the Mexican National System of Researchers (*Sistema Nacional de Investigadores*, SNI) E-mail: eduardo.roman@outlook.com.

That same year, a Federal Circuit Court ruled that the test of compatibility between a national law and a human rights treaty – the so called, *conventionality review* – "is carried out in substitution of the deficiency of the internal regulations". That is to say, that the judge must first analyze how the human right in controversy is recognized in the Constitution and Mexican law, and only when he or she concludes that the human right is either not protected at all or is not sufficiently protected is it justifiable to carry out the conventionality review (TCC, T.J. (III Región) 5o. J/8 (10a.)).

More recently, another Federal Circuit Court has held that the principles of universality, interdependence, indivisibility and progressiveness of human rights, established in Article 1 of the Mexican Constitution, are not applicable to personal freedom, since, although it is a fundamental right, it cannot be considered a human right (TCC, T.A. I.10o.P.13 P (10a.)).

The above are just three examples – of the many that we could document – of misconceptions of human rights law after the 2011 constitutional amendment on human rights. This reflects a lack human rights culture between legal operators, such as lawyers and judges, but also a lack of basic notions of human rights that should be acquired in law school, especially after the above-mentioned constitutional amendment.

The challenge of making the content of human rights reform a reality for all Mexicans is huge because it implies, among other things, a cultural change among legal operators. A cultural change that must be promoted by law schools. In this paper, I point out some of the most urgent challenges that Mexican law schools are facing in relation to human rights teaching in order to promote a new human rights culture among future lawyers.

10.2 Legal Education and Human Rights Culture

For several years, legal education in Mexico has been facing two major problems. First, the uncontrolled growth of the number of law schools and the lack of mechanisms that guarantee the quality of the legal education and the optimal preparation that its students are receiving for professional practice. Second, the traditional teaching techniques that are used in Mexican law schools and their effects on the legal profession.

10.2.1 *The Uncontrolled Growth of the Number of Law Schools and Their Quality*

According to the most recent Center for Studies on Teaching and Law Learning (CEEAD) data, in the 2017–2018 academic year there were about 1,822 law schools in Mexico. This number continues to grow, with one new law school every week, which is the rate of growth since 1991 (CEEAD 2017; CEEAD 2018a). Mexican States like Guerrero, Guanajuato and Nayarit have more law schools than Germany, Spain and Canada, respectively (CEEAD 2014).

Although there is no official data about the number of new lawyers per year, some information related to the expedition of licenses to practice law (*cédulas profesionales*)[1] is available. CEEAD (2018b) estimates that in the period between 2010 and 2014, approximately 179,790 new licenses to practice law were expedited. Also, the Mexican Supreme Court (@SCJN, 2017) published through its Twitter account an infographic which indicated that the number of licenses to practice law in ten States was more than 500,000. In contrast, information published by INEGI (2016) indicates that in 2016 the number of people employed as lawyers was approximately 342,000. The disparity between these figures can be explained by the well-known fact that many people who study law do not practice it professionally.

The above data makes it possible to estimate the number of people dedicated to the legal profession. In a country like Mexico, with high levels of corruption, a low degree of rule of law, and with multiple human rights violations, it may not seem a bad idea to have many lawyers. If we also consider, as demonstrated by Pérez Hurtado (2009: 103), that a high percentage of future lawyers enter law school with the desire to help other people and make a change, it could be thought that the large number of lawyers who are authorized each year to practice law will contribute significantly to solving some of the country's major problems.

Unfortunately, the high number of law schools and lawyers has not led to a greater strengthening of the rule of law, or to an improvement in the human rights situation. This is a clear indicator that something is not working in legal education and the access to the legal profession. Therefore the problem, as pointed out by Garza (2017), is not whether the number of lawyers we have is too many or too little, but whether legal education and the mechanism for access to the practice of law guarantees the quality of the legal profession. We believe it does not, since the requirements to open a law school are relatively easy to fulfill and the procedure itself does not guarantee the quality of the content of the program or the quality of professors. Another problem is the absence of any mechanism to guarantee that new lawyers have the necessary knowledge and abilities to practice law.

The high number of law schools which were opened with very few requirements, and of lawyers authorized to practice law without any additional requirement beyond the university title, have magnified deep-rooted problems within legal education, such as the use of traditional methods of teaching law.

---

[1]In Mexico, the only requirement for practicing law is an undergraduate law degree from an authorized institution. Once the person has the university qualification, he or she can obtain a license to practice as a lawyer (*cédula professional*) through a simple administrative procedure at the Federal Department of Education.

10.2.2 Teaching Law and Human Rights in Mexico

In most Mexican law schools, the kind of teaching methods used respond to the idea of the teacher as the exclusive owner of knowledge, whose function is to transfer it unidirectionally to the students. The education of future lawyers usually encourages the memorization of content, but not the development of analytical skills to understand how to face and solve legal problems (Magaloni 2006: 64–65).

The typical legal education that law schools offer in Mexico is, in general, disconnected from the legal and social problems that the lawyer will face in practice. This is because, as Magaloni (2003) points out, legal education is focused mainly on the theoretical and conceptual study of norms, and teaching methods emphasize memory over the development of any other skills in the students. In this educational system, "the law student dedicates most of his education to knowing the set of rules that make up the system, to deciphering its possible meaning in the abstract and to organizing the normative material in a coherent, complete, logical and without contradictions system" (Magaloni 2003: 3).

This way of teaching law is inadequate for the teaching of human rights and for the purpose of generating a culture of human rights in Mexican lawyers because, as García and Vaño (2015: 13) point out, human rights cannot be learned; they must be apprehended. Here reiteration, literality, even memory do not work, if what is desired is that students have their own critical capacity and are able to autonomously investigate the context and background of each problem, confront debates and support opinions, exchange opinions, know the main mechanisms and causes of complaint and act to safeguard them beyond official rhetoric.

Indeed, if the purpose is to educate lawyers with a greater human rights culture and knowledge, it is necessary to be sensitive to the problems of serious and systematic violations of human rights that our country is facing. And this can only be achieved if the teaching of human rights is done in a contextual way, analyzing the application of the human rights law to concrete cases and, above all, making the future lawyer see the usefulness of human rights law in preventing or remedying injustices. The abstract study of human rights law sensitizes very little, and does not allow students to notice the real extension of a right that is reflected in concrete cases (Asúnsolo et al. 2016). In this sense, Escamilla/De la Rosa López (2009) have argued that human rights are experienced as a human condition of citizens, both in the public sphere and in the private sphere, and therefore "cannot be taught as transmission of contents to be memorized decontextualized from those living conditions" (Escamilla/De la Rosa López 2009: 59).

In general, there are many historical deficiencies in Mexican legal education, and, in particular, in the teaching of human rights. The result of this is that Mexican law students do not receive pertinent education in human rights law, and, much more important, they do not develop a human rights culture at law school.

The implications of the 2011 constitutional amendment on human rights urges us to transform the teaching of human rights in Mexican law schools. Next, I will refer to some key aspects of the reform that, from my perspective, have the greatest impact on the teaching of human rights.

10.3 The 2011 Constitutional Amendment on Human Rights

The 2011 constitutional amendment on human rights establishes a new paradigm for the Mexican legal system and this should impact on legal education, especially in the teaching of human rights. The amendment introduces in the Constitution some principles and contents that change the way of interpreting and applying the law. In the following lines I'll explain some of the most important.

10.3.1 The New Supremacy Clause

The 2011 constitutional amendment changes the Mexican supremacy clause of the Constitution. On the one hand, Article 1, first paragraph, states that people who are in Mexican territory are entitled to enjoy the human rights recognized by the Constitution and the international treaties signed by Mexico. On the other hand, the second paragraph of the same Article establishes that the norms related to human rights must be interpreted in accordance with what the Constitution and the international treaties on human rights say, though it also asserts that the most favorable interpretation of the law for the guarantee of human rights should apply (the so called, *principio pro persona*).

That is to say that the new supremacy clause includes at the top level of the hierarchy of norms not only the Constitution but also the human rights norms of treaties signed by Mexico.[2] Therefore, it raises the need to reinterpret the hierarchy of norms in Mexico. Before the constitutional amendment the only relevant article for the interpretation of the supremacy clause was Article 133, but after the amendment this clause should be interpreted in conjunction with Article 1, since this article gives the human rights norms of treaties the status of constitutional norms.

It seems that there is a consensus in legal scholarship and judicial doctrine in the sense that human rights norms from international treaties are part of the supremacy clause. However, there is disagreement on the understanding of the way that norms belonging to the supremacy clause interact with each other. We have two possible

---

[2]It should be noted that the new text of Article 1 of the Mexican Constitution refers to human rights norms in international treaties and not to international human rights treaties, thus contemplating not only treaties whose main object are human rights, but also the human rights norms that should be found in international treaties of a different nature (Carmona 2011: 45).

interpretations: that all the norms of the supremacy clause have the same hierarchical level; or that the same hierarchy does not exist between those norms.

The first option implies that any hierarchical relationship between the Mexican Constitution and the human rights norms from international treaties has been erased. For some, like Arenas (2013), the supremacy clause includes any human rights norm regardless of its source – such as, for example, human rights recognized by the Constitutions of some Mexican States. From this perspective, any incompatibility between the norms that form part of the supremacy clause must be resolved according to the *pro persona* principle (applying the most favorable norm), because the hierarchies between them have disappeared.

The second option considers that the norms of the supremacy clause do not have the same hierarchy, because the Constitution maintains a superior status in relation to any other norm. From this perspective, any incompatibility between the Constitution and any other norm of the supremacy clause must be resolved according to the principle of constitutional supremacy. The Mexican Supreme Court has taken a position in favor of this last interpretation of the supremacy clause when resolving the contradiction of thesis 293/2010 (SCJN, P./J. 20/2014 (10a.)).

What I am interested in highlighting here is how the changes introduced by the 2011 constitutional amendment to Article 1 modify the hierarchical order of the legal system to place the human rights norms recognized in international treaties above any other legal provision, even international treaty norms relative to other disciplines. Since the amendment, human rights, both those recognized in the Constitution and international treaties, have been introduced to the supremacy clause, functioning as a parameter for the validity of any other norm of the legal system. This conditions the way that the legal system should be interpreted and applied, making it necessary for existing and future lawyers to develop a better knowledge of human rights law above all, a deeper culture of human rights.

10.3.2 Constitutional and Conventional Review

The constitutional amendment on human rights and the ruling of the Inter-American Court of Human Rights (IACHR) in the *Radilla* case[3] – in which the IACHR ordered that all the Mexican judges should analyze the compatibility of the laws they apply with the American Convention of Human Rights (ACHR) – forced the Mexican Supreme Court to overrule its own doctrine of judicial review.

For several years, the Mexican Supreme Court established that only federal judges could exercise constitutional review. After the constitutional amendment and the *Radilla* case, the Mexican Supreme Court changed its doctrine to establish that

---

[3]IACHR, *Radilla Pacheco vs. Mexico* (23 November 2009).

all judges – including state courts judges – should exercise a constitutional and conventionality review in every case.[4]

For the Mexican Supreme Court, the implementation of the conventionality review was inconsistent with the constitutional review model concentrated only in federal judges. In its own words, "the *ex officio* conventionality review on human rights should be in accordance with the general model of constitutional review", so it was necessary to recognize the existence of a new model of judicial review that combines the concentrated and the diffuse review.

In its new doctrine, the Court established that exercise of the double review (constitutional and conventional) should follow these three steps:

First, judges must interpret the law in accordance with the human rights recognized in the Constitution and international treaties signed by Mexico. Second, when there are several reasonable interpretations of the law, judges must prefer the most favorable interpretation for the protection of human rights. Third, if none of the reasonable interpretations of the law are compatible with the human rights norms (constitutional or conventional), judges must not apply the law to that case (SCJN, P. LXIX/2011(9a.)).

Besides the methodology for exercise constitutional and conventional review, the Supreme Court also defined the group of norms that must serve as a parameter for that review. According to the Court, this group is integrated by the Constitution, the constitutional interpretation given by the federal judges, the human rights recognized in international treaties and its interpretation given by the official interpreters of those treaties (international courts, commissions, committees, etc.) (SCJN, P. LXVIII/2011 (9a.) y P./J. 20/2014 (10a.)).

10.3.3 Pro Persona *Principle*

The *pro persona* principle is an interpretive tool by which one must select the most favorable norm, or, to use its most extensive interpretation, for the broadest protection of human rights. Also, this principle implies the selection of the more restricted norm or interpretation when it concerns restrictions on the exercise of human rights (Pinto 1997: 163).

This principle has several possibilities of application. The first one, says Henderson (2004), refers to the application of the most protective norm. This occurs when, in a specific case, it is possible to apply two or more current norms, national or international, and, whatever their hierarchy, the judge must select the one that contains a better or more favorable protection of human rights (Henderson 2004: 93).

On the other hand, Castilla (2009) points out that, in this case, the *pro persona* principle allows the use of the most protective or least restrictive norm, depending

---

[4]See: SCJN, Expediente Varios 912/2010 (14 June 2011).

on the case, regardless of their hierarchy. According to the same author, this principle makes it possible to overcome classic arguments about whether the national or international norms should prevail (Castilla 2009: 72).

The *pro persona* principle can also refer to the application of the most favorable interpretation. This is a case of different application, since it does not refer to the dichotomy of applying one norm or another, but different interpretations of the same norm. There are cases in which a judge "is faced with a human rights norm where there could be several possible interpretations, that is, when there is doubt about a plurality of possible interpretations of the norm" (Henderson 2004: 96). In these cases, the *pro persona* principle operates as a method of interpretive preference that implies "giving a norm that contains human rights its broadest interpretation...or, the minimum possible interpretative scope if it is to limit or suspend its exercise" (Castilla 2009: 76).

Finally, in what would be its most controversial dimension, the *pro persona* principle can be used for the conservation of the most favorable norm. For some authors, the *pro persona* principle can also be applied in cases of substitution of norms, as an interpretive mechanism to preserve the one that is most favorable for the protection of human rights, regardless of whether it is the norm that it is intended to replace. In these cases, by applying the *pro persona* principle to a substitution of norms, "a later norm would not repeal or disprove another previous norm, regardless of its hierarchy, while the former establishes better or greater protections that must be conserved for people" (Henderson 2004: 94). What is sought with this criterion is the prevalence of human rights, "above rules of hierarchy and temporality, in order to achieve the preservation of the most favorable norms for the exercise of human rights" (Castilla 2009: 75).

The ICHR recognized this principle in its first decision on a contentious case.[5] In another decision, the Court ratified the application of the *pro persona* principle based on Article 29 of the ACHR, in the sense that "if the American Convention and another international treaty apply to the same situation, the most favorable norm should prevail to the human person". Therefore, if the ACHR itself establishes that its interpretation cannot imply the restriction of human rights recognized more broadly in other treaties, it is not acceptable that the interpretation of other treaties establishes restrictions for the human rights recognized by the ACHR.[6]

All the above changes require Mexican lawyers to acquire knowledge and develop argumentative skills that are not typically taught in Mexican law schools.

On the one hand, the scope of protection of human rights is significantly expanded by incorporating international human rights law at constitutional level. Now, the Mexican lawyer requires greater knowledge of international human rights law, as well as interpretative and argumentative skills for the correct application of it.

---

[5]IACHR, *Viviana Gallardo et al. Costa Rica* (3 November 1985), paragraph 16.
[6]IACHR, *Opinión Consultiva 5/85* (13 November 1985), paragraph 52.

On the other hand, human rights norms operate as parameters of validity in any other law (criminal, civil, family, etc.). This is also an enormous challenge for the Mexican lawyer, since human rights have a transverse effect throughout the legal system.

The implications of the human rights constitutional amendment analyzed in this section represent a huge challenge for law schools. Legal education and, particularly, the teaching of human rights in law schools are key aspects of the success of the amendment. If law schools do not change the way they teach human rights, it will be impossible to achieve all the benefits that the amendment could have.

10.4 The Challenges of Human Rights Teaching

It is clear from the preceding discussion that there are great challenges for legal education in general and human rights education in particular. These are challenges that we have faced for many years but, particularly since the 2011 human rights constitutional amendment, they have become more acute. Next, I will refer to those that I find the most important in terms of the characteristics of legal education and human rights education in Mexico, and the main changes introduced by the constitutional amendment.

10.4.1 From Theoretical to Practical Teaching of Human Rights

One of the main problems of legal education in Mexico, as already mentioned, is the predominantly theoretical teaching, focused more on the study of the content of the law than on its application to specific cases. The teaching of human rights has not been exempted from this, and this is probably one of the main reasons why Mexican lawyers are less sensitive to the identification of human rights violations and not very empathetic with the defense of these cases. But it has also fostered a significant technical deficiency in the interpretation and application of human rights standards to specific problems.

Is not my intention to argue that the teaching of human rights cannot involve some predominantly theoretical issues. For example, a recent book (Román et al. 2017) suggests that, as part of the human rights course, contents such as history, foundations, legal theory and critical perspectives of human rights must be addressed. Nonetheless, it is important to specify that we propose its approach based on activities that foster in students awareness of a critical analysis of predominantly theoretical contents.

Of course, it is essential that students know the content of both constitutional and conventional norms where human rights are recognized. However, this knowledge is only part of what is necessary for a lawyer to know about human rights. Another fundamental part is the one that has to do with the different mechanisms and procedures that serve to process cases of human rights violations, as well as the way in which the authorities in charge of resolving these procedures are interpreting the content of constitutional and conventional norms.

This, of necessity, implies the use of jurisprudence and legal standards related to human rights, which results in a more practical than dogmatic approach to the study of rights. It involves analyzing human rights not as static normative figures, but as rules in action that, when applied to specific cases, display all their dimensions – something which cannot be seen from abstract analysis of them in legal texts. Thus, for example, the different dimensions and scope of freedom of speech can only be appreciated when analyzing a specific case concerning the exercise or violation of this freedom; it is insufficient to merely analyze the way it is recognized in constitutional or international norms.

To introduce students to a practical approach to human rights, the lecture class, which has been the traditional way of teaching law in Mexico, is insufficient. Even when a lecture deals with the analysis of human rights in light of specific cases, it does not allow students to develop critical analytical tools on their own for the interpretation and application of human rights norms in specific cases.

Alternative pedagogical tools – such as the case method and, even better, problem-based or challenge-based learning – are more effective ways to address the content of human rights norms and the functioning of protection systems. These allow students to not only appreciate the normative deployment of human rights in specific cases, but also to develop a certain interpretation about the scope of these human rights and the way they should be applied in specific cases.

This contributes to greater awareness among future human rights lawyers, since it allows them to detect in real situations the possible violation of human rights as recognized by the legal system, as well as to appreciate the legal system's practical utility for facing and solving social injustices. But it also contributes to better technical training of the lawyer in terms of his ability to interpret and apply human rights standards to specific situations.

Therefore, one of the main challenges in the human rights education of future lawyers is to overcome the predominantly theoretical and dogmatic approach to human rights, and instead implement a more realistic and significative way to teach human rights, developing more sensitive lawyers who are better equipped to identify human rights violations and technically better prepared to defend them in real cases.

10.4.2 The Use of Different Sources of Human Rights

One of the great challenges faced by both teachers and students of human rights, especially since the 2011 constitutional amendment, is to properly handle two different sources of human rights: constitutional and international human rights law. Each uses interpretive rules and principles that do not always coincide.

This is because human rights are recognized both in national (mainly in the Constitution) and in international (mainly in treaties) norms. Despite our lack of constitutional culture and our little experience in the management of a normative Constitution, it seems to me that it is not the constitutional norms that represent the main problems for Mexican teachers and students, but the still lower degree of knowledge that we have regarding Public International Law in general and International Human Rights Law in particular.

Thus, in the Mexican legal community, including academia, we are not as familiar with the diverse sources of Public International Law or the principles of interpretation of one of these sources: international treaties. Therefore, for example, it is difficult for us to differentiate between an international custom and a rule of *ius cogens*, between a declaration and an international treaty, between binding jurisprudence and international *soft law* in the field of human rights. The legal categories of Mexican law do not coincide with those of international law and this causes difficulties in both understanding and applying international standards.

An example of this is found in the methods of interpretation. In Mexico, traditionally, the main method of interpretation of the law has been to resort to the will of the legislator (González 2001: 244), a method that is not the main one for the interpretation of treaties according to the Vienna Convention of the Law of Treaties, where it has a subsidiary nature. In fact, in accordance with this Convention, the preparatory work for the treaties – which would be the most similar to the legislative debate where the will of the legislator is embodied – is something which, for the purposes of interpreting the treaty, must be used only when all the other rules of interpretation have been exhausted and the meaning remains ambiguous, obscure, absurd or unreasonable.[7] In other words, one of the most relevant methods of interpretation for a national law is only a complementary method for international law.

Another example of the different treatment given to the same source in the national and international legal system is custom. At national level, custom is usually of limited relevance: it is valid only in certain matters and to the extent and with the conditions defined by law. In international law, by contrast, it is an autonomous source from which general obligations can be derived for the entire international community, and therefore has the potential to be a more widespread legal force than treaties that only bind the parties.

From my perspective, neither law schools nor legal operators in general have given this diversity of sources and interpretative methods the importance they deserve. The consequence is several cases of sources of international law being used incorrectly at national level, such as claiming in *amparo* an autonomous violation of the Universal Declaration of Human Rights, as in the example referred to at the beginning of this work.

---

[7]See: Articles 31 and 32 of the Vienna Convention of the Lawlaw of Treaties.

In this sense, any human rights course taught in Mexican law schools should take into account these differences and make them apparent to future lawyers, so they can familiarize themselves with them and understand how to use both national and international sources properly.

10.4.3 The False Dichotomy between Constitutional and International Human Rights Law

Another problem facing human rights teaching in Mexican law schools is the apparent dichotomy between Constitutional and International Human Rights Law. This usually takes shape in various law degree programs that divide the teaching of human rights by, on the one hand, establishing a course, usually mandatory, that focuses on the human rights recognized by the Constitution and, on the other hand, another course, usually optional, that focuses on international human rights law.

The new content of Article 1 of the Constitution, especially with the integration of international human rights norms at constitutional level, and with the mandate to interpret constitutional and international human rights norms harmonically, establishes the need to address the teaching of human rights simultaneously. Human Rights courses whose approach is only constitutional or only international are no longer meaningful or useful to future lawyers. Each right must be addressed at all times in its double dimension (constitutional and international) because otherwise it can easily fall into the error of interpreting rights incompletely by failing to consider more advanced standards developed at constitutional or international level. The relationship between constitutional and international human rights law is not one of substitution – as judges seem to think in some of the cases referred to in the introduction of this paper – where the international dimension of human rights acquires relevance and meaning only when the national is insufficient or unsatisfactory, but of reciprocal complementarity and this must be fully reflected in the curricula of all law degrees.

From a practical perspective, it is also necessary to teach constitutional and international human rights law simultaneously, since most of the legal problems related to human rights that future lawyers will face will suppose the simultaneous application of constitutional and international norms. For example, the arbitrary detention carried out by a police officer supposes a violation of the arrested person's human rights that are recognized in both constitutional and international norms, and in respect of which both constitutional and international courts and organizations have developed standards that define its scope. With this reality faced by lawyers, it is little use for students to analyze in one course the human rights recognized in the Constitution and in another, if they decide to take it, the human rights recognized in international law. It is as though a doctor were taught, separately, to cure a broken arm and skin lesions, but never to attend an open fracture.

It is necessary, then, that law schools unify in one or several courses the simultaneous teaching of human rights with both a constitutional and an international approach. The only division that still makes sense regarding human rights education is that related to the teaching of national and international protection systems – a division that, in any case, should not lose sight of the generally subsidiary and complementary character of international systems. It should also not be forgotten that, ideally, national systems should be sufficient to effectively remedy any violation of human rights. This is why law schools should encourage future lawyers to acquire the proper knowledge and professional skills to operate both types of systems.

10.4.4 Encapsulation of Human Rights in the Law Degree Program

It has been mentioned above that the teaching of human rights in the training of future lawyers is encapsulated in one or a few courses. This represents a problem in a double sense.

In the first place, it is illusory to pretend that the teaching of human rights fits into one or a few courses. One of the evolutionary lines of human rights is its specification, which means the recognition of new human rights in contexts and with respect to more specific groups.[8] The constant signing of new international treaties, as well as the multiplication of protection systems, implies a greater number of international organizations that interpret these treaties, thereby generating new standards. The continuous expansion of human rights law makes it materially impossible for one or a few courses to be sufficient for future lawyers to enter this universe.

In the second place, human rights are present in virtually all areas of social life, therefore it is very likely that some of them are present in the vast majority of legal problems faced by lawyers. Of course, there are some areas of law, such as criminal or family law, where the incidence of human rights is greater, but we can also see their presence in almost any area of the law. Consequently, training in human rights cannot be limited to one or a few subjects, but must be transversal throughout the curriculum of the law degree. This means that law schools must review their curriculum not only to incorporate more human rights subjects, but also to identify in each of the subjects of the curriculum the human rights content that needs to be incorporated in every course.

---

[8]About this tendency, see: Peces-Barba Martínez (1999: 180–197) and Román et al. (2017: 29–31).

10.5 Conclusion

The 2011 constitutional amendment of human rights had a profound impact on the Mexican legal system because it imposed a new way of interpreting and applying legal norms under the paradigm of human rights. This necessitates a thorough transformation in the way law is taught in Mexico. It is necessary for law schools to contribute to the development of a human rights culture in future lawyers, providing law students with the knowledge and an appropriate environment to develop the professional skills needed for a better approach to human rights cases.

If the teaching of human rights in Mexican law schools does not change, the 2011 constitutional amendment is destined to fail or, at least, to limit its transforming potential or dilute it for many years. A country like Mexico, with a serious problem of systematic violations of human rights, cannot afford to waste any tool that could serve to reverse this lacerating reality, especially an educational one which has the power to eradicate some of the main causes of that problem. As we are beginning to appreciate with the criminal justice system constitutional amendment of 2008, changes implemented in the legal education of future lawyers make a significant contribution to the change in paradigms and the consolidation of a new culture in the practice of law.

This chapter identifies some of the main problems and challenges facing human rights education, especially since the 2011 constitutional amendment. It does not intend to be a comprehensive list but only illustrative of those that seem to me to be the greatest priority to address. In any case, all have the common denominator of shaping law schools as key actors for the implementation of the reform and, beyond that, they show that among the many measures that must be implemented to end the serious crisis of human rights facing the country, is the urgent transformation of human rights education and culture that future lawyers receive. It is time for law schools to assume their responsibility and reinforce their commitment in the formation of more sensitive, committed and technically capable lawyers who defend human rights more effectively. Until this happens, an essential part of the formula for the success of the constitutional amendment will be absent, and we will be waiting, in vain, for a change in the country's human rights situation that will otherwise never come.

References

Asúnsolo Morales, C.R.; Román González, E.; Martínez González, C. (2016). "La transformación de la enseñanza de los derechos humanos. Algunas conclusiones a partir del diagnóstico del CEEAD sobre la enseñanza de los derechos humanos en Nuevo León", Paper presented at *Primer Congreso Internacional en Metodología de la Investigación y Enseñanza del Derecho*, Instituto de Investigaciones Jurídicas de la UNAM, Mexico.

Carmona Tinoco, J.U. (2011). "La reforma y las normas de derechos humanos previstas en los tratados internacionales", in: Carbonell, M. and Salazar, P. (Coords.), *La reforma constitucional de derechos humanos: un nuevo paradigma* (Mexico: Instituto de Investigaciones Jurídicas de la UNAM): 39–62.

Castilla, K. (2009). "El principio *pro persona* en la administración de justicia", in: *Cuestiones Constitucionales. Revista Mexicana de Derecho Constitucional*, 20 (January-June): 65–83.

Centro de Estudios sobre la Enseñanza y Aprendizaje del Derecho, A.C. (CEEAD), (2018a). *Las escuelas de Derecho en México. Ciclo Académico 2017–2018*, at: http://www.ceead.org.mx/infografia_ies.html.

Centro de Estudios sobre la Enseñanza y Aprendizaje del Derecho, A.C. (CEEAD), (2018b). *Cédulas profesionales expedidas a egresados de la licenciatura en Derecho en sus distintas denominaciones, 1945–2016*, at: http://www.ceead.org.mx/infografia_ies.html.

Centro de Estudios sobre la Enseñanza y Aprendizaje del Derecho, A.C. (CEEAD), (2017). *Las escuelas de Derecho en México. Ciclo Académico 2016–2017,* at: http://www.ceead.org.mx/infografia_ies.html.

Centro de Estudios sobre la Enseñanza y Aprendizaje del Derecho, A.C. (CEEAD), (2014). *Las escuelas de Derecho en México. Ciclo Académico 2013–2014,* at: http://www.ceead.org.mx/ej-recursos-adicionales.html.

Escamilla Salazar, J.; De la Rosa López, O. (2009). "La praxis del pedagogo en la articulación entre DDHH y educación", in: Escamilla Salazar, J. (Ed.), *Los derechos humanos y la educación. Una mirada pedagógica en el contexto de la globalización* (Mexico: Miguel Ángel Porrúa): 55–66.

García Sáez, J.A.; Vaño Vicedo, R. (2015). "Presentación", in: García Saez, J.A.; Vaño Vicedo, R. (Eds.), *Educar la mirada. Documentales para una enseñanza crítica de los derechos humanos* (Valencia: Tirant lo Blanch).

Garza Onofre, J.J. (2017). "¿En México cuáles son los Estados con más abogados y con más escuelas de derecho? A propósito del mes patrio y los datos del CEEAD y de la SCJN" [Blog, 17 September]; at: https://entreabogadosteveas.wordpress.com/2017/09/.

González Oropeza, M. (2001). "La interpretación jurídica en México", in: Vázquez, R. (Ed.), *Interpretación jurídica y decisión judicial*, 2nd edn. (Mexico City: Fontamara): 237–254.

Henderson, H. (2004). "Los tratados internacionales de derechos humanos en el orden interno: la importancia del principio pro homine", in: *Revista del Instituto Interamericano de Derechos Humanos*, 39 (January–June): 71–99.

Instituto Nacional de Estadística y Geografía (INEGI), (2016). *Estadísticas a propósito del… día del abogado (12 July)*; at: http://www.miguelcarbonell.com/artman/uploads/1/jbr_Abogados.pdf.

Magaloni Kerpel, A.L. (2003). *Los Grandes Desafíos de la Educación Legal en México: El Programa de Derecho del CIDE*, USMEX 2003–04 Working Paper Series; at: http://escholarship.org/uc/item/7897f3wt.

Peces-Barba Martínez, G. (1999). *Curso de derechos fundamentales. Teoría General* (Madrid: Universidad Carlos III-Boletín Oficial del Estado).

Pérez Hurtado, L.F. (2009). *La futura generación de abogados mexicanos. Estudio de las escuelas y los estudiantes de Derecho en México* (Mexico: Instituto de Investigaciones Jurídicas de la UNAM-CEEAD).

Pinto, M. (1997). "El principio pro homine. Criterios de hermenéutica y pautas para la regulación de los derechos humanos", in: Abregú, Mario; Courtis, Christian (Eds.), *La aplicación de los tratados internacionales de derechos humanos por los tribunales locales* (Buenos Aires: Editores del Puerto): 163–171.

Román González, E.; Asúnsolo Morales, C.R.; Martínez González, C. (2017). *Manual docente del curso Derechos Humanos* (Monterrey: CEEAD); at: www.ceead.org.mx/manuales.html.

SCJN (2017). "Conoce cuáles son los estados con el mayor número de #abogados" [Twitter, 7 September]; at: https://twitter.com/SCJN/status/905930849346039808.

Case Law

Inter-American Court of Human Rights (IACHR). *Radilla Pacheco vs. México*. Preliminary Objection, Merits, Reparations and Costs. 23 November 2009. Series C, No. 209.
IACHR. *Opinión Consultiva 5/85*. 13 November 1985. Series A, No. 5.
IACHR. *Viviana Gallardo y otras*. 3 November 1985. Series A, No. 101.
Suprema Corte de Justicia de la Nación (SCJN). T.A. 1a. CCXVI/2014 (10a.). Declaración Universal De Los Derechos Humanos. Sus Disposiciones, Invocadas Aisladamente, No Pueden Servir De Parámetro Para Determinar La Validez De Las Normas Del Orden Jurídico Mexicano, Al No Constituir Un Tratado Internacional Celebrado Por El Ejecutivo Federal Y Aprobado Por El Senado De La República. *Gaceta del Semanario Judicial de la Federación*, 10a. Época, Book 6 (May 2014), Vol. I: 539. Registration No. 2006533.
SCJN. P./J. 20/2014 (10a.). Derechos Humanos Contenidos En La Constitución Y En Los Tratados Internacionales. Constituyen El Parámetro De Control De Regularidad Constitucional, Pero Cuando En La Constitución Haya Una Restricción Expresa Al Ejercicio De Aquéllos, Se Debe Estar A Lo Que Establece El Texto Constitucional. *Gaceta del Semanario Judicial de la Federación*, 10a. Época, Book 5 (April 2014), Vol. I: 202. Registration No. 2006224.
SCJN. P. LXVIII/2011 (9a.). Parámetro Para El Control De Convencionalidad Ex Officio En Materia De Derechos Humanos. *Gaceta del Semanario Judicial de la Federación*, 9a. Época, Book III (December 2011), Vol. 1: 551. Registration No. 160526. http://www.scielo.org.mx/scielo.php?script=sci_arttext&pid=S2448-64422018000100099.
SCJN. Expediente Varios 912/2010, 14 June 2011.
Tribunales Colegiados de Circuito (TCC). T.J. (III Región) 50. J/8 (10a.). Control Difuso De Convencionalidad Ex Officio. Su Aplicación Es De Naturaleza Subsidiaria O Complementaria Del Sistema Jurídico Mexicano. *Gaceta del Semanario Judicial de la Federación*, 10a. Época, Book 4 (March 2014), Vol. II: 1,360. Registration No. 2005942.
TCC. T.A. I.10o.P.13 P (10a.). Libertad Personal. Atento Al Principio De Supremacía Constitucional, Es Ilegal Aplicar Las Disposiciones Que Regulan El Sistema Procesal Penal Acusatorio A Los Actos Que Deriven De Procesos Iniciados En El Sistema De Justicia Tradicional, Aun Cuando El Gobernado Afirme Que Aquéllas Le Otorgan Una Mayor Protección Para El Ejercicio De Dicho Derecho. *Gaceta del Semanario Judicial de la Federación*, 10a. Época, Book 44 (July 2017), Vol. II: 1,043. Registration No. 2014726.

Part III
Structural Reforms and Their Implementation Challenges

Part III

Chapter 11
How Does Criminal Justice Work in Mexico?

María Novoa and Karen Silva Mora

Abstract Mexico's criminal justice reform aimed to drastically transform the country's criminal justice system, making it more efficient and effective in order to improve the quality of justice and to guarantee the rights of both victims and those accused of crimes. More than ten years after Mexico passed this constitutional reform, the results of the accusatory criminal justice system have come short of achieving these goals. As a result, Mexico currently ranks as one of the countries with the highest levels of impunity not just in Latin America, but worldwide. This has created a deep mistrust in the institutions responsible for providing justice and security. It is clear that the consolidation of Mexico's criminal justice system poses great challenges. Reform efforts must continue if Mexico wants to strengthen its rule of law, which is the foundation for peace and equality.

Keywords amparo · Criminal justice system · Impunity · Public policy · Rule of law

---

María Novoa is Coordinator of the Justice Project in México Evalúa. She has worked in the World Bank, the Inter-American Development Bank, PNUD, the European Union and USAID. She has also been part of different projects for institutional strengthening in El Salvador, Mexico, Paraguay, Guatemala, Venezuela, Honduras, Bolivia, Ukraine and Azerbaijan. She has a Master's degree in Public Policy from the Universidad Simón Bolívar. Email: maria.novoa@mexicoevalua.org.

Karen Silva is a researcher of the Justice Project in México Evalúa. Previously, she coordinated the Drugs Policy Program at the CIDE. She has a Bachelor's degree in Law from the UNAM. Email: karen.silva@mexicoevalua.org.

11.1 Context

Over the last decade, Mexico experienced one of the most severe security and justice crises since its transition to democracy. Impunity has been one of the main factors that has led to the fragmentation of the country's rule of law. In addition to decades of violence and criminality that have plagued society, the criminal justice system has not been able to effectively respond to its citizens' needs, despite significant regulatory reforms and institutional changes.

Today, Mexico is one of the countries with the highest rates of impunity not only in Latin America, but also in the entire world (UDLAP 2017). At the same time, the systematic violation of human rights, in particular through the commission of torture and mistreatment, is embedded in its public security and law enforcement institutions (Novoa/Silva Mora 2018). Furthermore, institutions are incapable of guaranteeing effective access to justice. According to the 2017 National Victimization and Public Security Opinion Survey (Envipe), in 49% of the investigations and preliminary probes carried out by the Attorney General's Office in 2016, either no resolution was reached or the investigation was dropped.

As a result, citizens deeply mistrust security and judicial institutions, which, in turn, contributes to the fact that the country's crime rate is one of the highest in Latin America. Only one in every ten crimes is reported to the authorities and thus recorded in the official crime rate. This distrust of authorities is the second reason why victims do not report crimes (16.5%), following the belief that filing a criminal complaint is a "waste of time" (33.1%) (Novoa/Silva Mora 2018).

In this context, there is a clear need to continue efforts to consolidate the criminal justice system as a mechanism to strengthen the rule of law, which is the basis for achieving peace and equality.

11.2 Rule of Law and Criminal Justice System

In order to address the strengthening of the rule of law, it is first necessary to clearly define the concept. What do we mean by "rule of law"? What are its implications? How does it relate to the criminal justice system? A minimalist definition of rule of law is the enforcement of publicized laws which are clear and evenly applied by independent courts that reach verdicts through an ordinary trial process. This definition, however, does not reference fundamental rights, equality, or justice (Maravall 2003).

A more modern definition points out that the rule of law has two fundamental pillars: limiting the state's power and abuse, and the recognition and protection of individuals' rights and freedoms (Rodríguez Zepeda 2001; De la Madrid 2004). The combination of these two ideas translates into what some scholars consider to be the fundamental value of the State: security and legal certainty.

In the words of Borja (1997), "the fundamental characteristic of the rule of law is its complete submission to legal norms. Only in this way can people's rights be guaranteed and society can be confident and free under the rule of law, not in arbitrariness. This principle describing the scope and effectiveness of the law is called legal certainty, which is a value that must be fundamental to the State. Without security, freedom, democracy and justice cannot flourish; without security, a country's development is not possible."

Although these definitions provide us with a starting point to analyze the rule of law, it is also essential to consider the definition and function of institutions (González Guerra 2009). Several authors have outlined a theoretical framework for the democratic rule of law. In addition to the uniform application of standards that guarantee rights, freedoms and legal security by independent courts, this broader notion takes into account the institutional design of the legal system and the performance of the justice system's institutions (Aguiar Aguilar/Azul 2015). This more comprehensive definition of the rule of law includes the following elements (Aguiar Aguilar/Azul 2015):

(a) Protection and guarantee of fundamental rights and freedoms.
(b) Exercise of power subject to a legal framework.
(c) Separation of powers.
(d) A modern justice system with independent, competent and impartial courts, prosecution services and public defenders.
(e) Institutional capabilities and the professionalization of public officials.
(f) An effective fight against corruption, illegality and the abuse of power by state authorities.
(g) Police that respect human rights, and civilian control over security forces.

This definition, which goes beyond law enforcement and considers the existence and development of criminal justice system institutions, gives us a broader picture of the foundations of the rule of law and what is at stake. Rule of law, in this case, is not limited to formal rules that apply to the courts and their independence, but also applies to a wide range of institutions and actors, including public security institutions, law enforcement agencies, public defenders, the penitentiary system and human rights commissions (Aguiar Aguilar/Azul 2015).

From the empirical perspective, the World Justice Project (WJP 2018) designed a conceptual framework and methodology in order to develop a *Rule of Law Index*, which serves as a quantitative tool that measures the rule of law in practice. The Index's methodology and comprehensive definition of the rule of law is based on the experiences and perceptions of the general public and in-country experts worldwide. It presents a portrait of the rule of law several countries worldwide by providing scores and rankings based on eight indicators: (1) constraints on government powers; (2) absence of corruption; (3) open government; (4) fundamental rights; (5) order and security; (6) regulatory enforcement; (7) civil justice; (8) criminal justice. Many of the dimensions of the index – particularly the last one – are directly related to the criminal justice performance (WJP 2018). In this instance, the rule of law is considered to work properly within a country if factors such as its effectiveness and impartiality are fulfilled.

In order to discuss democratic rule of law, establishing rules that guarantee the citizens' freedoms and human rights on paper is not enough. Comprehensive public policy on security and justice which translate into the capacity of institutions to efficiently and effectively deliver results must also be implemented. The criminal justice system, in this context, has a key role to play in preventing impunity, providing legal certainty to citizens, and ensuring respect for human rights. This can be achieved through building robust institutional capacities that generate citizens' trust (Novoa/Silva Mora 2017).

11.3 Criminal Justice Reform: From Implementation to the Consolidation of the Criminal Justice System

During the last decade, Mexico's criminal justice system has undergone an institutional transformation, following a process that other Latin American countries started years before. On June 18, 2008, the Criminal Justice and Public Security Reform (better known as criminal reform) was approved, through which Article 16 and paragraphs 2, 3, 4, 5, 7, 13, 17, 19, 20 and 21 of the Mexican Constitution were modified. This radically changed the country's criminal justice system, transitioning it from a discredited mixed-inquisitorial system to an adversarial and accusatory criminal justice system, in order to bring it in line with the democratic rule of law. The ultimate aim of this change to the justice system was to make it efficient and effective in order to improve the quality of justice and guarantee the protection of the fundamental rights of victims and defendants.

To achieve such a radical change, profound institutional and legal transformations were required that relied upon three main factors: time, resources, and political will. Taking this into consideration, the legislature established an eight-year timeline to carry out the necessary steps to implement the new justice system, and earmarked a large amount of resources in the federal budget for the criminal reform. It also created a national coordination body in order to implement the reform systematically and homogeneously on all three levels of government.

Congress set June 2016 as the deadline for the implementation of the criminal reform. Today, ten years after the reform was passed and two years since its implementation across the entire country was supposed to be completed, the accusatory criminal justice system remains in the early stages of consolidation. The reform was implemented heterogeneously at local and federal levels, which has produced good practices and success stories, but remains far from the system Congress envisioned ten years ago. This is partly due to a lack of clear political will during the early stages of the reform, when many authorities, including local governments, were reluctant to invest in one of the most ambitious projects of the last century, foreseeing the possibility that the reform would be reversed in the future. In fact, as a result of these reservations, most states did not begin implementation until 2014, when the deadline for the implementation of the reform was imminent (CIDAC 2016).

As a result of this uneven and incomplete implementation process, despite the enormous amount of resources invested in its transformation, the criminal justice system still has significant gaps and deficiencies and lacks institutional capacities, which hinders access to quality justice. Particularly since 2016, the uneven implementation has been a challenge for the consolidation of the criminal justice system. This stage has had to focus on addressing the existing gaps between states, rather than on evaluating and monitoring the justice system's operation and its results, and therefore identifying areas of opportunity and making the necessary improvements. These assessments must consider the context of a weakened rule of law that the new justice system has faced, which results from: a public insecurity crisis that impedes the measurement of the real impact of the system, the lack of a citizen culture and general knowledge about the reform, but most importantly, the defects carried over from the mixed inquisitorial system. These deficiencies, coupled with the uneven implementation in the states, make it difficult for institutions to implement the necessary work to achieve the accusatory system's objectives.

11.4 How Does the Criminal Justice System in Mexico Work Today?

Evaluations of the criminal justice system cannot ignore the fact that it is a public policy that forms part of a broader security and justice system which must be analyzed comprehensively. Its functioning depends on the interaction between various institutions, which would ideally all have symmetrical capacities. Therefore, before evaluating the justice system's results, it is necessary to study public policies, the decision-making process about how they are carried out, and available institutional capacities in order to produce satisfactory results.

11.4.1 Public Policy

From a public policy standpoint, effective coordination of the different institutions that are involved in the justice system is the foundation for its proper functioning, consolidation, and progress. Unfortunately, comprehensive coordination does not currently exist.

The Coordination Council and its Technical Secretariat (SETEC), which made up the coordination body during the implementation phase, were dissolved at the end of the implementation process. In 2016, the federal government designated the Executive Secretariat of the National Public Security System (Spanish acronym:

SESNSP) as the body in charge of coordinating the consolidation of the criminal justice system. Coordination has not been an easy task for SESNSP, since it has limited legal powers for distributing resources and planning. SESNSP cannot create policies that involve judiciary and public defenders, or give them federal funding in order to make improvements. This means that SESNSP can only impact public security institutions, which include the police, prosecutors and the penitentiary system (México Evalúa 2018). As a result, there are significant asymmetries between justice sector institutions, which have compromised the consolidation of the system as a whole.

At local level, progress has been uneven. At the conclusion of the implementation process, the logical step was for the implementing bodies in each state to transition into monitoring and evaluation bodies in order to ensure continuity and progress. Contrary to expectations, this process has been heterogeneous. In some states, the implementing bodies have been replaced by consolidation bodies, in others the institutions have not changed, and in the rest consolidation tasks have been transferred to the State Executive Secretariats, which are also unable to adopt policies that affect judicial powers and public defenders. It is necessary to provide the states that still have implementing institutions with legal certainty and legal powers to carry out monitoring and evaluation. This demonstrates that, in addition to the problem of coordination at national level, it is important to tackle the crisis of technical institutional coordination at local level. These two challenges obstruct the continuity of the system's operation and jeopardize its consolidation.

On the other hand, there is a clear lack of comprehensive and continuous planning for the consolidation of the system. SESNSP, the designated national body for consolidation, developed a plan that included ten action points that were related to the implementation or strengthening of necessary figures, offices or evaluation models regarding police functions and alternative justice in particular, and criminal justice in general.[1]

However, these actions alone do not constitute a consolidation plan. First, they are subject to annual change and do not consider the medium to long term. Secondly, the actions aim to close the gaps or address pending tasks in the implementation stage instead of achieving the monitoring and evaluation process that would help identify areas of opportunity in order to make the necessary adjustments to the system. On the other hand, a consolidation plan must be based on previous diagnosis and evaluation, defined goals, objectives and priorities, expected outputs and results, as well as the monitoring and evaluation of the system's results, which is not currently the case. In addition, the plan does not take into account the systemic and integral approach required for consolidation, and the actions instead focus on particular institutions. Likewise, the actions proposed by the SESNSP do not respond to the specific needs of each state and institution responsible for operating the system, since, as previously said, they do not take into

---

[1]See: https://www.gob.mx/justiciapenal/articulos/10-acciones-que-impulsara-en-2017-el-sesnsp-para-avanzar-en-la-consolidacion-del-sistema-de-justicia-penal-120501.

account the judiciary and public defenders. Again, this makes it an unsuitable consolidation plan.

Finally, the importance of monitoring and evaluation of the criminal justice system needs to be emphasized. One of the crucial public policy tasks is to create registration, processing and reporting systems that generate reliable, updated, verifiable and timely statistical data to ensure a comprehensive assessment of criminal justice. However, due to a variety of factors, monitoring and evaluation have been omitted since the accusatory system began to operate. First, there are no set guidelines for collecting data and, as a result, each state and institution collects data according to its own arbitrary method. On the other hand, the limited available data collection does not consider the logic of the accusatory model. Finally, since interconnected computer systems and shared databases that allow states and institutions to exchange information do not exist, it is impossible to have a comprehensive view of the justice system's operation (México Evalúa 2018).

11.4.2 Institutional Capacities

There are also critical deficiencies in institutional capacities that have directly impacted the operation and results of the justice system, and thus the perception of impunity.

In the first place, even after the conclusion of the implementation phase of the penal system, Congress has continued to pass reforms which have serious implications for the system's operation. Congress passed the latest reform in 2016, and, during the following months, various actors tried to promote a new reform that would tighten the rules of the accusatory system with the intention of limiting its guarantees. However, not all of the regulatory problems originate in the laws; judges' decisions and the federal courts' criteria have also influenced the operation. The jurisdictional function at times contradicts the logic and principles of the accusatory model – such as immediacy, continuity and contradiction – privileging the form over the substance and making the processes more inefficient. On the other hand, the *amparo* trial, as it is currently regulated, has led to the paralysis and prolongation of trials, affecting the essential principles of the criminal justice system, such as concentration, speed, immediacy, contradiction, and free evaluation of evidence. This interaction between the *amparo* trial and the criminal justice system has yet to be reviewed.

In relation to technical issues, there are continued shortcomings in collecting data and implementing computer systems. Although there are efforts to systematize data collection, standardized criteria that provide the necessary information for evaluation and measurement of results are still lacking. During this new stage, the mere collection of operational data is not enough. Rather, the data must also be useful for evaluating public policy from both quantitative and qualitative approaches. Many institutions continue to use improvised platforms that generally cannot be connected with other institutional operating systems. This puts consolidation at risk because, as mentioned previously, only monitoring and evaluation can detect areas of opportunity, in order to continuously adjust the system's operation.

Regarding the working institutional models, no comprehensive models have been developed to strengthen criminal investigation in prosecutors' offices; efforts have focused on managing the volume of cases, but not the quality of the investigation. As a result, although a small number of prosecutors' offices have increased their levels of efficiency in the resolution of cases, most of the cases they solve are either filed temporarily or are uncomplicated cases that involve a *flagrante delicto*, and therefore do not involve complex criminal investigations.

The federal government and the majority of the states (75%) are moving from a procuratorial to a prosecutorial system, with the aim of guaranteeing greater efficiency and independence in criminal prosecution. Nonetheless, these transitions have occurred without reconstructing institutional models to ensure their operational independence and criminal investigation capabilities. Until now, these 'transformations' have been limited to transferring staff and material resources from the former prosecutors' offices, resulting in a simple name change. Likewise, despite the existence of organizational manuals, the management models used by different areas and units have not been standardized. Although this can create space for beneficial improvisation and adjustment, it also makes it impossible to develop institutional evaluation, and for operators to become truly specialized and professionalized.

Although judiciaries continue to be the bodies with the greatest institutional development, they have encountered various problems related to their management models, which has put the operation of the system at risk in the medium and long term. These problems relate particularly to the delay, suspension and efficiency of hearings. That is, since there are no processes and mechanisms to distribute caseloads and monitor hearings, hearings tend to last longer, to be postponed, or to be re-scheduled over long periods of time. These problems, while managerial, also reflect the inability of operators to conduct themselves effectively during hearings.

On the other hand, despite the crucial role of Public Defenders' Offices in defending the rights of the accused, they are at a great disadvantage compared to other justice system operators. This is not only due to an asymmetric allocation of resources, but also to the lack of effective management models that are used in other institutions. Public defenders lack support staff for case management and investigation to assist them in managing their high caseloads, attending an average of 209 defendants simultaneously (México Evalúa 2018). This makes it impossible to allot sufficient time to each defendant to guarantee high-quality technical and legal defense.

Similarly, victims' support and legal assistance services are among the most disadvantaged institutions in the criminal justice system. In the first place, these services do not have their own institutional structure, and their location and distribution varies by state. While the Care Commissions provide these services in some states, public prosecutors' offices or even public defenders' offices offer them in other states. This situation leaves victims vulnerable because they are often unaware of their right to be represented by a lawyer and to obtain care and support.

In addition, a significant number of the State Victim Care Commissions only have a legal assistance area and do not have the capacity or personnel to provide comprehensive care and support for victims, as required by law.

On the other hand, the strengthening of the Supervisory Units for Precautionary Measures (Spanish acronym: UMECAS), which are essential for the establishment and monitoring of precautionary measures, continues to be a major pending concern. The UMECAS have, in general terms, two functions: (a) to provide reliable and verified information on the people being prosecuted, in order for the judge to determine the most appropriate precautionary measure for the specific case; and (b) to supervise compliance with the precautionary measures ordered by the judge at liberty, through follow-up with the prosecuted individuals by a specialized official. However, despite the fact that there is an UMECA in all thirty-two states, only five have made high-level progress, while eleven have made low-level progress and the remaining states mid-level progress. Weak institutional capacities have probably had a negative impact on the goal of minimizing the use of pre-trial detention, which continues to be the most requested and granted precautionary measure by the Public Prosecutors' Office.

Finally, with regard to public security institutions, the police remain a weak link in the system. However, mechanisms have been developed to strengthen and improve the function of the police, and new responsibilities, such as first responder and prosecutorial police, have also been considered. Among these new measures is the "optimal model of police operation", which simplified the Homologated Police Report (HPR), the form that police officers must fill out when they are the first responders. Criminal justice system training has also been implemented.

11.4.3 Results of the Operation

It is necessary to evaluate the data collected by the institutions in charge of operating the criminal justice system in order to assess the impact of the various public policies that have aimed to implement and consolidate the 2008 criminal justice reform on the management and resolution of issues. The results will reflect the capacities of all the institutions involved in the criminal justice system.

First, the primary purpose of the accusatory criminal justice system is to ensure access to effective and quality justice, yet this does not necessarily imply that all cases must be resolved through a lengthy criminal proceeding. Therefore, in order to respond to and satisfy the needs of victims efficiently, the accusatory system contemplates measures such as the use of alternative solutions.

The data show that the prosecutors' offices are not processing cases effectively and there is already a significant backlog only two years after the system went into effect countrywide. According to data from the National Census of Local Prosecution Offices (*Censo Nacional de Procuración de Justicia Estatal* – CNPJE) (INEGI 2017a, b, c), a decision was reached on only 50.8% of the investigations that were initiated in 2016. This indicator is not that different from the investigations initiated through the traditional system. According to the first census of local prosecution from INEGI, which contains information about 2010, at national level a decision was reached in only in 65.3% of the investigations (INEGI 2011).

However, this does not necessarily mean that cases that have been prosecuted are actually being dealt with by the justice system. If we analyze the way in which decisions are reached on prosecutions' investigation files, we observe that in 2016 most of the cases were temporarily archived (27%), while only 1.8% were dealt with by alternative justice (such as a reparatory agreement) and prosecutors use the discretionary prosecution principle in only 0.9% of the cases, even though alternative justice is the backbone of the justice system. This tendency has been maintained from the traditional system.

It is important to analyze the use of the temporarily archived files (known as 'reserve' under the traditional system). Procedural law allows public prosecutors to close a case temporarily when there is not enough data during the initial investigation to establish clear lines of investigation to clarify the facts. This is a temporary decision, as it involves only 'pausing' the investigation. The indiscriminate use of this measure highlights the inability of the police and public prosecutors to clarify the facts, that is, to complete the investigation. On the other hand, the authority benefits from pausing cases because they do not count as unresolved cases in the data, since technically a decision was already reached on them. This situation has not changed with the criminal justice system reform. Within the traditional system, 31.4% of the total of decisions reached on prosecutions' investigation files were determined through the reserve (a figure similar to temporarily archived), and only 24.5% were resolved as execution of criminal action, according to the CNPJE (INEGI 2011).

On the other hand, the type of cases prosecutors select reveals their poor investigative capabilities. As prosecutions' institutions develop the ability to perform higher quality investigations, they will be able to resolve more complex cases, in addition to those when the suspect is arrested at the time of the crime, which reduces the complexity of the investigation. Although the data show that the majority of cases that prosecutors bring before a judge did not involve an arrested suspect (54%), this does not necessarily imply that they are complex cases. In fact, according to data obtained by México Evalúa through an information request, in 2017 in some states almost all the cases that prosecutors brought before a judge were with a detainee, which suggests that they have little to no effectiveness in the investigation (México Evalúa 2018). In addition, that figure may also include cases in which a suspect was detained, but the prosecutor released him or her with a notice to appear before a judge in the future.

Another indicator that has impacted the perception of impunity is the frequency with which public prosecutors release suspects who were arrested in *flagrante delicto*. The procedural law gives this power to the prosecutors in order to prioritize managing the high workload and the individuals' freedom. This does not imply impunity, since even if the suspect is released, the prosecutor has the obligation to continue the investigation and bring the case before a judge. Nonetheless, this power is being used excessively, and not all these cases are being brought before a judge. This means that many of the investigations remain open, creating greater congestion in public prosecutors' offices.

According to INEGI, of the total number of investigation files initiated by prosecution offices in 2016, the local judiciaries handled only 4.6% of the cases, and only 0.2% of the investigations ended in oral trials. This data is not necessarily negative, since, as mentioned above, the accusatory model provides – and, in fact, privileges – the use of alternative and anticipated solutions, which allows matters to be resolved without reaching the last stage of a criminal proceeding. However, there is also a significant backlog in the resolution of cases before courts, with only 2.7% of the initiated criminal cases concluded in 2016.

Since the 2008 reform passed, and in accordance with the presumption of innocence principle, additional non-custodial precautionary measures were introduced in addition to pre-trial detention. The hope was that pre-trial detention would be used only in exceptional circumstances. In this regard, the task of the prosecutor is to ensure that only necessary precautionary measures are used to guarantee the purposes of the criminal proceeding and to avoid the excessive use of pre-trial detention. However, pre-trial detention is still the precautionary measure most frequently requested by public prosecutors and imposed by judges (México Evalúa 2018). This could be the result of inquisitorial practices that still remain from the former system and the lack of effective precautionary measure monitoring units that perform risk studies with adequate monitoring systems.

The results we analyzed provide us with an overview of how justice works in Mexico. The accusatory criminal justice system favors the use of alternative or early exits, in order to avoid resorting exclusively to the prosecution of cases. It also seeks to minimize legal resolutions that may reduce the pressure on the system but also incur a high social cost in terms of justice, since they do not resolve the core of the conflict. In this regard, impunity reflects the inability of the criminal justice system to seek and deliver justice. In addition to the unreported cases, impunity also persists when crimes are reported to the authorities but they do not provide a satisfactory response.

According to the *Accusatory Criminal Justice System Impunity Index* developed by México Evalúa (2018), high levels of impunity are widespread throughout Mexico, with a national average of 87.3%. This index measures the proportion of cases that were reported to the authorities and investigated, but went unpunished or unsolved. In this sense, impunity is understood as the percentage of cases in which there was no resolution or consequence. The following graph shows that even the states with the lowest rate of impunity exceed 50% (Table 11.1).[2]

---

[2]The following states were not included in the analysis because they did not provide the necessary information to create the indicator: Aguascalientes, Campeche, Colima, Michoacán, Puebla, Sinaloa, Sonora, and Tamaulipas.

Table 11.1 Impunity in the accusatory criminal justice system. *Source* México Evalúa

At a first glance, it could be inferred that these results are related to the states' progress of developing public policies to improve the criminal justice system and strengthen institutional capacities. In other words, as public policies are developed, the quality of justice improves, which leads to a lower level of impunity. Analyzing the public policies and impunity rates of each state shows us that there is indeed a relationship; states with the greatest deficiencies in public policies are those with the highest levels of impunity, while those with the lowest levels of impunity have the most robust public policies.

To summarise, the information currently available shows that the current justice system has not achieved the expected outcomes. This is a result of the fact that the system has not been able to operate under optimal conditions due to significant implementation gaps that make it impossible to evaluate its actual results. As a consequence, policy reforms and institutional transformations have not been enough to reduce impunity, as the new criminal justice system is not able to satisfactorily respond to citizens' demands for justice.

11.5 Conclusions

The current criminal justice system in Mexico jeopardizes the country's already fragile rule of law, since it is not able to respond to demands for justice. However, the greatest obstacles do not lie in legislation but in the system's operation. Before any additional reforms are passed, efforts must be focused on solving the day-to-day operational challenges, ranging from the creation and implementation of public policies to reorganization to strengthening legal operators' competencies.

But, above all, it will not be possible to observe progress in the system's results, much less to reduce impunity, if there are no comprehensive evaluation processes in place that assess how the system currently works in order to identify areas of opportunity.

References

Aguiar Aguilar, Azul A. (2015). "La Procuración de Justicia: El talón de Aquiles del Estado de Derecho en México", in: *Revista Mexicana de Análisis Político y Administración Pública*, 4(1): 159–172.

Borja, R. (1997). *Enciclopedia de la política* (Mexico City): Fondo de Cultura Económica.

Carbonell Sánchez, M. (Coord.), (2002). *Derechos Fundamentales y Estado. Memoria del VII Congreso Iberoamericano de Derecho Constitucional* (Mexico City: Instituto de Investigaciones Jurídicas UNAM).

Centro de Investigación para el Desarrollo [CIDAC]. (2016). *Hallazgos 2015: evaluación de la implementación y operación a ocho años de la reforma constitucional en materia de justicia penal* (Mexico City: CIDAC); at: http://cidac.org/wp-content/uploads/2016/05/HALLAZGOS_2015.pdf.

De la Madrid, M. (2004). *Constitución, Estado de Derecho y Democracia* (Mexico City: Instituto de Investigaciones Jurídicas, UNAM).

González Guerra, J.M.; Villegas Rojas, P. (2009). *Democratización, Estado de derecho y rol del movimiento de los trabajadores* (Mexico: Konrad Adenauer Stiftung).

Instituto Nacional de Estadística y Geografía [INEGI] (2011). *Censo Nacional de Procuración de Justicia Estatal* [Database]; at: http://www.beta.inegi.org.mx/programas/cnpje/2011/.

Instituto Nacional de Estadística y Geografía [INEGI] (2017a). *Censo Nacional de Procuración de Justicia Estatal* [Database]; at: http://www.beta.inegi.org.mx/programas/cnpje/2017/.

Instituto Nacional de Estadística y Geografía [INEGI] (2017b). *Encuesta Nacional de Victimización y Percepción sobre Seguridad Pública* [Database]; at: http://www.beta.inegi.org.mx/proyectos/enchogares/regulares/envipe/2017/.

Instituto Nacional de Estadística y Geografía [INEGI] (2017c). *Censo Nacional de Impartición de Justicia Estatal* [Database]; at: http://www.beta.inegi.org.mx/programas/cnije/2017/.

Le Clercq, Juan Antonio; Rodríguez, Gerardo (2017). *Dimensiones de la impunidad global, IGI 2017* (Puebla: UDLAP).

Maravall, J.M. (2003). "The Rule of Law as a Political Weapon", in: Maravall, J.M.; Przeworski, A. (Eds.), *Democracy and the Rule of Law* (Cambridge: Cambridge University Press).

México Evalúa. (2018). *Hallazgos 2017: Seguimiento y evaluación del sistema de justicia penal en México* (Mexico City: México Evalúa).

Novoa, M.; Silva Mora, K. (2018). "Transformar la Procuración de Justicia para reducir la Impunidad", in: Pantin, Laurence (Coord.) *Léase si quiere gobernar (en serio)* (Mexico City: Mexico Evalúa–CIDAC); at: https://www.mexicoevalua.org/2018/04/11/lease-quiere-gobernar-en-serio/.

Rodríguez Zepeda, J. (2001). *Estado de Derecho y Democracia* (Mexico City: Instituto Federal Electoral).

Chapter 12
The Monster Within: Mexico's Anti-corruption National System

Cristopher Ballinas Valdés

> *Otra característica notable del Estado mexicano: a pesar de que ha sido el agente cardinal de la modernización, él mismo no ha logrado modernizarse enteramente. En muchos de sus aspectos, especialmente en su trato con el público y en su manera de conducir los asuntos, sigue siendo patrimonialista [...] lejos de constituir una burocracia impersonal, forman una gran familia política ligada por vínculos de parentesco, amistad, compadrazgo, paisanaje y otros factores de orden personal. El patrimonialismo es la vida privada incrustada en la vida pública.*
> The Philanthropic Ogre, Octavio Paz
> Another notable feature of the Mexican state: although it has been the cardinal agent of modernization, it has not managed to modernize itself entirely. In many of its aspects, especially in its dealings with the public and in its conduct of affairs, it remains patrimonial [...] far from constituting an impersonal bureaucracy, forming a large political family linked by ties of kinship, friendship, *compardrazgo*, peasantry and other factors of a personal nature. Patrimonialsim is the private life embedded in public life. Paz (1978: 92)

Abstract Classic institutionalism claims that even authoritarian and non-democratic regimes would prefer institutions where all members could make advantageous transactions. Thus, structural reform geared towards preventing and combating corruption should be largely preferred by all actors in any given setting. The puzzle, then, is why governments decide to maintain, or even create, inefficient

---

Cristopher Ballinas Valdés is a specialist in the study of executive government, regulation and public sector reform. A Doctor of Philosophy in Politics from the University of Oxford, his research agenda explores the effects of politics and institutions on policy outcomes – the politics of policies. Dr. Ballinas Valdés presents a broad high-level experience in policy instrumentation. As a result, he has developed a portfolio focusing on the areas of public sector reform, regulation, social policy, re-engineering, transparency, corruption control and border security. Email: cristopher.ballinas@itam.mx.

institutions. A perfect example of this paradox is the establishment of the National Anti-corruption System (SNA) in Mexico. This is a watchdog institution, created to fight corruption, which is itself often portrayed as highly corrupted and inefficient. The limited scope of anti-corruption reforms in the country is explained by the institutional setting in which these reforms take place, where political behaviour is highly determined by embedded institutions that privilege centralized decision-making. Mexican reformers have historically privileged those reforms that increase their gains and power, and delayed and boycotted those that negatively affect them. Since anti-corruption reforms adversely affected rent extraction and diminished the power of a set of political actors, the bureaucrats who benefited from the current institutional setting embraced limited reforms or even boycotted them. Thus, to understand failed reforms it is necessary to understand the deep-rooted political institutions that shape the behaviour of political actors. This analysis is important for other modern democracies where powerful bureaucratic minorities are often able to block changes that would be costly to their interests, even if the changes would increase net gains for the country as a whole.

Keywords Democratic institutions · Mexican presidentialism · National Anti-corruption System · Partido Revolucionario Institucional (*PRI*)

12.1 Introduction

Studies regarding the impact of political institutions on government restructuring are hardly a novel idea, although they are relatively new in Mexico. They have been a central unit of research for institutional economists and political scientists for the last four decades, leading to multifarious conclusions. Mancur Olson (1982a, b, 1984), when analysing the rise and decline of Western economies, argues that "even in dictatorial systems, the dictator has an incentive to make the economy of the country he controls work better, since this will generate more tax receipts he can use as he pleases and usually also reduce dissent" (1984: 637). According to Olson, even authoritarian and non-democratic regimes prefer institutions where all members can make advantageous transactions, since any other situation is not an equilibrium. This would in turn lead to another set of institutional reforms until all members are satisfied. In his words: "any disequilibrium indicates that all mutually advantageous transactions have not been consummated".

Following this logic, no government, even an authoritarian one, has an incentive to generate serious recessions or disequilibria, and will steadily and slowly move onto efficient and equalitarian institutions, even if it implies losing some political control or economic gains. Yet, the world is full of cases where governments do, in fact, cultivate institutions that are less than ideal, or even economically and socially harmful. The puzzle, then, is why governments decide to maintain, or even create, inefficient institutions.

To solve this conundrum, it is important to understand the potential gains which some groups derive from a set of institutions, before turning our attention to the structure of incentives created by the said institutions and policies. We can then see how the structure of incentives creates powerful groups which stand to gain the most – in terms of power and privilege – from *the preservation of the existing order*, not from its alteration. When restructuring economic institutions, reformers have inducements to preserve those political institutions that allow them to gain, or at least maintain, power. What seems a contradiction to some is, in fact, a landmark of the political elite in many countries. We will use Mexico, and particularly the creation of the Mexican National Anti-corruption System, to exemplify this very real problem.

This perverse incentive to maintain or create inefficient institutions is something that has characterized reforming intents in Mexico for decades (if not centuries). Octavio Paz, the first Mexican writer to win the Nobel Prize in Literature, characterized the Mexican political system of the late Seventies as a *philanthropic ogre*. For Paz, the Mexican political system of the last century, characterized by the hegemonic control of the Partido Revolucionario Institucional (PRI), held a deep contradiction. On the one hand, politicians during this regimen were dedicated to providing services, building hospitals and schools, creating a social security system for workers, subsidizing agriculture and industrialization, and creating several publically owned firms to guarantee milk and other basic goods. On the other hand, the political system was renowned for its political control of all branches of government at all levels, the suppression of checks and balances, and the sometimes brutal neutralization of political opponents by way of serious violations to civil and human rights. In Paz's own words:

> Within the Mexican State there is an enormous contradiction that no one has been able, or even tried, to solve: the body of administrators and technocrats, the professional bureaucracy, shares the privileges and the risks of public administration with the President's friends, family and favourites, and with the Minister's friends, family and favourites. The Mexican bureaucracy is modern, it wants to modernize the country, and its values are modern values. Rising before it, sometimes as rival and others as associate, is a mass of friends, relatives and favourites, united by personal ties. This courtesan society is renewed partially every six years, every time a new President rises to power. Because of its implicit ideological situation, and its mode of recruitment, these bodies of courtesans are not modern; they are the survivors of hereditary privileges. The contradiction between the courtesan society and the technocratic bureaucracy does not immobilize the State, but it does make its course long and winding. There aren't two politics within the State: there are two ways of understanding politics, two sensitivities, two moralities (Paz 1978: 41).

Paz sees this contradiction inside the Mexican political system, and most particularly inside the central government, as leading to contradictory decision-making. We contend that, even after the defeat of the hegemonic system, this dynamic prevails, and continues to affect all efforts at profound government restructuring.

Such is the case of the Mexican National Anti-corruption System (Sistema Nacional Anticorrupción, or SNA). We contend that Mexican reformists of the second decade of the twenty-first century never truly wanted to transform the country's institutions to lead the nation to higher prosperity, but intended to use institutional changes as mechanisms to maintain power.

Fighting corruption appeared to be a contradiction for the reforming agenda of the twenty-first century. Historically, Mexico had no tradition of checks and balances or independent watchdogs, and corruption was endemic. In fact, corruption helped Mexico attain the political stability that allowed it to achieve long periods of economic growth. It also remains the glue that holds the country's establishment together. The system is so entrenched that even when the long-time opposition party, the National Action Party (PAN), took power, it quickly fell into line, but in different ways. In this case, a reform agenda and maintaining tainted institutions were two faces of the same coin. The reform team became focused on reforming the economy while ensuring that anti-corruption policies would not turn against them.

Therefore, this article argues that the creation of the SNA, even when it was never originally meant to be set up, faced a contradiction in its origin that prevented full implementation. The creation of the SNA was embedded within a corrupt structure of institutions. Bureaucratic groups shaped its design in such a way that their interests would not be affected. Thus, during the creation of the SNA, institutional and political limitations persisted. There was no *tabula rasa* or blank slate for the creation of the SNA; it had to be built through institutions which maintained and masked corrupt behaviour. More importantly, those in charge of implementing the reform were the most interested in designing it to fail.

The rest of this paper is organized thus: first, I will describe the inner dynamics of the Mexican central public administration born from the Mexican Revolution of 1910, and its further development during the long governmental tenure of the PRI. Second, I analyse the institutional limitations present during the creation of the SNA. The final section presents my conclusions.

12.2 Nursing the Beast: Mexican Political Institutions

Before the breakdown of the authoritarian regime and the transition to a more democratic one, the Mexican political system was renowned for the stability of its one-party political system. The country seemed to have found the elusive combination of political stability and economic growth in a region characterized by political disruptions and violence (Huntington 1968). Many scholars have argued that the relative stability was the product of institutional features not found in other, more democratic countries (Haggard/Webb 1994; Ros 1994; Santiso 2004).

Emphasis has been placed on the enormous power concentrated in the Mexican presidency. It is widely believed that Mexican presidents controlled all political, economic and social levers of the country. These extended faculties gave the President the power to control corporatist sectors, labour unions, and peasant organizations, and gave him the opportunity to negotiate directly with business associations. Based on these assumptions, several scholars have characterized the

Mexican political system as anti-democratic, corrupt and authoritarian – a 'perfect dictatorship' with a democratic façade.

Mexican presidents exercised an extraordinary range of powers. Although originally weak in design, the presidency collected legal and extra-legal faculties which prevented others from acting as collective players against it. The Party, the legislative and judicial branches, and the bureaucracy were brought into line, and became compliant. Then, three conditions were necessary for *presidencialismo* to occur. First, a unified government; second, Party discipline; and finally, the ability of the President to set the Party's agenda and to punish any uncooperative behaviour shown by the members of the PRI's legislative caucus (Molinar Horcasitas/ Weldon 2001; Weldon 1997b).

Based upon these elements, the regime achieved lasting stability, combining political survival and economic development. "The Mexican president was therefore the linchpin of an inter-temporal agreement that succeeded in reassuring key interests that the bargain they had struck with the regime would continue" (Lehoucq et al. 2004).[1] This resulted in a highly centralized decision-making process revolving around the Executive, and in a strong central bureaucracy characterized by narrow and secretive decision-making (Lehoucq et al. 2004).

Mexican presidents were certainly not omnipotent actors, and they did face several constraints on their authority. As scholars have documented, Congress, the Supreme Court, the central bureaucracy and corporatist organizations all challenged presidential powers at some point during the PRI regime (Castañeda 1995; Cordera/ Tello 1981; Weldon 1997b).[2] Yet, Presidents created a set of institutions that both *de jure* and *de facto* secured the loyalty of both the legislature and the judiciary.

As a consequence of the expansion of presidential power, the central public administration was relatively isolated from the pressures of the political system. The supremacy of the Executive Branch over all other branches of government and the centralization of political activity shaped the public administration's structure.

---

[1] These complement a set of elements topically quoted in the literature on the Mexican political system: first, the lack of electoral competition, based on an official Party as an "electoral ministry" and the regulator of political conflict; and second, a set of unwritten rules, also known as "meta-constitutional powers". These included the possibility of appointing and removing governors, members of the judicial branch, peasants and union leaders. With the President as the direct leader of the Party, it was also possible to appoint candidates for the Congress and the Senate, and to control Party actions.

[2] Weldon (1997a, b, 2004) has documented how Mexican legislators opposed the President's will despite the institutional matrix sustaining *presidencialismo*. Moreover, during *presidencialismo*, the PRI came to monopolise all committee chairs and all positions of influence within Congress and the judicial branch, which was advantageous in those situations in which they needed to gain a large majority approval. Something similar happened with the judicial branch. Although the 1917 Constitution guaranteed its formal independence, Congress exercised political control over it, mainly through the rules on the appointment, tenure and impeachment of judges. At the same time, the President obtained the power to request that Congress dismiss judges, as happened during Lázaro Cardenas's presidential term (1934–40) when he discharged all the members of the Supreme Court. Consequently, the tenure of judges of the Supreme Court was changed to a six-year term, concurrent with presidential terms.

The President consolidated political control of the bureaucracy, placing the Ministry of the Interior and its loyal staff as overseers of other government branches.

Through a series of unique characteristics, the PRI ensured internal stability, and combined it with mobility for its governing members. Paramount was the fact that the PRI's presidential candidate was selected from within the ranks of the administration. This introduced a powerful incentive for the system to attract and retain well-qualified candidates (Hernández Rodríguez 1987, 1993). Another factor contributing to stability was the regulation barring consecutive re-election within the Mexican Congress. Elected office was used as a stepping stone to other political positions, and candidate selection was used to control members (Smith 1975, 1979).

Additionally, cabinet officials were freely appointed by the President, and needed no ratification by any of the other branches of government. Indeed, the president appointed not only the cabinet, but also a wide assortment of middle-ranking officers in the ministries, other cabinet-level agencies, and state-owned enterprises (Carpizo 1983; Hernández Rodríguez 1994). This extensive appointment prerogative provided the President with a formidable degree of freedom. It also ensured discipline at all levels, including the Cabinet, since its members could be removed at any time.

The centralized character of decision-making engendered an asymmetry among bureaucratic agencies and, in many ways, resulted in a specialization by policy area or ministry.[3] Thus, Mexican presidents were the dominant actors in both decision-making and policy-making. During the PRI's tenure, this allowed presidents to shape policy around their preferences, and provided a measure of policy continuity across presidential terms (sexenios).

There was a symbiotic relationship between presidents and the bureaucracy. And, given the technical character of many policies, the bureaucracy enjoyed a certain level of independence from the President. They usually took unilateral action without consulting other branches of government or the Party. Given this, there was little investment in policy capacities in other spheres. In many cases, bureaucrats managed to place themselves at the top of the political axis and establish control over other branches of government.

Consequently, the central bureaucracy was not only a technical but also a political arena; decisions were taken, but many political struggles also took place there. Power-seekers had strong incentives to develop their careers by rising through the ranks of the central public administration. The rise and promotion of Mexican civil servants was regulated by a series of written and unwritten rules

---

[3]For instance, the Ministry of the Interior dealt mostly with political matters, while the Ministry of Finance focused on economic issues. The Ministry of the Interior played the most important political role, since the intelligence agencies that kept supporters and opponents under surveillance were located within it. Meanwhile, the Ministry of Finance, which controlled revenues and expenditure, exercised political power in that it could facilitate or block actions of state agencies (Ortiz Mena 1998). The Interior and Finance ministries together operated to check and balance the power of the President.

developed during the post-revolutionary period. This created groups and institutionalized coalitions within governmental bodies that shaped the internal dynamics of the Mexican public administration.

Controlling other branches of the government as well as societal groups and trade unions prevented opposition when reforming. This happened during the late 1980s and early 1990s, as a powerful central bureaucracy and central control of all the elements of the political system provided the ideal scenario for rapid and efficient implementation of structural reforms. The literature concurs that the success of these reforms was profoundly influenced by the ability of presidents to appoint cohesive reform teams, delegating to their members the authority both to craft policies and execute them, while at the same time insulating them from countervailing pressures.

Most scholars attribute the scope, pace and success of the Mexican reform program to centralized presidential power, control over the ruling party, and the administration's technocratic and political know-how. Powerful presidents and controlling central bureaucrats were also key to maintaining governability, and to undertaking profound change when necessary. Deep structural and economic reforms during these decades were only possible as they were carried by central bureaucrats, who controlled the institutions, and possessed the expertise. Economic reform in Mexico was swift and seen as highly successful, but the way it was done also had serious ramifications.

The concentration and centralization of power in some persons and agencies may have proved successful in the short term, but had consequences that jeopardized the further reforms of political institutions. In order to gain more control over the process, reformers altered deep-rooted institutions that regulated the central public administration. Mid-level bureaucrats were cut out of the decision-making process, though not initially from the implementation process.

What happened to be an advantage also turned into the most dramatic dead weight. As bureaucrats began to lose long-standing privileges and their source of power, they reacted. Bureaucrats started to alter the pace and extent of reforms, adapting, modifying, or even aborting them. The reform teams thus faced opposition not only from outside the government, but also from inside the bureaucracy itself, primarily from nationalists, experts, and traditional bureaucrats. This affected the scope of the reforms and distorted their original aim, especially those regarding government structure.

Electoral institutions had been reformed, yet the central government equilibrium remained intact, even after the democratic transition in 2000, and the 2006 elections. The economic reforms of the Nineties and the advent of democracy in the country brought no change to the main structures of government which, aside from some cosmetic changes, remained the same during the transition. Minor democratic controls were put into place, such as legislative ratification of some cabinet members, and some budgetary controls. A major reform of the Judicial Branch, driven by the increasing democratic wave, shaped a judiciary review process on a scale never before seen in the country. A new career civil service was created, but it was focalized, and had limited scope and impact.

Paradoxically, in a country characterized by a highly-disciplined bureaucracy, the most vociferous opposition to economic and political change came not from interest groups, legislators or voters, but from bureaucrats within the government. Carlos Salinas de Gortari (President of Mexico 1988–1994), widely considered the most successful liberal reformer in the Latin American region at the time, has frankly admittedly that the real adversaries were not outside, but within the government itself. Even after the presidency was won by a different party in 2000 (the PAN), high and mid-level bureaucrats remained in their posts doing the same thing in the same way as they did it before. Many reforms hinged on a bureaucracy committed to taking them to fruition. Yet, powerful mid-level bureaucrats controlled the implementation processes, and delayed them or, even aborted them.

The story repeated itself during the late 1990s and the first decade of the new century. The way to rise to the presidency may have changed, yet the powerful government bureaucracy remained intact. As observed by Ballinas (2011), Mexican presidents may have exerted control over the creation of reform agendas and autonomous watchdog agencies, but the central bureaucracies boycotted and limited the scope of these, resulting in failed institutions with limited power and mixed levels of autonomy. Intervention during the process of designing autonomous agencies resulted in a struggle between bureaucrats and reform teams. Political struggles determined the final institutional outcomes, which the case studies reveal to be a multifarious disarray of unexpected organizational forms.

This study illustrates how the creation of agencies that undermine the power structure within the public administration is affected by those same political factors. It also reveals that government restructuring is more likely to result in significant failure when domestic bureaucratic structures are well established. An important lesson is that it is a mistake to reform or create institutions that can be boycotted by entrenched central bureaucracies without strengthening counterbalances such as fiscal controls and legislative oversight.

As stated above, this phenomenon is not exclusive to Mexico. In his research on reform in Soviet-type economies, Winiecki (1996) found that Party apparatchiks and economic bureaucrats can greatly benefit from persistent interference in the economic sphere, and are consequently most interested in maintaining the status quo. These motivations can condemn reforms in Soviet-style economies, as the content of economic reforms is altered or dismantled by counter-reformers. The apparatchiks swiftly implemented those economic reforms that expanded their influences and privileges, and sabotaged and aborted those economic and political reforms counter to their interests. Such has been the case in Mexico and many other places.

12.3 The System That Never Was

The government of Enrique Peña Nieto began with exaggerated amounts of optimism. By 2012, the confident atmosphere surrounding the economic reforms attracted positive global attention towards the promising Mexican economy.

A reform program, alluringly named the "Pact for Mexico" was designed, and agreed to, by an array of political forces – many of them political rivals of Peña Nieto's PRI. It was also massively publicized. This Pact was a reform agenda similar to those implemented in Mexico during the Eighties and Nineties, and listed a series of issues that would serve as a legislative blueprint for the first part of the administration. The agenda included economic growth, competitiveness, security, democratic governance, and government reform. Backed by other political forces from the very beginning, the reform agenda was extensively and successfully implemented in a relatively short period. Sweeping educational, energy, telecom, governance, and budgetary reforms were passed. Also, part of the original pact were plans to eradicate corruption by building independent institutions and strengthening transparency, yet these were delayed for years and remain incomplete.

From the beginning, Peña Nieto presented himself as progressive reformer. The international media portrayed him as the Mexican saviour who would turn the country around, changing the Narco-stained narrative to one of a prosperous country. "Saving Mexico", ran a *Time* Magazine cover with a photograph of the Mexican President. Nevertheless, an analysis of the reform agenda of the Peña Nieto administration reveals that, while they had clear economic reform in mind, profound political reform was denied, and social reform completely ignored.

Peña Nieto's administration lived through two contrasting processes that explain why reforms regarding corruption were never finished while other more problematic ones, such as education or energy, were swiftly approved and implemented. On the one hand, Peña Nieto´s economic liberalization reforms were accomplished by promising larger profits to economic actors who supported them. On the other, political reform implied restructuring the very institutions that political actors used to maintain and remain in power. Thus, the former reforms were implemented, and the latter ignored.

Peña Nieto and his team never really wanted a reform on corruption; it was included in the "Pact for Mexico" by opposition parties. Peña Nieto's team wanted to secure the benefits of economic reform for their financial supporters. Legislative approval of the major liberalization reforms was achieved through graft, allowing favored economic and political actors to profit from access to privileged information. On the political side, as a member of the traditional Partido Revolucionario Institutional, the President wanted to restore the country's political system to something akin to the 1950s, a time when the federal government's paramount goal was economic growth, but when it also controlled all branches of the government at federal and local levels. Economic reform was seen as a way to secure loyalties throughout the political arena at virtually no cost in terms of popularity.

In 2013 Peña Nieto's administration presented to the Congress a proposal of constitutional reform which would increase the legal capacity of the agency for transparency and personal data protection and create a National and Autonomous Commission of Combating Corruption. The following year Peña Nieto and his close circle found themselves in a media whirlwind when it was discovered that a favored government contractor had built a multi-million-dollar mansion called Casa Blanca for his family. Corruption suddenly became the *raison d'être* of the country's activist and NGO community, and the topic threatened to overshadow all others.

The scandal's potential damage to the administration, and especially to the President's image, led to the decision that an anti-corruption reform had to be rolled out, shaped by them, and controlled by them. In consequence, the National and Autonomous Commission of Combating Corruption's proposal did not prosper, as it faced vociferous opposition from civil society organizations. Those organizations took the lead in the process of drafting a new proposal that would eventually develop into a proposal for the National System Anti-corruption.[4]

Mexico had been suffering a time of extreme violence, which had weakened credibility in public institutions. However, the administration's blatant corruption and abuse of power only made a bad situation worse. In 2017, Mexico was placed last among OECD countries in Transparency International's Corruption Perceptions Index, with an overall ranking of 135 out of 180 countries, at the same level as Paraguay, Kyrgyzstan, Ivory Coast and Russia. The increasing perceptions of corruption in the country were not only because of the Casa Blanca scandal, but because of widespread corruption across the country, at all levels. At least fourteen former or current governors from the governing party were under investigation for corruption or for colluding with organized crime, the very groups largely responsible for Mexico's rising violence.

It is well known in Mexico that corrupt officials divert millions of dollars in government funds away from the public and into their own pockets. This carries serious social and economic consequences, such as reducing foreign investment, hindering economic growth, and fuelling inequality. A comprehensive study by the Mexican Institute for Competitiveness (2015) indicated that corruption reduces foreign investment in Mexico by five percent each year, and the World Economic Forum (2017) ranks corruption as the single most important barrier to doing business in Mexico. The National Survey on Victimization by the National Institute for Statistics and Geography (INEGI 2017) found that judges, police, and prosecutors are perceived as some of the most corrupt actors in the country.

This is consistent with the findings of the Global Impunity Index (2017) from the Center for Studies on Impunity and Justice, University of the Americas Puebla, that states that impunity is a norm across Mexico, as it is throughout Latin America and the Caribbean. Although nearly every country in Latin America is struggling to combat high rates of impunity, Mexico's case is dramatic: high levels of corruption and impunity are connected not only to weak institutions, but to the fact that the very institutions in charge of containing corruption are working to undermine the efforts to contain it. For instance, almost 43% of the country's prison population hasn't been tried yet, which the report indicates is a measure of the low

---

[4]This largely explains the citizen nature, at least in law, of the SNA.

Table 12.1 Investigations of public servants suspected of misuse of public funds (administrative responsibility penalties, ARP)

Year	2009	2010	2011	2012	2013	Total
Investigation concluded	1,385	1,911	1,562	1,652	1,021	7,531
Under investigation	0	0	87	157	327	571
ARP	95	54	47	21	0	217
No ARP	769	932	546	315	56	2,618

Source Ortiz Ramírez (2016: 559)

functionality and inefficiency of the judicial system.[5] Despite the judicial review undertaken several years before, justice is not improving in Mexico (Table 12.1).

An example of impunity can be found in Ortiz Ramirez's analysis of Administrative Responsibility Findings (2016). Yearly audits of the executive branch are conducted by the Superior Auditor of the Federation. Cases of alleged misallocation or misuse of funds are investigated, and if a government official is found to have been responsible, he or she is found to have Administrative Responsibility and can be held responsible for the missing funds. Administrative Responsibility penalties go from slaps on the wrist to criminal prosecutions. Ortiz Ramirez found that, between 2009 and 2013, the number of cases in which a government official was found responsible for misallocation or misuse of funds went from 6 to 2%, despite a string of high-profile corruption scandals. It was under these circumstances that the anti-corruption reform was begun.

Under intense pressure to answer for the scandals jolting his administration, Peña Nieto's government rolled out an anti-corruption reform package, which was approved and then entered into force in July 2016 to a great fanfare. It was presented as a landmark foundation for a tougher and more comprehensive approach to combating corruption, and a major step forward in terms of increasing accountability for corrupt public officials. The SNA was created as an entity charged with coordinating anti-corruption efforts at federal and state level, harmonizing the efforts of civil society and Mexican federal agencies to improve oversights, sanction corrupt businesses, and promote the prosecution of cases.

Already existing institutions would take part in the SNA, but were hampered by a lack of clear coordination and autonomy, as well as by new offices that were created as part of the system. The System is headed by a Coordinating Committee in charge of analysing, designing and implementing anti-corruption actions and establishing a framework for coordination between the 96-plus entities at the federal, state, and municipal levels which are charged with combating corruption. The Central Committee is constituted by representatives from the Superior Auditor of the Federation, the Special Prosecutor's Office for Combating Corruption, the

---

[5]The Global Impunity Index Report pointed out that Mexico's ratio of police per capita was significantly higher than the global average (355 per 100,000 inhabitants); nevertheless having only 4.2 judges per 100,000 inhabitants, which is well below the average, creates serious clogging during trials and judicial reviews, and most crimes go unpunished.

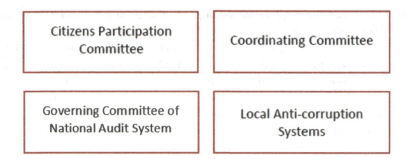

Fig. 12.1 Members of the national anti-corruption system. *Source* The author

Ministry of Public Administration, the Federal Tribunal of Administrative Justice, the National Institute for Transparency Access to Information and Personal Data Protection, the Federal Judicial Council, and a Citizen Participation Committee. The institutional objective was to put together groups that were not coordinating their efforts in order to identify and control corruption and, by including citizens in the Central Committee, repair the relationship between the government and the public (Fig. 12.1).

The reforms seemingly laide the foundation for a tougher and more comprehensive approach to combating corruption in Mexico. The objective was to demand greater government transparency, expand audit powers, and reduce political influence over investigations into corruption cases. The main tool was the creation of an autonomous Special Prosecutor's Office for Combating Corruption. Note that, at the time of writing, the head of this office has not yet been appointed.

The system also lacked important offices to institute a far more comprehensive approach to combating corruption in Mexico. These included other figures such as a Financial Intelligence office which could investigate money laundering, campaign financing, and the use of money to influence policy; and an Organized Crime office to delve into the use of cartel money for political purposes. A quick institutional review shows that the intention of creating a tangible system to control corruption was merely a façade. After nine months of pushing to examine the kind of corruption that ignited public outrage and brought the new watchdog into existence, some of the institutions' most prominent members say they have been stymied every step of the way, unable to make the most basic headway (Fig. 12.2).

Regardless of the publicity surrounding the anti-corruption reforms, and despite popular demands, little was achieved. Mandatory local anti-corruption systems were supposed to be set up as result of this reform. Nevertheless, Enrique Peña Nieto's administration failed to implement several important aspects of the anti-corruption reform package that are essential for making the National Anti-Corruption System fully operational, and more importantly, it deliberately attempted to prevent several important anti-corruption probes moving forward.

The Senate delayed the appointment of several key actors in the system, including the Special Prosecutor and eighteen Magistrates specialized in

Citizens Participation Committee	Coordinating Committee
Oversees and liaises between society and the institutions that comprise the system	Coordinates institutions in charge of preventing, investigating, and sanctionining corruption

Prevention	Investigation	Sanction
Ministry for Public Administration Internal Control Bodies National Institute for Transparency	Special Prosecutor for Combating Corruption Federal Auditor Superior	Federal Tribunal of Administrative Justice Federal Judicial Council

Note: This figure shows all the Mexican institutions that should be part of the system for counting all the phases of corruption control. According to the General Law of the SNA, the various parts of SNA include the Citizen Participation Committee, the Coordinating Committee, the Governing Committee of National Audit System, and local anti-corruption systems; it also includes the Executive Secretary of SNA, along with a technical secretary and the Executive Commission.

Fig. 12.2 Complete integration of the National Anti-corruption System. *Source* The author

investigating and prosecuting corruption cases. The delays happened because the Senate considered that candidates were not independent, and mainly identified as part of the Peña Nieto administration. Additionally, the Citizen Participation Committee, which was supposed to play a major role in suggesting and overseeing the actions of the anti-corruption system, has claimed that the administration has consistently undermined their efforts to do so. At state level, systems have not yet been implemented in most places. This is not a minor point, as corruption is endemic at state level. The above gives strength to many of the assertions in the document that emphasize the inertia of subnational political institutions.

Added to this were the administration's refusal to cooperate in some of the biggest cases of alleged government corruption, the scandals regarding the use of government surveillance technology against anti-corruption activists, allegations of widespread bribery to win construction contracts, and the purported embezzlement of millions of dollars. All this signalled that central government efforts to fight corruption were mainly phoney. One glaring example is the protection of Mexican government officials implicated in the United States Department of Justice's investigation of the Brazilian construction company, Odebrecht. This was a bribery scandal which rocked administrations across Latin America, but the Peña Nieto government did its best to sweep it under the rug.

Why create a complex system of institutions to fight corruption that will not be fully implemented? Why hobble them and make them inefficient and ineffective? Shouldn't public pressure have led the government to create institutions which would give better results and lead to greater social equilibrium?

First, public opinion, citizens and civil society leaders, including some who helped engineer the creation of the anti-corruption system, may have fallen prey to a familiar trick: the government creates a panel to address a major issue, only to starve it of resources, inhibit its progress or ignore it, or make rules so convoluted that the system is unworkable. In the case of the SNA, the system is not a collection of processes, but a group of institutions without a coherent set of procedural rules.

For example, the Citizens' Committee technically oversees the entire process, yet it is overseer in name only. All significant decisions must be made by a collection of seven different agencies. Even when supervising other members' actions, the institutional construction leaves the Citizens' Committee heavily outvoted. Six of the agencies come from different branches of government, with different incentives, different objectives, and different processes. There is no homogenous procedure established for inter-agency interactions. When one part of a process is finished, there is no established procedure to pass on to the next part. Another example: the SNA communicates the results of an investigation to the prosecution, which then needs to begin its own enquiry. The system is designed not to work, or to do so as slowly as possible.

Second, and more important, Mexico has no tradition of independent watchdogs, so there is no quick fix here. The creation of the SNA is embedded in the tradition of Mexican centralized public administration. Solutions come from the President and the central bureaucracy which designs them. Thus, 'solutions' are fashioned to suit the incentives of the government, not of the public. Reformers knew that including these six visible yet disconnected agencies created a perfect façade for the SNA, and excluding crucial actors, such as financial intelligence, was part of the plan.

The Mexican political system has never created real counterbalances or checks and balances. This has resulted in a highly centralized decision-making process around the Executive. All deep structural reforms in Mexico have been exclusively presidential driven. The President and central government bureaucrats shape reforms in such a way as to avoid being affected by them. This is the case with the SNA. Full implementation of the System would have limited the gains derived from the economic reforms pushed by the same Peña Nieto administration. It's no coincidence that the most vociferous calls for action against corruption were against government officials involved in infrastructure and oil contracts, yet those same were a huge part of the support for Peña Nieto's reforms. Fighting corruption would have stymied plans for gaining control of a strategic economic sector, therefore corruption control resulted in just farce.

12.4 Final Remarks

Classic institutionalism claims that even authoritarian and non-democratic regimens would prefer institutions where all members could make advantageous transactions. According to this argument, structural reforms that focus on preventing, limiting and combating corruption will be largely preferred by all actors in any given setting. Nevertheless, the Mexican political system was comprised of bureaucrats who were system-specific, implying that these actors would be worse off under a fully implemented anti-corruption scheme. Thus, those in charge of implementing such a reform who were at-risk of losing the privileges granted to them by the current system dedicated themselves to limiting the scope of the reform.

In Mexico, political behaviour is highly determined by embedded institutions that privilege centralized decision-making. Mexican reformers have historically privileged those changes that increase their gains and delayed and boycotted those that negatively affect them. This is the result of a path dependency on President-driven reforms and entrenched central bureaucracies, without strengthening real counterbalances, which the Mexican political system has never done. Corruption control represented a contradiction in the government's plans to continue extracting rents. The SNA resulted in a façade, characterized as "a group of people who meet for coffee and biscuits".

This result holds not just for Mexico, but also for soviet-style economies, and even for modern democracies where powerful bureaucratic minorities are often able to block changes that would be costly to their interests, even if the changes would increase net gains for the country as a whole. To understand how reforms to government, anticorruption included, are limited or interrupted, it is necessary to understand the basic political institutions of a country.

References

Ballinas Valdés, Cristopher (2011). *Political Struggles and the Forging of Autonomous Government Agencies* (Basingstoke: Palgrave Macmillan).
Carpizo, Jorge (1983). *El presidencialismo en México* (Mexico: Siglo XXI).
Castañeda, Jorge G. (1995). "The Political Economy of Mexico, 1940–1988: A Game Theoretical View", in: *European Journal of Political Economy*, 11: 291–316.
Cordera, Rolando; Tello, Carlos (1981). *México: La disputa por la nación: perspectivas y opciones del desarollo* (Mexico: Siglo XXI).
Haggard, Stephan; Webb, Steven (Eds.) (1994). *Voting for Reform: Democracy, Political Liberalization, and Economic Adjustment* (Oxford: Oxford University Press).
Hernández Rodríguez, Rogelio (1987). "Los hombres del presidente De la Madrid", in: *Foro Internacional*, 28,2: 5–38.
Hernández Rodríguez, Rogelio (1993). "La administración al servicio de la política: la Secretaría de Programación y Presupuesto", in: *Foro Internacional*, 33,1: 445–473.
Hernández Rodríguez, Rogelio (1994). "Inestabilidad política y presidencialismo en México", in: *Mexican Studies/Estudios Mexicanos*, 10,1: 187–216.
Huntington, Samuel P. (1968). *Political Order in Changing Societies* (New Haven, Yale University Press).
Instituto Mexicano para la Competitividad (2015). *La corrupción en México: Transamos y no avanzamos* (Mexico, Instituto Mexicano para la Competitividad).
Le Clercq, Juan Antonio; Rodríguez, Gerardo (2017). *Dimensiones de la impunidad global. IGI 2017* (Puebla: UDLAP).

Lehoucq, Fabrice; Aparicio, Francisco; Benton, Allyson; Nacif, Benito; Negretto, Gabriel (2004). "Political Institutions, Policymaking Processes and Policy Outcomes in Mexico", Latin American Research Network Working Paper No. R-512 (Washington, D.C.: Inter-American Development Bank [IBD]).
Molinar Horcasitas, Juan; Weldon, Jeffrey (2001). "Reforming Electoral Systems in Mexico", in: Shugart, Matthew; Wattenberg, Martin (Eds.), *Mixed-Member Electoral Systems: The Best of Both Worlds?* (Oxford: Oxford University Press): 209–231.
Olson, Mancur (1982a). *The Rise and Decline of Nations: Economic Growth, Stagflation, and Social Rigidities* (New Haven: Yale University Press).
Olson, Mancur (1982b). "Microeconomic Incentives and Macroeconomic Decline", in: *Weltwirtschaftliches Archiv* 120,4: 631–645.
Ortiz Ramirez, Jorge Alejandro (2016). "Sanciones Administrativas derivadas de la Fiscalización Superior: una revision de su eficacia", in: Romero Gudiño, Alejandro; Bolaños Cárdenas, Leonardo Arturo (Eds.), *Fiscalización, Transparencia y Rendición de cuentas*, Vol. 3 (Mexico City: Comisión de Vigilancia de la Auditoría Superior de la Federación – Cámara de Diputados del H. Congreso de la Unión): 543–564.
Paz, Octavio (1978). "El Ogro Filantrópico", in: *Vuelta*, 21: 13–26.
Ros, Jaime (1994). "Mexico's Trade and Industrialization Experience Since 1960: A Reconsideration of Past Policies and Assessment of Current Reforms", in: Helleiner, G.K. (Ed.), *Trade Policy and Industrialization in Turbulent Times* (New York: Routledge): 170–216.
Santiso, Carlos (2004). "The Contentious Washington Consensus: Reforming the Reforms in Emerging Markets", *Review of International Political Economy*, 11,4: 827–843.
Smith, Peter (1975). 'La movilidad politica en el México contemporáneo', *Foro Internacional*, 15,3: 379–413.
Smith, Peter (1979). *Labyrinths of Power: Political Recruitment in Twentieth-Century Mexico* (Princeton, NJ: Princeton University Press).
The World Economic Forum (2017). *The Global Competitiveness Report 2017–2018* (Geneva: The World Economic Forum).
Weldon, Jeffrey (1997a). "El presidente como legislador, 1917–1934" in: Picato, Pablo Atilio (Ed.), *El poder legislativo en las décadas revolucionarias, 1908–1934* (Mexico City: Universidad Nacional Autónoma de México, Instituto de Investigaciones Legislativas): 117–145.
Weldon, Jeffrey (1997b). "The Political Sources of Presidencialismo in Mexico", in: Mainwaring, S.; Shugart, Matthew (Eds.), *Presidentialism and Democracy in Latin America* (Cambridge: Cambridge University Press).
Weldon, Jeffrey (2003). "El Congreso, las maquinarias políticas locales y el Maximato: las reformas no-reeleccionistas de 1933", in: Dworak, Fernando (Ed.), *El legislador a examen: el debate sobre la reelección legislativa en México* (Mexico City: Fondo de Cultura Económica): 33–53.
Weldon, Jeffrey (2004). "Changing Patterns of Executive-Legislative Relations in Mexico", in: Middlebrook, K.J. (Ed.), *Dilemmas of Political Change in Mexico* (London, Institute of Latin American Studies, University of London): 133–67.
Winecki, Jan (1996). "Why Economic Reforms Fail in the Soviet System: A Property Right-Based Approach", in: Alston, Lee J.; Eggerston, Thrainn; North, Douglass C. (Eds.) *Empirical Studies in Institutional Change* (Cambridge: Cambridge University Press): 63–91.

Chapter 13
Institutional Path Dependence in the Failure of the "War on Drugs" in Mexico

Jorge Javier Romero

Abstract There have been many critics of the way the Mexican government has confronted the problems related to drug market regulation but just a few of those critics have focused on the legacy of different institutions and the development of local powers such as the figure of the *caciques*. This chapter provides a critique of the so-called "war on drugs" from an institutionalist perspective which considers the existing tensions in Mexico between the formal legal order and the informal institutions that really prevail in the country.

Keywords Cacicazgo · Clientelism · Drugs regulation · Violence · War on drugs

Many criticisms have been written about the prohibitionist approach that the Mexican government has adopted with respect to drug market regulation, an approach that ended with the Army, the federal police and the Navy in open frontal war against the drug trade. Those criticisms have been launched from very diverse fronts: human rights, social costs, market inefficiency, as well as in terms of objectives achieved as public policy like security and the "recovery" of the rule of law. Nevertheless, few of them, if any, have focused on the influence of institutional history on drug policy and the institutional trajectory of the local power allocation that constrains it.

This article is a critique of the so-called "war on drugs" from an institutionalist perspective, which considers the existing tensions in Mexico between the formal legal order and the informal institutions that really prevail in the country. I argue that the keys to understanding the failure of the strategy assumed by the last two governments underlie the process of institutionalization of local authority: the way

---

Research Professor C, of the Department of Politics and Culture at the Universidad Autónoma Metropolitana Xochimilco attached to the Public Policies area, and professor of the postgraduate division of the Faculty of Political and Social Sciences of the UNAM. Professor Romero has carried out research visits at the Institute of Advanced Social Studies of the Spanish National Research Council and has given lectures at different universities and study centers in Mexico and Spain. He is currently on sabbatical at the Drug Policy Program of the CIDE Centro Region, where he directs the Diploma in Drug Policy and the Internal Seminar of the PPD; Email: jromero@correo.xoc.uam.mx.

© Springer Nature Switzerland AG 2020
J. A. Le Clercq and J. P. Abreu Sacramento (eds.), *Rebuilding the State Institutions*,
https://doi.org/10.1007/978-3-030-31314-2_13

in which local political intermediation has been institutionalized in Mexico since the nineteenth century. The local power in Mexico is based, to this day, on the way of doing things inherited from the figure of the *cacique*. The formal institutionalization of the Mexican state has finally assimilated the informal mechanisms of reduction of violence characteristic of the *cacicazgo*, that consolidates (as an informal institution) a framework of negotiation and disobedience parallel to the legal order. The *cacicazgo* emerges as a mechanism of clientele administration that exercises control over local populations as a bargaining chip in perpetual negotiation with federal political leaders.

Any prohibitionist approach is doomed to fail, while the *de facto* distribution of power that exists between the caciques and their localities remains unchanged.

In this article I consider the implications of analysing the *cacique*[1] *form of political intermediation* from a path-dependent perspective and analyse the historical trajectory of drug regulation in Mexico and how it reflects the constraints established by the *cacicazgo* path dependency. Finally, the concluding section iscusses the implications of the study on Calderon's policy decisions, as well as any other prohibitionist approach.

13.1 The Informal Institutionalization of the Cacique Intermediaries

With the independence of Mexico and the subsequent formal institutionalization of the liberal republic, a contradiction arose between the legal order and the traditional forms of local power, which during the Viceroyalty lay with the traditional authorities, who had operated as translators between different orders: those of the

---

[1]The word *cacique* comes from the Caribbean aboriginal languages and is adopted by the Spanish Empire as part of a legal scheme that seeks to regulate the administration of the colonies in America (Zermeño Padilla 2017: 297). In its origins it refers to a formal institution legitimized by the political organization of the conquest. The first lexicographical reference in which the concept is mentioned dates from 1729 and describes cacique:

> as a synonym of lord among the Indians. From the same concept derives "cacicazgo" to designate the territory under the rule of the *cacique*. Therefore, *cacique* is the dynastic feudal lord who had legal privileges and the right of family succession. It was a noun used by the Spaniards to identify [...] those who commanded, the chiefs of the people (Zermeño Padilla 2017: 298).

> What I am interested in highlighting in this first definition is that the *cacique* is not yet seen as a despotic ruler who operates outside the law or in a kind of "middle" between the established legal order and informal political negotiation. He is not yet "the little despot who distributes at his whim all the positions in his territory [...] in the community nothing is done without first having his approval" (Zermeño Padilla 2017: 305). Its existence is recognized by the Old Regime and the Crown and regulated by law in the *Recopilación de Leyes de los Reynos de Indias*, as referred by Guerra (1988: 201).

communities, with their uses and customs recognized by the Crown, those of the manorial order of the haciendas, and that of the colonial bureaucracy. These were formally recognized authorities, but with the dissolution of the Spanish legality they were demoted to informality. The advent of the new liberal legal order displaced the figure of the *cacique*, excluding him from the legal organization of the territory (Zermeño Padilla 2017: 310–312).

However, this displacement did not mean the end of the *cacicazgo* as an institution; it only transitioned from the formality of the law to the informality of the political turmoil. François-Xavier Guerra rightly notes that the *cacique* (whether his authority is legal or not) serves as an intermediary between the governed people and the representatives of the new liberal state and, therefore, it is necessary:

For the governed, for traditional society, whose system of authority is totally different, someone is needed to act as an intermediary with the representatives of the modern State, to translate the language of politics, demands, rejections, reactions … This relationship between two heterogeneous worlds is assured by the *cacique*. He is at the same time an authority of the traditional society and a member of the political culture of the political people and machinery of the modern State. The existence of the *cacique* is all the more indispensable as the separation between the two worlds is greater. [...] Articulation between two heterogeneous 'peoples' is an illegal power, hidden, shameful, but inevitable (Guerra 1988: 201).

It should come as no surprise that, despite being displaced from the legal order, the *cacique* has been an essential part of the new regime. Since its formation, during the nineteenth century, the Mexican State has been a social order of limited access, where the basis of social organization has been personal relationships: who one is and who one knows. Personal interaction, particularly between powerful individuals, has determined access to wealth and limited opportunities for the weakest – a natural state[2] in which access to the law has been limited to a few, and has been, in any case, a framework for negotiating disobedience according to the resources, power or influence of each one. The reduction of violence has been carried out as a result of pacts concerning the distribution of parcels of income extraction among those included in the power coalition. The state protections have extended only to those who pay directly for them or to the political clienteles in which the members of the pact of domination sustain their domain. In order to do business, to obtain services or to disobey the law, particular protections obtained through personal relationships with those who have the capacity to extend patronage have been required.

---

[2]The *limited access order* (or *natural state*) emerged between five and ten thousand years ago, and was associated with increasing scale of human societies. Increasing scale is accomplished through a hierarchy of personal relationships between powerful individuals. Personal relationships among the elite form the basis for political organization and constitute the grounds for individual interaction. A natural state is ruled by a dominant coalition; people outside the coalition have only limited access to organizations, privileges, and valuable resources and activities (North et al. 2009: 56).

The uneven process of building an organization with a competitive advantage in violence, capable of controlling the population and the territory of the whole country, took more than fifty years, until finally a state organization with a predominance of social relations organized by personal lines was institutionalized, which included privileges, very marked social hierarchies, a very unequal application of the law, arbitrarily defined property rights, and racial, culturally based, discrimination. Inheritor to the institutional trajectory of the Viceroyalty, the State that emerged from the liberal victory, consolidated during the dictatorship of Porfirio Díaz, generated mechanisms to reduce violence based on the sale of particular protections and the control of clienteles.

13.2 The Negotiation of the Law Through Intermediaries as a Path-Dependent Dynamic for Drug Regulation

Although the institutional displacement described in the previous section should not be a surprise given the foundational conditions of the Mexican State, it is especially relevant that the political discussion between the federal elites and the local authorities has abandoned the domain of the law in favor of informality. As we argue below, this transition constitutes a critical moment in the development of drug regulation policy, since it is during this historical juncture that local and federal incentives were established to give rise to black market and reinforce it.

A path-dependence approach[3] makes it possible to identify a critical historical juncture in the institutional trajectory of *cacicazgo*. Given the limitations of this article, the criterion for identifying this historical juncture is the clear and consolidated establishment of a new incentive scheme for the main actors involved in the institution – in this case, the transition from the *cacicazgo* of a formal institution to a competing informal institution.

This transition covers the years between the consolidation of the liberal republic and the end of Porfiriato by the Mexican Revolution. During this period the *caciques* now deprived of the legitimacy of legality accumulated power, gained loyalties and fought against liberals, conservatives and French alike. After the war against French intervention, caudillos with territorial control of a *cacique* character maintained a tense relationship with the central power. Many of them supported the rebellion that led Porfirio Diaz to power, which preserved their local strength, and although it is true that they were gradually replaced by operators loyal to the national leader, they ended up using the same methods of reducing violence based on the negotiation of disobedience and the sale of particular protections that

---

[3]The idea of a path-dependent trajectory encloses a logic of increasing returns which could also be described as self-reinforcing or positive feedback processes. A process in which the "costs of switching from one alternative to another will, in certain social contexts, increase markedly over time" (Pierson 2000: 251).

allowed them to maintain control, given the high transaction costs and the huge agency problem that prevailed in Mexican politics.

Eventually, those strategies gave way to Porfirian pax and the *cacicazgo* consolidated in what Helmke/Levitsky (2004) called a competing informal institution: socially shared rules, usually unwritten, that are created, communicated, and enforced outside officially sanctioned channels that coexist with ineffective formal institutions that are not systematically enforced, which enables actors to ignore or violate them, producing results which diverge from those that the formal institution was supposed to obtain. "These informal institutions structure incentives in ways that are incompatible with the formal rules: to follow one rule, actors must violate another" (Helmke/Levistky 2004: 729).

During the Porfirian pax the *cacique* forms of political intermediation reached a point of equilibrium. The new incentive scheme became inert and, consequently, the costs of deviating from the trajectory that it drew increased (Pierson 2000: 263). Paradoxically, the concentration of power around the person of Díaz gave greater territorial extension, freedom of action and discretion to their *caciques* than they would have enjoyed under the Old Colonial Regime (Guerra 1988: 202).

At this point we can see a clear path-dependent logic that was deepened thanks to different aspects of the new relationships between the three main actors that make up the *cacicazgo*: settlers, *caciques* and representatives of the federal government. The new arrangement increased the power asymmetry between the settlers and the *caciques* who *de facto* ruled the land. Territorial divisions were drawn in the municipalities to meet local power arrangements. The reduction of violence and the sale of protections allowed economic growth, although this followed the pattern described by John Coatsworth:

> The interventionist and pervasively arbitrary nature of the institutional environment forced every enterprise, urban or rural, to operate in a highly politicized manner, using kinship networks, political influence, and family prestige to gain privileged access to subsidized credit, to aid various stratagems for recruiting labour, to collect debts or enforce contracts, to evade taxes or circumvent the courts, and to defend or assert titles to land. Success or failure in the economic arena always depended on the relations of the producer with political authorities – local officials for arranging matters close at hand, the central government for sympathetic interpretations of the law and intervention at the local level when conditions required it. Small enterprise, excluded from the system of corporate privilege and political favours, was forced to operate in a permanent state of semiclandestinity, always at the margin of the law, at the mercy of petty officials, never secure from arbitrary acts and never protected against the rights of those more powerful. (Coatsworth 1990: 94)

The legal order that was constructed at the time was clearly biased in favor of those with sufficient negotiation capacity to buy the protection of the state organization, embodied in local agents of different hierarchy and in the governors and military chiefs, institutionalized forms of the former caudillos with local territorial control. The disobedience of the law was negotiated everywhere, and its protection was bought, either with rent parcels or with political reciprocity.

This legal order designed to resolve the conflicts of power between the different regions of the country (but nothing else) provided the incentives for the emergence of illegal markets based on the power of the figure of the *cacique*. Some even used these markets to strengthen their influence in their regions.[4]

This was the institutional context in which *caciquism* became rooted in society and in the political structure of the country in such a way that it could survive the cataclysm of the Mexican Revolution. The civil war was followed by the reconstruction of a basic natural state that reproduced the characteristics of the previous arrangement. The successive crises of violence, however, were resolved in a process of gradual institutionalization, over more than two decades, until it reached its final form in the 1940s, which in the end solved the problem of the circulation of political elites and presidential successions without modifying the basic features of the institutional pattern based on the rentier control of a narrow coalition of interests (Acemoglu/Robinson 2012).

The political pact that was consolidated in 1946, from which emerged the definitive form of the regime's party, the Institutional Revolutionary Party (PRI), represented the arrival of the social order of limited access to maturity.[5] The stability of the classical period of the PRI regime (1946–1982) was characterized by an intricate institutional arrangement, structured around formal and informal rules that regulated both the particularistic appropriation of sources of income and the circulation of political elites. The legal order of the PRI regime was a direct heir of the way in which the law in Mexico had been institutionalized since the Porfiriato: as a framework for the negotiation of disobedience and the sale of particular protections. That was the mechanism for reducing violence and the framework in which business could be successful, which, under these conditions, did not have to be exclusively 'legal'. During the years of economic and political stability after the 1946 agreement, those protected by the regime obtained great benefits: the entrepreneurs dedicated to production for the domestic market, who were protected from foreign competition; the union leaders who were granted the monopoly of labour representation and exclusive usufruct of union dues while being allowed to charge

---

[4]Such is the case of Mucio Martínez in Puebla:

> In Puebla, an old comrade in arms of Diaz, Mucio Martinez, held the governorship for 18 years (this was not a record: Cahuantzi, in Tlaxcala, served for 26 years and others, more than 20), was enriched by the illegal operation of canteens, brothels and the state monopoly of pulque. With the complicity of its officials – notably that of its police chief, Miguel Cabrera – it was, even for Porfirian parameters, the prototype of a corrupt and arbitrary ruler; "When in a country the President of the Republic is called Porfirio Díaz, and the Minister of Finance José Yves Limantour, the King of Journalism, Rafael Reyes Spíndola and a State Governor, Mucio P. Martínez [declared an opposition speaker], the revolution is a must..." (Knight 2010: 34).

[5]A *mature* natural state is characterized by durable institutional structures for the State and the ability to support elite organizations outside the immediate framework of the State. Both characteristics distinguish the mature natural state from the basic natural state, but to reiterate, the differences are of degree rather than of kind. At the limit of the spectrum, a mature natural state is able to create and sustain perpetually surviving organizations, but that is not a common feature of mature natural states.

employers for the docility of workers; bureaucrats who sold public services; and organizations that were granted some monopoly of services in exchange for their political allegiance, to name just a few.

The sale of private protections was carried out through two networks: bureaucratic and corporate. During the classic era of the regime, the bureaucracy peacefully controlled the territory, marginalized the military from power – although it granted them control of certain protection sales plots – and depersonalized the presidency by making it the apex of a career managed from a system of clientelist incentives that rewarded discipline and political loyalty over any other bureaucratic virtue. The knowledge or the administrative efficiency could return, but without belonging to a network of clientelist reciprocity nobody could ascend in the hierarchical scale.

The second network, dependent on the first, but with a lot of bargaining power, was constituted by political intermediaries – trade unions or peasants' leaders, leaders of marginalized groups, like market tenants, street traders, taxi drivers or shoe shiners – who maintained the peace of their clienteles and administered the state protections and budget spill-overs that the bureaucracy destined to serve the popular sectors. Both networks came together in the PRI, a cloak of identity and a mechanism for resolving conflicts and distributing rent plots. The head of the network of networks – the final arbitrator of the settlement – was the President of the Republic, an heir to the attributes of the founding leader of the basic natural state, Porfirio Diaz, but only for six years.

The administration of justice was strongly politicized, since at both the federal and local levels the public prosecutors and the judiciary were extremely dependent on the executive powers, incarnated in the states of the republic in the governors, who were nothing more than institutionalized *cacicazgos* of sexennial duration, in the image and likeness of national power, but completely subordinated to it. The judicial systems were networks of clienteles with strong ties of reciprocity that eliminated any possibility of independence of judges or magistrates.

13.3 The Flimsy Rule of Law and "Substances that Degenerate the Race"

Thus, in Mexico, the laws have always been a framework of negotiation of disobedience, rather than a socially accepted set of rules of the game to solve the problems of cooperation and competition in Mexican society. The legislation on drugs was not, of course, an exception. The prohibition of drugs began in Mexico almost from the approval of the Constitution of 1917, after the Revolution (Romero 2017), even though it was not a matter of special relevance for public policy. Although the issue of "substances that poison the individual and degenerate the race" was a concern of the Constitution makers, who explicitly ordered the General

Congress, the legislatures of the States and the Council of General Health – dependent of the Presidency of the Republic – to carry out anti-alcoholic actions and oppose the sale of nerve-damaging substances, the legislation derived from that constitutional mandate was only applied with rigor in exceptional cases. In fact, the faculties on the matter were given to the General Health Council and were not established as criminal matters until more than a decade later.[6]

The first specific regulations of the constitutional mandate in the matter were the *Provisions on the trade of products that can be used to foment vices that degenerate the race and, on the cultivation of plants that can be used for the same purpose* of 15 March 1920. The Provisions were essentially of a health nature, as they did not imply criminal sanctions. Opium could even be cultivated in the country, despite the international alarm over the substance, decreed since the international treaty signed at the Second International Opium Conference, held in The Hague in 1912, of which Mexico was a signatory. To cultivate opium in Mexican territory, it was enough to have the permission of the Department of Public Health, while the text established that "the cultivation and trade of marijuana was strictly prohibited", despite its use for centuries in traditional Mexican therapies. Thus, an illegal cannabis market was born, which generated profits for both those who trafficked the plant and those State agents who protected the clandestine market, as shown in an episode in the *tremendista* novel *Epitalamio del Prieto Trinidad*, first published in 1942 by the Spanish writer exiled in Mexico, Ramón J. Sender, in which he describes how corruption had become the agreement regarding drugs. The protagonist of the story, a bad-tempered military man in charge of an insular prison inspired by the Marias Islands, walks through the corridors of a market in the capital and approaches the stall of the herbalist who sells marijuana. He threatens to report her it if she does not tell him who her provider was:

> The old woman refused. Without losing stiffness she dropped a fifty-peso bill at Trinidad's feet.
>
> – Excuse me, my boss. Something fell out of your pocket. Trinidad picked it up.
> – I dropped two. Where is the other one?
>
> "Here it is," the old woman said quickly. I had taken it from the ground without knowing (Sender: 1966).

It was the Penal Code of 1931 that established with precision that crimes against health were a matter of federal jurisdiction. New forms of delinquency were defined around the drug trade, and penalties were hardened. That code would set the tone for the approach to drug policy during the following years: addicts were considered

---

[6]In that order, while morphine, opium, heroin and cocaine were recognized as medicinal, so they must be subject to state regulation for sale, marijuana was completely banned, thus Mexico anticipated the prohibitionist wave because in the United States it was not until 1937 that the prohibition of cannabis was consolidated with the *Marihuana Tax Act*.

ill, not criminals, although the legal formulation left a lot of room to criminalize them, which opened the space for consumer extortion.[7]

The sanitarian vision regarding drugs was consolidated with the Sanitary Code of 1934. However, in the final months of the government of Lazaro Cárdenas, in 1940, a new regulation of drug addiction was approved, which meant a pioneering attempt to start what is known today as harm reduction policy. According to that ordinance, of ephemeral validity since it was suspended just six months after it was approved owing to pressure from the United States, the government would provide drugs to those addicted at cost price in order to eliminate the clandestine market.[8]

The pressure exerted by the United States against the regulation did not waver. Roosevelt's government halted the export of medicines to Mexico until the measure was repealed and, as the other major producer of pharmaceutical products was Germany, which was at war and therefore trade with it was interrupted, Cardenas had no choice but to suspend the regulation just a few months after its entry into force. It remained suspended until it was repealed by the enactment of a new Health Code in 1973. However, the regulation had been effective, during its short term, in reducing the clandestine market and police extortion.

Throughout the classic period of the PRI regime (1946–1982), drug policy towards consumers remained pragmatic without major changes in the legal framework. The forced internment for the rehabilitation of addicts was abandoned, and the prohibition established in the Penal Code was maintained, without formally criminalizing consumers, but with huge margins of arbitrariness, so that, in practice, they were constant victims of extortion or imprisonment. Thus, the clandestine internal market was managed in accordance with the generalized mechanism of the relationship between the State and society: the particular negotiation of disobedience with authority agents. Consumers could be imprisoned or not by simple possession, at judges' discretion, if they did not reach an agreement beforehand with the police or the public prosecutor. The judge decided if the amount possessed could be considered commensurate with personal consumption or if it merited penal sanction. To be exempted from crimes, users of substances had to declare themselves addicted.

---

[7]To close this margin somewhat, the Federal Code of Criminal Procedures established a "procedure for drug addicts", which stated that if the Public Prosecutor's Office found that the purchase or possession of drugs was solely for "the personal use of them by the accused", it would not exercise criminal action. This is an important precedent of the legislation currently in force, which uses the non-exercise of criminal action for people who possess the prohibited substances in quantities within the thresholds established by a table in the *General Health Law* of the maximums regarded as personal doses for immediate use.

[8]That regulation was perhaps the first norm in the world to adopt what is now known as the harm reduction approach, which is based on the recognition that the best way to deal with the problematic consumption of substances is from a health perspective, with measures that keep users away from criminal circuits and do not consider users criminals – to avoid extortion and harassment by the police – with the provision of substances produced in adequate sanitary conditions and without adulterations, which are more dangerous than the substances themselves.

This changed as a result of the reforms called "small drug smuggling law" of 2008, already in full "war against drugs" unleashed by President Felipe Calderón. Various articles of the penal code and the General Health Law were modified to differentiate drug trafficking from small drug dealing, to empower local authorities to pursue the second and to differentiate consumers from small traffickers. A table of thresholds for the amount of possession recognized as acceptable as a dose for immediate consumption was then established in the General Health Law. Thus, it was established that the maximum dose of personal and immediate consumption of marijuana would be 5 g, opium 2 g, heroin 50 mg and cocaine 500 mg. Regarding other substances listed, the established thresholds are equally low. Any amount above the threshold is already considered simple possession, worthy of imprisonment, even if the intention to trade it is not proven.

13.4 Traffic to the United States and the Sale of Local Protections

By the mid-1930s, the issue of illicit drug trafficking to the United States began to gain importance, as the prohibition in that country advanced. During the years in which the XVIII Amendment of the Philadelphia Constitution was in effect, the clandestine alcohol market from Mexico to the neighbour of the north had been significant, but once the prohibition was abolished, it was the turn for trade in illegal psychotropic substances.

Until then, Mexico had not been a relevant producer of prohibited substances, with the exception of cannabis; however, during the Second World War, with the return of the US soldiers who had participated in the conflict, the demand for illegal opiates increased notably in the United States. Many wounded servicemen who had been treated with morphine had become hooked and were not given any substitute treatment. Hence, poppy production destined for the clandestine market skyrocketed in northern Mexico, especially in the region known as the "golden triangle", at the confluence of the states of Sinaloa, Durango and Chihuahua. That trade soon became protected by the Army, with low levels of violence, after the governor of Sinaloa was allegedly killed in 1944 by order of opium producers in the region (Resa Nestares 2005).

The armed forces were part of the arrangement of the classic era of the regime and their leaders and officers obtained, in exchange for their discipline and loyalty, margins for the private use of their positions of power in defined areas of influence. Like the rest of the agents of the State, the military were able to use plots to extract payments privately, among them the administration of the illegal drug markets. Indeed, this is a difficult conjecture to prove convincingly due to the clandestine nature of the activity and the veil of secrecy with which the armed forces were protected during the classic era of the regime. During most of the PRI regime, the issue of drug trafficking was treated as a matter of low importance, as an issue that was regulated by the traditional protection-selling mechanisms with which the different instances of the State operated.

During the 1940s and 1950s, opium was the main illegal substance exported to the United States, but beginning in the 1960s, marijuana began to be the most exported drug through illegal networks. The popularization of cannabis use among young Americans during the so-called "prodigious decade", whether among the hippy movement, among the opponents of the Vietnam War, or among the rock and roll fanatics, caused Mexican production to grow substantially and their market to spread.

The levels of violence connected with clandestine drug trafficking to the United States remained low until Richard Nixon declared the "war on drugs" in 1971 and began to pressure the Mexican government to undertake campaigns to eradicate poppy and marijuana crops. The so-called "Operation Condor", begun in 1975 during the government of Luis Echevarria, implicated the Army in the destruction of crops and the confiscation of shipments, although this stopped neither production nor traffic, nor ended the sale of protection by the authorities. Later, during the government of Ronald Reagan, the pressure on the Mexican government increased again, especially after the murder of DEA agent Enrique Camarena in 1985. During those years the Drug Certification Process was established. It subsisted until 2002 and evaluated the cooperation efforts of the producing or transit of substances countries with the drug policy of the United States; if a country was not certified, bilateral assistance was suspended, and financial and commercial sanctions were imposed. Although between 1987 and 1999 there were five years in which resolutions against certification were initiated in the US Congress, Mexico managed to pass the test during all the years of its validity.

The United States pressures focused on the seizure of caches and the eradication of plantations, not in respect of legality or the strengthening of the rule of law; thus, the "war on drugs" only increased the costs of the protection sales, exacerbated the corruption of the arrangement and increased its levels of violence.

During all those years, since 1977, Mexico experienced a gradual democratization process that culminated in a new political pact in 1996, from which the PRI lost the political monopoly and the government stopped controlling elections. Although the democratization process reduced the degree of arbitrariness in the application of the law, this was only reflected in the scope of the elections and in the issues that reach the Supreme Court of Justice, converted since 1995 into a constitutional court. In the rest of exercise of power areas, the application of the law has continued to be discretionary, the negotiation of disobedience continues to predominate and the selling of the State protection in particularistic manners has not stopped.

The new arrangement did not change the rentier character, based on clientelist reciprocity, of the political settlement, because it kept the spoils system in the distribution of public employment and did not generate enough solid institutional mechanisms to replace the private negotiation of the obedience with the law with an effective and legitimate rule of law.

With the end of the political monopoly and the defeat of the PRI in 2000, the local and municipal governments acquired autonomy to manage the sale of private protections without the limits imposed by the strict party discipline and centralized arbitration in the Presidency of the Republic. Political competition did not reduce the rentier scramble but instead increased the demand for public resources to privatize. The distribution of power no longer had a centralized mechanism, as in the classic times of PRI presidentialism, but instead had multiple actors with decision-making power over money and budgets.

13.5 The loss of Territorial Control by the State and the Increase in Violence

This recovered autonomy, which reproduced the mechanisms of control of parcels of income existing before the 1929 agreement (the pact of pacification from which the regime of the PRI emerged), had particularly notable consequences in the management of clandestine markets, especially that of drugs. The arrangement which developed during the classic era of the PRI regime in relation to the clandestine market for drugs generated mutual benefits for drug traffickers, police and the Army. It became the pragmatic way of dealing with the nonsense of the prohibition imposed from abroad, while the demand for substances in the United States maintained a growing trend. Cyclically, the American pressure required persecution actions, more aimed at showing public opinion the commitment to fight drug trafficking than to achieve eradication, which was impossible. That perverse arrangement allowed the enrichment of drug lords and increased their capacity to recruit personnel to their service and to arm themselves.

With the end of the monopoly of the PRI, without the previous control mechanisms, the local appropriation of the rents was exacerbated, and the local security agencies were out of control, inasmuch as the operative force of organized crime grew, thanks to the benefits obtained from the clandestine drug markets, whose protection costs were reduced due to the fragmentation of the negotiation. The strengthened cartels, already with a good organizational infrastructure and weapons, began to diversify their operations towards predatory crimes, while the high degree of impunity generated by a system of crime control based on arbitrariness and the corruption of the police opened windows of opportunity for the growth of crime not linked to drug trafficking.

The model of authoritarian order had already reached crisis point when Felipe Calderón became President in 2006, but instead of opting for in-depth reform, his government intentionally chose to replace local forces and their pacts with a consortium of the Army, the federal police and the Navy to open a frontal war on the drug trade – no matter how much he tried to justify himself later by saying that it was against organized crime as a whole – but without developing strong judicial control mechanisms for its action, based on respect for the legal order, which resulted in an outdated form of exercising State power that eventually provoked one of the greatest violence crises in the already violent history of Mexico and a disproportionate increase in the violation of human rights (Madrazo et al. 2018), already inherently violated by the traditional forms of police arbitrariness. The emergence of federal forces in the fight against drug trafficking not only disrupted existing agreements between traffickers and local authorities, but also broke the traditional order of clientelist reciprocity that contained other forms of crime and violence. The frontal war did not reduce, however, the economic incentives for the production and trafficking of drugs (Romero 2018); on the contrary, it increased them, because the rise in prices caused by the attack meant that where a *capo* fell, and an organization was destroyed, several others arose with the intention of fighting for the market.

The way in which the mechanisms for reducing the violence of the old regime deteriorated with the eruption of plurality can be observed in what happened in the state of Michoacán. There is a need for serious and well-documented studies on how the rupture of the PRI that was experienced in that entity in 1988 and the faction struggle that developed in a large part of its regions after the split from which the PRD was born affected the rules of the game of the traditional order. The role played by the decomposition of the settlement in the increased capacity for violence of the groups of traffickers, who controlled the region to dominate the routes for transferring cocaine and other narcotics to the United States, is clearer. The resulting situation of chronic economic stagnation that made Michoacán one of the greatest expellers of workers towards the North American market is no less relevant in the decomposition of the political network.

The fact is that gradually, over the last three decades, in Michoacán the predatory bandits, no doubt some of them descendants of those who exercised power under the protective mantle of the PRI agreement, have been acquiring autonomy and controlling territories because of its capacity for violence; it is they who impose order. The huge profits of the clandestine drug market were the main source of its original accumulation; that is where the resources that allowed them to arm themselves and fight to impose their domain come from, although today they have diversified their sources of income extraction and use their power as authentic State substitutes. Why has the formal State lost control? There must be many causes to explain it, but I think one of the fundamental ones is that, instead of a process of democratization that strengthens the local order with a good base of social legitimacy, what happened was the dissolution of the old order in a messy and highly disputed manner.

The attempt of the Calderón government to impose order based on federal forces – it was in Michoacán that the first massive intervention of the Army and the federal police took place to recover the lost ground in front of the cartels – ended by dissolving the local mechanisms of the negotiated order and generated huge asymmetries of information in the fight against criminal gangs. Instead of the recovery of the state order, what happened was a kind of civil war that led to the replacement of one band of bandits by another and a greater decline of state control.

The emergence of self-defence groups as a reaction to the State's inability to reverse the criminal control of the territory is not a good sign. Undoubtedly it is a complex phenomenon, which has as one of its components social discontent at the arbitrary extortion of the gangs, but the order thus imposed is not going to lead to an efficient arrangement based on the legal order. It could serve, as Trejo (2014) has pointed out, to reduce information asymmetries in the fight against bandits, based on close knowledge of the local situation, which federal forces lack, and to wash the face of the State in a frontal combat that implies violations of human rights and intolerable actions by the forces of the legal order, but nothing guarantees that once these groups control the territory they do it according to the principles of the rule of law (Guerra 2018).

The route started in Michoacán was generalized in different areas of the country, but more than a decade after the strategy of "frontal and effective combat against drug trafficking" was launched, the so-called "war on drugs" has not achieved the proposed objectives – recover the strength of the State and security in social coexistence – nor others commonly associated with the repression of drug trafficking, such as reduction in the production, trafficking and sale of illegal substances (UNODC 2017). Rather, the strategy has contributed to the metastasis of violence that the country has experienced. That is, the "war against drugs" – the substantive militarization of the repression of drug trafficking and organized crime – has not only failed to strengthen the State and provide security for social coexistence, but, according to the growing accumulation of evidence, the effects of this policy have been very negative, because the logic of the strategy to combat drug trafficking has not been to use the law to stop offenders, but to eliminate opponents by means of a war logic, even though this is outside the law (Madrazo et al. 2018).

The increase in violence has had several causes; for example, as organized crime groups have transformed their activities and become more dependent on the control of local territories, the alternation of political parties in the municipal power increases the violence related to organized crime in the short term by destabilizing state protection networks. The municipal alternation generates uncertainty among organized crime groups around the protection pacts and consequently wars can be generated between and within criminal gangs (Bejarano 2018). Undoubtedly, the intervention of the armed forces has been a trigger for violence and the Army and Navy have contributed to the growth of the homicide rate in the country (Silva Forné et al. 2012) (Madrazo et al. 2018), which by 2017 had reached around twenty-four homicides per hundred thousand inhabitants.

The "war on drugs" has had a notable impact on the formal institutional framework of the Mexican State, since from the approval in 1996 of the first Federal Law against Organized Crime, the individual guarantees established in the Constitution began to be affected. The "constitutional costs" of the war became clearly evident with the creation of:

> (…) a special criminal regime – of reduced rights, and amplified police powers and discretion – to prosecute "organized crime". This regime was adopted in the same process of reform in which the ordinary criminal procedure was reconfigured radically in order to make it transparent and strengthen the rights of the victims and the defendant, based on an

adversarial logic and through the oral requirement of the process. Transparency and guarantees as guiding principles of the criminal process, however, were not admissible for all citizens (…) (Barreto/Madrazo 2015: 165).[9]

The "constitutional costs" of the war against drug trafficking have continued to accentuate, because in 2017 the government of Enrique Peña Nieto managed to get the majority of the Congress of the Union to approve the Internal Security Law, despite the arguments presented against from the academy, most of the civil organizations dedicated to security and human rights issues, the UN High Commissioner for Human Rights, the Inter-American Commission on Human Rights, as well as a good number of intellectual personalities with an impact on opinion public.

The armed forces have been aware that their deployment by the country to offset the incapacities of the police and investigative bodies in the fight against crime was clearly in violation of the constitutional Article 21, reformed in 2008 – hence their insistence that they be given a legal framework for action, in anticipation that their actions could be the object of accusations in the international justice system. In the absence of a solid constitutional argument able to sustain the discretionary operations that have so far been carried out, because Article 21 is very clear in reserving the tasks of public security to civil bodies and in putting the investigation of crimes under the responsibility of the public prosecution, they accepted an archaic constitutional concept, lost in the sixth section of Article 89 of the Constitution, whereby the President of the Republic is empowered to "dispose of the totality of the permanent armed forces: the Army, the Navy and of the Air Force, for the internal security and external defence of the Federation". Thus, in the law of 2017 the term "internal security" was used as a subterfuge to overturn the express prohibition that the armed forces intervene in public security tasks, but without giving it a clear definition.

The law was declared unconstitutional by the Supreme Court in December 2018, but that same day the new President, Andrés Manuel López Obrador, presented a proposition to reform the Constitution and create a militarized National Guard. The reform that creates the National Guard reproduces the essence of the failed Internal Security Law, but removes the restrictions so far raised by Article 21 of the Constitution, to avoid a new intervention of the Judicial Power against it.

---

[9]The special criminal regime created for organized crime and drug trafficking includes the possibility of subjects being detained without communication and without formal charges for up to eighty days if deemed necessary for any investigation of "organized crime"; an incarceration withholding extended twice as long (four days) as in the ordinary penal system, before being made available to the judge; incommunicado in jail (except communication with their defense lawyers); the compurgation of sentences in "special" detention centers, separate from the general population; an authorization to establish measures, not specified, of "special" surveillance and without the right to know who the accuser is. All these measures are constitutionally prohibited in the "ordinary" criminal justice process and attack the general meaning of the first title of the Constitution, dedicated to human rights (ibid.).

13.6 Conclusion

Mexico is immersed in a process of transition from a social order of limited access to one of open access. The traditional forms of violence reduction, based on the sale of private protections and the clientelist distribution of public benefits, are sinking throughout the country, but formal institutions capable of reducing violence based on the universal application of legality and the use of state force in a way that is fully attached to the legal order and with widespread social acceptance has not yet been completed. Democratization has had an adverse effect on violence, insofar as it has not occurred on the basis of a solid, professional and trained civil service that does not depend on the permanence of elected officials. The spoils system that characterizes the Mexican State in terms of the distribution of public employment has sharpened its defects with the alternation in power produced by competition between parties.

The war on drugs has weakened federalism and local governments, instead of strengthening them based on increased management capacities and adherence to the legal order. Instead of promoting the creation of an effective state organization, with local roots and committed to compliance with the law, the result has been a legal order of exception and the maintenance of traditional mechanisms of negotiation of disobedience and the sale of particular protections.

References

Acemoglu, Daron; Robinson, James (2012). *Why Nations Fail: The Origins of Power, Prosperity, and Poverty* (New York: Crown).

Bejarano Romero, Raúl (2018). *Competencia electoral, redes de protección y violencia del crimen organizado en México, 2006–2016* (Master's dissertation, Centro de Investigación y Docencia Económica, Mexico).

Coatsworth, J. (1990). *Los Orígenes del Atraso. Nueve Ensayos de Historia Económica de México en los Siglos XVIII y XIX* (Mexico City: Alianza Editorial Mexicana).

David, Paul A. (2007). "Path dependence: A foundational concept for historical social science", in: *Cliometrica: The Journal of Historical Economics and Econometric History*, 1,2: 91–114; at: https://doi.org/10.1007/s11698-006-0005-x.

Galindo López, Carlos; Gómez, Mara; Zepeda Gil, Raúl; Castellanos Cereceda, Noé Roberto (2017). *Seguridad Interior: elementos para el debate* (Mexico City: Instituto Belisario Domínguez del Senado de la República).

Guerra, Edgar (2018). "Organización armada. El proceso de toma de decisiones de los grupos de autodefensas tepacaltepequenses", in: *Estudios Sociológicos*, 36,106.

Guerra, François-Xavier (1988). *México: Del Antiguo Régimen a la Revolución*, Vol. 1, transl. Sergio Fernández Bravo (Mexico City: Fondo de Cultura Económica).

Helmke, Gretchen; Levitsky, Steven (2004). "Informal Institutions and Comparative Politics: A Research Agenda", in: *Perspectives on Politics* 2,4, 725–740; at: https://www.jstor.org/stable/3688540.

Knight, Alan (2010). *La Revolución mexicana. Del porfiriato al nuevo régimen constitucional*, transl. Luis Cortés Bargalló (Mexico City: Fondo de Cultura Económica).

Madrazo Lajous, Alejandro; Romero Vadillo, Jorge Javier (2018). "Seguridad Interior: La regresión", *Nexos* (February).

Madrazo Lajous, Alejandro; Calzada Olvera, Rebeca; Romero Vadillo, Jorge Javier (2018). "La 'guerra contra las drogas'. Análisis de los combates de las fuerzas públicas 2006–2011", in: *Política y Gobierno*, 25,2, (Mexico City: Centro de Investigación y Docencia Económica [CIDE]).

North, Douglas C.; Wallis, John Joseph; Weingast, Barry N. (2009). *Violence and Social Orders: A Conceptual Framework for Interpreting Recorded Human History* (Cambridge: Cambridge University Press).

Pierson, Paul (2000). "Increasing Returns, Path Dependence and the Study of Politics", in: *The American Political Science Review*, 94,2: 251–267; at: http://www.jstor.org/stable/2586011.

Resa Nestares, Carlos (2005). "Nueve mitos del narcotráfico mexicano (de una lista no exahustiva)", in: *Nota de investigación* (March) (Madrid: Universidad Autónoma de Madrid).

Romero, Jorge Javier (2016). *Violencia y régimen político* (Mexico City: Friedrich Ebert Stiftung).

Romero, Jorge Javier (2017). "A partir de la Constitución de 1917, cien años de política de droga en México", in: Esquivel, Gerardo; Ibarra, Francisco; Salazar, Pedro: *Cien Ensayos para el Centenario*, Vol. 3 (Mexico City: IIJ, UNAM).

Sender, Ramón J. (1966). *Epitalamio del Prieto Trinidad* (Madrid: Destino).

Silva Forné, Carlos; Pérez Correa, Catalina; Gutiérrez Rivas, Rodrigo (2012). "Uso de la fuerza letal. Muertos, heridos y detenidos en enfrentamientos de las fuerzas federales con presuntos miembros de la delincuencia organizada", in: *Desacatos* (México: Centro de Investigaciones y Estudios Superiores en Antropología Social); at: http://www.redalyc.org/articulo.oa?id=13925007004.

Trejo, Guillermo (2014). "La arriesgada apuesta por las autodefensas en México", in: *El País* (12 October), (Madrid).

United Nations Office on Drugs and Crime (2017). *World Drug Report 2017* (Wien: UNODC).

Zermeño Padilla, Guillermo (2017). *Historias Conceptuales* (Mexico City: El Colegio de México).

Chapter 14
Reversal of Fortunes: Changes in the Public Policy Environment and Mexico's Energy Reform

Tony Payan

Abstract From recent reexaminations of the relationship between politics and public policy, it has been found that the structure of public policy produces its own politics, just as politics produces its own type of public policy. The argument is that public policy generates its own incentives and resources and provides actors with information and cues that encourage their political views and convictions, but they also influence other actors – including political opposition groups, interest groups, and the masses – to articulate their own alternatives more accurately and push back, sometimes threatening public policies that appeared to have enjoyed a broad political consensus.

Recent developments in Mexico do suggest that the public policies of the last three decades have indeed produced significant political consequences – and resistance – all of which now threaten the sustainability of the public policies of democratization and liberalization that the country has pursued over the last three decades. The main political consequence is observable in the electoral results of 2018. The last general election caused a major change in the political and policy alignment of the country because the winning party of the presidency and both chambers, The National Regeneration Movement (MORENA), is a relatively new Leftist political party that ran against the country's status quo.

To explore these feedback loop dynamics and the resulting shift in the policy environment we focus on energy reform precisely because it came to be identified as the last (and major) step in what had been a steady pursuit of economic liberalization – or, as MORENA put it, the ultimate symbol of neoliberal politics that had to be reversed.

Keywords Corruption · Democratic participation · Energy reform · MORENA · NAFTA · Organized crime · PAN · Pact for Mexico · PEMEX · PRI

Tony Payan, Ph.D., is the Françoise and Edward Djerejian Fellow for Mexico Studies and director of the Mexico Center at the Baker Institute. He is also a professor at the Universidad Autónoma de Ciudad Juárez. He has a doctorate degree in international relations from Georgetown University and his research focuses primarily on border studies, particularly the US-Mexico border, border governance, border flows and immigration, as well as border security and organized crime. Email: tony.payan@rice.edu.

14.1 Introduction

Even before taking office as President of Mexico, Enrique Peña Nieto (2012–2018) invested much of his political capital in piecing together a coalition of political parties and leaders – a *Pact for Mexico* – to push for a number of structural reforms to the country's economic and political institutions.[1] Once in office, President Peña Nieto worked with both houses of Congress to make significant changes to the Mexican constitution and pass a slew of legislation on telecommunications, education, finance and fiscal policy, political institutions and elections, and energy – a sector which had remained clad with nationalistic symbolism and largely closed to private and foreign investment. Overhauling these sectors was to propel Mexico into higher economic growth, which had been relatively low for the last three decades, averaging barely above 2% per year (Fig. 14.1), and certainly insufficient to lift millions out of poverty. In addition, these structural reforms were another chapter in the remarkably long-lasting political and economic opening of the country since the 1980s. In effect, compared with much of Latin America, Mexico had enjoyed a broad political and social consensus on slow and imperfect but steady progress toward democratization and the implementation of a market-based economy.[2]

This broad consensus that underpinned the political and economic opening of the country for thirty years was indeed notable and electorally tangible. Between 1988 and 2017 roughly two-thirds of all Mexicans consistently voted for the National Action Party (PAN) and the Institutional Revolutionary Party (PRI), both of which endorsed political and economic structural reforms very much along the same lines. Figure 14.2 shows the total vote for these two right-of-center parties.

Mexico's presidential elections, showing the total number of votes by PAN and PRI, favoring a right of center agenda and a final collapse of their total vote in 2018. When PAN and PRI total tallies are added, roughly two-thirds of Mexicans had clearly supported the reforms over nearly thirty years.

---

[1] Secretaría de Relaciones Exteriores (2012). *Pacto por México*; at: https://embamex.sre.gob.mx/bolivia/images/pdf/REFORMAS/pacto_por_mexico.pdf (8 January 2019).

[2] This is a general observation, as Mexico has received various rankings on both scores by different organizations. On politics, *Varieties of Democracy* shows substantive progress on certain components of Mexico's liberal democracy (see https://www.v-dem.net/en/news/liberal-democracy-mexico/), but others show a deterioration on many scores, including *The Economist*, which labels Mexico a flawed democracy (https://www.economist.com/graphic-detail/2018/01/31/democracy-continues-its-disturbing-retreat), *Freedom House*, which ranks Mexico as only partly free (https://freedomhouse.org/report/freedom-world/2018/mexico), and Transparency International, which places Mexico 29th out of 100 countries, primarily due to high levels of corruption (https://www.transparency.org/country/MEX#), as well as The World Justice Project, which downgrades Mexico on rule of law issues (https://worldjusticeproject.org/sites/default/files/documents/WJP-ROLI-2018-June-Online-Edition_0.pdf). On economic freedom, Mexico has been ranked as number 60 out of 177, indicating that progress has been made, but there is much more to be done (https://www.theglobaleconomy.com/rankings/economic_freedom/) (All accessed on 8 January 2019).

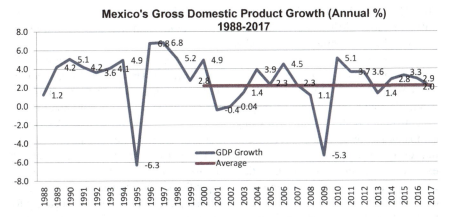

Fig. 14.1 Mexico's gross domestic product growth (annual %) 1988–2017. *Source* World Bank

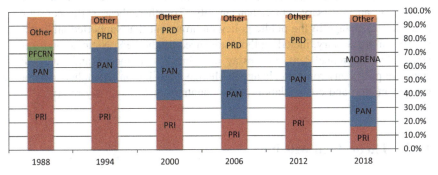

Mexico's presidential elections, showing the total number of votes by PAN and PRI, favoring a right of center agenda and a final collapse of their total vote in 2018. When PAN and PRI total tallies are added, roughly two-thirds of Mexicans had clearly supported the reforms over nearly thirty years.

Fig. 14.2 Mexico's presidential election results. Percentage of votes by party 1988–2018. *Source* INE

Moreover, unlike other countries in Latin America, which have gone through several political and economic transitions toward liberalization and numerous reversals, Mexico anchored its own transformation by pursuing a path of integration with the United States and Canada in North America. The North American Free Trade Agreement (NAFTA), which was negotiated between 1989 and 1993 and entered into effect on 1 January 1994, was simultaneously the cornerstone and the crowning achievement of that pursuit. NAFTA was also a guaranteed way to commit Mexico, presumably irreversibly, to a path of economic and political liberalization by hitching its fate to that of its North American neighbors. Even though Mexico was already well on its way to a market economy (Axelrad 1993:

201–222), NAFTA was Mexico's way of legislating its own transformation from outside (Rubio 2017). Thus, until recently, it would seem that politics and public policy in Mexico reinforced each other.

The last election, as evident in Fig. 14.2, brought about a major shift in the political and policy alignment of the country, however. The National Regeneration Movement (MORENA), a relatively new Leftist political party that ran against the country's status quo, managed to get over half of the vote and now controls the executive and both Chambers of Congress. Given that one of MORENA's central campaign promises was to reverse the policies of the last three decades, it is clear that every structural reform that Mexico put in place over the last thirty years is experiencing a serious challenge – this time from within the government. The July 2, 2018 elections may in the end reflect a public policy fatigue, including a deep dissatisfaction with the results of the politics and policy direction of the country for the last three decades and a desire for change. Others concern sudden changes in the international environment, including the significant political shift in the United States under President Donald Trump, who has criticized free trade and views Mexico as an adversary rather than an ally. Together, these shifts constitute a fundamental change in the public policy environment that supported all structural reforms in the country, including those advanced by the Peña Nieto administration. Under this theoretical lens, this essay examines the domestic and international causes of policy environment change in Mexico, focusing on its implications for the implementation and consolidation of the country's historic energy reform.

14.2 Theoretical Musings

Students of public policy have recently re-examined the relationship between politics and public policy, suggesting that the structure of public policy produces its own politics, much as politics produces its own kind of public policy. The argument is that public policy generates its own incentives and resources and provides actors with information and cues that encourage their political views and convictions, but they also influence other actors – including political opposition groups, interest groups, and the masses – to articulate their own alternatives more accurately and push back, sometimes threatening public policies that appeared to have enjoyed a broad political consensus (Pierson 1993: 595–628). Recent developments in Mexico suggest that the policies of the last three decades have indeed produced significant political consequences – and resistance – all of which now threaten the sustainability of the public policies of democratization and liberalization that the country has pursued over the last three decades. It can certainly be argued that the mixed results of the policies themselves produced over time their own kind of politics, ultimately resulting in a considerable shrinkage of the political coalition that had in turn produced the public policy consensus outlined above. The ability of the PAN-PRI coalition may have also ignored significant unintended consequences of their public policies, resulting in a more articulate political alternative in

MORENA. Political hubris cannot be discarded either as a possible contributor to the desire for change, particularly as specific economic and rule of law issues appeared to have worsened rather than gotten better over time. If so, this would confirm that the public policies of recent decades produced a slow-brewing political storm that now threatens the very reforms that recent governments have pursued – including energy reform.

The electoral results of 2018 appear to confirm just this policy and politics feedback loop. To be sure, public policy stability and change cannot be easily predicted (Wilson 2013: 391–402). Public policies, even those which have endured for decades, can be overturned or reversed altogether, or undergo substantial changes at any moment or be transformed over time, depending on many different factors (Capano/Howlett 2009). Domestically, coalitions behind the direction of a particular public policy can change and gain or lose power and influence or their credibility can erode. Public opinion may swing quickly, based on specific events or outcomes, or gradually if the policies put in place cannot deliver the results promised or expected. New actors with a different ideological bent or different interests and preferences can arrive on the scene. Market, social and technological conditions can shift, opening windows of opportunity for a different set of policies. Policy fatigue can envelop a specific field of action. Policies may also depend excessively on the agenda of one or a few individuals, without building the right institutions to sustain them in the long term. Similarly, the international context may change, making a specific policy irrelevant, unpopular or otherwise untenable, due to an erosion of international legitimacy for a country's leadership.

14.3 The Objective of This Chapter

To show how public policy and politics produce feedback loop dynamics that end up changing the policy environment and threatening the implementation and consolidation of a policy path, this chapter uses as a case study the 2013–2016 historic structural reform of the energy sector. It explores the central factors that developed over time and gained momentum and now constitute a reaction to the public policy projects of the PRI and PAN administrations of the years 1988–2018. It focuses on the results, intended and unintended, of the public policy path the country had pursued for thirty years and how they contributed to articulating the opposition, which eventually coalesced within MORENA. To explore these feedback loop dynamics and the resulting shift in the policy environment, we focus on energy reform precisely because it came to be identified as the last (and major) step in what had been a steady pursuit of economic liberalization – or, as MORENA put it, the ultimate symbol of neoliberal politics that had to be reversed. Indeed, the new policy environment sums up the failures of previous administrations – and quite possibly their political and policy hubris – and today constitutes the most significant danger to the consolidation of energy reform in Mexico – a reform that, regardless of its nature, the country sorely needs if it is to meet its future energy needs. To organize these factors in a coherent way, the paper classifies them into two categories: domestic and international.

14.4 Case Study: Energy Reform

Starting in 2008, the Mexican government realized that oil production was declining relatively fast even as Mexico's energy consumption was increasing (Fig. 14.3). At that time, the Calderón administration sought to reform the energy sector by introducing an important although less ambitious reform.[3] The 2008 energy bill recognized that the energy sector required institutional modernization and added investment to reserve its decline. It also sought to modernize PEMEX, the parastatal oil company. That reform, however gradual, was not successful. The decline in oil production continued.

In 2013, President Enrique Peña Nieto, convinced that his election signaled approval of the public policy path Mexico had been on since the 1990s, committed to pushing for structural reform in the energy sector very early in his administration. In fact, the structural reform to the energy sector was to be a crowning achievement of his administration and further Mexico's economic opening. There was enormous enthusiasm for the opening of the energy sector around the world, and President Peña was viewed as a talented leader by the international press.[4] To prepare the groundwork for the reform, President Peña signed the *Pact for Mexico* during his first month in office. He spent most of 2013 pushing a series of reforms through Congress and agreed to send an energy reform legislative proposal to Congress as soon as possible. By August 2013, he had sent the proposed constitutional changes required to open the energy sector to private investment, securing congressional passage of all changes in December that year, and signing the law amid great optimism in the country and the national and international markets. This was no mean feat. The Constitution was changed substantially, reversing the 1940 and the 1960 changes to the Constitution which impeded the opening-up of the energy sector. Articles 25, 27 and 28 of the Mexican Constitution underwent substantial changes (Cossío Díaz/Cossío Barragán 2017). The reform abrogated that part of Article 27 of the constitution which prohibited private and foreign investment in oil exploration and production. Similarly, the reform abrogated that portion of Article 28 that designated the petrochemical industry a strategic sector for the country, allowing full participation from private capital into it. Parastatal companies were

---

[3]Centro de Estudios Sociales y de Opinión Pública (2008). "Iniciativa de Reforma en Materia Energética" (April).

[4]"Make or Break for Peña Nieto: Mexico's President Should Push for a Bolder Energy Reform." 2013. *The Economist* (23 November). See at: https://www.economist.com/leaders/2013/11/23/make-or-break-for-pena-nieto (8 January 2019). *Time* magazine showed Mr. Peña Nieto on its 13 February 2014 cover with the headline reading *Saving Mexico*.

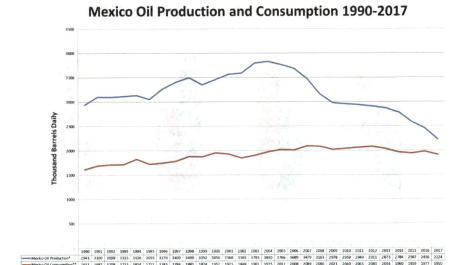

Fig. 14.3 Mexico's oil production decline and consumption from 1990 to 2017. *Source BP Statistical Review of World Energy 2019*, 68th edition; at: https://www.bp.com/content/dam/bp/business-sites/en/global/corporate/pdfs/energy-economics/statistical-review/bp-stats-review-2019-oil.pdf. Includes crude oil, shale oil, oil sands and NGLs (natural gas liquids – the liquid content of natural gas where this is recovered separately). Excludes liquid fuels from other sources such as biomass and derivatives of coal and natural gas. **Inland demand plus international aviation and marine bunkers and refinery fuel and loss. Consumption of bio-gasoline (such as ethanol), bio-diesel and derivatives of coal and natural gas are also included

redefined as "state productive companies," as opposed to government-owned and operated companies. The reform expelled the Mexican national oil company (PEMEX) workers' union from the governing board of the company, and beefed up a slew of agencies to regulate the auctioning, concession, exploration, and sale of oil and gas. It created the Mexican Petroleum Fund, an organization designed to capture some of the industry's profits for a national sovereign fund. And it now regulates the production of renewable energies (Government of Mexico 2013). The secondary legislation was approved by the Mexican Congress in 2015 and 2016. Almost simultaneously, the government invested heavily in crafting all the regulatory apparatus and creating and reforming the agencies that would oversee the implementation of the historic changes to the energy sector. The reform, as public policy change goes, was exemplary in its speed, transparency, and efficiency. By early 2015, the Mexican government began auctioning the first oil blocks in the Gulf of Mexico (Government of Mexico 2018). While the Mexican public expressed few concerns regarding the key structural changes to the energy sector, it was soon clear that the public remained divided on the reform (Fig. 14.4). And

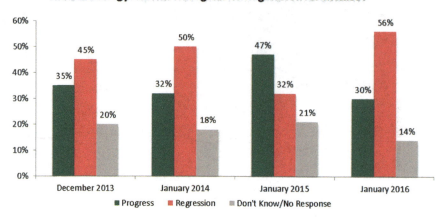

Fig. 14.4 *Parametría* poll conducted between 16 and 20 January 2016. *Source Parametría.* See: http://www.parametria.com.mx/carta_parametrica.php?cp=4840

although the reform had many vocal critics, and support for it eroded over time, the absence of public activism against it emboldened the Peña administration to push ahead to consolidate it, primarily through rushing the first block auctions in the Gulf of Mexico.

By the end of 2018, Mexico had conducted three auction rounds, and signed 107 contracts with foreign and domestic companies, including deep water, shallow water, and natural gas blocks and farm outs. In general, the perception of the international markets has been that the Mexican government has been fair and transparent in the implementation of the reform.

However, given this initial success, why is it that energy reform is now one of the most endangered structural changes to Mexico's economy? What deteriorated the policy environment to the point at which then-candidate and later President Andrés Manuel López Obrador was able to use the energy reform to his political advantage? What gave pause to the Mexican public so that between December 2013 and January 2016 the negative perception of the energy reform went from 45 to 56% and within a year – from January 2015 to January 2016 – its approval fell from 47 to 30%? The answers to these questions are important because they may determine the fate of Mexico's energy sector through a mere stoppage of all auctions and private participation in the sector or even a reversal of the reform. The next sections tackle both the domestic and the international challenges to the success of the reform, arguing that Mexico's own energy sector is now compromised.

14.5 Domestic and International Factors of Change in the Public Policy Environment in Mexico

Again, public policy environments do not change overnight. Many different issues emerge and mature over time to sow doubts on the benefits of specific policies, in this case energy reform. The 2018 election results can only be seen as a reflection of the deep concerns with the public policy path the country had been on. Clearly, Mexicans chose a new government that deliberately stated that it would take the country in a different direction, presumably the Left, away from the reforms that both the PAN and the PRI had pushed for. The 53.2% of the vote that Mr. López Obrador got carries with it an implicit mandate for public policy change, including energy. After all, Mr. Andrés Manuel López Obrador of the National Regeneration Movement Party (MORENA) obtained a majority of the national vote, even if 22.3% voted for PAN and 16.4% for PRI (Fig. 14.2). This is not to argue that it will be easy. The new government (2018–2024), headed by Mr. Andrés Manuel López Obrador, for example, will have to find a balance between the country's future energy needs, which require a modernized and diversified system of energy supplies, and the political-electoral mandate, which appears to dictate a narrower and more nationalistic approach to energy. He will also have to decide whether the energy reform stands as it is and implements it without changes; whether he makes substantial changes to it but moves ahead with modernization and diversification; or whether he reverses it altogether. It is possible to read all those options into the mandate that emerged from the July 1, 2018, elections. Whatever he decides to do, however, will have important consequences for Mexico's future economic development.[5] The domestic reasons for this political shift in the electoral preferences of the Mexican public are broken down further below.

The second category of factors threatening the consolidation of energy reform concerns Mexico's economic development model and its excessive dependence on the country's insertion in North America for much of its political legitimacy. NAFTA was, in fact, meant to tie Mexico's fate to its North American neighbors – dependence by choice, so to speak. The 2016 US presidential elections, however, threw that into question and, with the presidency of Donald Trump, Mexico is no longer seen as an indispensable partner and strong ally of the United States. With Donald J. Trump's anti-Mexico rhetoric, the Mexican government has lost an important source of political legitimacy, which ultimately gave the Mexican government a great degree of support for its policy choices. International policy legitimacy, in the end, does translate into domestic policy legitimacy, particularly in countries with higher levels of dependence, like Mexico on the United States.

---

[5]There is a demonstrable link between economic growth and energy. This is certainly the case in Mexico. It is sufficient to examine the link between Mexican power production and manufacturing and the Texas natural gas that fuels it. See Travis Bradford (2017) Adrian Duhalt (2018).

14.6 Winds of Change: Domestic Challenges to Energy Reform

This section explores the key domestic challenges to the success of energy reform in Mexico – all of which have contributed to the erosion of the policy consensus of the last thirty years. One of these is related to the policy cycle and the factors that accelerated the decline in support for neoliberal policies in the country, especially over the last twelve years. It concerns the persistent inequality and poverty in a country that granted its leadership maximum leeway to implement policies directed at globalizing the country's economy. After that, the essay explores the end of support for the Peña administration's ambitious reforms, primarily due to perceptions of corruption, impunity, and the government's inability to hold itself accountable to the law. Thirdly, the essay examines issues related to organized crime, as the activities of criminal groups appear to be a serious concern not only for the government's company, PEMEX, but also for private and foreign investors. Organized crime has become a major issue in the implementation of energy reform and has laid bare the government's inability to prevent, detect and effectively punish crimes which target the energy industry. It has also exhibited the weakness of the police forces charged with this key problem. Finally, the essay explores the fundamental lack of democracy through public participation in the process by which energy projects are approved and deployed, particularly when they affect indigenous and farming communities throughout the country. All these issues are directly related to economic governance and the weakness of the rule of law in the country.

14.6.1 The End of the Policy Consensus and Persistent Poverty and Inequality in Mexico

The work of the Mexican government in reforming the energy sector was hailed as historic in its scope and momentous in its significance. In effect, for the first time in seven decades, Mexico would allow private and foreign capital to participate in the energy sector without having to do so through the national oil company, PEMEX. Expectations rose high and the agencies implementing the reform were relatively speedy, efficacious, and transparent in their work. The Mexican government strengthened the regulatory powers of two agencies – the Energy Regulatory Commission (CRE) and the National Hydrocarbons Commission (CNH) – and created other regulatory agencies, including the Agency for Industrial Safety, Energy and the Environment (ASEA), the National Center for Energy Control (CENACE), the National Center for Natural Gas Control (CENAGAS), and the Mexican Petroleum Fund (FMP), and produced new norms for the energy markets in record time. Consequently, domestic and foreign companies became increasingly interested in the country's energy sector. By the time the first bid round to auction oil and gas blocks took place in July 2015, several companies had decided to participate and a few of them were able to purchase the rights for exploration and production of several of these blocks in the Gulf of Mexico. Successively, other bid rounds took place and 107 exploration and production contracts had been signed as of the first half of 2018 (National Hydrocarbons Commission 2018). The reviews on the overall performance of the Mexican government in the sector were highly positive (International Energy Agency 2016).

Despite the Mexican government's major accomplishments in implementing substantial changes in the energy sector constitutional, legislative, and regulatory frameworks, many Mexicans remained skeptical. Substantial numbers of citizens disagreed with the change and their skepticism grew over time. *Parametría*'s poll shows that by early 2016, Mexicans were becoming increasingly doubtful of the benefits of the energy reform (Fig. 14.4). But it would be unfairly simplistic to attribute this skepticism to a mere shift in public opinion on the contents of the energy reform itself.

Deeper undercurrents were already in place, threatening the implementation and consolidation of the reform. Doubts around Mexico's economic development model were already growing. According to a Pew Research Center poll conducted in mid-2017, 85% of Mexicans were dissatisfied with the way things were going in the country and 70% had a negative view of the economy (Vice/Chwe 2017). And they had reasons to do so. According to the National Council on the Evaluation of Social Development Policy (CONEVAL), poverty levels in Mexico remained steady from 2008 to 2016. The council's most recent study shows that the population living in *poverty* remains at about 45% and, in sheer numbers, it actually rose from 49.5 million to 53.4 million Mexicans (CONEVAL 2016).

Likewise, on inequality and income, Mexico ranks at the bottom of the member nations of the Organization for Economic Cooperation and Development (OECD 2015). The persistence of poverty and inequality has not gone unnoticed by its citizens. According to a 2017 poll conducted by Consulta Mitofsky, economic issues, security, and corruption have ranked consistently among the top three concerns of all Mexicans since at least 2013, with poverty and unemployment being two important concern subsets (Consulta Mitofsky 2017). And, as already stated, economic growth remained at a mediocre 2.1% per year – hardly a stellar performance and well below the country's needs.

Mexico economic underperformance has been amply debated,[6] but the reality remains the same. Thus, as many Mexicans were evidently failing to see the promised benefits of previous reforms, for which they had shown patient support, they were becoming increasingly unconvinced that the overall economic system was working for ordinary citizens. That skepticism was naturally transferred to the new slew of reforms. Along these lines, Mr. Peña made a strategic public relations mistake in searching for public support for the reform. He promised that the reform would bring the price of energy (especially fuels and electricity) down for the

---

[6]See, for example, Kehoe (2010) and Hanson (2012).

consumer. The opposite was true. The price rose, adding to the outrage and doubts about the benefits of the reform (Okeowo 2017). This would only add to the doubts that many Mexicans had regarding the eventual benefits of the reform, regardless of its virtues.

14.6.2 The End of the Policy Consensus and Corruption in Mexico

In addition to their overall dim view of the country's economic outlook, Mexicans' skepticism and eventual public opinion shift on the energy reform was underpinned by frustration with the country's progress on key rule of law issues. Corruption, lack of transparency, and impunity are some such concerns. The first of these is particularly worrisome. Most Mexicans, though they may not have the numbers at hand, are fully aware that the country's position on corruption and transparency is slipping away.

According to Transparency International, Mexico dropped in its *Corruption Perceptions Index* to 135th place out of the 180 countries measured, and its score was 29 out of 100 (Transparency International 2017). Moreover, according to the World Justice Project, Mexico ranks among the bottom third of all countries studied, with a score of 0.45 in the overall index, which measures government powers, absence of corruption, open government, fundamental rights, order and security, regulatory enforcement, civil justice and criminal justice (World Justice Project 2017–2018). Consequently, it should not be a surprise that this skepticism was quickly transferred to Mr. Peña's approval ratings. According to a poll by *Consulta Mitofsky* published in August 2018, 77% of Mexicans disapproved of Mr. Peña's government and only 18% approved of it. Those numbers had been steady for several years before this latest poll (Consulta Mitofsky 2018). And it cannot come as a surprise that this deep skepticism was also transferred to the energy reform that Mr. Peña had espoused in 2013 and 2014. If it is true that indicators on poverty, inequality, corruption, and lack of transparency are directly related to shifts in the policy environment, it should hardly come as a surprise that Mexico's elections appear to indicate that there is a strong desire for change, as reflected by the vote for MORENA in Fig. 14.2.[7]

Interestingly, the policy environment in Mexico did not change quickly. In fact, Mexico may be a good case of slow but steady growth of pessimism regarding broad changes in public policy, reaching a sufficiently critical level to push a solid majority of Mexican citizens to vote for a political party that proposed the reversal

---

[7]In a poll conducted in May 2018 Consulta Mitofsky also asked: "Do you believe that the next president of the republic must carry out a complete change, some change, or no change?" Around 58% of Mexicans answered that the next president must carry out a complete change and 26% expressed their desire for some change. Only a little over 6% believed that the country should stay the course. See Consulta Mitofsky (2018).

of several key policies, including energy reform. It is difficult to discern whether such changes are indeed possible or, if they are possible, where they are desirable. It is also difficult to know how much change can really happen under the significant economic constraints that Mr. López Obrador faces on taking office. It will certainly be very hard for Mr. López Obrador to reverse the energy reform without damaging the sector and the country's credibility among international investors, but what is certain is that the status quo is unlikely to prevail.

The issue of corruption is so salient in the minds of Mexicans that a key question that remains to be explored is the failure of the previous administrations (Salinas, Zedillo, Fox, Calderón, and Peña) to cement Mexico's economic development model and the policies that underpinned it by ensuring not only that more Mexicans enjoyed the benefits of the country's economic opening but also that they put in place the right institutions to prevent the country's slip on corruption. This is important because for three decades – judging by the electoral results – Mexican citizens were willing to give the policies derived from a neoliberal model a chance to produce results but by July 1, 2018, most Mexicans (53%) had concluded that the government and by extension the economic structural reforms of the last thirty years were simply not working. They had also concluded that corruption was only getting worse – a frustration supported by Mexico's rankings on corruption worldwide (Transparency International 2018). Mr. López Obrador was able to capture these concerns during his campaign. Even so, it is noteworthy that this conclusion was ultimately translated into votes through the very same political structural reforms of the last thirty years and in a largely peaceful process. But whichever the way the message may have been conveyed politically, it became clear that, even if the Mexican government's political opening rendered important accomplishments, over time its economic opening was insufficient to create higher endogenous growth, a bigger middle class, and the kind of human development that can aid in the development of institutions capable of resolving most of the country's problems, and that Mexicans had reached a critical tolerance limit with regard to corruption.

Unsurprisingly, policy fatigue began to accelerate, and most Mexicans viewed the State as increasingly weak and unable to respond to social demands. In other words, if we assume that the impact of negative public opinion on the ability of the government to consolidate its policy preferences increases as issues related to the rule of law and poverty and inequality become more salient (Burstein 2003: 21–40), the 2018 election results should not surprise anyone. Moreover, the ineffectiveness of the Mexican government to respond to public demands was made more evident by the rise in crime and crime and violence – more on this below. By the elections of 2018, Mexicans were ready for a change and well over half voted to reintroduce the State more aggressively into solving the country's economic and social problems. What the Mexican government failed to understand is that when the public is willing to grant the government the ability to set the policy agenda, and thirty years later the results are less than acceptable, office-holders cannot ask for additional opportunities to make sweeping changes, such as occurred with energy reform.

To summarize, so far this essay has explored two of the major threats to the consolidation of energy reform – economic underperformance and corruption. Both have contributed significantly to the erosion of the public policy consensus that had prevailed in Mexico for the last three decades. One is a phenomenon related to the inability of the economic model – of which energy reform was an important chapter – to deliver what it promised: prosperity for most Mexicans. By the end of the Peña administration, most of the public began to regard energy reform with great skepticism and viewed it as another way of transferring public wealth into the hands of a national (and international) elite – a story they had already witnessed in the privatization of the telecommunications sector in the late 1980s and 1990s (Clifton 2000: 63–79).

MORENA and Mr. López Obrador successfully made that one of their most important political arguments during the 2018 presidential campaign. The other concerns the dramatic drop in public approval of the Mexican government, broadly speaking, and of the Peña administration, specifically. This loss of political capital was largely due to the failure to institutionalize the rule of law with measures against corruption, lack of transparency, and government unaccountability. Mr. Peña, for example, refused to prosecute scores of corrupt governors from his own party or members of his own cabinet involved in corruption. To be sure, this was not a new problem. During an August 15, 2018, conference delivered in El Paso, Texas, former President Ernesto Zedillo acknowledged that his most profound error was his failure to procure a strengthening of the rule of law in the country. When President Felipe Calderón determined to tackle organized crime frontally while building the administration of justice institutions, the result was a spike in violence, including kidnappings, extortions, and murder, which tested the patience of most Mexicans (Fig. 14.5). During the Peña administration, the failure to combat corruption was further heightened by Mr. Peña's own scandals.

14.6.3 The End of the Policy Consensus: Organized Crime

The concept of *rule of law* is a complicated concept because it encompasses multiple issues: public safety and security, relative absence of corruption, low levels of impunity, transparency and accountability of all governmental activity, respect for human and due process rights, and especially strong governance institutions and a robust culture of lawfulness. In general, it is the principle that all people and organizations, including the government itself, are subject to the law and its enforcement (Bingham 2007: 67–85). In Mexico's case, as in much of Latin America, every single one of these indicators of the rule of law is worrisome to a greater or lesser degree. And although weaknesses in the rule of law in Mexico have been part of the history of the country for centuries, recently, most indicators have moved in the wrong direction.

As already discussed above, on corruption and transparency, the country's rankings have rapidly deteriorated. Levels of impunity have also risen considerably.

14 Reversal of Fortunes: Changes in the Public Policy ...

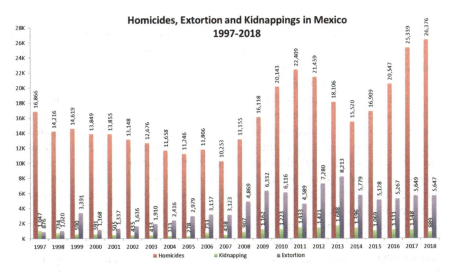

Fig. 14.5 Homicides, Extortion and Kidnappings in Mexico (1997–2018). *Source* National Security System. The 2018 numbers show crime statistics through July only. The projected annual victims at the current pace were estimated to reach 32,000 before the end of the year

The *Global Impunity Index* published by the *Universidad de las Americas Puebla* shows, for example, that Mexico suffers from serious structural and functional deficiencies in its ability to prevent, to detect and to punish criminal activities (Le Clercq/Rodríguez 2017). On respect for human and due process rights, Mexico's ranking is abysmal. Article 19, an international organization that monitors freedom of expression and the safety of journalists, considers Mexico one of the worst countries to practice journalism, for example.[8] Equally – or perhaps more – worrying are the high and increasing levels of crime and violence that Mexico has experienced over the last twelve years.

The public safety and security landscape has, in fact, worsened considerably during those years and has reached levels not seen in decades. Measured by the murder rate, kidnapping, and extortion, the country has experienced an extensive decline in its ability to protect not only its own citizens but also national and foreign investment and to guarantee the safety of all involved (Fig. 14.5). In fact, most polls show lack of public safety and security as one of the top two and three concerns of all Mexican citizens, often right next to poverty and corruption and poverty and inequality.

In addition to the descriptive statistics, it is important to note a qualitative shift in the trends in crime and violence. During the last two decades of the twentieth century and the first years of the twenty-first century, most of the crime and violence in Mexico was heavily concentrated in areas where organized criminal groups

---

[8]Article 19. "Mexico and Central America." See: https://www.article19.org/regional-office/mexico-and-central-america/ (8 September 2018).

were quartered and competed with one another for territorial control – Ciudad Juárez and Tijuana or the states of Tamaulipas and Michoacán. The activities of these criminal organizations focused on illegal drug smuggling to the United States and increasingly on the domestic illegal drug retail market.

Under this assumption, President Felipe Calderón (2006–2012) began a major assault on organized crime (Calderón Hinojosa 2015). President Calderón argued that organized crime was becoming a shadow government in many regions of the country, capable of challenging the very survivability of the Mexican State. By 2010, and largely as a result of the government's major assault on criminal groups, the drug cartels and their allies had started to break up into dozens of criminal groups, expanded to other areas of the country, and diversified their criminal enterprises (Heinle et al. 2017). Extortion, kidnapping, robberies, theft, etc., rose to unprecedented levels.

The levels of criminal activity and violence that the country has been experiencing soon reached deep into the energy sector, particularly in certain parts of the country where organized crime has a strong grip on government and society (Payan/Correa Cabrera 2014). By the end of the Peña administration, organized criminal groups had made the theft of fuels one of their major activities. They showed their ability and willingness to make energy projects and infrastructure the target of their activities, largely aided by the government's inability to stop them (Payan/Correa Cabrera 2016). In response to that, new vocabulary entered the scene. Criminal groups dedicated to targeting crude oil, fuel and gas pipelines came to be known as *huachicoleros*, and they were particularly pernicious to PEMEX (Calderón 2017). In an interview with a PEMEX employee in the area of logistics, the financial loss was reaching into the billions of dollars. In mid-2016, Etellekt, a consulting firm, had already warned that fuel theft was becoming a major concern for corporations seeking to invest in Mexico (Etellekt 2016).[9] The author's conversations with several energy company executives, particularly Chief Security Officers, in Houston, Texas further confirmed that this had become a major concern. Criminal activities targeting energy infrastructure now extend to nearly the entirety of the national territory, although they are heavily concentrated in those areas where PEMEX's pipelines criss-cross the country (Table 14.1). Interestingly, the *huachicol* crisis is the first serious rule of law crisis that President Andrés Manuel López Obrador is confronting. To stop the hemorrhage of fuel, he chose to dry out the pipelines that supply gasoline to most of Central Mexico. An unintended consequence is that PEMEX logistics were simply unable to supply gasoline by truck to the entire region, so fuel shortages ensued. This clearly reinforces the view that public policies – their pursuit or their neglect – often come with consequences which cannot be foreseen but which can easily test the patience of the public.

The government, at all levels, has been unable to curtail their activities and the losses to PEMEX now reach billions of dollars. These criminal groups are also adding to their attacks on energy infrastructure a willingness to extort resources

---

[9]Etellekt (2016).

Table 14.1 Clandestine Pipeline Taps in Mexico

Mexican State	2017	2018 January-June
Guanajuato	1,852	865
Puebla	1,443	1,175
Tamaulipas	1,100	626
Hidalgo	1,064	909
Veracruz	1,012	844
Mexico	976	731
Jalisco	530	758
Sinaloa	384	345
Morelos	378	208
Querétaro	304	161
Nuevo León	236	142
Michoacán	232	136
Tabasco	167	74
Baja California	154	59
Tlaxcala	122	210
Sonora	97	93
Mexico City CDMX	91	78
Chihuahua	85	77
Oaxaca	69	62
Coahuila	43	18
Durango	9	12
San Luis Potosí	6	1
Chiapas	5	3
Aguascalientes	3	1
Yucatán	1	2
Baja California Sur	0	0
Campeche	0	0
Colima	0	0
Guerrero	0	0
Nayarit	0	0
Quintana Roo	0	0
Zacatecas	0	0
Total	**10363**	**7,590**

Source PEMEX; see: https://www.pemex.com/acerca/informes_publicaciones/Paginas/tomas-clandestinas2017.aspx and http://wwwpemex.com/acerca/informes_publicaciones/Paginas/tomas-clandestinas.aspx

States marked in red and orange show that the activity of organized criminal groups targeting energy projects and infrastructure has reached nearly the entire country. States like Guanajuato, Puebla, Tamaulipas, Hidalgo, Mexico State, Jalisco and Veracruz, where oil and gas pipelines are an important part of the infrastructure, have been particularly targeted

from businesses and to kidnap personnel for ransom. This has been a major concern for investors who have observed the trends carefully as they prepare to deploy projects on land. A recent conversation with a major transnational investing in Mexico revealed that they are having to go to extreme measures to protect their businesses and their personnel, including the use of armed guards and additional kidnapping insurance. And although most transnational corporations are accustomed to operating in difficult security environments, most of them are having trouble figuring out the right safety and security measures for an environment where there is apparent rule of law but in practice there are enormous deficiencies. At the same time, when the government has moved public forces against them, the result has been direct confrontation and considerable bloodshed. Many foreign investors now fear that general organized crime will be one of their major obstacles to doing business in Mexico and, in private conversations with several of these companies, it has become clear that their business models and in-country activities heavily consider problems with public safety and security as an integral variable.

In general, elevated crime and violence in the country and the government's increasing neglect of its responsibility to protect both its citizens and the economic activity of nationals and foreigners from falling victim to them is one of the biggest challenges to the reform. It will be difficult to understand how much investment will be deterred from coming into the country due to crime and violence and how the costs of safety and security will affect business models when investing in Mexico, but these costs are not zero and companies will have to consider this to the detriment of Mexico's own image and its ability to attract the kind of investment the country requires for its own economic development and the acceleration of the pace of economic growth.

So far, this essay has argued that there has been a major shift in the policy environment in Mexico. And this shift will have a negative impact on energy reform. The root cause of this change is persistent economic underperformance, with high levels of poverty and inequality; corruption and impunity; and rising levels of crime and violence. In the end, the Mexican government has focused much of its capital on securing the structural reforms of the last thirty years, but has neglected to ensure that wealth and income are more evenly and sustainably distributed and that the rule of law is strengthened. This has now put all the accomplishments of the last decades at risk, made the country vulnerable to international criticism and made Mexico a major political football in the United States, the very country on which the economic development model the country has implemented depends. The next section explores the added risk to Mexico's path stemming from a change in the global political landscape, particularly in the United States.

14.7 Change in the International Environment

The major obstacles to the consolidation of energy reform in Mexico are not just domestic in nature. The international environment is also changing radically. In general, it has always been difficult to understand Mexico's economic and political transformations without linking them closely to the country's foreign policy, particularly its relations with the United States. The tacit support – and sometimes outright intervention – of the United States government has historically mattered for the direction the country has taken. This certainly was the case in the 1980s, when Mexico stumbled into financial crisis after financial crisis, and most of the conditions for economic and political liberalization came from the United States and international organizations in exchange for financial rescue packages (Fourcade-Gourinchas/Babb 2002: 533–579). This was also true in 1994, during the "Tequila Crisis" (Springer/Molina 1995: 57–81). The major push for energy reform was not much different. While serving as Secretary of State, Hillary Clinton appears to have been advising the Mexican government on how to proceed on liberalizing its energy sector, according to documents released by WikiLeaks.[10]

Thus, for decades, the state of the binational relationship has turned out to be an indispensable factor in deploying and consolidating Mexico's development path. Its insertion in North America has further reinforced this trend. Some thinkers have even argued that the North American Free Trade Agreement is quintessentially a *political* agreement, even more so than a commercial agreement, because it commits Mexico to a development path and precludes policies that might not serve the strategy established in the 1980s (Rubio 2018). Thus, the United States provides and has provided enormous legitimacy to the policy decision of the Mexican government for at least three decades.

But the political environment in the United States is now changing dramatically. During the 2016 presidential campaign, Mr. Donald J. Trump made Mexico a major object of his acerbic political rhetoric. Mexico, he argued, had taken advantage of the United States and that had to end. He promised to upend the North American Free Trade Agreement, a near-quarter century commercial accord between all three North American countries. Moreover, he promised to expel millions of unauthorized Mexican migrants and build a wall between the two countries. He did away with the rhetoric of a "competitive North American platform", and rejected any kind of strategic partnership with Mexico. His positions have only hardened since he took office in early 2017, and his rhetoric has continuously shown a degree of hostility that Mexico had not experienced in decades.

NAFTA renegotiations, called for by the Trump administration in August of 2017, have also resulted in something that promises to be an agreement more disadvantageous to Mexico, and likely contentious in the new MORENA-dominated legislature. Given Mexico's economic dependence on US foreign investment and the importance of the support of the United States government for the Mexican government's broad decisions on the country's direction, Mr. Trump has essentially pulled the political rug from under Mexico's feet and made the energy reform more vulnerable to reversal, particularly as one of MORENA's key promises was to reconsider that structural change to the country's energy sector.

Given this significant change in the political environment in the United States, the assumption that the Mexican government could always receive support from abroad to make structural changes, sometimes against domestic public opinion, can

---

[10]See WikiLeaks at: https://search.wikileaks.org/plusd/ (8 September 2018).

no longer be sustained. This shift makes it easier for the MORENA party and the administration of Mr. López Obrador to tinker with the basic structure of the reform as well as slow down or stop its implementation – at a minimum – or reverse it altogether, especially considering the fact that the new Mexican president will have a majority in both houses of Congress and control of seventeen state legislatures, just enough to change the Constitution all over again. This political threat to energy reform cannot be underestimated because, even if the basic constitutional and legal framework were to remain in place, the implementation of the reform could take a completely different path. Unfortunately, it is likely that Mexico will simply not have the capital to reverse the dramatic declines in its oil production or, more likely, investing public resources in oil production is likely to be less productive than allowing private capital to do it or find a hybrid system for public-private partnerships to manage oil production.

14.8 Conclusion

Table 14.2 summarizes the central factors that contributed to a shift in the public policy environment in Mexico – factors which allowed a breakdown in the policy consensus and opposition to the policies of the last thirty years to gel. This shift is what now threatens the viability of energy reform.

Shifts in public policy environments are crucial to understanding the path of social, economic, and political developments in any country. These shifts introduce a number of variables in each of these ambits that add considerable uncertainty to the ability of established policies to survive and thrive and create windows of opportunity for new policies, although they may not necessarily be an improvement. Latin America is plagued by examples of starts and reversals in public policy, many of them for the worse. In Mexico, the growth in skepticism regarding the

Table 14.2 Major challenges to the successful implementation and consolidation of energy reform in Mexico. While, broadly speaking, it is an erosion of the policy consensus in Mexico – a major public policy environment shift – that now threatens the consolidation of energy reform, this consensus broke down on the basis of specific issues that contributed to the gradual but eventually clear shift. The table summarizes the most obvious domestic and international factors

Challenges to Mexico's energy reform implementation and consolidation	Domestic	International
Factors contributing to the erosion of the public policy consensus in Mexico	Weaknesses of the economic model: poverty and inequality Rule of law issues: Corruption Organized crime Democratic participation	Shifts in the political environment in the United States

direction of the country, primarily with regard to economic and rule of law issues, which resulted in the electoral results of 2018 in Mexico and the troubled relationship with the United States under the Trump administration, crystallize just such a shift and bring a considerable degree of uncertainty to the future path of what is possible in Mexico. By extension, this significant change in the policy environment poses a major challenge to all of the country's structural reforms, including energy sector reform. In that sense, to simply speak of the Mexican public losing its patience with political elites is insufficient to explain the new direction of the country, which now puts energy reform on the chopping block. To understand what has happened in Mexico, one must go further back in space and time and understand that these essential weaknesses in the economic and rule of law models are what eventually allowed opposition to the policy environment to grow into a political movement which now controls both the Executive and both houses of Congress and can easily reverse energy reform, as well as other structural reforms.

At a time when greater legal and regulatory certainty is a desirable public good, the President, Mr. López Obrador, and his energy team have yet to set a clear and achievable plan for the country's future energy development. The López Obrador team has, for example, made contradictory statements regarding its designs for energy, and his advisors have even discounted each other's public statements. Thus, it is worth asking whether the election results, the product of a shift in the policy environment, mandate a complete shift in the model of economic development or simply a government that can ensure that the benefits of the open market can extend to more Mexicans and reduce levels of poverty and inequality. With regard to energy, it is not yet clear that the incoming team has reached a consensus on what it plans to do.

Unfortunately, none of the issues behind the policy environment shift can be corrected over the short term. It will require a long-term plan to fix all institutions charged with combating corruption, reducing impunity, ensuring an expeditious and efficient administration of justice, diminishing the levels of crime and violence, and fighting poverty and violence – and, of course, a competent team to handle the turbulent relationship with the United States for the next few years. In the meantime, a clear vision and a steady hand in implementing the country's reform are becoming critical. Currrent conditions are inciting analysts of Mexican society, politics, and the economy to ask: What is at stake if the only added ingredient to the shifting policy environment is greater uncertainty than the country was already facing?

Over the last thirty years, in spite of its significant shortcomings, Mexico has made enormous strides in its social, economic and political development. Its electoral system could be considered among the best in the world (FairVote 2018); its political system had been growing in its capacity to represent diverse voices, including giving MORENA the possibility of a landslide in the 2018 elections; its society has grown increasingly tolerant of diverse lifestyles; its economy has become an export powerhouse; and so on. All these achievements are based on the credibility that the country has amassed through trade agreements, monetary discipline, and fiscal restraint, in addition to other key virtues. That credibility is now at risk, as the country engages in what appears to be a major course correction, with a greater degree of uncertainty on the potential outcome.

The country will need to continue to build on these strengths, while attempting to solve its core weaknesses. The alternative is to lose all international credibility, followed by a flight of foreign investment required to achieve the stated goal of the energy reform: to increase production of energy and to do so in a way that contributes towards solving environmental issues and ultimately global warming. It would be a disservice to the country to turn back energy reform at this point. The country simply does not have the resources to accomplish its energy goals on its own – even if it is understandable why Mexicans turned the PRI and the PAN out of power.

References

Article 19 (2018). "Mexico and Central America"; at: https://www.article19.org/regional-office/mexico-and-central-america/ (8 September 2018).
Axelrad, Lee (1993). "NAFTA in the Context of Mexican Economic Liberalization", in: *Berkeley Journal of International Law*, 11,2: 201–222.
Bingham, Lord (2007). "The Rule of Law", in: *The Cambridge Law Journal*, 66,1 (March 2007): 67–85.
Burstein, Paul (2003). "The Impact of Public Opinion on Public Policy: A Review and an Agenda", in: *Political Research Quarterly*, 56,1 (March 1): 21–40.
Calderón Hinojosa, Felipe (2015). *Los retos que enfrentamos: Los problemas de México y las políticas públicas para resolverlos* (Mexico City: Debate).
Calderón, Laura (2017). "Huachicoleros on the Rise in Mexico", Justice in Mexico Project (20 May); at: https://justiceinmexico.org/huachicoleros-rising-mexico/ (3 September 2018).
Capano, Giliberto; Howlett, Michael (2009). "The Determinants of Policy Change: Theoretical Challenges", in: *Journal of Comparative Policy Analysis: Research and Practice*, 11: 1.
Centro de Estudios Sociales y de Opinión Pública (2008). *Iniciativa de Reforma en Materia Energética* (April).
Clifton, Judith (2000). "On the Political Consequences of Privatization: The Case of Teléfonos de México", in: *Bulletin of Latin American Research*, 19: 63–79.
Consulta Mitofsky (2017). *Así Es México 2017*; at: http://consultamitofsky.com.mx/Publicaciones/AsiesMexico2017/AsiesMexico_2017.pdf (4 September 2018).
Consulta Mitofsky (2018). "Evaluación 23 Trimestres de Gobierno de Enrique Peña Nieto"; at: http://consulta.mx/index.php/estudios-e-investigaciones/evaluacion-de-gobierno/item/1077-evaluacion-23-trimestres-mexico (2 September 2018).
Cossío Díaz, José Ramón; Cossío Barragán, José Ramón (2017), "The New Energy System in the Mexican Constitution" (Houston: Rice University, James A. Baker III Institute for Public Policy); at: https://www.bakerinstitute.org/media/files/files/68d55ed8/MEX-pub-RuleofLaw_JR2-042417.pdf (8 January 2019).
Etellekt (2016). "Situación actual y perspectivas de sobre el robo de hidrocarburos en México 2016: Reporte Sectorial" (15 July) (Mexico City: Etellekt).
Government of Mexico (2013). *Energy Reform Summary 2013*; at: https://www.gob.mx/cms/uploads/attachment/file/164370/Resumen_de_la_explicacion_de_la_Reforma_Energetica11_1_.pdf (8 January 2019).
Government of Mexico (2018). *Rondas*; at: https://rondasmexico.gob.mx/esp/rondas/ (8 January 2019).

Heinle, Kimberly; Rodríguez Ferreira, Octavio; Shirk, David A. (2017). "Drug Violence in Mexico: Data and Analysis through 2016" (San Diego: University of San Diego); at: https://justiceinmexico.org/wp-content/uploads/2017/03/2017_DrugViolenceinMexico.pdf (4 September 2018).

International Energy Agency of the Organization for Economic Cooperation and Development, (2016). *Mexico Energy Outlook* (Paris: OECD, IEA); at: https://www.iea.org/publications/freepublications/publication/MexicoEnergyOutlook.pdf (4 September 2018).

Kehoe, Timothy J. (2010). "Why Have Economic Reforms in Mexico Not Generated Growth?" (Minneapolis: Federal Reserve Bank of Minneapolis); at: http://citeseerx.ist.psu.edu/viewdoc/download?doi=10.1.1.194.1391&rep=rep1&type=pdf (4 September 2018).

Kehoe, Timothy J.; Hanson, Gordon H. (2012). "Understanding Mexico's Economic Underperformance" (Washington, D.C.: The Regional Migration Study Group); at: https://www.migrationpolicy.org/research/mexico-economic-underperformance (4 September 2018).

Le Clercq Ortega, Juan Antonio; Rodríguez Sánchez Lara, Gerardo (2017). GII-2017 *Global Impunity Index* (Puebla: Universidad de las Américas Puebla); at: https://www.udlap.mx/cesij/files/IGI-2017_eng.pdf (3 September 2018).

National Council for the Evaluation of Social Development Policy (CONEVAL) (2016). "Medición de la pobreza"; at: https://www.coneval.org.mx/Medicion/Paginas/PobrezaInicio.aspx (2 September 2018).

National Hydrocarbons Commission (2018). *Bóveda Nacional de Contratos* [National Energy Contracts Archive]; at: https://www.gob.mx/cnh/articulos/boveda-digital (2 September 2018).

Okeowo, Alexis (2017). "The Grass-Price Protests Gripping Mexico", in: *The New Yorker* (24 January); at: https://www.newyorker.com/news/daily-comment/the-gas-price-protests-gripping-mexico (3 September 2018).

Organization for Economic Cooperation and Development (OECD) (2015). "Inequality and Income" (Paris: OECD); at: http://www.oecd.org/social/inequality.htm (2 September 2018).

Payan, Tony; Correa Cabrera, Guadelupe (2014). *Energy Reform and Security in Northeastern Mexico.* Issue Brief No. 05.06.14 (Houston: Rice University, Baker Institute for Public Policy); at: https://www.bakerinstitute.org/media/files/files/21e1a8c8/BI-Brief-050614-Mexico_Energy Security.pdf (3 September 2018).

Payan, Tony; Correa Cabrera, Guadelupe (2016). *Security, the Rule of Law, and Energy Reform in Mexico* (Houston: Rice University, Baker Institute for Public Policy); at: https://www.bakerinstitute.org/media/files/research_document/89cb3282/MEX-pub-RuleofLaw_PC-121316.pdf (3 September 2018).

Pierson, Paul (1993). "When Effect Becomes Cause: Policy Feedback and Political Change", in: *World Politics*, 45,4: 595–628.

Rubio, Luis (2017). "El TLCAN un instrumento de política interna", in: *Proceso* (21 November); at: http://luisrubio.mx/wp/?p=5647 (7 January 2019).

Secretaría de Relaciones Exteriores (2012). *Pacto por México*; at: https://embamex.sre.gob.mx/bolivia/images/pdf/REFORMAS/pacto_por_mexico.pdf (8 January 2019).

Transparency International (2017). *Corruption Perceptions Index: 2017*; at: https://www.transparency.org/country/MEX (2 September 2018).

Transparency International (2018). *Corruption Perceptions Index: 2018*; at: https://www.transparency.org/country/MEX.

Vice, Margaret; Chwe, Hanys (2017). "Mexicans Are Downbeat about Their Country's Direction" (Washington, D.C.: Pew Research Center); see at: http://www.pewglobal.org/2017/09/14/mexicans-are-downbeat-about-their-countrys-direction/ (2 September 2018).

Wilson, Carter A. (2013). *Public Policy: Continuity and Change*, 2nd Edn. (Long Grove, IL: Waveland Press): 391–402.

World Justice Project (2017–2018). *Rule of Law Index: Mexico*; at: http://data.worldjusticeproject.org/ (2 September 2018).

Chapter 15
The Rule of Law in Economic Competition

María Solange Maqueo Ramírez

Abstract This chapter addresses the evolution process of the law of economic competition in Mexico, with special emphasis on the so-called structural reforms of 2013 and the enactment of a new Federal Law of Economic Competition. The aims of this writing are to highlight the aspects which have contributed to the consolidation of the rule of law, as well as to identify some tasks to be attended to, including not only potential legislative reforms, but also a proper implementation, the coordination of public policies, and the creation of precedents that will provide greater legal certainty.

Keywords Market system · Economic competition · Competition law · Antitrust · Economic constitution · Structural reforms · Rule of law · Federal Competition Commission · Federal Telecommunications Institute

15.1 Introduction

The advent of the neoliberal economic model entailed a profound transformation in the role of the State, which becomes subsidiary to the very capacities of the market (Lindblom 2001: 156). The paradigm of this position lies in the idea that the market is the *ad hoc* mechanism to coordinate economic activity and only its imperfections warrant the visible hand of the State. From this standpoint, State intervention in the economy is explained to the extent that: (i) it ensures the very subsistence of the market; and (ii) it lays down the conditions for the interaction of economic agents to allocate resources efficiently.

Accordingly, the rule of law becomes a precondition of the functioning of the market: "[it] is an indispensable foundation for market economy, which provides an essential environment for the creation and preservation of wealth, economic

---

María Solange Maqueo Ramírez, Associate Research Professor at the Legal Studies Division of the Economic Research and Teaching Center (CIDE) and Chair of the Advisory Board of the National Institute for Transparency, Access to Information and Personal Data Protection (INAI); Email: maria.maqueo@cide.edu.

security, and well-being, and the improvement of the quality of life" (Bufford 2006: 303) and, in turn, feeds on economic efficiency[1] as a goal to be fostered by legal rules.

With regard to the rule of law as a precondition to the functioning of the market, it is worth pointing out that the legal system lays the foundations for the conduct of business transactions. This is clearly evidenced by the creation of property rights, the guarantees for the promotion of contractual relationships, the duty of protection and surveillance in order to provide individuals with legal certainty over their property, as well as the impartiality and independence of court dispute settlement mechanisms. Each of these aspects of the legal system constitute the fundamental basis for the functioning of the market, to the extent that even the most radical liberal positions which favor the deregulation of economic activity admit the need to create minimum legal structures which enable its sustainability.

However, modern economic theory recognizes certain administrative, regulatory and surveillance functions in the very government that go beyond the minimum State. Under this scheme, its intervention is warranted so as to contribute to improving the functioning of the market in the face of its imperfections, whether in the case of market failures *per se* affecting economic efficiency, or to meet redistribution goals under social justice criteria. That implies, *inter alia*, the capacity of the State to mitigate, if not eradicate, imperfect competition, asymmetric information and incomplete markets.

Against that backdrop, the law of economic competition aims to protect the competition process through the free interplay of market forces, and, in the event of market failures, fight pricing; ensure a multiplicity of buyers and sellers as price takers, not price makers; forestall cases of abuse of a dominant position or market concentrations harmful to the competition process; and, lastly, intervene when the market experiences structural failures preventing the efficient allocation of resources.

In view of the foregoing, the "rule of law" "as applied to the law of economic competition" can be conceived as limiting State power in economic activity by submitting it to a legal system including assessment principles or criteria that purport to maximize economic welfare as a whole. It is not about denying State intervention in the market, but about determining its who, how and why. For such purposes, the rule of law comprises at least three main elements: (i) a constitutional and legal framework that favors economic competition; (ii) an administrative and institutional system, which defines the powers of regulatory bodies and their relationships with other relevant actors[2] (whether also government bodies, economic

---

[1]Generally speaking, economic efficiency as a goal of competition policy includes allocative efficiency, productive efficiency, and dynamic efficiency. In that respect, see Motta (2004: 52ff).

[2]In Sarsfield's opinion (2010: 15), a condition necessary for the rule of law to exist is an institutional equilibrium which "permits to define the set of *possible actions of actors*. Actors' behaviors are, then, predictable, understandable, and limited by law. In other words, there is an institutional equilibrium when institutions can tame, transform or constrain the power of organized group."

agents or consumers), and, lastly, (iii) a jurisdictional system that ensures effective judicial protection (Bufford 2006: 306ff).

In turn, the rule of law thus conceived becomes interdisciplinary in nature, economic competition becoming a natural meeting field between Law and Economics where both disciplines feature reciprocal influence.[3]

This is exactly the paradigm on which the origin of the law of economic competition in Mexico, the purposes of which were established from the outset by the now abrogated Federal Law of Economic Competition of 1992, is based: "to protect the competitive process and free market access by preventing monopolies, monopolistic practices, and other restraints of the efficient functioning of markets for goods and services". Hence, the assessment criterion for market regulation in order to promote free competition and maximized turnout to the marketplace lies primarily in the search for efficiency and, thus, economic development. In the words of Motta (2004: 30), the main goal of economic competition is ensuring "that competition in the marketplace is not restricted in such a way as to reduce economic welfare", which is understood as the "*total super plus,* that is the sum of consumer superplus and producer superplus" (2004: 18).

Nevertheless, from its beginnings to date, the law of economic competition in Mexico has been transformed. As will be seen in the following sections, this transformation has been progressive, albeit steady. From an origin which may be labeled artificial,[4] alien to Mexican idiosyncrasy and the economic context of the country, it is currently a powerful instrument in favor of the rule of law. Not only do economic competition and its regulation channel State influence on the market, as in its original meaning, but they also limit the abuse of power by large companies for the benefit of society at large, in which consumers perform an increasingly pivotal role. Nonetheless, as will be seen below, there remain some tasks to be performed that go beyond potential legislative reforms, so as to pave the way for the proper implementation of the rules and regulations in force.

15.2 Competition Law in Mexico: 1992–2013

15.2.1 *The Reception of Competition Law*

The reception of competition law in Mexico is within the framework of the market liberalization process introduced in the mid-1980s. This process entailed a profound transformation of the adopted economic model. It implied a transition from a protectionist economic model, characterized by considerable State intervention in

---

[3]On the relationship between law and economics from an institutional perspective, see Medema et al. (2000: 418ff).

[4]The idea that the introduction of economic competition may have been artificial does not constitute a unanimous position. In this regard, see Castañeda-Gallardo (2014: 337ff).

production processes and price control, to a market-based economy model (OECD 2004: 10).

However, the privatization process that Mexico was undergoing and the removal of trade barriers were still insufficient. It was necessary to create a regulatory framework ensuring free economic competition among market agents. Consequently, the first *Federal Law of Economic Competition* (Spanish acronym: LFCE)[5] was enacted in Mexico in 1992. Nevertheless, as Elbittar/Mariscal (2018: 17) highlight, this law did not stem from awareness of monopoly-related problems, the restraints arising from market power, or the practice of monopolistic behavior, but as a condition to access other markets. In particular, the enactment of this law was imperative for Mexico to become a party to the *North American Free Trade Agreement* (NAFTA), together with the United States of America and Canada.

In fact, Chapter Fifteen of the NAFTA, entitled "Competition Policy, Monopolies and State Enterprises", includes commitments for the State's Parties to adopt and maintain "measures to proscribe anticompetitive conduct and take appropriate action with respect thereto". It also incorporates common definitions about monopoly, non-discriminatory treatment and state enterprises, among other definitions.

By means of the LFCE, Mexico introduced for the first time in its legal system "provisions against cartels and abuses of dominant positions, and allow[ed] for mergers review and competition advocacy" (Aydin 2016: 165). Moreover, this law set out a catalog of anti-competitive behaviors in both the public and private sector, which would be expanded across successive legislative reforms. From the outset, this law drew a distinction between absolute monopolistic practices (concerning "hard-core cartels", "or agreements between competitors on price, output, market division, and bid rigging") (Aydin 2016: 165) and relative monopolistic practices (which "are what would be treated under monopoly or abuse of dominance provisions in other jurisdictions") (Aydin 2016: 165). In turn, this differentiation entailed adopting the US case law construction that draws a distinction between the rule *per se* (for absolute monopolistic practices) and the rule of reason (for relative monopolistic practices).

The creation of the Federal Competition Commission (Spanish acronym: COFECE) was a decisive step in the configuration of economic competence policy in Mexico. Pursuant to Article 23 of the now abrogated LFCE, the COFECE was a decentralized administrative body of the Secretariat of Economy, with "technical and operational autonomy", the function of which was to "prevent, investigate and contest monopolies, monopolistic practices and concentrations" in the terms of the law.[6] Basically, this autonomy relied on how commissioners (whose appointment depended on the Federal Executive Branch, not the Ministry) were appointed and

---

[5]Law published in the *Diario Oficial de la Federación* on 24 December 1992.

[6]In terms of Article 16 of the Mexican Federal Law on Economic Competition, "a concentration shall be understood as a merger, or acquisition of control, or any other act whereby companies, partnerships, shares, equity, trusts or assets in general are concentrated among competitors, suppliers, customers or any other economic agent."

on the allowance for a specific period for the commitment. Nonetheless, the COFECE had no budgetary independence, since the preparation of its budget depended on the Ministry of Economy (OECD 2004: 64).

Since its inception, the COFECE was vested with regulatory, investigation and sanctioning powers. However, much of the criticism during the first years of operation was about its inability to restructure a monopolized industry and, in general, the division of powers among different regulatory bodies, which undermined the scope of power granted to the COFECE in particularly complex areas (Aydin 2016: 165). This was the case, for example, of the regulatory body in the telecommunications area, under the responsibility of the now-defunct Federal Commission for Telecommunications (COFETEL). In this regard, "the FCC was responsible for identifying whether a firm had market power in a sector, but it was a sector regulator that had the responsibility to address this behavior, without the FCC's participation in the negotiations or the preparation of regulations to deal with the competitive conduct" (Aydin 2016: 168). Moreover, at the beginning, the Commission had slight influence on the regulatory improvement process. The relationship between the COFECE and the Regulatory Improvement Council (OECD 2004), also under the authority of the Ministry of Economy, was weak, although the regulation could have an impact on the economic competition process.

With regard to the COFECE's investigation powers, the COFECE had no power to conduct on-site searches (Aydin 2016: 168) . Furthermore, there was no system distinction between the authority investigating the alleged breaches of law and the authority determining such breaches and the relevant penalties (García 2003: 125). This situation did not support a perception of fairness in the procedures conducted by the COFECE.

In these early years, Mexico lacked a culture of economic competition, not only because it had adopted it artificially in order to access other markets,[7] but also because, as stated by García (2003: 125), those directly affected by anticompetitive behavior had no direct action before the Judiciary to claim damages. The fact that market competitors themselves and consumers, where applicable, might not claim damages caused by anticompetitive behavior led to the society in general distancing itself from the then unknown COFECE.

In addition, the inadequacy of sanctions as a disincentive to engage in anticompetitive practices, the lack of immunity programs to facilitate the identification of cartels, and the continual legal or administrative decisions reversing the Commission's decisions (Aydin 2016: 168–170), reduced the effectiveness of its roles.

---

[7]For another perspective, see Castañeda-Gallardo (2014: 337ff).

15.2.2 Legislative Reforms of 2006

Although, in general terms, the international perception of the LFCE was positive, there were still significant areas to improve, as evidenced by the 2004 OECD Report on Competition Law and Policy in Mexico. Moreover, at national level, "[g]overnment and private actors criticized the FCC for being weak, court proceedings triggered by companies' complaints slowed down investigations, and a number of the FCC's decisions were reversed by the district courts on procedural grounds" (Aydin 2016: 155). In general terms, the COFECE was considered an administrative body whose investigation tools and sanctioning powers were insufficient to deter anticompetitive practices (Gallardo/de la Mora 2014: 37).

In response to this situation, on June 28, 2006, an extensive reform of the Federal Law of Economic Competition (LFCE) was published in the *Diario Oficial de la Federación*, which: (i) increased the penalties for breaches of the law; (ii) extended the list of relative monopolistic practices; (iii) strengthened the COFECE's powers related to the investigation of monopolistic practices by means of the introduction of powers to conduct on-site searches; (iv) implemented the immunity program to identify cartels more easily; (v) reduced the cases of concentrations that required notice to be served upon the Commission; and, finally, (vi) introduced some institutional modifications and corrections to specific provisions of the law (Diego-Fernández 2010: 79). In addition, the 2006 reform included new powers for the COFECE to render binding opinions on the regulation that might have effects contrary to economic competition (OECD 2012: 35). This strengthened its participation in regulatory processes and required more cooperation with the Regulatory Improvement Council.

Additionally, this legislative reform clarified the circumstances where relative monopolistic practices could be exempted from sanction. Indeed, a paragraph was added at the end of Article 10 of the law then in force, which provided that the COFECE could choose not to punish those practices, provided that the economic agent proved the existence of efficiency gains and a favorable impact on the process of free competition resulting from its behavior. A list of different situations that could involve efficiency gains, such as the introduction of new products, the reduction of production costs, or the inclusion of technological advances, included net contributions to consumers' welfare, whenever these outweighed the anticompetitive effects of the behavior. This addition to the law assumed express acknowledgement, though extremely limited and on a secondary basis, by consumers as beneficiaries of the economic competition policy.

Despite the advances entailed by the 2006 legislative reform, some of its additions were found invalid by the Mexican Supreme Court of Justice, by reason of the Action of Unconstitutionality 33/2006 filed by Mexico's Attorney General. In particular, all provisions that set forth the participation of the Congress of the Union and jurisdictional authorities in matters related to the COFECE's structure and exercise of powers became void. This was because the Supreme Court considered that it might amount to a violation of the principle of separation of powers, since the COFECE was a decentralized agency, assigned to the public administration and thus under the control of the Federal Executive Branch.[8]

Moreover, the 2006 legislative reforms still faced some difficulties. One of them was on-site searches. While their introduction strengthened the competition agency's ability to investigate anticompetitive behavior, "the COFECE had to announce searches in advance, reducing the effectiveness of its cartel detection work" (OECD 2012: 35). Additionally, the amount of fines was still insufficient to deter anticompetitive behavior and the filing of increasingly complex cases showed new requirements from the authority (Diego-Fernández 2010: 79).

15.2.3 Legislative Reforms of 2011

The experience acquired so far and, hence, the accuracy in identifying the problems faced by the COFECE to achieve its goals led to the 2011 legislative reform.[9] Indeed, many of the concerns pending after the 2006 reform were addressed by this amendment. This is apparent in the modifications introduced to simplify the notification process of certain types of mergers and reduce the situations that require it; to extend the scope of the immunity program in order to include both individuals and companies (OECD 2012: 34); to strengthen the COFECE's powers to conduct investigations and procedures intended to determine sanctions for monopolistic practices and unlawful concentrations; as well as to increase the amount and nature of sanctions.

It should also be noted that these amendments to Mexico's antitrust law addressed the concept of "joint dominance". Prior to these amendments, the LFCE just prohibited "unilateral abuses of dominance by one firm with market power" (Fitzpatrick/Aziz 2010). The 2011 reform extended the meaning of significant power "to multi-agent setting, in which a set of economic agents can be identified to have, collectively, significant market power" (Pavón-Villamayor 2010).

The 2011 reform of the LFCE introduced a distinction between the investigation phase (by the COFECE's Technical Secretary) and the procedural phase to determine applicable sanctions (assigned to a Reporting Commissioner to prepare a draft resolution submitted for vote at an *En Banc* Session). Thus, the decision-making on potential unlawful behavior was spread across different actors, so as to create intra-institutional checks and balances. Emphasis was further placed on the importance of strengthening on-site searches, in order that they would no longer have to be announced in advance. The reform introduced the COFECE's power to order precautionary measures for the purpose of temporarily suspending certain practices that might harm competition, or rather consumers, even during the

---

[8]Supreme Court of Justice of the Nation (2007). Action of Unconstitutionality 33/2006.
[9]Published in the *Diario Oficial de la Federación* on 10 May 2011.

investigation phase (Senate 2010).[10] Furthermore, other improvements, such as oral hearings or "settlement mechanisms in unilateral conduct cases and commitments for merger reviews", were made to the proceedings (OECD 2012: 34). In addition, these amendments introduced an anticipated termination mechanism to conclude the procedures followed in cases of relative monopolistic practices or undue concentrations. For those purposes, the economic agents were allowed to formally declare their commitment to suspending or not performing the corresponding anticompetitive behavior, and the COFECE was empowered to do so. With regard to sanctions, it was again noted that they were inadequate to deter improper behavior by economic agents (particularly, large companies), wherefore their amounts were increased, based on an estimate of economic agents' income (Senate 2010). Also, some behaviors deemed absolute monopolistic practices were referred to as crimes, and the COFECE was empowered to file complaints with the relevant authorities in charge of prosecuting crimes.

One of the main goals of the reform was to create mechanisms that made the competition agency's decisions more transparent and certain. Therefore, the COFECE imposed several duties related to the disclosure of its acts and the issuance of technical criteria.

Finally, the 2011 legislative reform provided for the need to create courts specialized in economic competition within the jurisdictional scope of ordinary administrative proceedings. Despite the advantages of the courts' specialization and the simplification of the means of appeal, "the length of time that courts took to review cases remained a problem since the specialized courts with expert judges that were envisioned by the reform were not set up and the ordinary administrative judicial procedure before these courts was never implemented" (OECD 2016: 20).

That same year, another reform was introduced to several legal systems that allowed class actions to be filed and damages to be claimed through civil proceedings by those who have suffered some damage as a consequence of monopolistic practices or unlawful concentrations.[11] Thus, the way was paved for strengthening the position of consumers against the negative effects of anticompetitive practices.

All these legislative reforms not only made Mexico a case in point on account of its ability to adopt economic competition policies progressively and successfully

---

[10]Joint opinion issued by the Trade and Industrial Promotion Commission and the Second Legislative Studies Commission on the draft Executive Order to amend, add and repeal different provisions of the Federal Law of Economic Competition, the Federal Criminal Code, the Fiscal Code of the Federation, the Federal Law of Contentious-Administrative Procedure, and the Organic Law of the Federal Court of Fiscal and Administrative Justice], *Gaceta Parlamentaria LXI/2PPO-195/28050*, December 9, Mexico; at: http://www.senado.gob.mx/index.php?ver=sp&mn=2&sm=2&id=28050.

[11]Executive Order to amend and add the Federal Code of Civil Procedure, the Federal Civil Code, the Federal Law of Economic Competition, the Federal Consumer Protection Law, the Organic Law of the Judicial Power of the Federation, the General Law of Ecological Balance and Environmental Protection, and the Law for the Protection and Defense of the User of Financial Services, published in the *Diario Oficial de la Federación* on 30 August 2011.

(Aydin 2016: 157), but also placed the country on a par with best international practices in the area, through the institutional strengthening of the agency, the continuous improvement of its procedures to investigate and impose sanctions, and the introduction of measures to promote transparency and accountability (OECD 2012: 35).

15.3 Structural Reforms in Economic Competition

In December 2012, the main political forces at that time, together with the Federal Government, signed the so-called Pact for Mexico, whereby they undertook, *inter alia*, to: (i) enhance economic competition in all sectors, but especially in those regarded as strategic – telecommunications, transportation, financial, and energy; (ii) strengthen the COFECE; (iii) create courts specialized in economic competition and telecommunications; and (iv) guarantee equal access to telecommunications through measures that strengthen the autonomy of the regulatory body of that sector and increase competition in radio, television, telephone and data services.[12] The purpose of the Pact for Mexico was to ensure the implementation of a series of structural reforms in order to comply with the commitments undertaken. It was precisely in that context that the 2013 constitutional reforms on economic competition and telecommunications and radio broadcasting were presented.[13] These reforms, in turn, would be developed by enacting a new Federal Law of Economic Competition[14] and the Federal Telecommunications and Radiobroadcasting Law.[15]

While these reforms focused on the problems faced by the telecommunications sector (Elizondo 2015: 44), the truth is that significant modifications were introduced in: the institutional design of competition agencies (2.1); the scope of their powers (2.2); and the realization of the specialization of jurisdictional bodies (2.3).

15.3.1 *Institutional Design*

As far as institutional design is concerned, the 2013 constitutional reforms created two antitrust agencies to deal with economic competition matters. On the one hand, the COFECE was re-founded with power over any sector or market on an interlinked basis, and, on the other hand, the Federal Telecommunications Institute, the

---

[12]*Pacto por México. Todos trabajando por ti* (2012). Signed on December 2 by the presidents of the executive committees of the political parties *Acción Nacional, Revolucionario Institucional* and *Revolución Democrática*. See clause 2. "Acuerdos para el crecimiento económico, el empleo y la competitividad" [Agreements on economic growth, employment and competitiveness].
[13]Published in the *Diario Oficial de la Federación* on 11 June 2013.
[14]Published in the *Diario Oficial de la Federación* on 23 May 2014.
[15]Published in the *Diario Oficial de la Federación* on 14 July 2014.

functions of which were limited to telecommunications and radio broadcasting, was created (to replace the COFETEL). Both entities were vested with constitutional autonomy and, therefore, were neck and neck with the executive, legislative and judicial branches. Thus, they abandoned their position of hierarchical subordination as decentralized bodies of the Ministry for Economy and the Ministry for Communications and Transportation, respectively.

This legal modification of the COFECE finally enabled the many attempts undertaken during both the 2006 legislative reform and the 2011 legislative procedure to be realized, so as to strengthen the Commission's independence. At present, the Federal Executive Branch is in charge of appointing commissioners from both the COFECE and the Federal Telecommunications Institute (Spanish acronym: IFETEL), subject to the Mexican Senate's approval. Moreover, its appointment scheme is designed to select commissioners based on candidates' merits and technical expertise. For such a purpose, Section 28 of the Political Constitution of the United Mexican States, as amended, provides for the creation of an Evaluation Committee in charge of examining expertise and submitting proposals for appointment by the Executive Branch.

Likewise, Section 28 lists some measures intended to strengthen the autonomy of the COFECE and the IFETEL, such as the autonomous exercise of their budget and the constitutional guarantee of budgetary adequacy, the removal of commissioners only for serious offenses established by laws and by a qualified majority voting of the Mexican Senate, and the creation of an incompatibility system that guarantees their independence and fairness in the decision-making process.

In that regard, it should be noted that while the structure of the COFECE and the IFETEL as autonomous constitutional bodies strengthens their autonomy and independence, the truth is that it poses significant "challenges of coordination of public policies" (Elizondo 2015: 45).[16] Also essential is the relationship between economic competition bodies and the institutions promoting regulatory improvement at both federal and state level. While the former are autonomous – i.e. not subordinate to the powers of the union – the latter are part of the Public Administration that forms the basis of the Executive Branch at both federal and state level. Accordingly, their closeness and the cooperation mechanisms that govern them are subject to political will, although "the most harmful restrictions on competition are precisely the regulatory barriers imposed by the authorities themselves" (COFECE 2018: 5).

Another aspect that prevents bodies engaged in economic competition and telecommunications from being captured by economic agents and other stakeholders is the adoption of government transparency policies, under the principles of

---

[16]"The constitutional text did not foresee that, in practice, there would be difficulties in determining the scope of action of each agency" (Núñez 2017a, b). An example of this is the AT&T-Time Warner merger case, in which the economic agents had to notify both agencies (IFETEL and COFECE), since the merger did not just affect the telecommunications sector; see at: https://www.eleconomista.com.mx/opinion/Cofece-e-IFT-delineando-responsabilidades-20170320-0006.html.

digital government and open data, as well as the incorporation of accountability mechanisms through reporting and appearance before the Congress of the Union and even the Federal Executive Branch, in compliance with Section 28 cited above. All that relates to another structural reform that deals with transparency and the right of access to public information, entrusted to another body recently considered constitutionally autonomous (that is, the National Institute for Transparency, Access to Information and Personal Data Protection, INAI).[17]

Finally, it is worth pointing out that, in an internal scheme of checks and balances, the economic competition system is built on the idea of separating the investigating authority from decision-making bodies. This reinstates one of the rationales that guided the 2011 reform and grants it constitutional status.

15.3.2 Scope of Powers

With regard to the powers of the COFECE and the IFETEL in terms of competition, the amendment of Section 28 of the Mexican Constitution grants constitutional status to the goals outlined in secondary legislation, that is to: "[…] guarantee free competition and maximized turnout to the marketplace, as well as prevent, investigate and police monopolies, monopolistic practices, economic concentrations and any other restrictions to the efficient operation of markets, in accordance with the Constitution and the law."[18] For such a purpose, this section provides that the Commission, as well as the IFETEL, has all the necessary powers to accomplish their task efficaciously.

Although the new LFCE incorporates, to a great extent, those powers of investigation and sanctioning that had been strengthened since the former law, new powers are introduced, such as the power to "regulate access to essential facilities, and order divestment of certain assets, rights, stakes or shares of economic agents, in the proportion needed to remove anti-competitive effects" (Section 28, Mexican Constitution). The inclusion of this aspect, in addition to encouraging compliance with the goals of economic competition bodies, was envisaged as a sanction in order to deter anticompetitive behavior (Guajardo 2014: 40).

These new powers, which, in turn, entail the introduction of unprecedented concepts in the Mexican legal system, as in the case of essential facilities, have been

---

[17]*See* "Decreto por el que se reforman y adicionan diversas disposiciones de la Constitución Política de los Estados Unidos Mexicanos, en materia de transparencia" [Executive Order to amend and add different provisions of the Political Constitution of the United Mexican States on transparency], published in the *Diario Oficial de la Federación* on 7 February 2014.

[18]In terms of Article 61 of the Mexican Federal Law on Economic Competition, published in the *Diario Oficial de la Federación* on 23 May 2014, a concentration "shall be understood as a merger, acquisition of control, or any other act by means of which companies, associations, stock, partnership interest, trusts or assets in general are consolidated, and which is carried out among competitors, suppliers, customers or any other Economic Agent."

subject to questioning by scholars and lawyers due to the legal uncertainty posed by their recent development (CIDAC 2015: 3). Although these powers have already been implemented by antitrust agencies, they are still subject to discussion and there is little case law that provides full certainty as to their scope.

Concerning the new powers of the *economic competition agency,* in 2014 two special procedures were included in the LFCE: (a) one to determine the existence of essential facilities; and (b) another to prevent and eliminate barriers to free market access and economic competition.

In addition, economic competition bodies have no power to file unconstitutionality claims in relation to both federal and local regulations that might be contrary to economic competition (COFECE 2018: 13). This is particularly relevant considering that unconstitutionality claims are a means of constitutional control whereby the Mexican Supreme Court of Justice may decide on the potential contradiction between the constitutional text and a legal provision of a lower status; moreover, they are a power granted to other autonomous constitutional bodies under Section 105 of the Political Constitution of the United Mexican States.

15.3.3 Specialization of Jurisdictional Bodies in Economic Competition

One of the main goals of the 2013 constitutional reform[19] and the subsequent LFCE was to prevent litigation being used to escape the effectiveness of the measures taken by economic competition bodies to reduce the companies' market power and anticompetitive practices.[20] For such purposes, applicable regulations significantly reduce the opportunities and means to challenge the decisions rendered by the Commission and the IFETEL. This eliminates the possibility of questioning them through federal contentious-administrative proceedings before the Federal Court of Administrative Justice (formerly, the Federal Court of Fiscal and Administrative Justice) and the administrative motion – for reconsideration or review – filed before the economic competition bodies. Therefore, since the reform, the decisions issued by antitrust agencies may only be challenged through indirect *amparo* proceedings, instituted before courts of the Judiciary specialized in economic competition, radio broadcasting and telecommunications. This is in addition to the inability to request a stay of the relevant act.

---

[19]With a draft Executive Order to reform and add different provisions of the Political Constitution of the United Mexican States. *Gaceta Parlamentaria,* XVI, 3726-II (12 March), Mexico, Legislative Palace of San Lázaro.

[20]See: Chamber of Deputies, LXIL Legislature (2013). "Iniciativas del Titular del Poder Ejecutivo. Con proyecto de decreto, que reforma y adiciona diversas disposiciones de la Constitución Política de los Estados Unidos Mexicanos" [Executive Branch Initiatives. With a draft Executive Order to reform and add different provisions of the Political Constitution of the United Mexican States], *Gaceta Parlamentaria,* XVI, 3726-II (12 March), Mexico: Legislative Palace of San Lázaro: 20ff.

The creation of courts specialized in economic competition, radio broadcasting and telecommunications means that judges must have experience and technical expertise in these fields and that their number is necessarily limited (OECD and Ministry of Economy 2016: 46). Additionally, this specialization – given the characteristics of the matters addressed – means that court decisions need to integrate an interdisciplinary vision that considers the impact of such decisions on the market in terms of economic efficiency.

In general terms, the specialization of the courts dealing with matters related to economic competition, broadcasting and telecommunications is associated with many advantages, such as more efficient procedures, better quality decisions, and enhanced uniformity of decisions with a resulting higher legal certainty (OECD and Ministry of Economy 2016: 57). However, the professionalization and ongoing training of the members of these courts are essential to maintain their effectiveness.

Lastly, it is worth highlighting one of the powers granted under the new LFCE to these specialized courts, which could substantially change the role of consumers in economic competition processes. It is the possibility of dealing, either individually or collectively, with claims for damages caused by monopolistic practices or unlawful concentrations, once the decisions issued by economic competition bodies have become final (Article 134 of the law). This addition strengthens the measures outlined since the 2011 reforms in different legal systems, intended to generate favorable conditions so that consumers could obtain compensation for behavior contrary to free competition and maximized turnout to the marketplace.

The inclusion of redress in relation to anticompetitive behavior could entail, in practice, a means of narrowing the distance between economic competition policies and society in general, thus encouraging the adoption of a true competition culture. However, its acceptance is still at an early stage of consolidation. Besides, there are aspects that create some uncertainty over the scope of its effectiveness, such as the courts' ability to determine proper compensation and the disincentives that this scheme could create for economic agents to stick to the immunity program under the law (Núñez 2017a, b). In addition, there have been some situations that call into question the possibility that the specialized courts may comply with the objectives foreseen by the amendments, given the uncertainty about the length of judges' appointments and the lack of transparency in the criteria for their removal. This is the case of Judge Tron Petit, who was removed before the end of the period for which he was appointed after issuing a resolution against a major company with significant market power in the telecommunications sector (Levy 2011).

15.4 Conclusions

Economic competition in Mexico is the consequence of ongoing evolution which, five lustra after its reception, has achieved high international standards. The different legislative reforms on this matter, as well as the 2013 constitutional reform and its secondary legislation, have strengthened the autonomy and independence of economic competition bodies, their powers to meet their goals, and the judicial protection procedures that discourage litigation without restricting access to justice. All this contributes to consolidating the rule of law in this field. Nevertheless, there are still tasks which need to be completed, not only to promote new regulatory amendments, but also because many of the goals depend on their effective implementation, the coordination of public policies and the development of precedents that provide more legal certainty.

References

Anaya, Jorge; Ruiz, Eugenio; Trejo, Ricardo (2009). "Evolución del Derecho de la Competencia en México" [Evolution of Competition Law in Mexico], in: *Boletín Mexicano de Derecho Comparado*, new series, 52,126 (September–December): 1,169–1,200.

Aydin, Umut (2016). "Competition Law and Policy in Mexico: Successes and Challenges", in: *Law and Contemporary Problems*, 79,55: 155–186.

Bufford, Samuel (2006). "International Rule of Law and the Market Economy – An Outline", in: *Southwestern Journal of Law & Trade in the Americas*, 12: 303–312.

Calsamiglia, Albert (1988). "Justicia, Eficiencia y Derecho" [Justice, Efficiency and Law], in: *Revista del Centro de Estudios Constitucionales*, 1: 305–335.

Carlton, Dennis; Picker, Randal C. (2007). "Antitrust and Regulation". Working Paper 12902, *National Bureau of Economic Research*, Massachusetts, United States of America (February); at: http://www.nber.org/papers/w12902.

Castañeda-Gallardo, G. (2014). "Orígenes, avances y dificultades de la política de competencia económica en México (1993–2003)" [Origins, advances and difficulties of the economic competition policy in Mexico (1993–2003)], in: García Alba, Pascual; Gutiérrez, Lucino; Torres Ramírez, Gabriela (Eds.): *El Nuevo Milenio Mexicano. Tomo 3: El Cambio Estructural* (México: Universidad Autónoma Metropolitana, Azcapotzalco): 337–376.

Centro de Investigación para el Desarrollo, A.C. (CIDAC) (2015). *Mejores Prácticas Internacionales en Insumos Esenciales en Industrias de Red*; at: http://cidac.org/mejores-practicas-internacionales-en-insumos-esenciales-en-industrias-de-red/.

Chamber of Deputies, LXIL Legislature. (2013). "Iniciativas del Titular del Poder Ejecutivo. Con proyecto de decreto, que reforma y adiciona diversas disposiciones de la Constitución Política de los Estados Unidos Mexicanos" [Executive Branch Initiatives].

Dam, Kenneth W. (2007). *The Law-Growth Nexus: The Rule of Law and Economic Development* (Washington, D.C.: Brookings Institution Press).

Diego-Fernández, Mateo (2010). "Brevísima Explicación y Análisis de las Reformas a la Ley Federal de Competencia en México" [Overview of the Reforms of the Federal Competition Law in Mexico], in: *Revista de Derecho Económico Internacional*, Instituto Tecnológico Autónomo de México (ITAM), 1,1 (November): 77–84.

Doering, Detmar. (2011). *Freedom, The Rule of Law and Market Economy: Concerning a cognitive dissonance* (Potsdam: Liberal Institute Friedrich-Naumann-Stiftung für die Freiheit).

Elbittar, Alexander; Mariscal, Elisa (2018). "Prólogo a la primera edición en español" [Foreword to the first edition in Spanish], in: Motta, Massimo (Ed.): *Política de competencia: Teoría y práctica* (Mexico City: FCE, UNAM, COFECE and CIDE).

Elizondo, Carlos (2015). "¿Una Nueva Constitución en 2013? El Capítulo Económico" [A New Constitution in 2013? The Economic Chapter], in: *Cuestiones Constitucionales. Revista Mexicana de Derecho Constitucional*, 31 (July–December): 29–56.

Federal Economic Competition Commission (COFECE) (2018). *Plataforma para el Crecimiento 2018–2024*; at: https://www.cofece.mx/wp-content/uploads/2017/12/plataforma-de-crecimiento.pdf#pdf.

Fitzpatrick, Danielle; Aziz, Luis Alberto (2010). "Amendments to Mexico's Federal Law on Economic Competition", in: *Lexology* (10 November); at: https://www.lexology.com/library/detail.aspx?g=47d50dd2-d5cc-4944-88e6-25ecf7715fc0.

Gallardo, Adrián; de la Mora, Luz María (Eds.) (2014). *Reforma de Telecomunicaciones y Competencia Económica. México más productivo y más competitivo*, Vol. 3 (Mexico City: Fundación Colosio – MA Porrúa).

García, Tonatiuh (2003). *Ley Federal de Competencia Económica. Comentarios, concordancias y jurisprudencia* (Mexico City: National Autonomous University of Mexico).

Guajardo, Ildefonso (2014). "Necesidad y racionalidad de la Reforma de Competencia Económica" [Necessity and rationale of the Economic Competition Reform], in: Gallardo, Adrián; de la Mora, Luz María (Eds.): *Reforma de Telecomunicaciones y Competencia Económica. México más productivo y más competitivo*, Vol. 3 (Mexico City: Fundación Colosio – MA Porrúa).

Levy, Irene (2011). "Tron Petit: the inconvenient judge", in: *El Universal* (4 December); at: https://www.eluniversal.com.mx/columna/irene-levy/cartera/tron-petit-el-magistrado-incomodo.

Lindblom, Charles E. (2001). *The Market System* (Harrisonburg, New Haven & London: Yale University Press).

Maqueo, María Solange (2011). "Las imperfecciones del Mercado" [The Market imperfections], in: *Revista de Investigaciones Jurídicas* (Mexico City: Escuela Libre de Derecho): 601–647.

Mariscal, Judith (2014). "Los retos que enfrenta la Reforma de Telecomunicaciones" [The challenges faced by the Telecommunications Reform], in: Gallardo, Adrián; de la Mora, Luz María (Eds.): *Reforma de Telecomunicaciones y Competencia Económica. México más productivo y más competitivo*, Vol. 3 (Mexico City: Fundación Colosio – MA Porrúa).

Medema, Steven G.; Mercuro, Nicholas; Samuels, Warren J. (2000). "0520 Institutional Law and Economics", in: Bouckaert, Boudewijn; De Geest, Gerrit (Eds.): *Encyclopedia of Law and Economics, Vol. I: The History and Methodology of Law and Economics* (Northampton: Edward Elgar Publishing Inc.): 418–455.

Motta, Massimo (2004). *Competition Policy: Theory and Practice* (Cambridge: Cambridge University Press) [1st edn. in Spanish (2018). *Política de competencia: Teoría y práctica*, (Mexico City: FCE, UNAM, COFECE and CIDE)].

Núñez, Javier (2017a). "COFECE e IFETEL: Delineando responsabilidades" [COFECE and IFETEL: delineating responsabilities], in: *El Economista* (20 March); at: https://www.eleconomista.com.mx/opinion/Cofece-e-IFT-delineando-responsabilidades-20170320-0006.html.

Núñez, Javier (2017b). "Reparación del daño: avance en la aplicación de la política de competencia" [Redress: progress in the application of the competition policy], in: *El Economista* (31 October); at: https://www.eleconomista.com.mx/opinion/Reparacion-de-dano-avance-en-la-aplicacion-de-la-politica-de-competencia-20171031-0049.html.

Organization for Economic Co-operation and Development (OECD) and Inter-American Development Bank (IDB) (2004). *Competition Law and Policy in Mexico: An OECD Peer Review* (Washington, D.C.: OECD and Inter-American Development Bank).

Organization for Economic Co-operation and Development (OECD) and Inter-American Development Bank (IDB) (2012). *Follow-up the Nine Peer Reviews of Competition Law and Policy of Latin American Countries: Argentina, Brazil, Chile, Colombia, El Salvador, Honduras, Mexico, Panama and Peru* (Washington, D.C.: OECD and Inter-American Development Bank).

Organization for Economic Co-operation and Development and Ministry of Economy of Mexico (2016). *The Resolution of Competition Cases by Specialised and Generalist Courts: Stocktaking of international experiences* (Washington, D.C.: OECD).

Pavón-Villamayor, Víctor (2010). "Competition Law Reform in Mexico: A note on Joint Dominance", *Competition Policy International* (3 September); at: https://www.competitionpolicyinternational.com/competition-law-reform-in-mexico-a-note-on-joint-dominance/.

Roldán, José; Mena, Carlos; Méndez, Laura (Eds.) (2015). *Derecho de la Competencia en México* (Mexico: Porrúa).

Sarsfield, Rodolfo (2010). "What is the Rule of Law (And Is Not)?", Paper for the 2010 Annual Meeting of the American Political Science Association, 2–5 September, American Political Science Association; at: http://ssrn.com/abstract=1667682.

Senate of the Congress of the Union, LXIII Legislature. (2010). "Dictamen de las Comisiones Unidas de Comercio y Fomento Industrial y de Estudios Legislativos, Segunda, a la Minuta con Proyecto de Decreto por el que se Reforman, Adicionan y Derogan diversas Disposiciones de la Ley Federal de Competencia Económica, del Código Penal Federal, del Código Fiscal de la Federación, de la Ley Federal de Procedimiento Contencioso Administrativo y de la Ley Orgánica del Tribunal Federal de Justicia Fiscal y Administrativa".

Supreme Court of Justice of the Nation (2007). "Decision and individual opinion by Minister Olga Sánchez Cordero de García Villegas, Action of Unconstitutionality 33/2006", in: *Diario Oficial de la Federación* (12 July).

Witker, Jorge (2017). "El Capítulo Económico de la Constitución de Querétaro" [The Economic Chapter of the Querétaro Constitution], in: *Revista de la Facultad de Derecho de México*, 67,267: 567–599.

Universidad de las Américas Puebla (UDLAP)

With over 75 years of experience, Universidad de las Américas Puebla (UDLAP) is an academic institution with more than 70 undergraduate and graduate study programs in diverse areas. It offers a multicultural experience to its students, including the 55 nationalities represented on campus due to its exchange agreements with nearly 40 countries.

UDLAP has a beautiful and unique campus located in Cholula, the oldest city in Latin America. The laboratories, library, computer rooms, and classrooms have the latest technology, allowing students to transform their theoretical knowledge into practice, thus strengthening their abilities and competencies. Aside from ample knowledge and experience, 99% of UDLAP's faculty have graduate degrees. They also devote time to research and artistic creation, and one in every three full-time professors belongs to Mexico's National Research System. Quality at UDLAP is backed by international accreditations, such as the one granted by the Southern Association of Colleges and Schools Commission on Colleges (SACSCOC) since 1959. This accreditation has been ratified to its highest level, being one of only two universities outside the United States to have a level 6. UDLAP is the only one-campus university in Latin America to have 5 stars overall from QS Stars in 2017, earning 5 stars in teaching, internationalization, inclusion, infrastructure, and employability.

Address: Ex Hacienda Sta. Catarina S/N. San Andrés Cholula, Puebla, C.P. 72810. Mexico.
Website: www.udlap.mx

About the Editor

Juan Antonio Le Clercq has a Ph.D. in Political and Social Sciences, a Master's in Political Sciences and a Bachelor's in Political Sciences and Public Administration from the *Universidad Nacional Autónoma de México (UNAM)* with a Specialization in Politics and Energy and Environmental Management from the *Facultad Latinoamericana de Ciencias Sociales (Flacso)*. He is full-time professor of Political Science and International Relations, Academic Director of the Department of International Relations and Political Science, UDLAP; Coordinator of the *Centro de Estudios sobre Impunidad y Justicia* (CESIJ); and Coordinator of the Global Impunity Index and Global Impunity Index Mexico, UDLAP. Since 2017, Dr. Le Clercq has been a Non-resident Scholar in the Mexico Center of the Baker Institute at *Universidad de Rice*. He is co-author of the Global Impunity Index (IGI) 2015 and 2017, as well as the Global Impunity Index Mexico (IGI-MEX) 2016 and 2018, all edited by UDLAP. His publications include:

Le Clercq, Juan Antonio (2018), "El complejo impunidad", in Laura Loeza and Ana Liese Richard (eds.), *Derechos Humanos y violencia en México*, Mexico: UNAM.

Le Clercq, Juan Antonio. (2017), "The Relationship Between Impunity and Inequality Globally and in Mexico", in Úrsula Oswald Spring and Serena Eréndira

Serrano (eds.), *Risks, Violence, Security and Peace in Latin America: 40 Years of the Latin American Council of Peace Research (CLAIP)*, Cham: Springer, pp. 195–205.

Le Clercq, J.A., Chaidez, A., Rodríguez, G. (2016) "Midiendo la Impunidad en América Latina", in *Iconos de la Facultad Latinoamericana de Ciencias Sociales* (FLACSO-Ecuador), No. 55, March 2016, pp. 69–91. ISSN: 1390-1249. http://dx.doi.org/10.17141/iconos.55.2016.1934.

Le Clercq, J.A., (2015) "Regime Change, Transition to Sustainability and Climate Change Law in Mexico", in Brauch, Hans Günter, Oswald Spring, Úrsula; Grin, John; Scheffran; Jürgen (Eds.), *Handbook on Sustainability Transition and Sustainable Peace*, pp. 505–523.

Abreu, J.P., Le Clercq, J.A. (Coords.); Porrúa, M.A. (Ed.) (2011) "La reforma humanista. Derechos Humanos y cambio constitucional en México" City. Publisher/institution.

He contributes a weekly column to the online news portal *Eje Central* (www.ejecentral.com.mx).

Address: Ex hacienda de Sta. Catarina Mártir, 72810, San Andrés Cholula, Puebla, Mexico.

Email: juan.leclercq@udlap.mx

About the Co-Editor

José Pablo Abreu Sacramento has a Bachelor's Degree in Law from the Universidad Marista (Merida, Mexico, 2004), a Diploma in Political Science and Constitutional Law from the Centro de Estudios Politicos y Constitucionales (Madrid, Spain, 2005); an M.Sc. in Philosophy and Public Policy from the London School of Economics and Political Science (London, UK, 2017) and a Ph.D. from the Universidad Complutense (Madrid, Spain, 2009). He has served as an advisor to congressmen at the Chamber of Deputies (2006–2010) and Senate (2010–2012) and as an advisor to the Chief Justice at the Electoral Court of the Federal Judicial Branch (2012–2015). He has taught Constitutional and Electoral Law at different private and public univeristies in Mexico and is now the Director of the Bachelor Degree in Law at the Tecnológico de Monterrey, Campus Santa Fe.

Address: Av. Carlos Lazo 100, Santa Fe, La Loma, 01389, Ciudad de Mexico, Mexico.
Email: jpabreu@tec.mx

About the Contributors

Cristopher Ballinas Valdés is a specialist in the study of executive government, regulation and public sector reform. A Doctor of Philosophy in Politics from the University of Oxford, his research agenda explores the effects of politics and institutions on policy outcomes – the politics of policies. Dr. Ballinas Valdés presents a broad high-level experience in policy instrumentation. As a result, he has developed a portfolio focusing on the areas of public sector reform, regulation, social policy, re-engineering, transparency, corruption control and border security.
Email: cristopher.ballinas@itam.mx

Rafael Estrada Michel is a lawyer from the Escuela Libre de Derecho (ELD), Mexico, and received his doctorate in the History of Law and Legal, Moral and Political Philosophy program at the University of Salamanca (USAL) in Spain. He studied a Diploma in Legal Anthropology at the National School of Anthropology and History (ENAH). Between 2009 and 2016 he was a Counselor of the National Commission of Human Rights, appointed by the Senate, and between 2012 and 2016 he served as Director General (dean) of the National Institute of Criminal Sciences (INACIPE), appointed by the President of Mexico. In 2018 he was designated Visiting Research Professor at the University of Pisa, Italy. A member of the National Researchers System, level 2.

Since 1997 has been teaching public law and legal history at his alma mater and at Universidad Iberoamericana [Iberoamerican University] (UIA), Universidad Panamericana [Panamerican University] (UP), Universidad Nacional Autónoma de México [National Autonomous University of Mexico] (UNAM), Universidad Autónoma Metropolitana [Metropolitan Autonomous University] (UAM), Instituto Tecnológico Autónomo de México [Autonomous Technological Institute of Mexico] (ITAM), Universidad La Salle (ULSA) [La Salle University], Instituto Tecnológico y de Estudios Superiores de Monterrey [Monterrey Institute of Technology and Higher Education] (ITESM), Universidad Latina de América [Latin University of America] (UNLA), Universidad Autónoma de Nuevo León

[Nuevo León Autonomous University] (UANL), and Universidad Pontificia de México [Pontifical University of Mexico] (UPM).
Email: program.restradam@up.edu.mx

Ana Elena Fierro is a Doctorate in Law from the Instituto de Investigaciones Jurídicas de la UNAM. LLM from the Georgia University and Master in Philosophy from the Universidad Anáhuac, campus Mayab. Bachelor in Law from ITAM. Nowadays, Ana E. Fierro is Coordinator of the Master in Managment and Public Policy and research professor at the CIDE. Her interests are transparency, accountability and responsibility of civil servants.
Email: ana.fierro@cide.edu

Camilo Gutiérrez worked at the World Justice Project from 2016 to early 2019, where he managed data analysis for the Rule of Law Index. Prior to joining the WJP, he worked as a professor and research assistant at Universidad de los Andes, in Bogotá, Colombia. He holds a B.A. and Masters in Economics from Universidad de los Andes
Email: camilo.guti.p@gmail.com

Fernando Herrera holds a B.A. in Marketing and International Business from the Universidad Autónoma de Yucatan (UADY), and a Master in Latin American Studies from Université Paris III Sorbonne Nouvelle. He has collaborated at Higher Education Institutions such as UADY and CIDE. He has also worked as a consultant for non-profit organizations participating in projects related to transparency and accountability, education and social policy. He currently works at the School of Social Sciences and Goverment of Tecnológico de Monterrey.
Email: fernandoherrerarosado@gmail.com

María Solange Maqueo Ramírez, Associate Research Professor at the Legal Studies Division of the Economic Research and Teaching Center (CIDE) and Chair of the Advisory Board of the National Institute for Transparency, Access to Information and Personal Data Protection (INAI).
Email: maria.maqueo@cide.edu

Joel Martinez is the Director of Engagement at the World Justice Project. Prior to joining the WJP, Mr. Martinez worked with the Massachusetts Commission Against Discrimination in its enforcement of anti-discrimination laws, focusing on outreach to low income communities. He earned his B.A. in Economics and Political Science from Middlebury College
Email: jmartinez@worldjusticeproject.org

María Novoa is Coordinator of the Justice Project in México Evalúa. She has worked in the World Bank, the Inter-American Development Bank, PNUD, the European Union and USAID. She has also been part of different projects for institutional strengthening in El Salvador, Mexico, Paraguay, Guatemala, Venezuela, Honduras, Bolivia, Ukraine and Azerbaijan. She has a Master's degree in Public Policy from the Universidad Simón Bolívar.
Email: maria.novoa@mexicoevalua.org

Mauricio Olivares-Méndez, is a researcher-in-training especially interested in social cohesion, diversity, political rights and migration studies. National Council for Science and Technology fellow, 2013–2015 and Recipient of an Erasmus Mundus Scholarship to pursue a Joint Masters degree at the Universities of Amsterdam, Deusto and Osnabrück. Currently working at Universidad Autónoma de Querétaro coordinating the undergraduate program in Political Science and Public Administration.
Email: mauricio.olivares@uaq.mx

Tony Payan is the Françoise and Edward Djerejian Fellow for Mexico Studies and director of the Mexico Center at the Baker Institute. He was adjunct associate professor at Rice University, professor at the Universidad Autónoma de Ciudad Juárez and professor of political science at The University of Texas at El Paso between 2001 and 2015. He has a doctorate degree in international relations from Georgetown University and his research focuses primarily on border studies, particularly the US-Mexico border, border governance, border flows and immigration, as well as border security and organized crime.
Email: tony.payan@rice.edu

Alejandro Ponce is the Chief Research Officer of the World Justice Project. He joined the WJP as Senior Economist and is one of the original designers and a lead author of the WJP Rule of Law Index. Prior to joining the World Justice Project, Dr. Ponce worked as a researcher at Yale University and as an economist at the World Bank and the Mexican Banking and Securities Commission. Dr. Ponce has conducted research in the areas of behavioral economics, financial inclusion, justice indicators, and the rule of law, and has been published in collected volumes as well as top academic journals such as the American Economic Review and the Journal of Law and Economics. He holds a BA in Economics from ITAM in Mexico, and an MA and Ph.D. in Economics from Stanford University.
Email: aponce@worldjusticeproject.org

Eduardo Román González is a Doctor in Law, Government and Public Policy from Universidad Autónoma de Madrid, Spain; Coordinator of Research at CEEAD, a Mexican independent research center focused on legal education; Professor of Constitutional Law, Human Rights and Public International Law at Facultad Libre de Derecho de Monterrey and Tecnológico de Monterrey, Monterrey Campus. Member of the Mexican National System of Researchers (*Sistema Nacional de Investigadores*, SNI).
Email: eduardo.roman@outlook.com

Jorge Javier Romero is Research Professor C, of the Department of Politics and Culture at the Universidad Autónoma Metropolitana Xochimilco attached to the Public Policies area, and professor of the postgraduate division of the Faculty of Political and Social Sciences of the UNAM. Professor Romero has carried out research visits at the Institute of Advanced Social Studies of the Spanish National Research Council and has given lectures at different universities and study centers in Mexico and Spain. He is currently on sabbatical at the Drug Policy Program of

the CIDE Centro Region, where he directs the Diploma in Drug Policy and the Internal Seminar of the PPD.
Email: jromero@correo.xoc.uam.mx

Vidal Romero is Professor at the Political Science Department at ITAM and Visiting Fellow (2018–2019) at the Latin America and Caribbean Centre (LACC) at the London School of Economics and Political Science. He holds a Ph.D. in Political Science from Stanford University. He was visiting Professor at Stanford University (2012–13). Romero is Co-Director of ITAM's Center of Studies on Security, Intelligence, and Governance. His current research examines the conditions under which governments can establish (democratic) order in their territories. He has collaborated on different research projects with the World Bank, the Wilson Center, México Evalúa, the National Endowment for Democracy, and the Inter-American Development Bank.
Email: vromero@itam.mx

Rodolfo Sarsfield is an Associate Professor at the Autonomous University of Queretaro. He received his Ph.D. in Political Science from the Facultad Latinoamericana de Ciencias Sociales [Latinamerican Faculty of Social Sciences] (FLACSO) in 2004. He has been Associate Researcher of the Latin American Public Opinion Project at Vanderbilt University, and Affiliated Researcher of the Department of Legal Studies at the Centro de Investigación y Docencia Económicas [Center for Research and Teaching in Economics] (CIDE). He is currently a Board Member of the Committee on Concepts and Methods at the International Political Science Association (IPSA), and he collaborates with the Mass Survey team for Team Populism.

His research focuses on the study of social norms, preference formation, and political attitudes, with an emphasis on the attitudes toward democracy, corruption, informal rules, and the rule of law in Latin America. Also, he studies concepts and methods in political science. He is the editor of the special issue for Justice System Journal on "The Rule of Law" (with Ryan E. Carlin). He also is the author of Research Design (with G. Dave Garson, Statistical Associate Publishing, Asheboro, NC). He has published more than two dozen journal articles and contributions to edited volumes.
Email: rodolfo.sarsfield@uaq.mx

Karen Silva is a researcher of the Justice Project in México Evalúa. Previously, she coordinated the Drugs Policy Program at the CIDE. She has a Bachelor's degree in Law from the UNAM
Email: karen.silva@mexicoevalua.org.

Leslie Solís joined the World Justice Project in the fall of 2016, after spending five years as a criminal justice analyst at the prominent think tank México Evalúa in Mexico City. She was also an editorial advisor for the Justice Section at Diario Reforma, one of Mexico's largest daily newspapers, for two consecutive years. She holds a BA in Political Science and International Relations from CIDE.
Email: lsolis@worldjusticeproject.org

Radu-Mihai Triculescu, Early Stage Researcher under the Marie Skłodowska-Curie actions, Horizon 2020 of the E.U., University of Twente, Enschede, Netherlands.

He holds a Master Degree in International Affairs from Florida State University (2013), and a Joint Master in International Migration and Social Cohesion from the University of Amsterdam, Universidad de Deusto, and Osnabruck University (2015). He completed his Bachelor studies in Political Science and International Affairs at Florida State University (Magna Cum Laude, Phi Beta Kappa, 2011). *Email*: r.triculescu@utwente.nl

Index

A
Abimourched, Rola, 136
Abreu, Jose P., 171, 285
Accountability, 4, 10, 11, 30, 31, 53, 61, 68, 85, 103, 137, 138, 141–153, 167, 217, 254, 273, 275, 288
Accusatory Criminal Justice System, 193, 196, 201, 203, 204
Acemoglu, Daron, 228
Ackerman, John, 143
Adcock, Robert, 24, 25, 33
Administrative Courts, 11, 46, 66, 145–148, 153
Administrative Justice, 46–48, 54, 218, 272, 276
Administrative Responsibility Penalties, 217
Agnew, John, 125
Agrast, Mark, 4
Aguiar Aguilar, Azul A., 195
Aguilar Rivera, José Antonio, 88
Ahmad, Nabeela, 114
Amendments, 8, 11, 14, 81–83, 87–92, 97, 102, 103, 129, 130, 142, 175, 176, 178–180, 183, 184, 188, 232, 271, 272, 275, 277, 278
American Convention of Human Rights, 152, 180
Amparo, 11, 12, 46, 130, 134, 141–143, 146, 149–153, 175, 185, 199, 276
Anaya, Jorge, 278
Anaya Muñoz, Alejandro, 136
Anstett, Élisabeth, 41, 43
Antitrust, 271, 273, 276
Aparicio, Francisco, 211
Argyris, Chris, 144

Armed Forces, 13, 28, 45, 51, 164, 232, 236, 237
Arneson, Richard J., 161
Arnson, Cynthia, 114, 116
Article 19, 255
Asúnsolo, C. R., 178, 183, 187
Asimov, Michael, 145
Atak, Idil, 127, 136, 138
Atuesta Becerra, Laura H., 115
Autonomous Technological Institute of México, 40, 57, 58, 141, 287–290
Axelrad, Lee, 243
Aydin, Umut, 268–270, 273
Aziz, Luis Alberto, 271

B
Ballinas, C., 12, 214, 287
Barris, Accul, 169
Barros, Rober, 20, 24
Bates, Robert H., 108
Becker, Lawrence, 170
Beeson, Mark, 125
Begné Guerra, Cristina, 51
Behavior, 1, 2, 4, 7, 9, 12, 20, 27–30, 66, 85, 108, 112, 118, 156, 168, 169, 171, 266, 268–272, 275, 277
Behn, Robert D., 144
Bejarano, Raúl, 236
Bellamy, Richard, 85
Belton, Rachel, 20, 32, 34
Benton, Allyson, 211
Bergman, Marcelot, 114
Bingham, Lord, 254
Bingham, Tom, 2, 20, 32, 84, 128
Black's Law Dictionary, 143

© Springer Nature Switzerland AG 2020
J. A. Le Clercq and J. P. Abreu Sacramento (eds.), *Rebuilding the State Institutions*,
https://doi.org/10.1007/978-3-030-31314-2

Blanco, Luisa R., 114
Blanton, Robert, 126
Blanton, Shannon L., 126
Booth, John A., 168
Borja, R., 195
Borrego Estrada, Felipe, 52
Botero, Juan, 62
Bovens, Mark, 143
Brandt, Richard B., 160
Bufford, Samuel, 266, 267
Burgoa, Ignacio, 146
Burstein, Paul, 253

C
Caballero, José Luis, 87, 89
Cacicazgo, 13, 224–227, 229
Caldeira, Gregory A., 20, 28, 29
Calderón Chelius, Leticia, 51
Calderón, Gabriela, 111
Calderón Hinojosa, Felipe, 91, 232, 234, 235, 246, 253, 254, 256
Calderón, Laura, 256
Caldwell, Bruce, 32
Calsamiglia, Albert, 278
Calzada Olvera, Rebeca, 235, 236
Cameron, Maxwell, 30
Capano, Giliberto, 245
Carbonell, Miguel, 87
Carlos Salinas de Gortari, 91, 92, 214
Carmona, J. U., 179
Carlton, Dennis, 278
Carothers, Thomas, 24, 59
Carpizo, J., 212
Casar, María Amparo, 87, 101
Castañeda-Gallardo, G., 267, 269
Castagnola, Andrea, 129
Castilla Juárez, Karlos A., 131
Castillo, Manuel Angel, 51
Caulkins, Jonathan, 115
Cavina, Mario, 41
Cejudo, Guillermo, 67
Center for Research and Teaching in Economics, 290
Center for Studies on Teaching and Law Learning, 176
Ceobanu, Alin M., 114
Chacón Rojas, Orlando, 92
Chaihark, Hahm, 35
Challenge, 4, 8–11, 28, 45, 46, 48, 49, 59–62, 84, 88, 102, 103, 118, 123, 125, 126, 141, 142, 144, 149, 150, 152, 163, 175, 176, 183, 184, 188, 193, 197, 198, 205, 244, 248, 250, 258, 260, 261, 274, 276
Chavez, Rebecca Bill, 20, 28, 29

Checks and balances, 2, 12, 30–32, 34, 84, 86, 143, 153, 209, 210, 212, 220, 271, 275
Chemerinsky, Erwin, 60
Chwe, Hanyu, 251
Citizen Council of the National Institute of Migration, 134
Citizenry, 10, 32, 156, 157, 162, 166, 167
Civic culture, 156, 166–169
Civic education, 10, 155–157, 165–167, 169–171
Civil justice, 5, 7, 58, 59, 61, 63, 66, 68, 70, 74, 82, 97, 195, 252
Civil law, 39, 41, 50
Clientelism, 229, 233, 235, 238
Clifton, Judith, 254
Coatsworth, J., 227
Cohen, G. A., 166, 170
Cohen, Jean L., 125
Collective goods, 160, 161
College of México, 158, 159
Collier, David, 19–21, 24, 25, 29
Collins, James, 115
Community life, 155–157, 159–162, 164–166, 168–171
Competition law, 14, 267, 270
Computer-assisted personal interviewing, 67
Concha Cantú, Hugo, 101
Conde, Silvia L., 156, 168
Constitutional amendment, 83, 102, 142, 175, 176, 178–180, 183, 184, 188
Constitutional Change, 8, 81, 83, 84, 87, 88, 90–92, 99–101, 103, 246
Constitutionalism, 41, 84, 85
Constitutional Reforms, 8, 41, 42, 48, 87–95, 102, 129, 142, 145, 149–151, 193, 215, 273, 276, 277
Constitutions, 5, 8, 9, 11, 30, 32, 40, 41, 44–46, 48, 81–92, 94, 97, 98, 101–103, 128–130, 134, 142, 145–148, 150, 151, 157, 168, 171, 176, 179–181, 185, 186, 196, 211, 229, 232, 236, 237, 242, 246, 260, 274–276
Consulta Mitofsky, 251, 252
Cooter, Robert C., 85
Coppedge, Michael, 19, 33, 34
Cordera, R., 211
Correa Cabrera, Guadalupe, 136, 256
Corruption, 2–5, 7, 9, 11–13, 28, 39, 44, 46, 48–50, 54, 57, 58, 60, 62, 64–66, 68–70, 74, 82, 83, 88, 97, 102, 103, 113, 115–119, 136, 143, 159, 166, 167, 177, 195, 207, 208, 210, 215–221, 230, 233, 234, 242, 250–255, 258, 260, 261, 287, 290

Cossío Barragán, José Ramón, 246
Cossío Díaz, José Ramón, 88, 101, 129, 142, 246
Court of Justice of the Nation, 146–152, 175, 177, 180, 181, 271
Crépeau, François, 127, 138
Crime, 9–13, 20, 27, 42, 45, 49–52, 61, 62, 66–68, 83, 107, 110, 112–119, 131, 132, 134–137, 159, 162, 164–166, 193, 194, 202, 203, 216–218, 230, 231, 234–237, 241, 250, 253–256, 258, 260, 261, 272, 289
Criminal Justice Reform, 68, 193, 196, 201
Criminal Justice System, 11, 12, 47, 50, 61, 64, 66, 76, 188, 193–205
Criminal Organization, 9, 111, 112, 114, 115, 117, 118, 136, 137, 256
Csete, Joanne, 115
Culture, 2, 41, 58, 135, 155, 166, 168–170, 175, 176, 178, 180, 185, 188, 197, 223, 225, 254, 269, 277, 289
Culture of Legality, 2, 103
Czarnota, Adam, 28

D

Dahl, Robert, 113
Dale, Roger, 125
Dam, Kenneth W., 278
Dauvergne, Catherine, 127, 128
David, Paul A., 238
Davis, Diane, 135
de la Garza, Isidro, 87, 88, 101
de la Madrid, M., 90, 194
de la Mora, Luz María, 270
de la Rosa, O., 178
Dell, Melissa, 111, 113
Democracy, 1–3, 7, 20, 24, 25, 28, 30–32, 34, 86, 103, 108, 110, 111, 113, 114, 117, 119, 156–159, 164, 166, 167, 169, 194, 195, 208, 213, 221, 242, 250, 290
Democratic institutions, 83, 84
Democratic participation, 260
Diamond, Larry, 113, 136, 166, 169–171
Díaz-Cayeros, Alberto, 111
Díaz de León, Alejandra, 135
Díaz Saenz, Rodrigo, 102
Diego-Fernández, Mateo, 270, 271
Distrito Federal Electoral Institute, 159
Documentation Network of Migrant Advocacy Organizations, 123, 134–136
Doering, Detmar, 278
Dreyfus, Jean Marc, 43
Drucker, Ernest, 115
Drug cartel, 13, 111, 115, 136, 256

Drug legalization, 107, 119
Drug market regulation, 223
Drug Policy Program (PPD), 223, 289, 290
Drug prohibition, 115
Drugs regulation, 224, 226
Dunoff, Jeffrey, 127
Dworkin, Ronald, 20, 24, 26, 27

E

Eastwood, Niamh, 119
Economic competition, 11, 13, 14, 47, 88, 265–270, 272–278
Economic constitution, 265
Economist Intelligence Unit, The, 3
Economist, The, 3, 242, 246
Elbittar, Alexander, 268
Elizondo, Carlos, 273, 274
Elkins, Zachary, 86, 87
Elster, John, 157
Enciso, Froylán, 115, 119
Energy Reform, 241, 244–246, 248–254, 258–262
Energy Regulatory Commission, 250
Enrique Peña Nieto, 12, 91, 92, 132, 214, 218, 237, 242, 246
Equality, 2, 6, 21–23, 26, 34, 41, 46, 47, 126, 193, 194
Ernesto Zedillo Ponce de León, 91, 92
Escamilla Salazar, J., 178
Esquivel, Gerardo, 87, 88, 101, 102, 229
Estrada Michel, Rafael, 7, 42, 287
Etellekt, 117, 256
Executive Commission for Victims Assistance, 45
Executive Secretariat of the National Public Security System Factor, 198

F

Fallon, Richard, 20, 24
Federal Competition Commission, 14, 268–276
Federal Court of Administrative Justice, 46–49, 276
Federal Institute of Competition, 46
Federal Law of Economic Competition, 265, 267, 268, 270, 271, 273, 275–277
Federal Prosecutor, 50, 149
Federal Telecommunication Commission, 14, 269, 274
Federal Telecommunications Institute, The, 273, 274
Felipe Calderón Hinojosa, 92
Ferejohn, John, 31, 32
Fernandez, Kenneth E., 114
Ferrajoli, Luigi, 41, 146

Ferrante, Riccardo, 41
Ferreira, Octavio, 256
Fierro, Ana, 141, 144, 288
Fioravanti, Maurizio, 41
Fiscal disconnect, 109, 116, 118, 119
Fiss, Owen M., 29
Fitzpatrick, Danielle, 271
Fix-Fierro, Héctor, 87, 88
Flores, Imer B., 22
Foot, P., 169, 170
Formal legality, 20, 26, 27, 29, 32, 34, 83
Foster, Michelle, 128
Fox, Edward, 119
Freedom House, 3, 62, 242
Freeman, Gary P., 137
Free School on Law, 40, 287
Friedmann, Wolfgang G., 20
Friedrich, Carl J., 84
Fukuyama, Francis, 20
Fuller, Lon L., 20, 22, 24, 33
Fundamental Rights, 5, 7, 39, 40, 42–48, 52, 57–61, 64, 65, 69, 74, 89, 97, 123, 124, 128, 148, 176, 194–196, 252

G
Gallardo, Adrián, 270
Gallie, W. E., 20, 21
Galindo López, Carlos, 238
García, Adriana, 147, 153
García Enterría, Eduardo, 145
García Sáez, J. A., 178
García, Tonatiuh, 269
Garibian, Sévane, 43
Garza Onofre, J. J., 177
General Assembly, 137
General Population Poll, 62–64
Gil Botero, Enrique, 149
Ginsburg, Tom, 86–88, 129, 145, 148
Global Commission on Drug Policy, 119
Global Compact for Safe, Orderly and Regular Migration, 137
Global Impunity Index, 4, 5, 8, 82, 216, 217, 255
Globalization, 9, 123–128, 132, 136
Gloppen, Siri, 28
Goertz, Gary, 24
González Guerra, J. M., 195
González Oropeza, M., 185
Governability, 40, 41, 54, 213
Governance, 3, 40, 62, 85, 102, 124, 127, 137, 138, 143, 215, 241, 250, 254, 289, 290
Government of Mexico, 247
Grimm, Dieter, 84
Guajardo, Ildefonso, 275

Guarnieri, Carlo, 28, 30
Guerra, François-Xavier, 224, 225, 227
Gutiérrez Rivas, Rodrigo, 236

H
Habermas, Jürgen, 20, 32
Haggard, Stephan, 24, 210
Hamara, Courtney T., 22
Hampton, Jean., 22, 30
Hanson, G., 251
Hardin, Russell, 85, 161
Hart, J., 157, 160
Hayo, Bernd, 24
Heinle, Kimberly, 256
Helmke, Gretchen, 227
Henderson, H., 181, 182
Heredia Zubieta, Carlos, 135
Heritage Foundation, 62
Hernández, Maya, 116
Hernández, R., 212
Herrera González, Vladimir, 116
Herron, Erik S., 28
Hidalgo, Fernando Daniel, 20
Himma, Kenneth E., 22
Hoff, Karla, 24
Holland, Alisha C., 114
Holmes, Stephen, 23, 26, 28, 98
Homicides, 63, 66, 67, 107, 109–113, 117, 118, 236, 255
Homologated Police Report, 201
Howlett, Michael, 245
Hubickey, Victoria, 114
Human Rights, 2, 7, 9–12, 20, 32, 34, 39, 40, 42–48, 50, 54, 58, 60, 61, 82, 83, 88, 89, 103, 123, 124, 126, 128–134, 136–138, 141, 142, 144–146, 149–152, 155, 156, 159, 165, 166, 168, 171, 175–188, 194–196, 209, 223, 235–237, 287, 289
Human Rights Reform, 7, 9, 130, 149, 150
Huntington, Samuel P., 113, 210
Hursthouse, Rosalind, 156, 169
Hyper-reformism, 81, 88, 97, 103

I
Ibarra, Francisco, 87, 88, 101, 102, 229
Iberoamerican University, 40, 287
Impunity, 3–5, 7–9, 12, 13, 45, 48, 50, 60, 68, 82, 83, 102, 103, 136, 165, 166, 193, 194, 196, 199, 202–205, 216, 217, 234, 250, 252, 254, 255, 258, 261
Index, 3–5, 7–9, 12, 57–70, 73–76, 82, 97, 110, 111, 128, 195, 203, 216, 217, 252, 255, 288, 289

Index

Indicators, 3, 7, 8, 13, 39–41, 43, 44, 46, 49, 50, 54, 57, 58, 61–63, 76, 91, 97, 126, 144, 177, 195, 201–203, 252, 254, 289
Individual Rights, 27, 31, 32, 34, 39, 83, 85, 156
Inequality, 2, 3, 13, 29, 111, 216, 250–253, 255, 258, 260, 261
Insecurity, 9, 52, 107, 109, 111–115, 118, 119, 197
Insensee, Josef, 171
Institution, 1–4, 9, 12, 13, 27, 28, 30, 42, 53, 54, 61, 62, 66–68, 81–86, 88, 89, 101–103, 109, 113, 118, 124, 126, 128, 137, 138, 145, 156, 158, 168, 169, 177, 193–202, 207–211, 213–221, 223–227, 238, 242, 245, 253, 254, 261, 266, 274, 287, 288
Institutional capacities, 9, 131, 196, 197, 199, 201, 204
Institutional Revolutionary Party, 211, 228, 242
Institution Equilibrium, 7, 27–29, 85, 156, 266
Instituto Federal de Telecomunicaciones, 46, 274–276
Instituto Nacional de Acceso a la Información, 46, 49, 67, 265, 275, 288
Inter-American Court of Human Rights, 150, 180
Inter-American Human Rights Commission, 133, 136
Interconnected worlds, 126
International Political Science Association, 290
International Transparency, 159
Irregular migration, 123, 124, 127, 128, 130, 134, 136, 137

J
Jiménez Rodríguez, Paola G., 112
Joireman, Sandra Fullerton, 24
Judicial Independence, 29–31, 89, 149, 153
Judicial Institutions, 194
Judiciary, 28–31, 53, 54, 60, 62, 65, 94, 129–131, 137, 143, 144, 198, 199, 211, 213, 229, 269, 276
Judiciary control, 31
Justice, 1–7, 11, 12, 21, 23, 29, 32, 34, 44–48, 50–54, 57–59, 61, 63, 64, 66, 68, 70, 73, 74, 76, 82, 83, 85, 89, 95, 97, 103, 111, 112, 128–130, 132, 134, 138, 146, 147, 149, 152, 153, 166, 188, 193–205, 216–219, 229, 233, 237, 242, 252, 254, 261, 266, 270–272, 276, 278, 288–290

K
Kapiszewski, Diana, 29
Kaufmann, Daniel, 77
Kavka, Gregory S., 30
Kehoe, T., 251
Kelemen, Daniel R., 35, 37
Kelly, Patty, 132
Kelsen, Hans, 20, 25
Khan, Haroon A., 126
Kitrosser, Heidi, 141–144
Kleinfeld, Rachel, 59, 61
Klosko, Georges, 157, 161–165
Knight, Alan, 228
Kovic, Christine, 132
Kraay, Aart, 77
Krause, Krystin, 114
Krygier, Martin, 37
Kuenzi, Michele, 114

L
Lamarche, Gara, 169
Lapsley, Irvine, 144
La Salle University, 40, 287
Latin America and Caribbean Centre, 290
Latinamerican Faculty of Social Sciences, 290
Latin University of America, 40, 287
Lauth, Hans-Joachim, 20, 22, 25, 33
Law, 1–11, 13, 14, 19–34, 39–46, 48–52, 54, 57–70, 73–76, 81–89, 97–103, 107–120, 123, 124, 126–131, 135–138, 141–153, 155–157, 159–161, 164–166, 168, 169, 171, 175–188, 193–197, 199, 201, 202, 205, 216, 219, 223–229, 231–233, 236–238, 242, 245, 246, 250, 252–254, 256, 258, 260, 261, 265–278, 287–290
Law schools, 11, 175–178, 182, 183, 185–188
Lawyer, 11, 40, 47, 63, 152, 175–178, 180, 182–184, 186–188, 200, 237, 276, 287
Le Clercq, Juan Antonio, 8, 82, 83, 97, 102, 171, 255
Legal behavior, 20, 27, 29
Legal education, 175–179, 183, 188, 289
Legalism, 39, 40
Lehoucq, Fabrice, 211
Lessing, Benjamin, 111, 115
Levitsky, Steven, 19–21, 24, 25, 29, 227
Levy, Irene, 277
Lindblom, Charles E., 265
Lockhart, Sarah, 137
London School of Economics and Political Science, 119, 285, 290

López-Noriega, Saul, 147, 153
Lovett, Frank, 20, 24
Lowndes, Vivien, 158
Lyons, David, 160

M
Maciuceanu, Andra Olivia, 20
MacIntyre, Andrew, 24
Mackie, J. L., 164
Madrazo, Alejandro, 235–237
Madrazo, Jorge, 102
Magaloni, Ana, 152, 178
Magaloni, Beatriz, 113, 114
Mahon, James E., 19, 21, 24, 25
Manin, Bernard, 31
Maqueo, María Solange, 13, 265
Maravall, José María, 20, 27, 28, 30
March, James G., 158
Mariscal, Elisa, 268
Mariscal, Judith, 268
Market regulation, 2, 223, 267
Market system, 265
Martínez, C., 178, 183, 187
Martínez, Jorge, 168
Martin Reyes, Javier, 87
Martin, Susan, 136
Mastruzzi, Massimo, 77
Marván, Ignacio, 87, 101
Matanock, A., 114
May, Rachel A., 124, 139
McAllister, William B., 119
McCubbins, Mathew D., 145
McElwain, K. M., 116
McNamara, Francis, 114
Measurement, 2, 6–8, 24, 25, 39, 40, 51, 59–62, 64, 69, 73, 76, 166, 197, 199
Medellín, Ximena, 152
Medema, Steven G., 267
Melone, Albert P., 28
Melton, James, 86–88
Mena, Carlos, 280
Méndez, Francisco, 102
Méndez, Juan E., 29
Méndez, Laura, 280
Mercuro, Nicholas, 267
Merryman, John Henry, 36
Metropolitan Autonomous University, 40, 287
Mexican Constitution, 8, 9, 11, 41, 81–84, 86–90, 97, 103, 146, 147, 150, 157, 176, 179, 180, 196, 242, 246, 275
Mexican Council on Administration of the Federal Judicial Branch, 48, 49, 52, 53
Mexican Petroleum, 246, 247, 250, 256, 257
Mexican Petroleum Fund, 247, 250

Mexican Political System, 9, 209–211, 220, 221
Mexican Presidentialism, 87
Meyer, John W., 125
Migration, 2, 9, 10, 123, 124, 127, 128, 130–138, 289, 291
Mill, John Stuart, 165
Ministry of National Affairs, 4, 132, 133, 168
Ministry of Public Function, 48
Mirilovic, Nikola, 137
Miron, Jeffrey A., 115
Modern State, 1, 225
Molinar Horcasitas, Juan, 211
Møller, Jørgen, 19–21, 24–26, 31, 34
Money, Jeannette, 137
Monterrey Institute of Technology and Higher Education, 40, 287
Moral, 10, 26, 27, 40, 155–157, 159–161, 165, 166, 168, 170, 287
Morales, Víctor, 168
Moral obligation, 10, 156, 157, 159–161, 165, 166, 170
Morsi, Z., 149
Motta, Massimo, 266, 267
Mudde, Cas, 20
Mulgan, Richard, 143
Munck, Gerardo L., 20
Murillo, Stefana, 158

N
Nacif, Benito, 211
Narváez Medécigo, Alfredo, 129
National Action Party, 13, 113, 141, 210, 214, 242, 244, 245, 249, 262
National Anti-corruption System, 12, 52, 208–210, 216–221
National Autonomous University of Mexico, 40, 141, 223, 287–290
National Census of Local Prosecution Offices, 201, 202
National Center for Energy Control, 250
National Center for Natural Gas Control, 250
National Commission for Human Rights, 43, 45
National Council Against Discrimination, 159, 168
National Council on the Evaluation of Social Development Policy, 251
National Electoral Institute, 168
National Hydrocarbons Commission, 250, 251
National Institute for Educational Evaluation, 167, 168
National Institute for Statistics and Geography, 67, 109, 117, 159, 177, 201–203, 216

National Institute of Criminal Sciences, 40, 287
National Institute of Migration, 131, 134
National Regeneration Movement, 153, 241, 244, 245, 249, 252, 254, 259–261
National Security, 39, 45, 50, 131, 135, 137, 161, 163, 255
National System of Researchers, 289
National Victimization Survey, 67, 114, 117, 194
Negretto, Gabriel, 211
Neild, Rachel, 135
Nijman, Janne Elisabeth, 127
Nohlen Dieter, 145
Nonet, Philippe, 23
North American Free Trade Agreement, 243, 259, 268
North, Douglas C., 1, 85, 108, 225, 232
Novoa, M., 11, 194, 196, 288
Nozick, Robert, 157, 161–163
Nuevo León Autonomous University, 287
Nully trial, 141, 142, 146, 147
Núñez, Javier, 274, 277

O
O'Donnell, Guillermo, 143
Okeowo, Alexis, 252
Olsen, Johan P., 158
Olson, Mancur, 160, 208
Olsson, O., 24
Open government, 4, 5, 7, 57, 58, 65, 67, 74, 97, 195, 252
Operation Condor, 233
Opium, 230, 232, 233
Oralia, Sandra, 116
Organisation for Economic Co-operation and Development, 68
Organized crime, 13, 45, 51, 113, 117, 118, 132, 135, 137, 216, 218, 234, 236, 237, 241, 250, 254, 256, 258, 260, 289
Orkeny, Antan, 28
Ortiz, Jorge, 212, 217
Osorio, Javier, 111, 113, 115
Otsuka, Michael, 157, 161–163
Outcomes, 57, 59, 61, 62, 68, 73, 144, 151, 166, 204, 214, 245, 287

P
Pact for Mexico, 215, 242, 246, 273
Paffenholz, Thania, 135
Panamerican University, 40, 287
Parker, Geoffrey, 125
Pasquino, Pasquale, 31, 32
Pavón-Villamayor, Víctor, 271
Payan, Tony, 13, 256

Paz, Octavio, 209
Peces-Barba, G., 187
Peerenboom, Randall, 20
Pérez Correa, Catalina, 236
Pérez Hurtado, L. F., 177
Pérez, Orlando J., 114
Pettigrove, Glen, 156, 169
Phillips, Brian J., 111
Picker, Randal C., 278
Pierson, Paul, 226, 227, 244
Pinheiro, Paulo Sergio, 29
Pinto, M., 181
Poiré, Alejandro, 116
Political pluralism, 9, 111
Ponce, Alejandro, 57, 58, 62, 156, 289
Pontifical University of Mexico, 40, 288
Pou Giménez, Francisca, 87, 88
Poverty, 13, 58, 111, 113, 242, 250–253, 255, 258, 260, 261
Pozas-Loyo, Andrea, 129
Presidentialism, 87, 234
Principle of Fairness, 10, 155, 157, 160–163, 165
Pro persona principle, 48, 180–182
Przeworski, Adam, 20, 27, 28, 30
Public affairs, 10, 86, 155–160, 162, 165–167
Public goods, 2, 10, 40, 85, 86, 160–165
Public policy, 13, 14, 60, 89, 102, 141, 155, 169, 196, 197, 199, 223, 229, 241, 244–247, 249, 252, 254, 260, 285, 288, 289
Putnam, Robert D., 164, 169–171

Q
Quah, Danny, 115
Qualified Respondent's Questionnaires, 63
Quintana, Karla, 152

R
Radilla Pacheco Case, 180
Ramírez, Telésforo, 138
Rawls, John, 162, 170
Raz, Joseph, 7, 20, 22, 24, 26, 34
Reciprocity, 155, 169–171, 227, 229, 233, 235
Reform, 3, 7–9, 11–14, 41–48, 52, 53, 68, 81–96, 102, 129–132, 135, 142, 145, 149–151, 166, 175, 176, 179, 188, 193, 194, 196, 197, 199, 202–205, 207, 208, 210, 213–218, 220, 221, 232, 234, 236, 237, 241, 242, 244–253, 258–262, 265, 267, 268, 270–277, 287
Regulation, 2, 12, 40, 45, 61, 66, 119, 127, 131, 176, 212, 223, 224, 226, 230, 231, 266, 267, 269, 270, 276, 287

Reich, Rob, 169
Resa Nestares, Carlos, 232
Research Center for Development, 197, 276
Restrepo, Pascual, 115
Reychler, Luc, 135
Reynolds, Noel B., 26
Ribeiro, Ludmila, 114
Riggs, Fred Warren, 24
Ríos-Figueroa, Julio, 24, 29, 129
Ríos, Viridiana, 102, 111, 113
Rivera León, Mauro Arturo, 87
Roberts, Mark, 158
Robinson, James A., 62, 228
Robles, Gustavo, 114
Rodríguez, Daniel, 77
Rodríguez, Gerardo, 8, 82, 83, 97, 255
Roldán, José, 280
Role of Constitution, 84, 101
Román, Eduardo, xiii, 11, 175–190, 278
Romero Gudiño, Alejandro, 50
Romero Vadillo, Jorge Javier, 235, 236, 289
Romero, Vidal, 9, 13, 290
Rose-Ackerman, Susan, 37
Ros, Jaime, 210
Rosmarin, Ari, 119
Rotberg, Robert, 40
Rovira, Cristóbal Rovira, 20
Rubio, Luis, 244, 259
Ruiz, Eugenio, 278
Rule by law, 25–27, 29, 31, 34, 61
Rule of law, 1–11, 13, 14, 19–34, 39–41, 43, 45, 46, 48, 50, 54, 57–65, 67, 69, 70, 73, 74, 76, 81–87, 89, 97–103, 107–120, 123, 124, 126–129, 138, 141–145, 148, 149, 151–153, 155–157, 159–161, 164–166, 168, 169, 171, 177, 193–197, 205, 223, 229, 233, 236, 242, 245, 250, 252–254, 256, 258, 260, 261, 265–267, 278, 288–290
Rule of law deficit, 97
Rule of Law Index (RLI), 4, 5, 7–9, 57–65, 67, 69, 70, 73, 74, 76, 82, 97–100, 110, 111, 128, 195, 288, 289
Rule of men, 21, 22

S
Sadowski, Christine M., 169
Salazar Ugarte, Pedro, 87
Samuels, Warren J., 267
Sánchez-Cuenca, Ignacio, 27
Sandel, Michael, 155
Sandholtz, Wayne, 24
Santiso, Carlos, 210

Sarabia, Heiddy, 132
Sarsfield, Rodolfo, 6, 7, 24, 156, 266, 290
Sartori, Giovanni, 6, 21, 24, 25, 33, 34, 85
Sassen, Saskia, 125
Scanlon, T. M., 162
Schaffer, Frederic Charles, 24
Schedler, Andreas, 22, 24, 143
Scheppele, Kim Lane, 28
Schwartz, Herman, 28
Schwartz, Thomas, 154
Security, 3–5, 7, 9, 13, 39, 44, 45, 50, 51, 57, 58, 60, 61, 65, 67, 69, 74, 82, 83, 95, 97, 103, 108–110, 113, 114, 116–119, 128, 131, 132, 135, 137, 159–163, 166, 171, 193–198, 201, 209, 215, 223, 234, 236, 237, 241, 251, 252, 254–256, 258, 266, 287, 289, 290
Security crisis, 3, 9, 108–110
Sehring, Jenniver, 25
Self-defense groups, 236
Seligson, Mitchell A., 168
Selznick, Philip, 23
Sender, Ramón J., 230
Serna, José María, 87–89, 92, 101
Shapiro, Ian, 22, 30
Shapiro, Martin, 37
Shirk, David A., 256
Shon, D. A., 144, 153
Silva Forné, Carlos, 236
Silva-Herzog, Jesús, 88
Silva Mora, K., 194, 196
Skaaning, Svend-Erik, 19–21, 24–27, 30–34, 84
Smith, Peter, 212
Soberanes, José M, 152
Social Contract, 1, 2, 86
Society, 1, 6, 9, 10, 12, 20, 22, 23, 27–29, 41, 58, 60–62, 65, 81, 82, 86, 98, 101, 103, 108, 112, 113, 118, 123, 126, 134, 137, 138, 153, 155, 156, 164, 166–169, 171, 194, 195, 209, 216, 217, 220, 225, 228, 229, 231, 256, 261, 267, 269, 277
Society for Community Research and Action, 144, 153
Solís, Patricio, 156, 159
Sovereignty, 9, 20, 32, 34, 123–128, 131, 136, 137
Sowell, Thomas, 21
State liability trial, 141, 142, 146, 148, 149, 153
Staton, Jeffrey K., 24, 29
Stein, Robert, 126
Stiglitz, Joseph E., 24

Index

Stotzky, Irwin P., 29
Structural reforms, 3, 11, 52, 207, 213, 220, 242, 244–246, 253, 258, 261, 265, 273, 275
Subcommittee on Prevention of Torture and other Cruel Inhuman or Degrading Treatment or Punishment, 134
Sunstein, Cass R., 23, 85, 98
Superior Federal Audit, 48–50
Supervisory Units for Precautionary Measures, 201
Surveys, 4, 8, 25, 62–64, 67–69, 114, 117, 155, 194, 216, 290

T

Taagepera, Rein, 24
Tamanaha, Brian, 21, 22, 24–27, 31, 32, 34
Tamir, Moustafa, 145, 148
Tatar, María, 77
Tavilla, Elio, 41
Taylor, Matthew M., 29
Teaching, 40, 176–179, 183, 184, 186–188, 265, 281, 287, 288, 290
Technical Secretariat for the Implementation of the Criminal Justice Reform, 197
Tello, C., 211
Tena, Felipe, 146
Teune, Henry, 24
Thornton, Mark, 115
Tiede, Lydia, 24
Transit country, 45, 130, 132, 133, 135, 138, 233
Transparency International, 3, 60, 216, 242, 252, 253
Trejo, Guillermo, 236
Trejo, Ricardo, 278

U

Uildriks, Niels, 135
Ungar, Mark, 29
United Nations, 10, 134
United Nations Development Programme, 63
United Nations Human Rights Council, 137
United Nations Office on Drugs and Crime, 112, 119, 236
United Nations Security Council, 77
University of Salamanca, 40, 287
University of the Americas Puebla, 194, 216, 281

V

Valadés, Diego, 40, 41, 54, 87, 88
Valdés Castellanos, Guillermo, 115
Valdés Ugalde, Francisco, 101
Vaño Vicedo, R., 178
Velasco Rivera, Mariana, 87
Velázquez Flores, Rafael, 135
Vera Institute of Justice, 77
Verkuilen, Jay, 20
Versteeg, Vera, 77
Vice, Margaret, 251
Vicente Fox Quezada, 91, 92
Vile, M. J., 31
Villegas, P., 195
Violence, 9, 20, 27, 28, 40, 42, 51, 52, 60, 62, 66, 107, 110, 111, 113–115, 118–120, 132, 134–136, 194, 210, 216, 224–228, 232, 233, 235, 236, 238, 253, 255, 256, 258, 261
Voigt, Stefan, 24

W

Waldron, Jeremy, 2, 20, 23, 24, 85
Wall, Steven, 165
Waluchow, W. J., 22
War on drugs, 12, 107–109, 113, 115, 116, 223, 233, 236, 238
Webb, S., 210
Weingast, Barry R., 85, 108, 116, 120, 225
Weldon, Jeffrey, 211
Werner, Wouter, 127
Western, Shaina, 137
Weyland, Kurt, 20, 33
Whittington, Keith E., 35, 37
Wilson, Carter A., 245
Winecki, Jan, 222
Winston, Kenneth I., 33
Witker, Jorge, 280
Wood, Charles H., 114
Wood, Duncan, 102
World Bank, 3, 57, 58, 62, 68, 243, 288–290
World Justice Project, The, 3–5, 7–9, 57–65, 67, 68, 73, 76, 111, 166, 195, 288, 289
World Value Survey, 155, 159, 167
Worldwide Governance Indicators, 62

Y

Yankelevich, Pablo, 130

Z

Zagrebelsky, Gustavo, 41
Zavala, Dirk, 148, 149
Zepeda Gil, Raúl, 111
Zepeda Lecuona, Guillermo, 112
Zwiebel, Jeffrey, 115